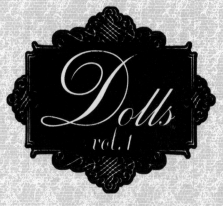

Story & Art by Yumiko Kawahara

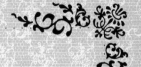

Contents

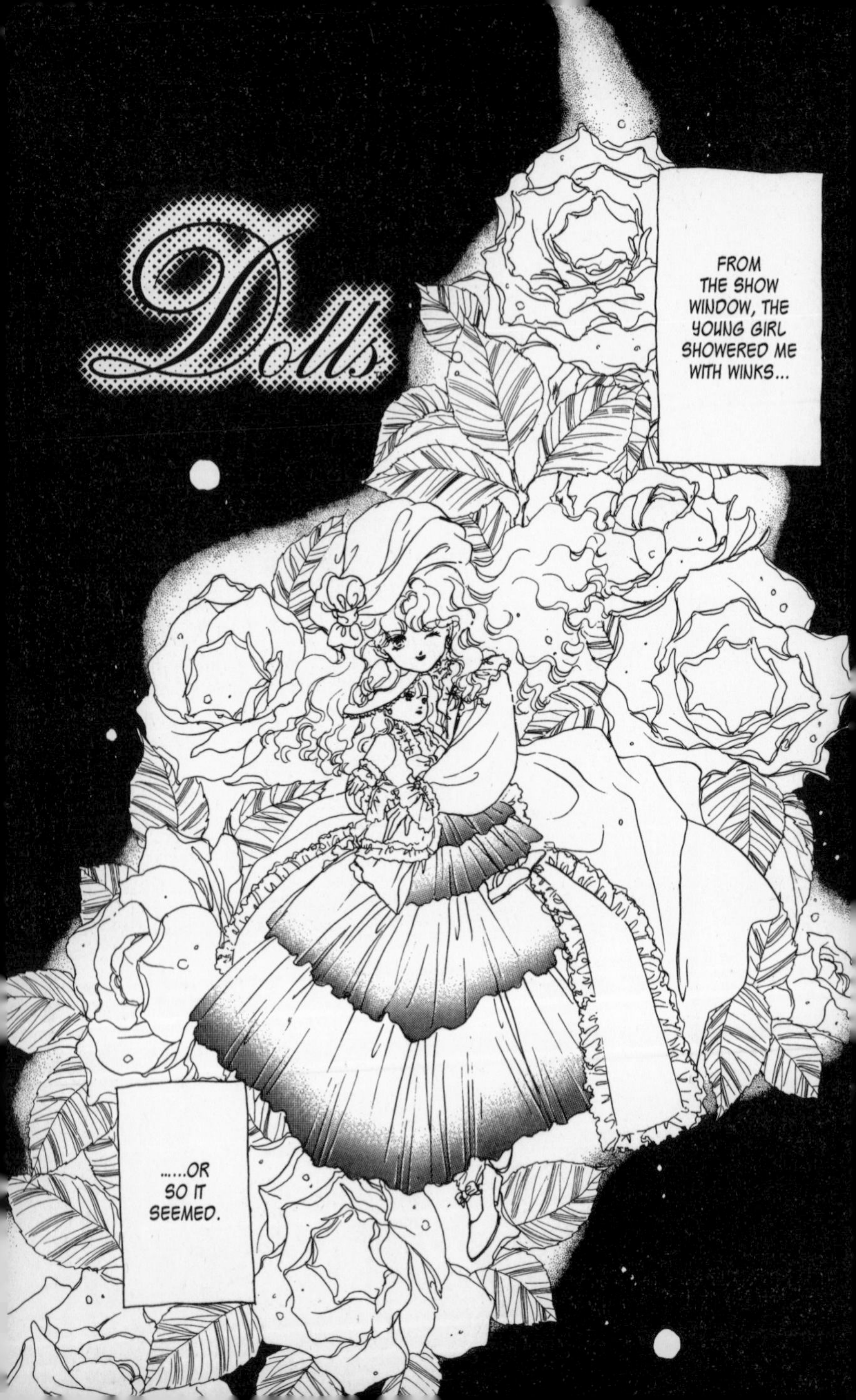
FROM THE SHOW WINDOW, THE YOUNG GIRL SHOWERED ME WITH WINKS...
Dolls
......OR SO IT SEEMED.

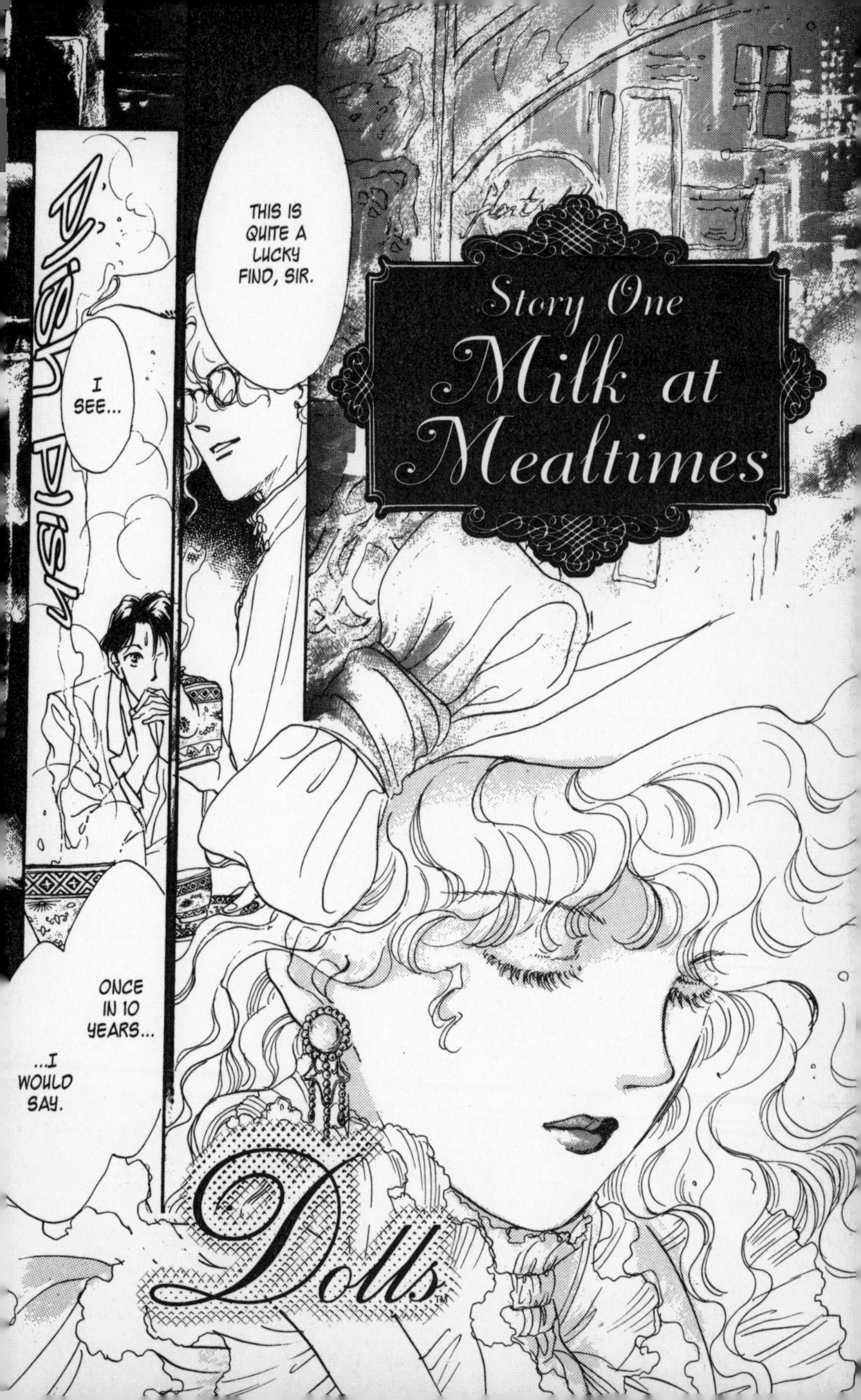
Story One
Milk at Mealtimes
Dolls™
THIS IS QUITE A LUCKY FIND, SIR.
I SEE...
Pish Pish
ONCE IN 10 YEARS...
...I WOULD SAY.

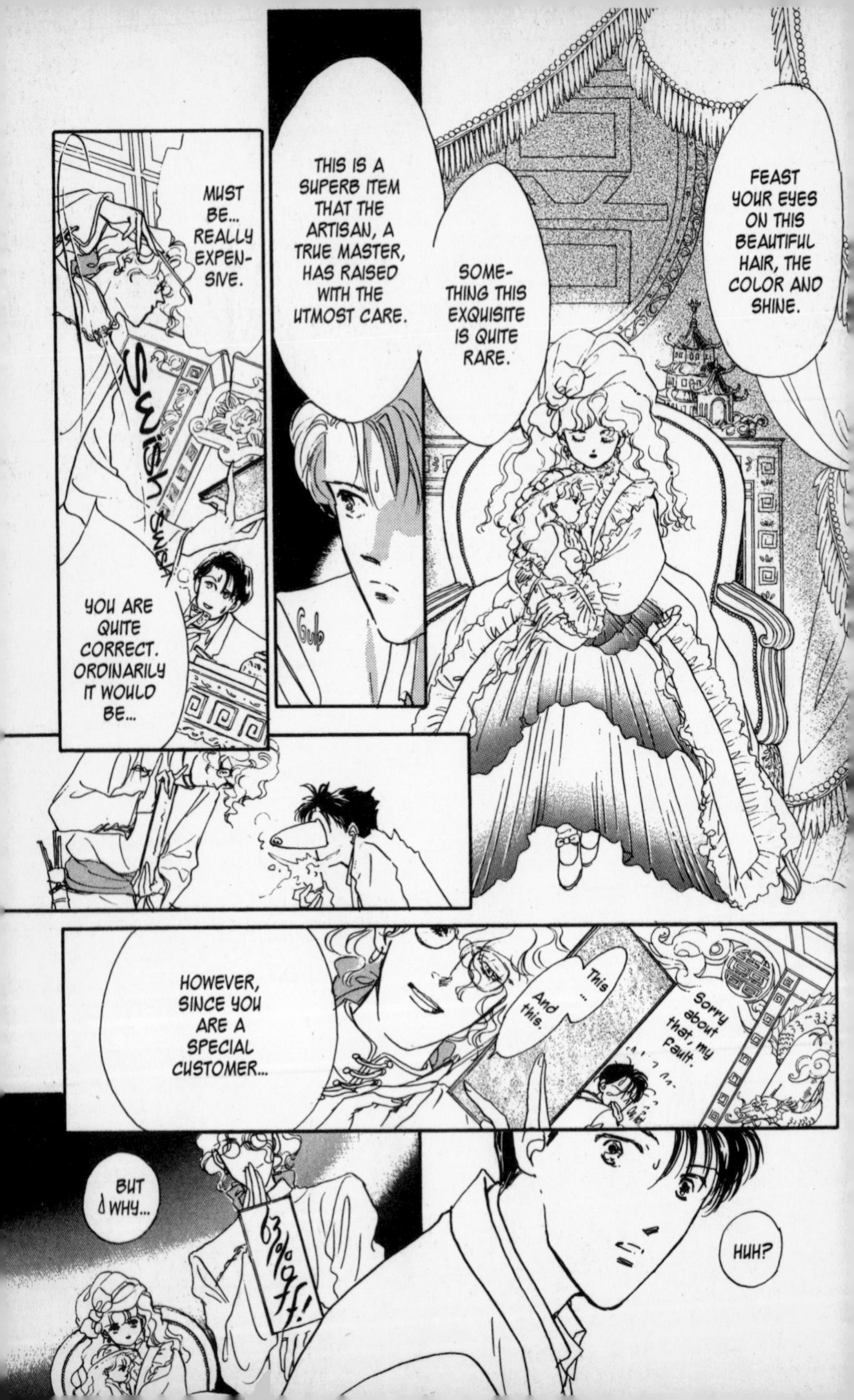
FEAST YOUR EYES ON THIS BEAUTIFUL HAIR, THE COLOR AND SHINE.
SOME-THING THIS EXQUISITE IS QUITE RARE.
THIS IS A SUPERB ITEM THAT THE ARTISAN, A TRUE MASTER, HAS RAISED WITH THE UTMOST CARE.
Gulp
MUST BE... REALLY EXPEN-SIVE.
Swish
swish
YOU ARE QUITE CORRECT. ORDINARILY IT WOULD BE...
Sorry about that, my fault.
This...
And this.
HOWEVER, SINCE YOU ARE A SPECIAL CUSTOMER...
HUH?
63% off!
BUT WHY...

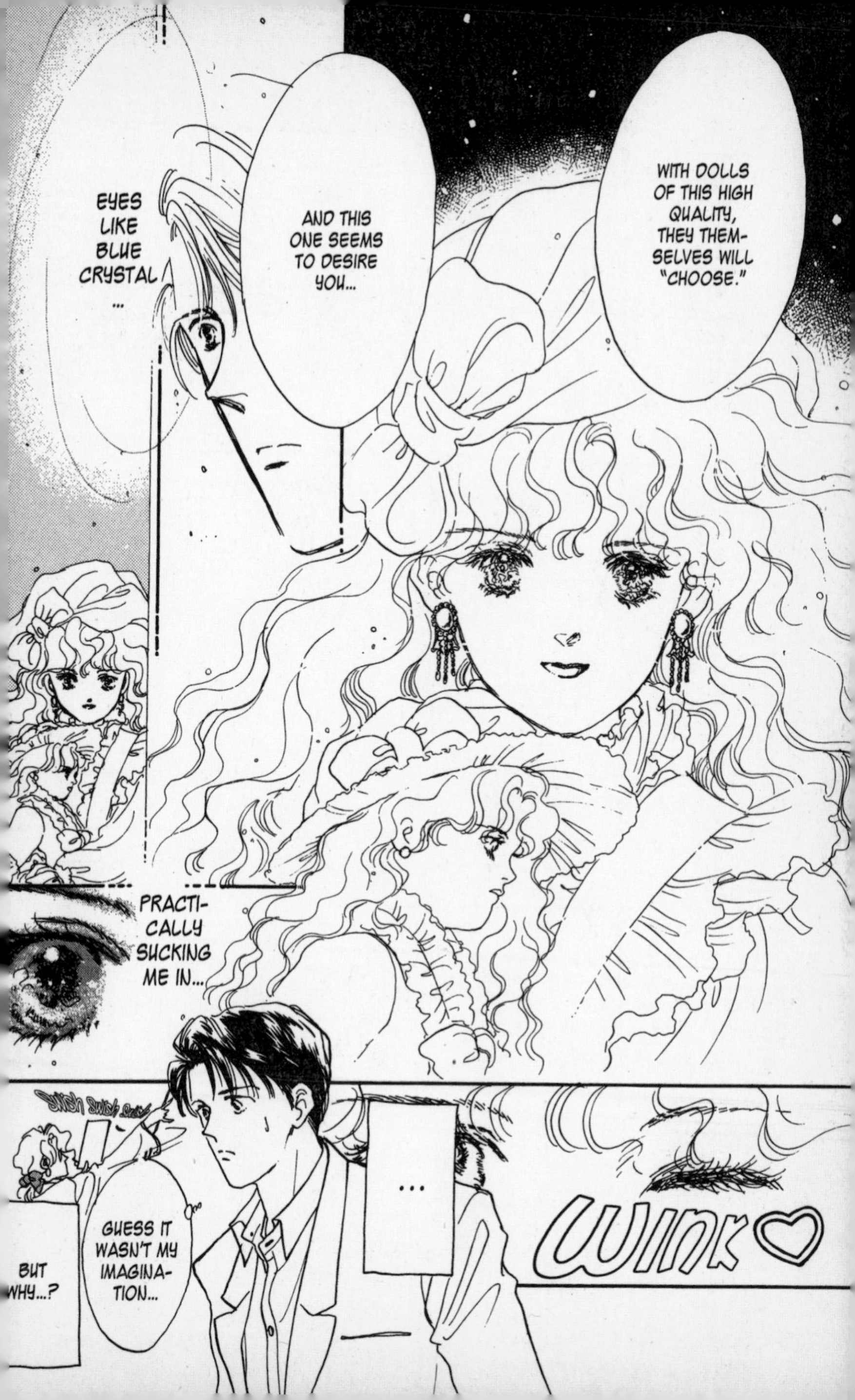
WITH DOLLS OF THIS HIGH QUALITY, THEY THEMSELVES WILL "CHOOSE."
AND THIS ONE SEEMS TO DESIRE YOU...
EYES LIKE BLUE CRYSTAL ...
PRACTICALLY SUCKING ME IN...
WINK♡
...
GUESS IT WASN'T MY IMAGINATION...
BUT WHY...?

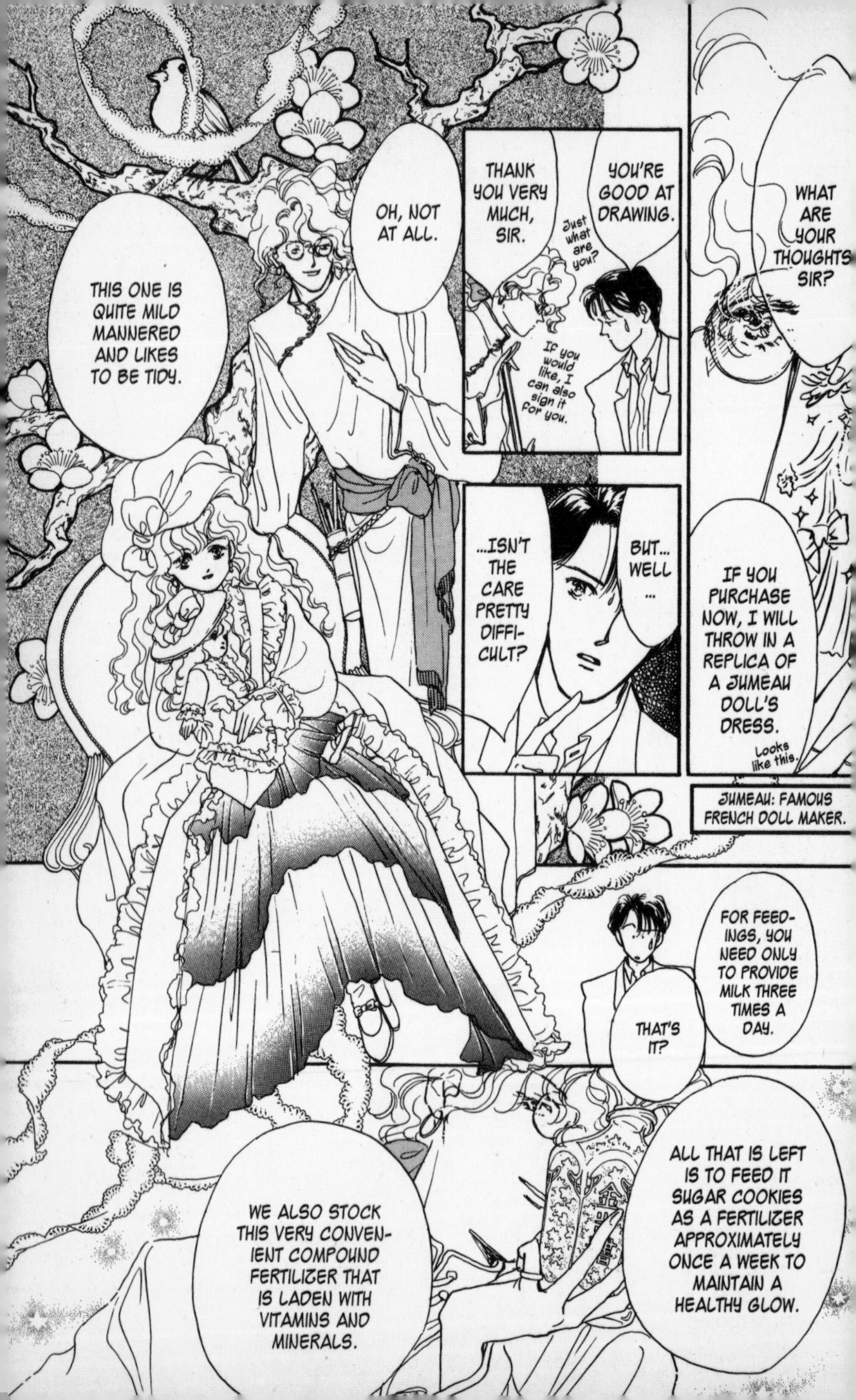
WHAT ARE YOUR THOUGHTS SIR?
IF YOU PURCHASE NOW, I WILL THROW IN A REPLICA OF A JUMEAU DOLL'S DRESS.
Looks like this.
JUMEAU: FAMOUS FRENCH DOLL MAKER.
YOU'RE GOOD AT DRAWING.
THANK YOU VERY MUCH, SIR.
Just what are you?
If you would like, I can also sign it for you.
BUT... WELL ...
...ISN'T THE CARE PRETTY DIFFI-CULT?
OH, NOT AT ALL.
THIS ONE IS QUITE MILD MANNERED AND LIKES TO BE TIDY.
FOR FEED-INGS, YOU NEED ONLY TO PROVIDE MILK THREE TIMES A DAY.
THAT'S IT?
ALL THAT IS LEFT IS TO FEED IT SUGAR COOKIES AS A FERTILIZER APPROXIMATELY ONCE A WEEK TO MAINTAIN A HEALTHY GLOW.
WE ALSO STOCK THIS VERY CONVEN-IENT COMPOUND FERTILIZER THAT IS LADEN WITH VITAMINS AND MINERALS.

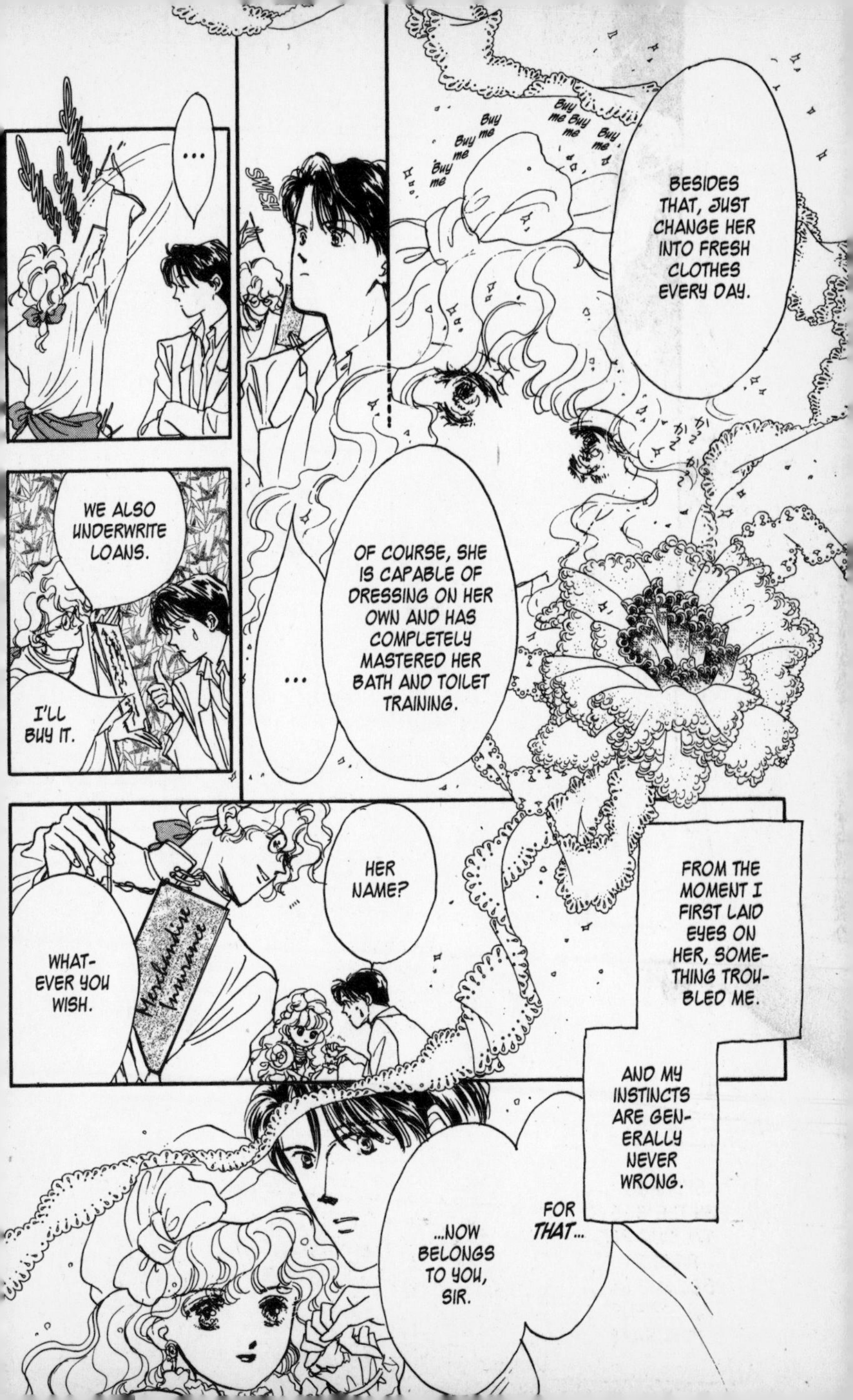
Buy me Buy me Buy me Buy me Buy me Buy me
BESIDES THAT, JUST CHANGE HER INTO FRESH CLOTHES EVERY DAY.
OF COURSE, SHE IS CAPABLE OF DRESSING ON HER OWN AND HAS COMPLETELY MASTERED HER BATH AND TOILET TRAINING.
SWISH!
...
...
WE ALSO UNDERWRITE LOANS.
I'LL BUY IT.
FROM THE MOMENT I FIRST LAID EYES ON HER, SOMETHING TROUBLED ME.
HER NAME?
WHAT-EVER YOU WISH.
Merchandise Insurance
AND MY INSTINCTS ARE GENERALLY NEVER WRONG.
FOR *THAT*...
...NOW BELONGS TO YOU, SIR.

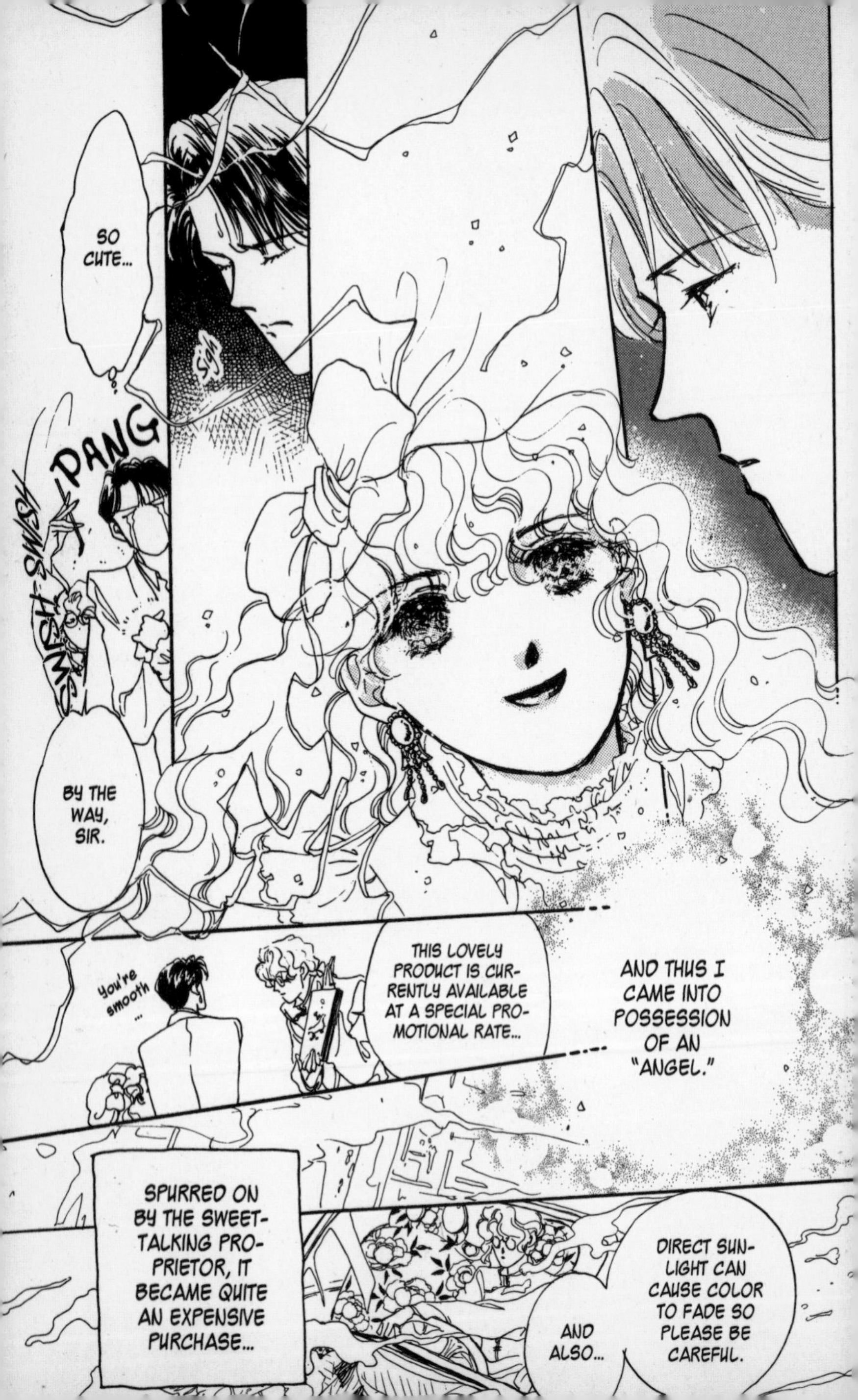
SO CUTE...
sigh
PANG
SWISH-SWISH
BY THE WAY, SIR.
AND THUS I CAME INTO POSSESSION OF AN "ANGEL."
THIS LOVELY PRODUCT IS CUR-RENTLY AVAILABLE AT A SPECIAL PRO-MOTIONAL RATE...
You're smooth...
DIRECT SUN-LIGHT CAN CAUSE COLOR TO FADE SO PLEASE BE CAREFUL.
AND ALSO...
SPURRED ON BY THE SWEET-TALKING PRO-PRIETOR, IT BECAME QUITE AN EXPENSIVE PURCHASE...

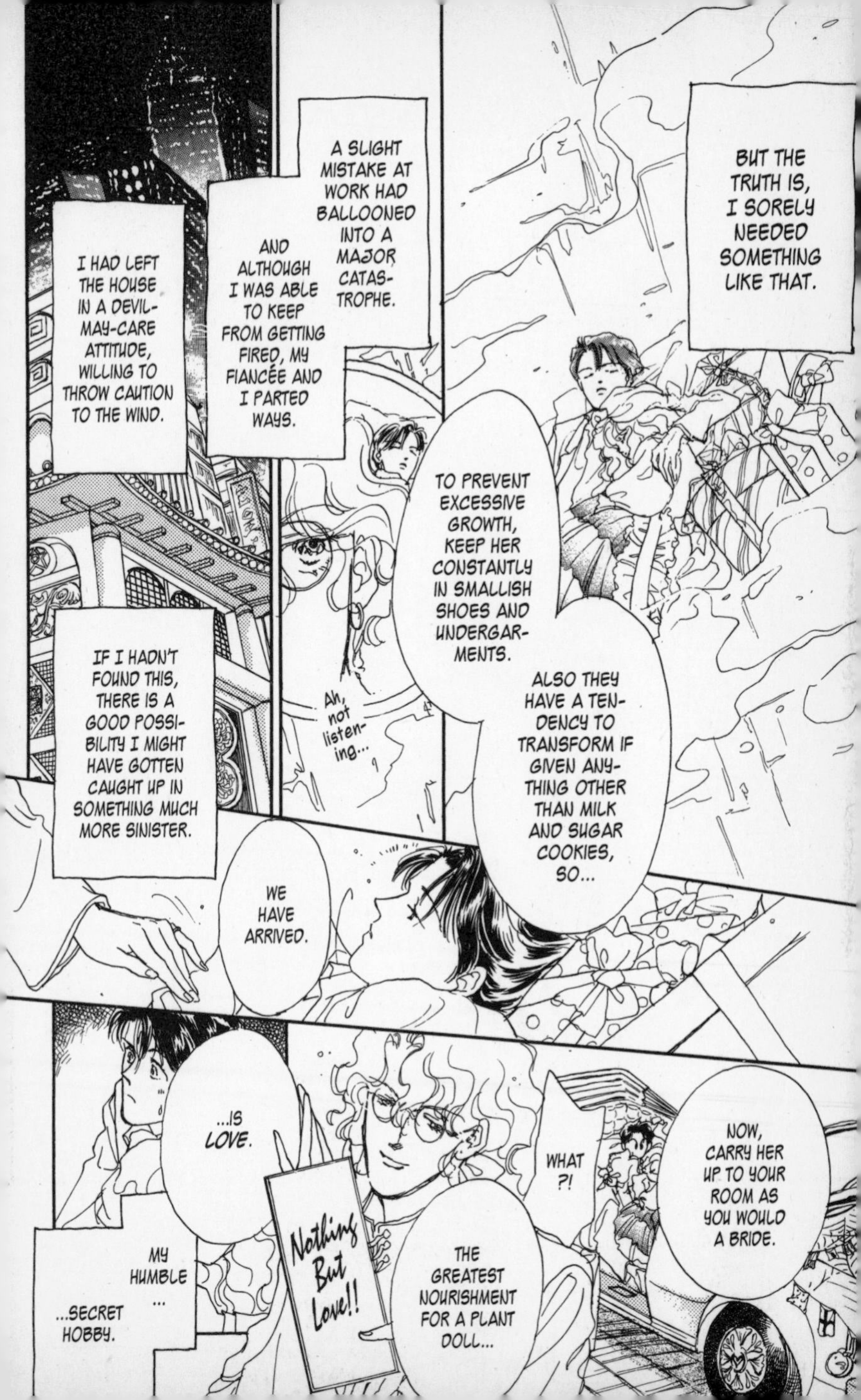
BUT THE TRUTH IS, I SORELY NEEDED SOMETHING LIKE THAT.
TO PREVENT EXCESSIVE GROWTH, KEEP HER CONSTANTLY IN SMALLISH SHOES AND UNDERGAR-MENTS.
ALSO THEY HAVE A TEN-DENCY TO TRANSFORM IF GIVEN ANY-THING OTHER THAN MILK AND SUGAR COOKIES, SO...
A SLIGHT MISTAKE AT WORK HAD BALLOONED INTO A MAJOR CATAS-TROPHE.
AND ALTHOUGH I WAS ABLE TO KEEP FROM GETTING FIRED, MY FIANCÉE AND I PARTED WAYS.
Ah, not listen-ing...
I HAD LEFT THE HOUSE IN A DEVIL-MAY-CARE ATTITUDE, WILLING TO THROW CAUTION TO THE WIND.
IF I HADN'T FOUND THIS, THERE IS A GOOD POSSI-BILITY I MIGHT HAVE GOTTEN CAUGHT UP IN SOMETHING MUCH MORE SINISTER.
WE HAVE ARRIVED.
NOW, CARRY HER UP TO YOUR ROOM AS YOU WOULD A BRIDE.
WHAT ?!
THE GREATEST NOURISHMENT FOR A PLANT DOLL...
...IS *LOVE*.
Nothing But Love!!
MY HUMBLE ...
...SECRET HOBBY.

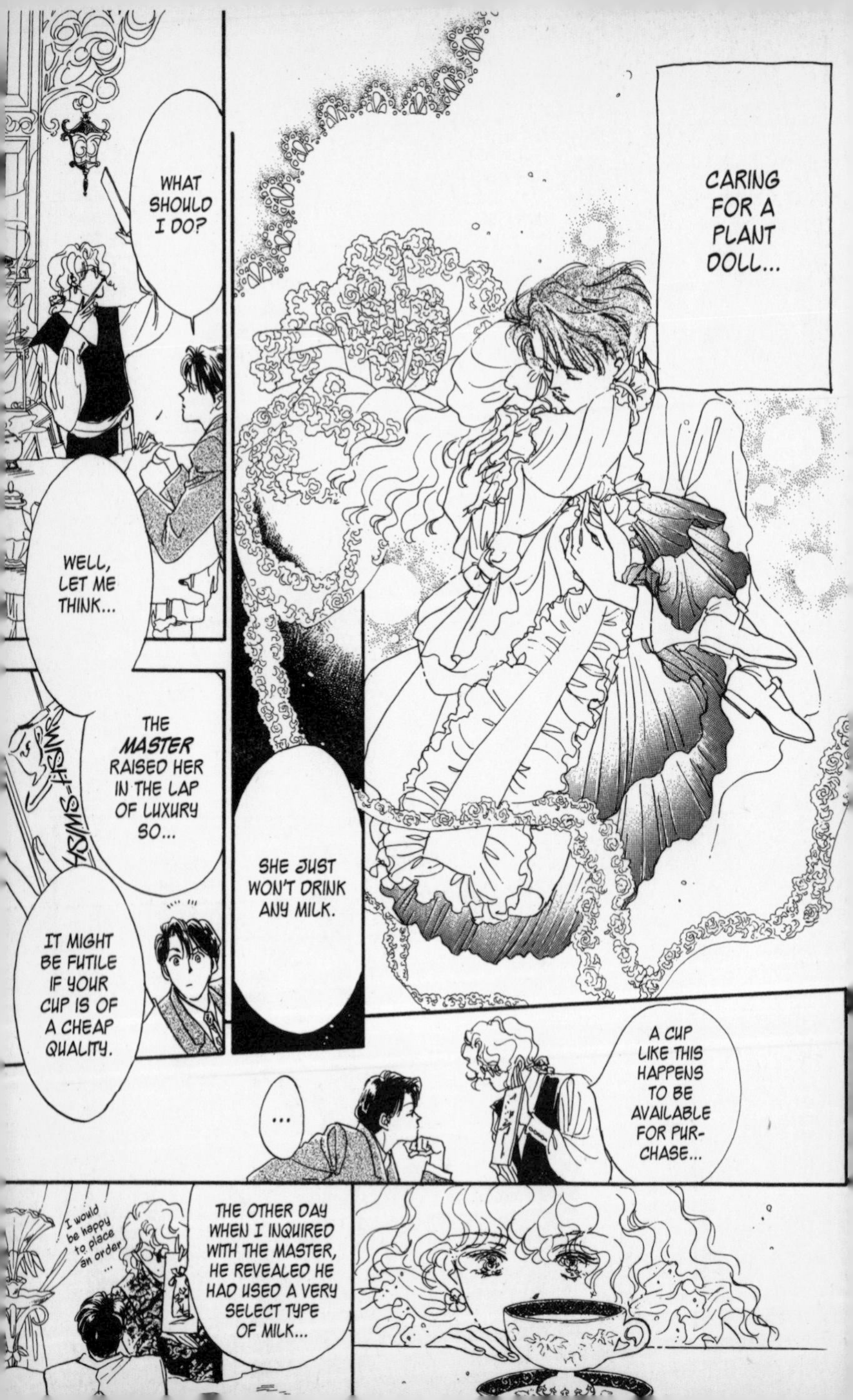

CARING FOR A PLANT DOLL...
SHE JUST WON'T DRINK ANY MILK.
WHAT SHOULD I DO?
WELL, LET ME THINK...
THE *MASTER* RAISED HER IN THE LAP OF LUXURY SO...
SWISH-SWISH
IT MIGHT BE FUTILE IF YOUR CUP IS OF A CHEAP QUALITY.
A CUP LIKE THIS HAPPENS TO BE AVAILABLE FOR PUR-CHASE...
...
THE OTHER DAY WHEN I INQUIRED WITH THE MASTER, HE REVEALED HE HAD USED A VERY SELECT TYPE OF MILK...
I would be happy to place an order...

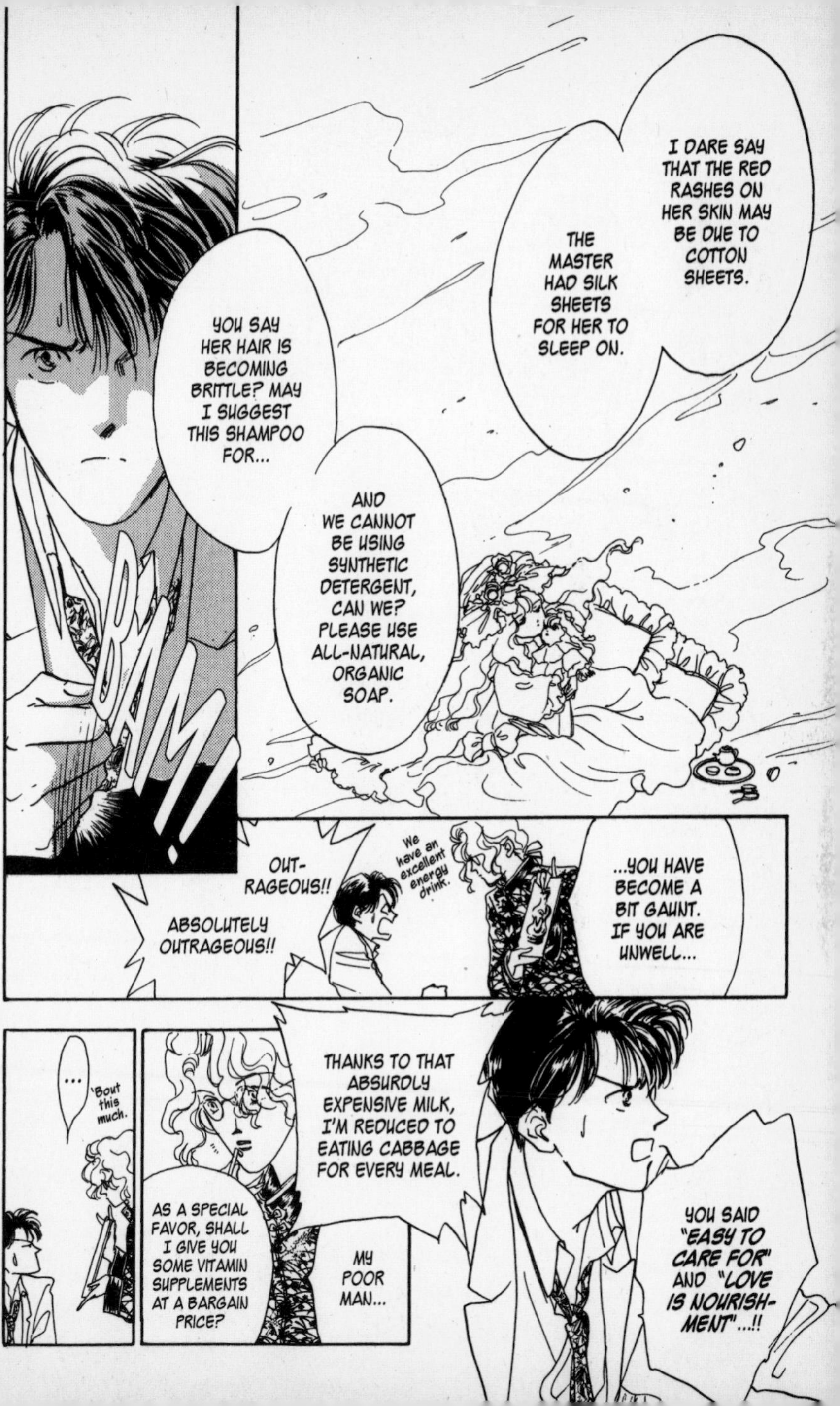
I DARE SAY THAT THE RED RASHES ON HER SKIN MAY BE DUE TO COTTON SHEETS.
THE MASTER HAD SILK SHEETS FOR HER TO SLEEP ON.
YOU SAY HER HAIR IS BECOMING BRITTLE? MAY I SUGGEST THIS SHAMPOO FOR...
AND WE CANNOT BE USING SYNTHETIC DETERGENT, CAN WE? PLEASE USE ALL-NATURAL, ORGANIC SOAP.
BAM!!
...YOU HAVE BECOME A BIT GAUNT. IF YOU ARE UNWELL...
We have an excellent energy drink.
OUT-RAGEOUS!!
ABSOLUTELY OUTRAGEOUS!!
YOU SAID "EASY TO CARE FOR" AND "LOVE IS NOURISHMENT"...!!
THANKS TO THAT ABSURDLY EXPENSIVE MILK, I'M REDUCED TO EATING CABBAGE FOR EVERY MEAL.
MY POOR MAN...
AS A SPECIAL FAVOR, SHALL I GIVE YOU SOME VITAMIN SUPPLEMENTS AT A BARGAIN PRICE?
...
'Bout this much.

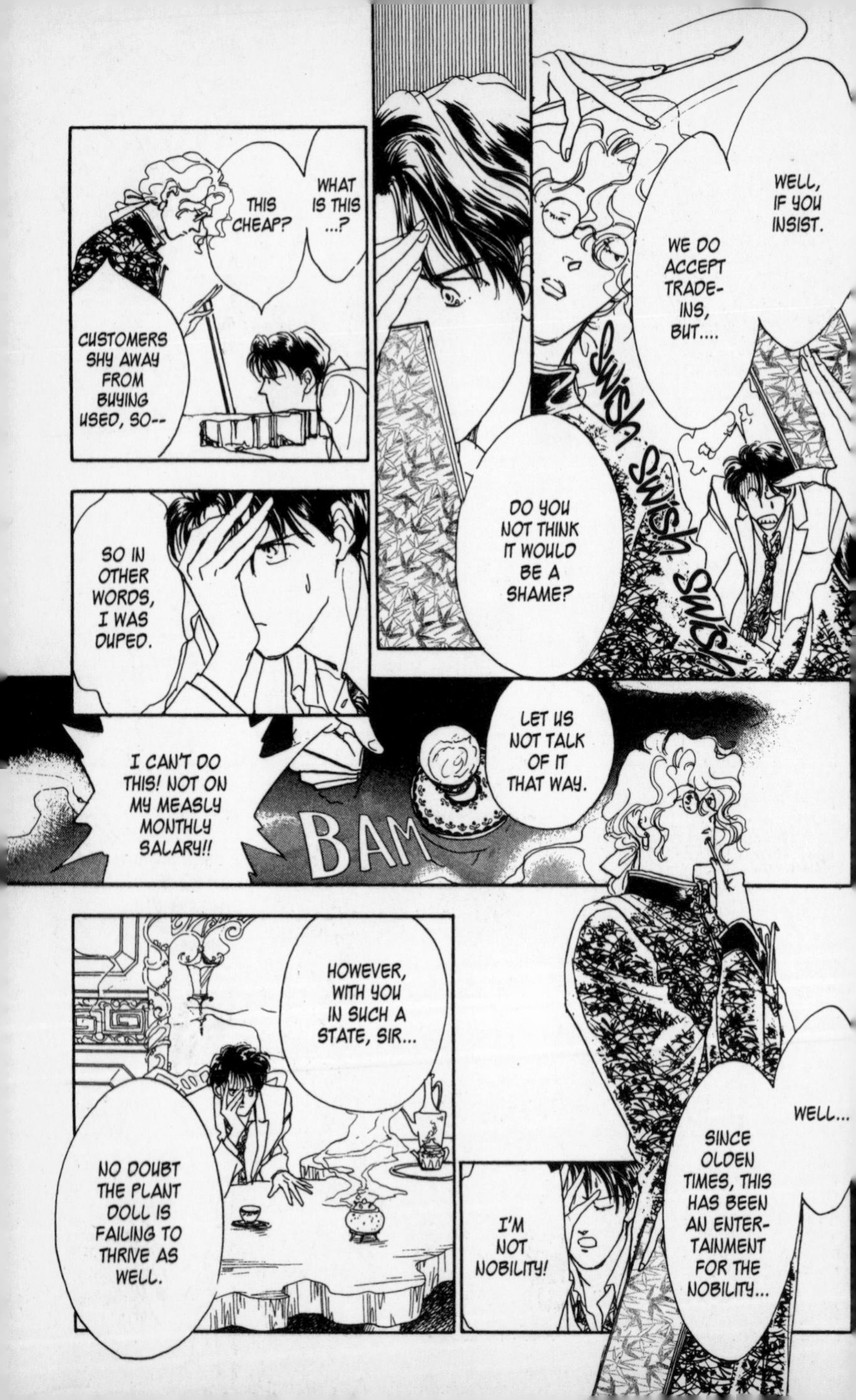
WELL, IF YOU INSIST.
WE DO ACCEPT TRADE-INS, BUT....
SWISH
SWISH
SWISH
DO YOU NOT THINK IT WOULD BE A SHAME?
WHAT IS THIS ...?
THIS CHEAP?
CUSTOMERS SHY AWAY FROM BUYING USED, SO--
SO IN OTHER WORDS, I WAS DUPED.
LET US NOT TALK OF IT THAT WAY.
BAM
I CAN'T DO THIS! NOT ON MY MEASLY MONTHLY SALARY!!
WELL...
SINCE OLDEN TIMES, THIS HAS BEEN AN ENTER-TAINMENT FOR THE NOBILITY...
I'M NOT NOBILITY!
HOWEVER, WITH YOU IN SUCH A STATE, SIR...
NO DOUBT THE PLANT DOLL IS FAILING TO THRIVE AS WELL.

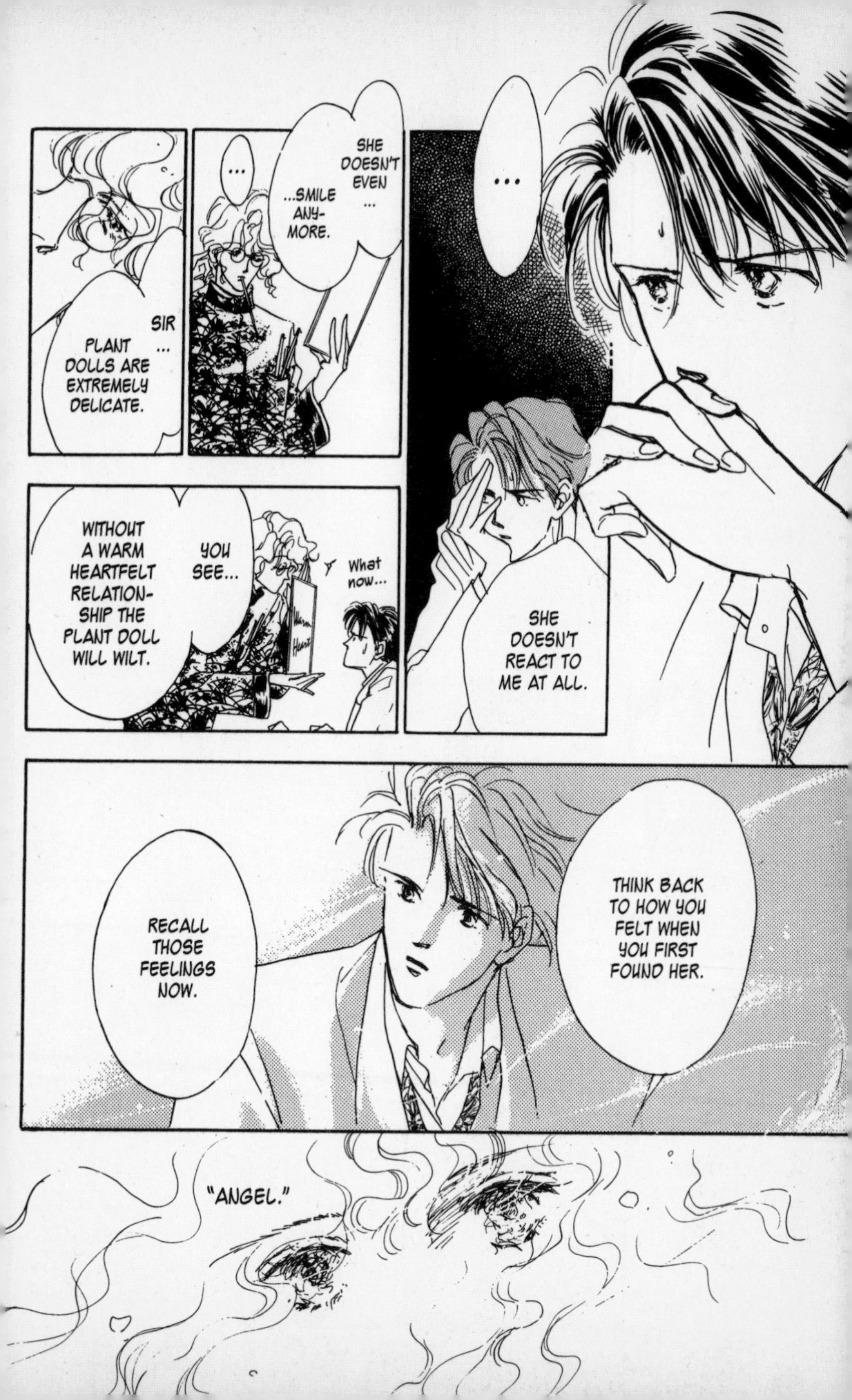
...
SHE DOESN'T REACT TO ME AT ALL.
SHE DOESN'T EVEN ...
...SMILE ANYMORE.
...
SIR ...
PLANT DOLLS ARE EXTREMELY DELICATE.
What now...
YOU SEE...
WITHOUT A WARM HEARTFELT RELATIONSHIP THE PLANT DOLL WILL WILT.
THINK BACK TO HOW YOU FELT WHEN YOU FIRST FOUND HER.
RECALL THOSE FEELINGS NOW.
"ANGEL."

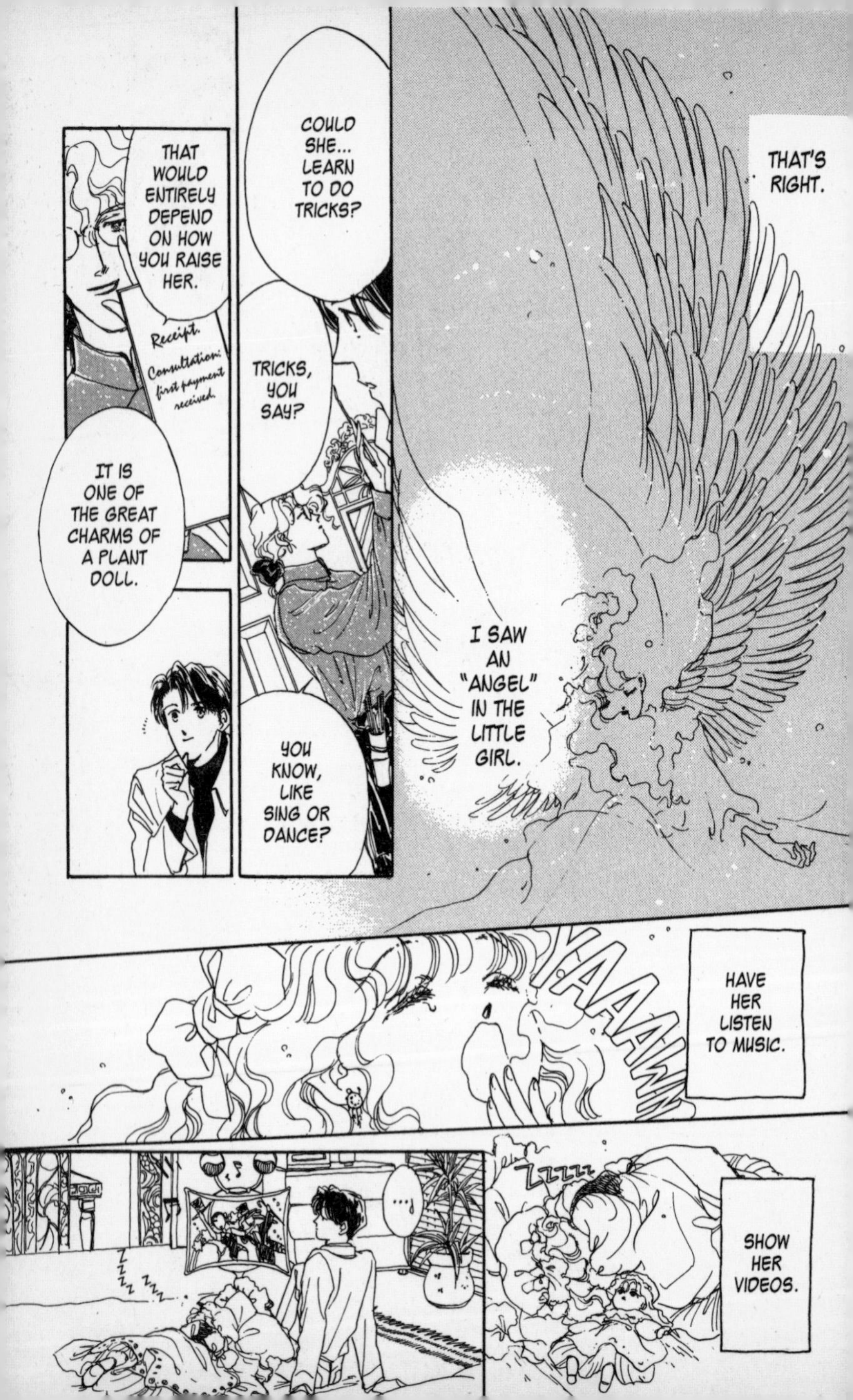
THAT'S RIGHT.
I SAW AN "ANGEL" IN THE LITTLE GIRL.
COULD SHE... LEARN TO DO TRICKS?
TRICKS, YOU SAY?
YOU KNOW, LIKE SING OR DANCE?
THAT WOULD ENTIRELY DEPEND ON HOW YOU RAISE HER.
Receipt.
Consultation: first payment received.
IT IS ONE OF THE GREAT CHARMS OF A PLANT DOLL.
HAVE HER LISTEN TO MUSIC.
YAAAAWN
SHOW HER VIDEOS.
ZZZZZ

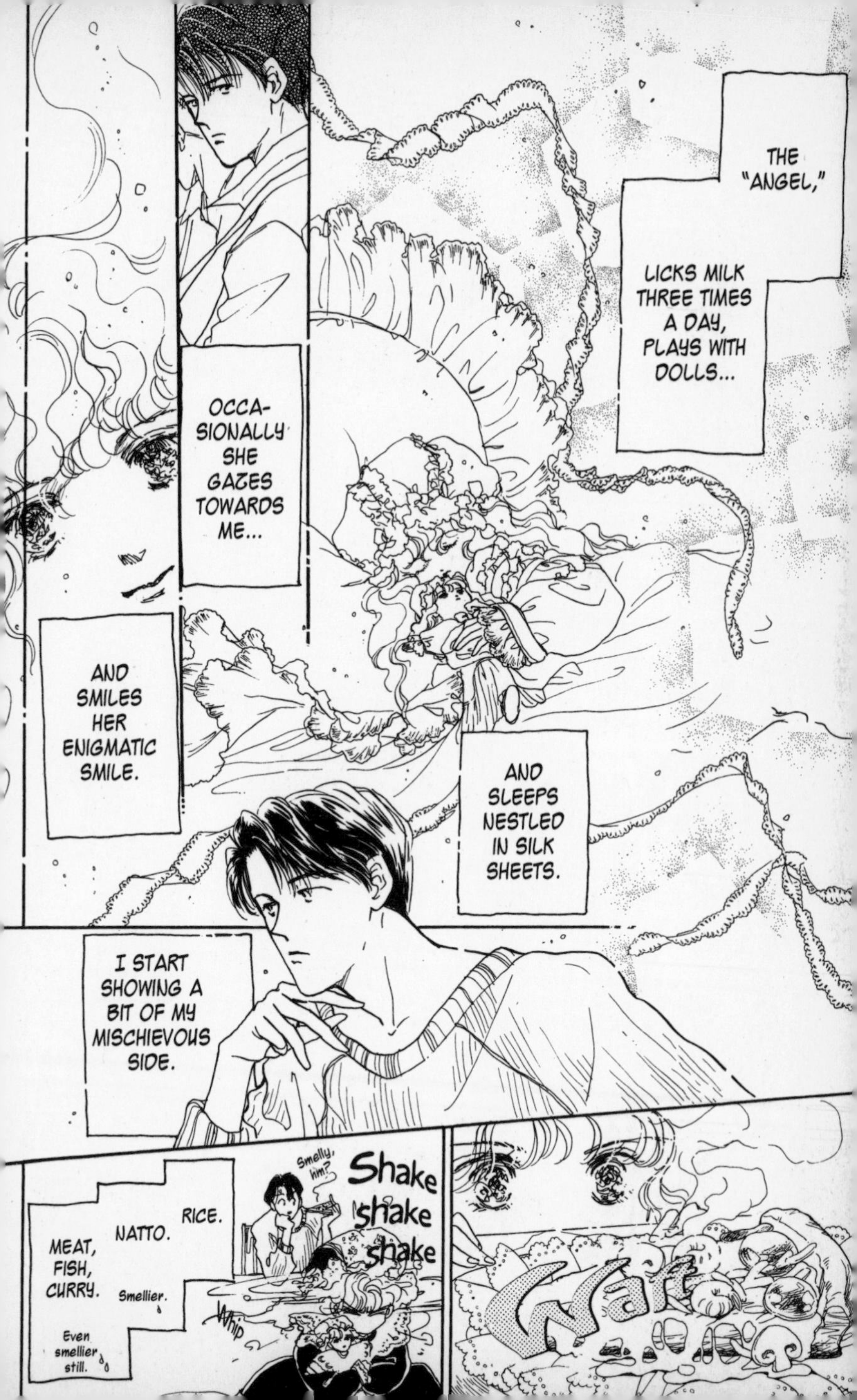
THE "ANGEL,"
LICKS MILK THREE TIMES A DAY, PLAYS WITH DOLLS...
AND SLEEPS NESTLED IN SILK SHEETS.
OCCA-SIONALLY SHE GAZES TOWARDS ME...
AND SMILES HER ENIGMATIC SMILE.
I START SHOWING A BIT OF MY MISCHIEVOUS SIDE.
Smelly, hm?
Shake shake shake
RICE.
NATTO.
MEAT, FISH, CURRY.
Smellier.
Even smellier still.
Whip

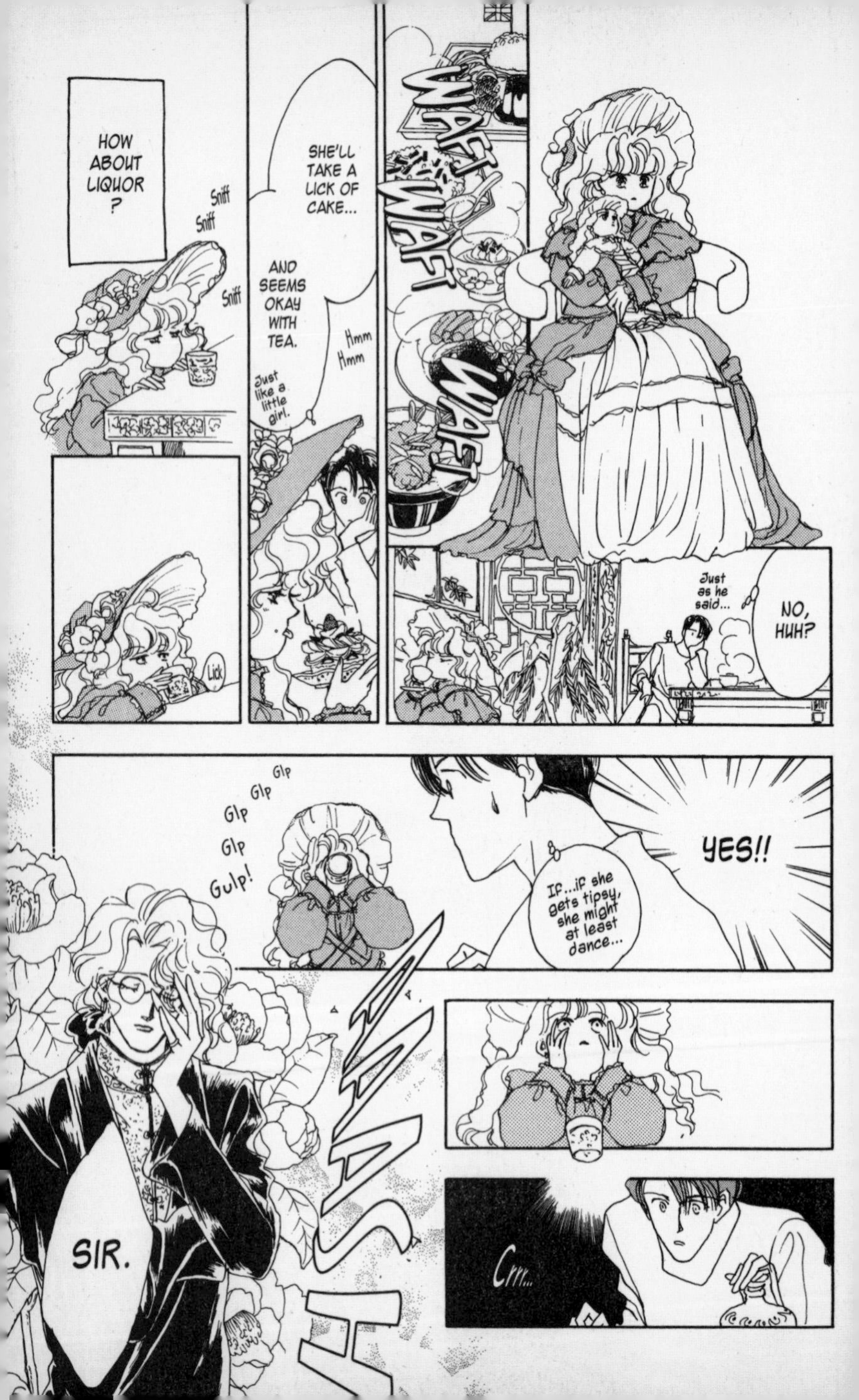
WAFT
WAFT
WAFT
Just as he said...
NO, HUH?
SHE'LL TAKE A LICK OF CAKE...
AND SEEMS OKAY WITH TEA.
Hmm
Hmm
Just like a little girl.
HOW ABOUT LIQUOR?
Sniff
Sniff
Sniff
Lick
YES!!
If...if she gets tipsy, she might at least dance...
Glp
Glp
Glp
Glp
Gulp!
Crrr...
SIR.

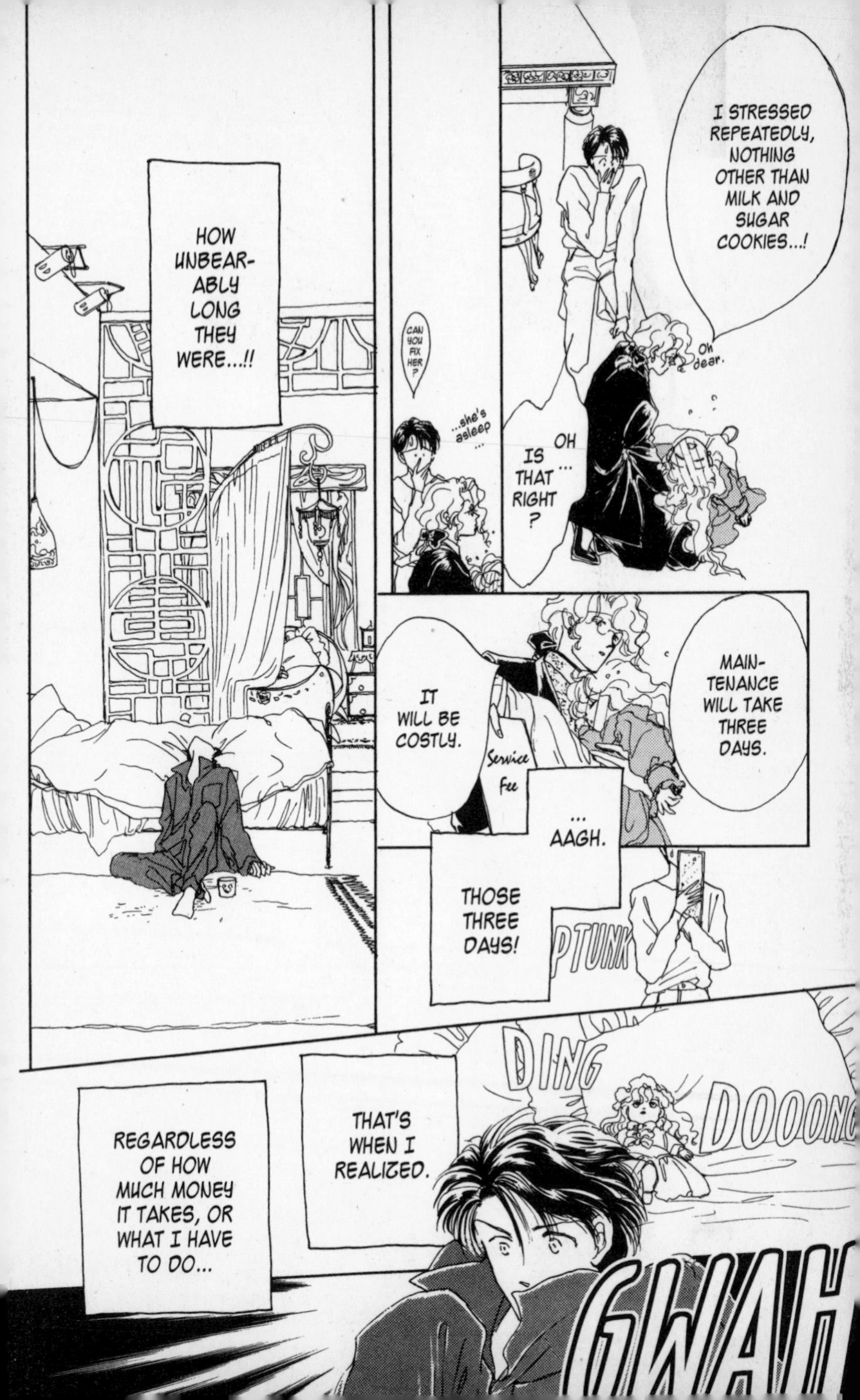
I STRESSED REPEATEDLY, NOTHING OTHER THAN MILK AND SUGAR COOKIES...!
Oh dear.
OH ... IS THAT RIGHT ?
CAN YOU FIX HER ?
...she's asleep ...
MAIN-TENANCE WILL TAKE THREE DAYS.
IT WILL BE COSTLY.
Service Fee
... AAGH.
PTUNK
THOSE THREE DAYS!
HOW UNBEARABLY LONG THEY WERE...!!
DING
DOOONG
GWAH
THAT'S WHEN I REALIZED.
REGARDLESS OF HOW MUCH MONEY IT TAKES, OR WHAT I HAVE TO DO...

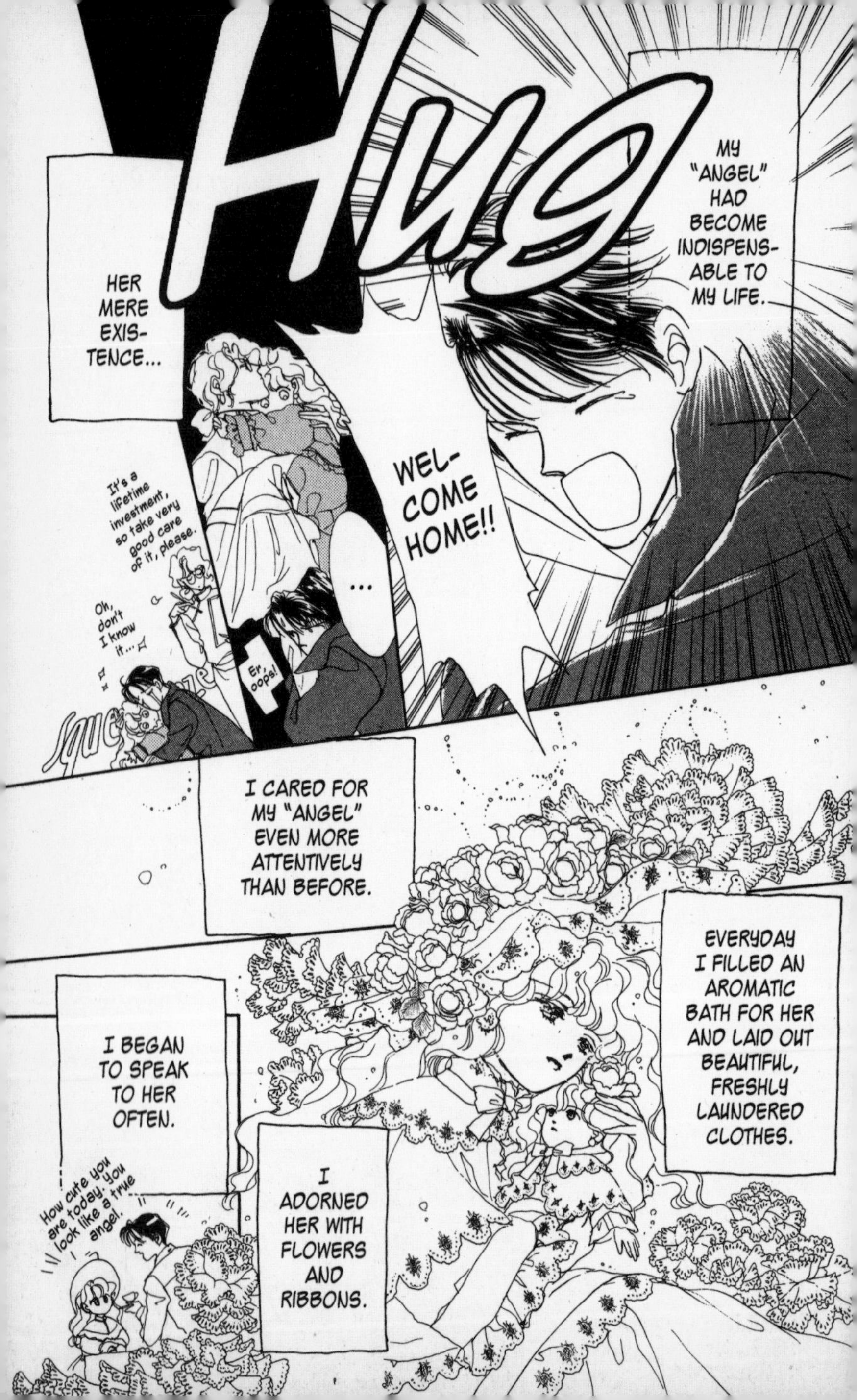
Hug
MY "ANGEL" HAD BECOME INDISPENS-ABLE TO MY LIFE.
WEL-COME HOME!!
HER MERE EXIS-TENCE...
...
Er, oops!
It's a lifetime investment, so take very good care of it, please.
Oh, don't I know it...
I CARED FOR MY "ANGEL" EVEN MORE ATTENTIVELY THAN BEFORE.
EVERYDAY I FILLED AN AROMATIC BATH FOR HER AND LAID OUT BEAUTIFUL, FRESHLY LAUNDERED CLOTHES.
I ADORNED HER WITH FLOWERS AND RIBBONS.
I BEGAN TO SPEAK TO HER OFTEN.
How cute you are today. You look like a true angel.

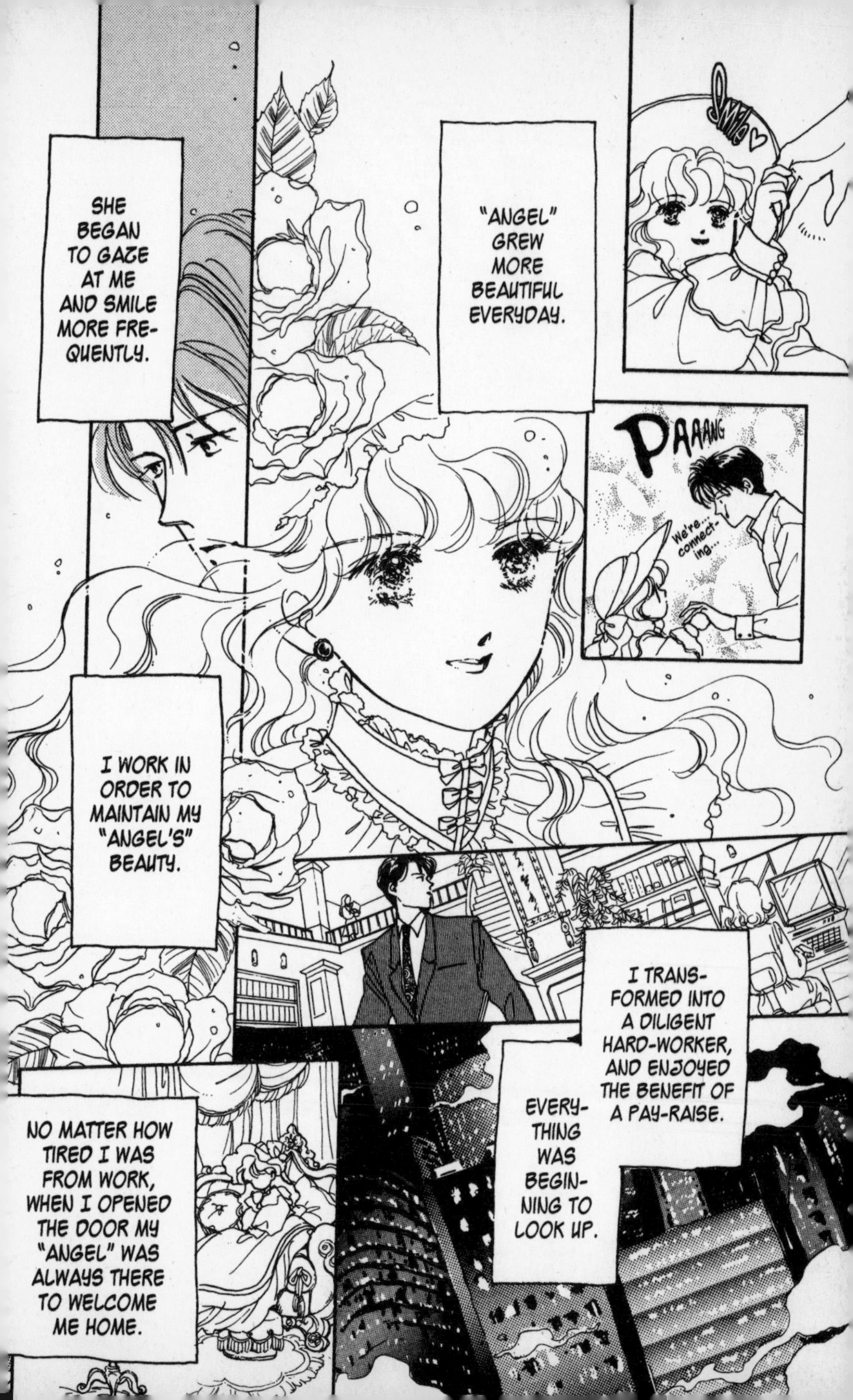
"ANGEL" GREW MORE BEAUTIFUL EVERYDAY.
PAAANG
We're... connect-ing...
SHE BEGAN TO GAZE AT ME AND SMILE MORE FRE-QUENTLY.
I WORK IN ORDER TO MAINTAIN MY "ANGEL'S" BEAUTY.
I TRANS-FORMED INTO A DILIGENT HARD-WORKER, AND ENJOYED THE BENEFIT OF A PAY-RAISE.
EVERY-THING WAS BEGIN-NING TO LOOK UP.
NO MATTER HOW TIRED I WAS FROM WORK, WHEN I OPENED THE DOOR MY "ANGEL" WAS ALWAYS THERE TO WELCOME ME HOME.

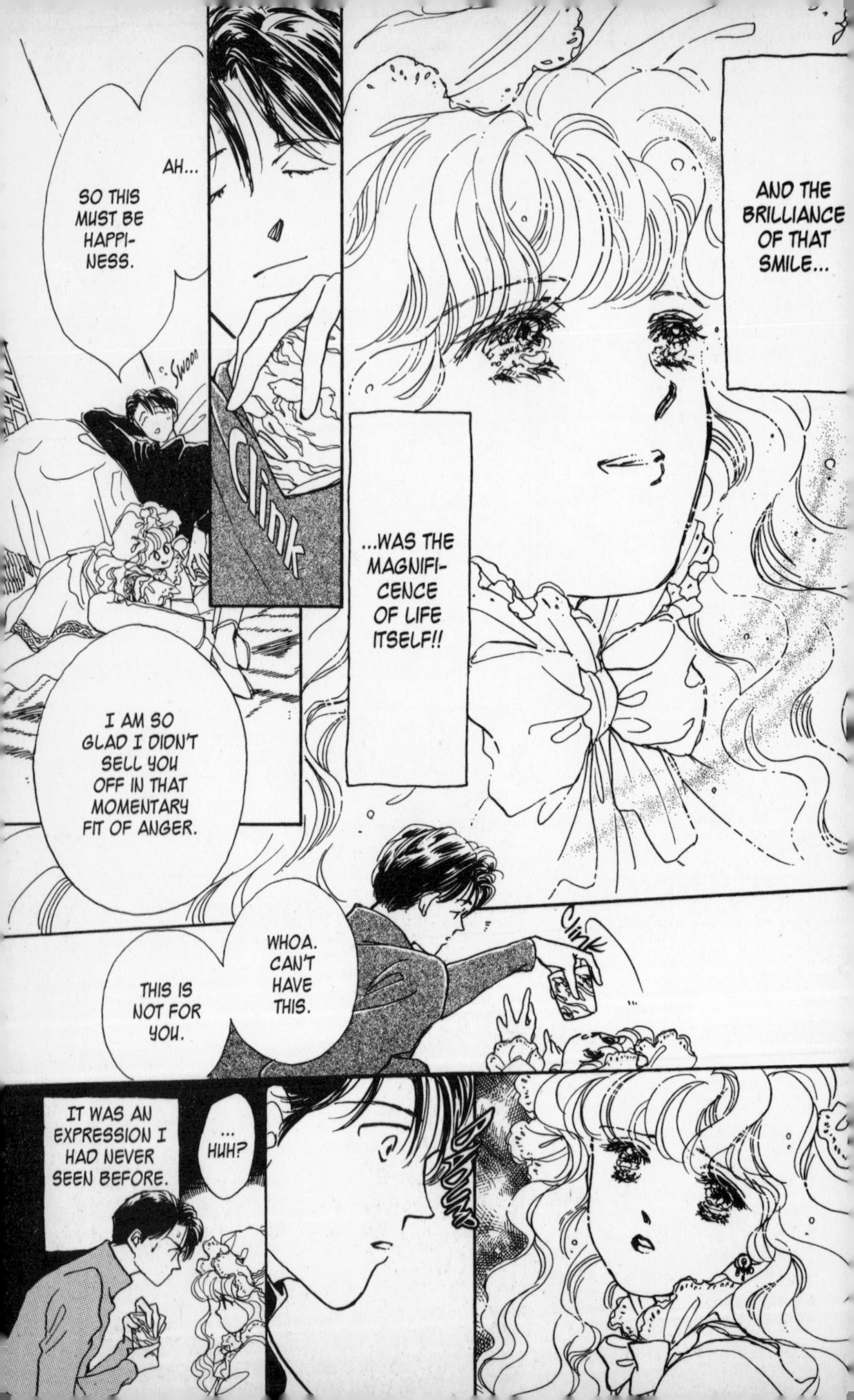
AND THE BRILLIANCE OF THAT SMILE...
...WAS THE MAGNIFICENCE OF LIFE ITSELF!!
Clink
AH...
SO THIS MUST BE HAPPINESS.
Swoon
I AM SO GLAD I DIDN'T SELL YOU OFF IN THAT MOMENTARY FIT OF ANGER.
Clink
WHOA. CAN'T HAVE THIS.
THIS IS NOT FOR YOU.
...HUH?
IT WAS AN EXPRESSION I HAD NEVER SEEN BEFORE.

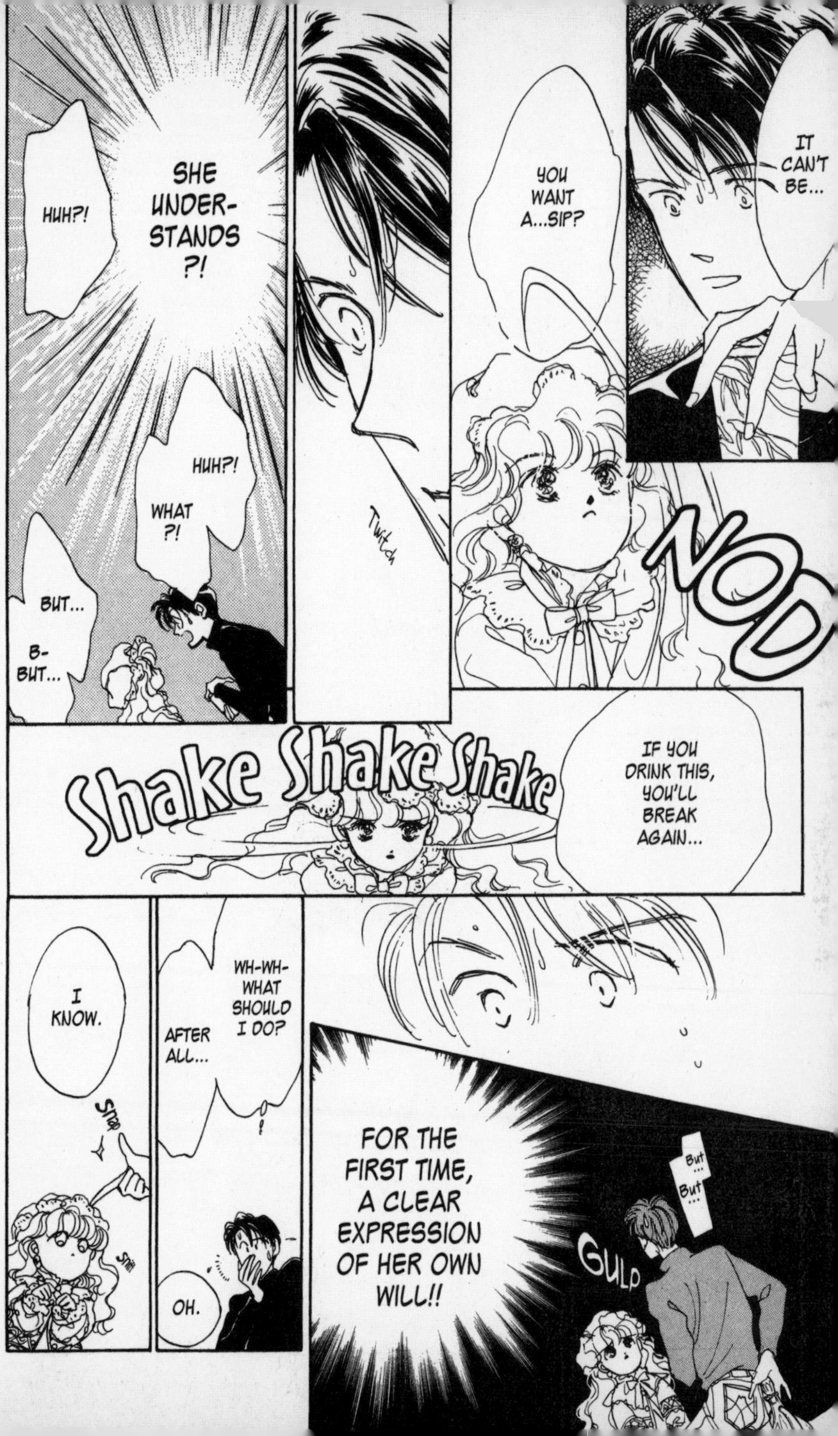
IT CAN'T BE...
YOU WANT A...SIP?
NOD
Twitch
SHE UNDERSTANDS?!
HUH?!
HUH?!
WHAT?!
BUT...
B-BUT...
IF YOU DRINK THIS, YOU'LL BREAK AGAIN...
Shake Shake Shake
FOR THE FIRST TIME, A CLEAR EXPRESSION OF HER OWN WILL!!
But... But...
GULP
WH-WH-WHAT SHOULD I DO?
AFTER ALL...
OH.
I KNOW.

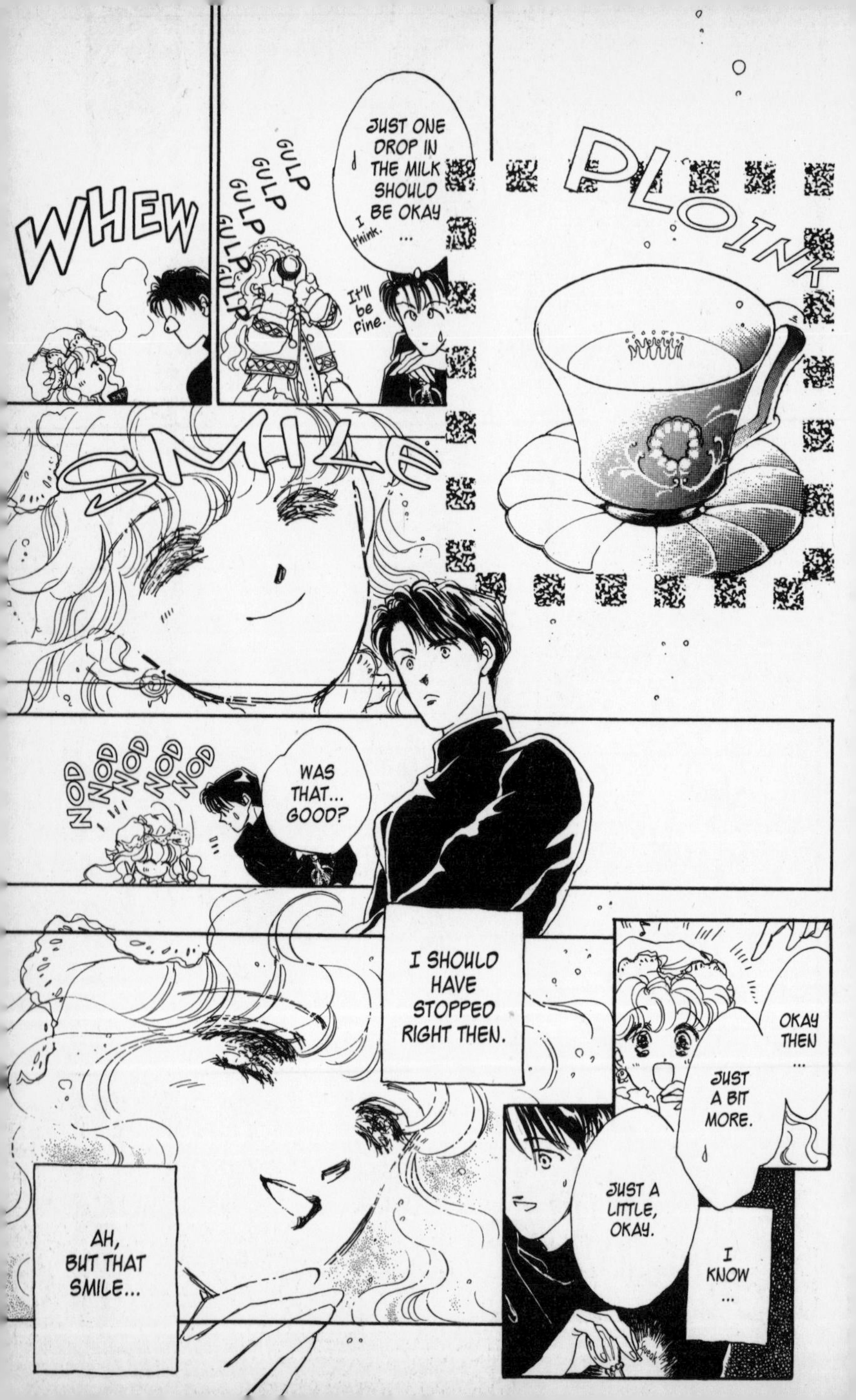
PLOINK
JUST ONE DROP IN THE MILK SHOULD BE OKAY ...
I think.
It'll be fine.
GULP GULP GULP GULP GULP
WHEW
SMILE
WAS THAT... GOOD?
NOD NOD NOD NOD NOD
OKAY THEN ...
JUST A BIT MORE.
JUST A LITTLE, OKAY.
I KNOW ...
Squeak
I SHOULD HAVE STOPPED RIGHT THEN.
AH, BUT THAT SMILE...

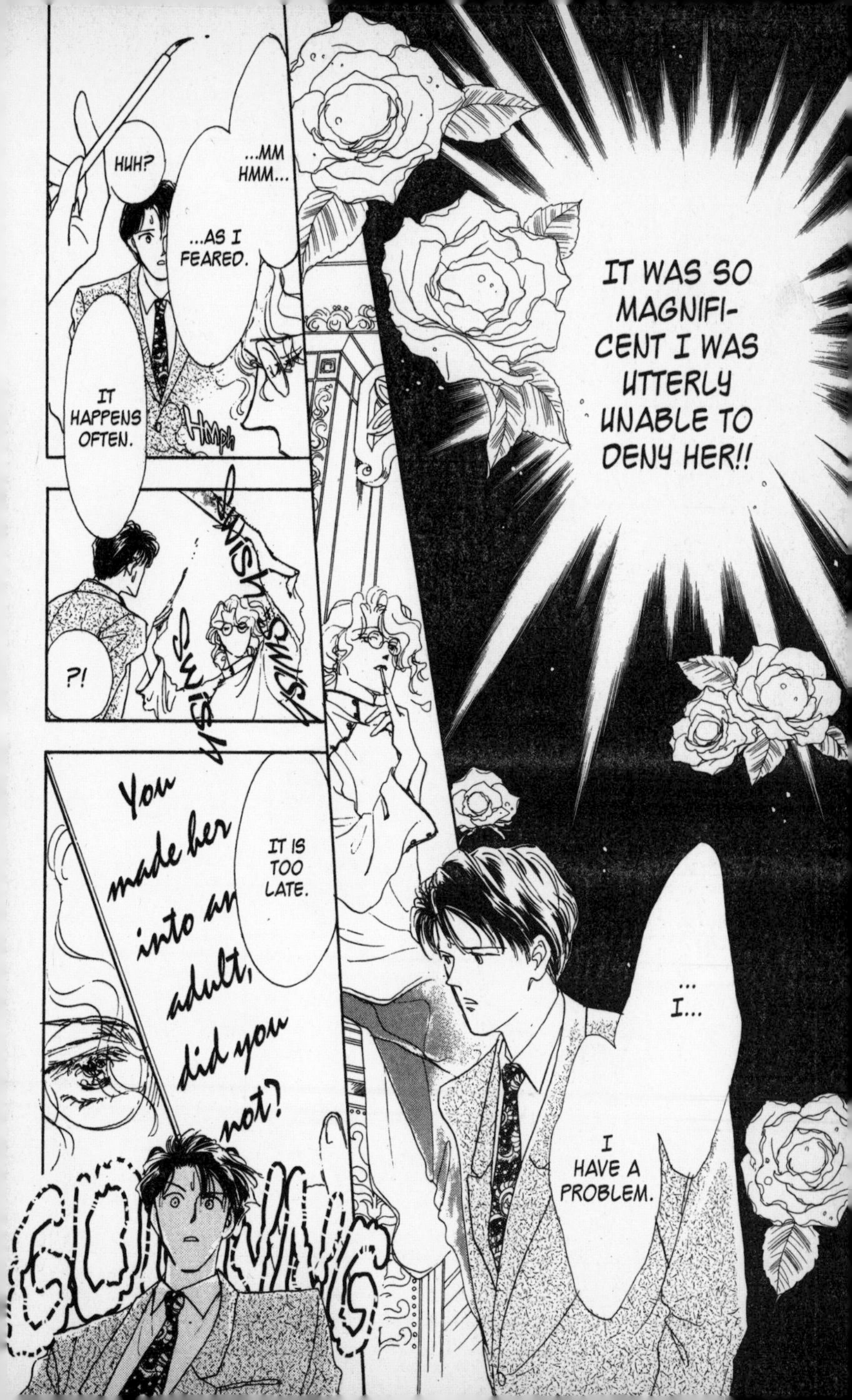
IT WAS SO MAGNIFICENT I WAS UTTERLY UNABLE TO DENY HER!!
... I...
I HAVE A PROBLEM.
...MM HMM...
HUH?
...AS I FEARED.
IT HAPPENS OFTEN.
Hmph
SWISH SWISH
?!
IT IS TOO LATE.
You made her into an adult, did you not?

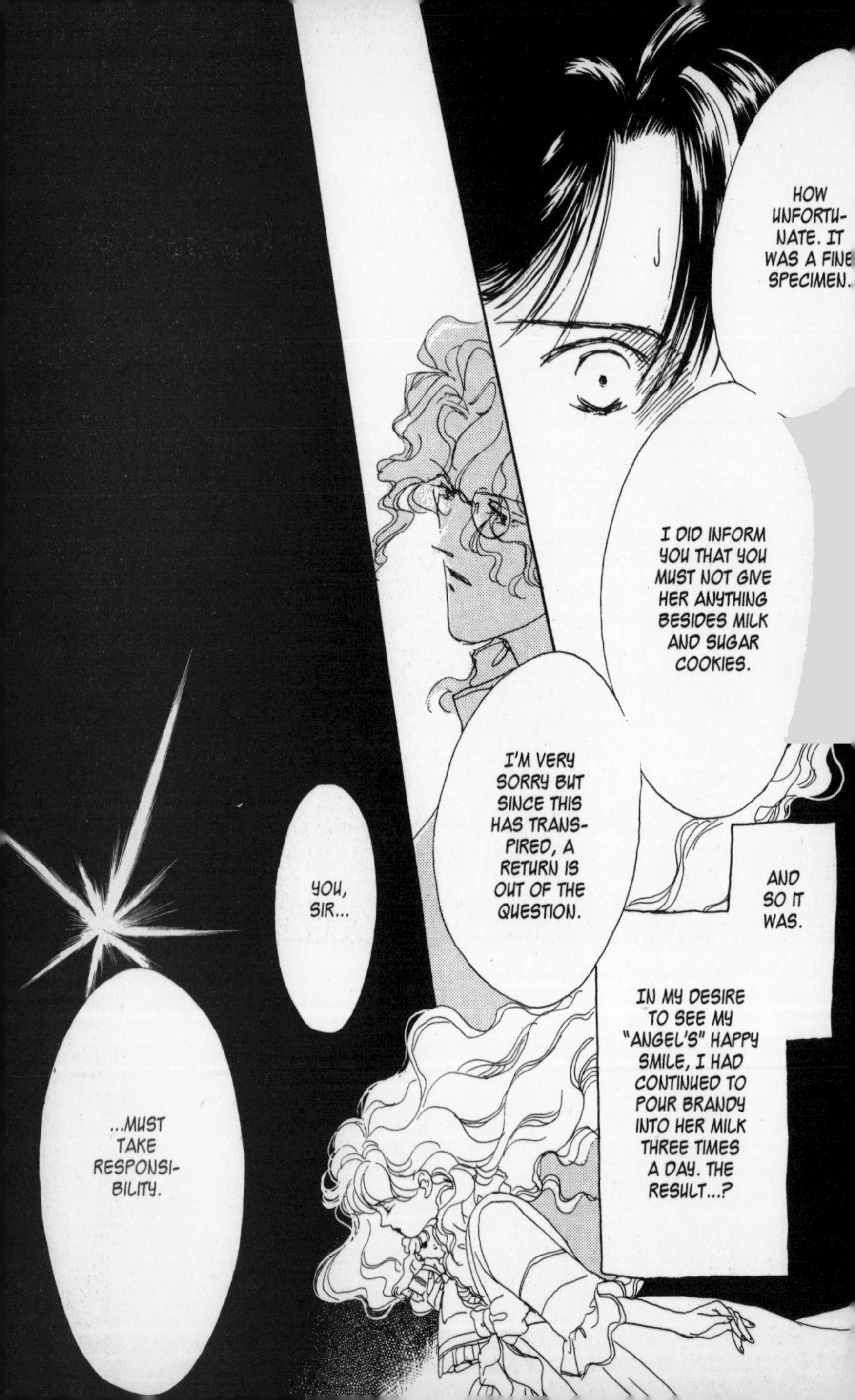
HOW UNFORTUNATE. IT WAS A FINE SPECIMEN.
I DID INFORM YOU THAT YOU MUST NOT GIVE HER ANYTHING BESIDES MILK AND SUGAR COOKIES.
I'M VERY SORRY BUT SINCE THIS HAS TRANSPIRED, A RETURN IS OUT OF THE QUESTION.
AND SO IT WAS.
IN MY DESIRE TO SEE MY "ANGEL'S" HAPPY SMILE, I HAD CONTINUED TO POUR BRANDY INTO HER MILK THREE TIMES A DAY. THE RESULT...?
YOU, SIR...
...MUST TAKE RESPONSIBILITY.

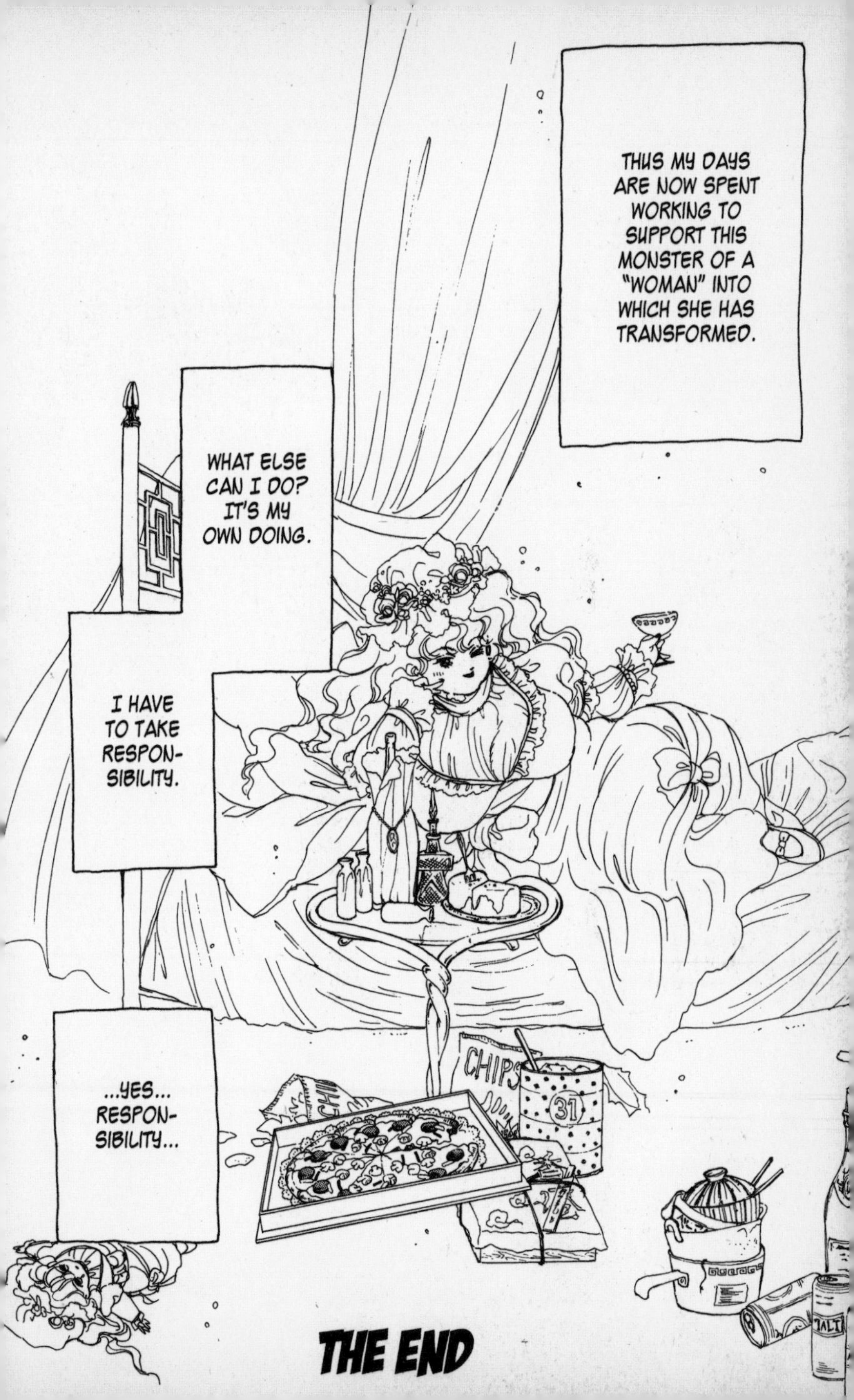
THUS MY DAYS ARE NOW SPENT WORKING TO SUPPORT THIS MONSTER OF A "WOMAN" INTO WHICH SHE HAS TRANSFORMED.
WHAT ELSE CAN I DO? IT'S MY OWN DOING.
I HAVE TO TAKE RESPON-SIBILITY.
...YES... RESPON-SIBILITY...
CHIPS
31
THE END

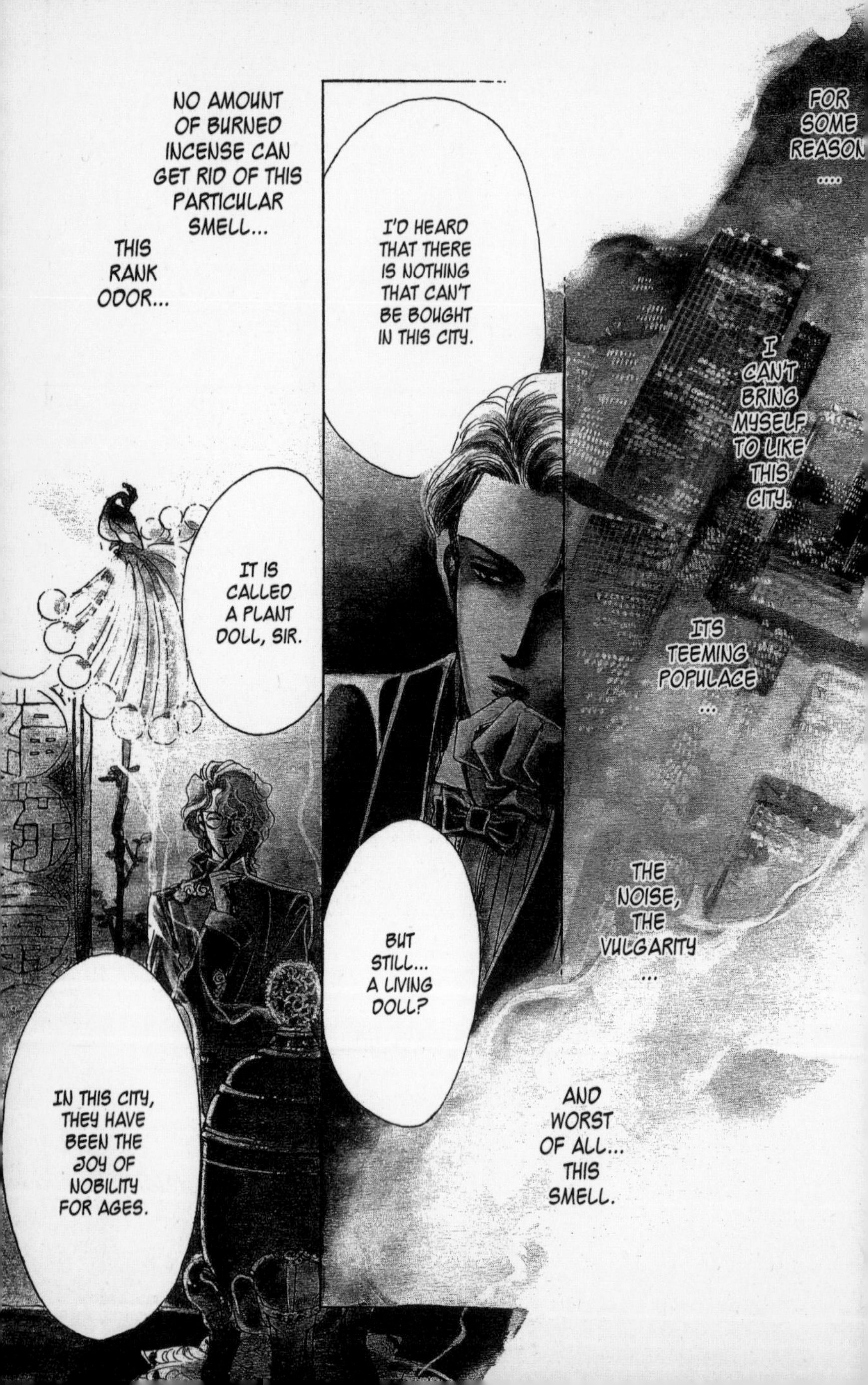
FOR SOME REASON....
I CAN'T BRING MYSELF TO LIKE THIS CITY.
ITS TEEMING POPULACE...
THE NOISE, THE VULGARITY...
AND WORST OF ALL... THIS SMELL.
I'D HEARD THAT THERE IS NOTHING THAT CAN'T BE BOUGHT IN THIS CITY.
BUT STILL... A LIVING DOLL?
NO AMOUNT OF BURNED INCENSE CAN GET RID OF THIS PARTICULAR SMELL...
THIS RANK ODOR...
IT IS CALLED A PLANT DOLL, SIR.
IN THIS CITY, THEY HAVE BEEN THE JOY OF NOBILITY FOR AGES.

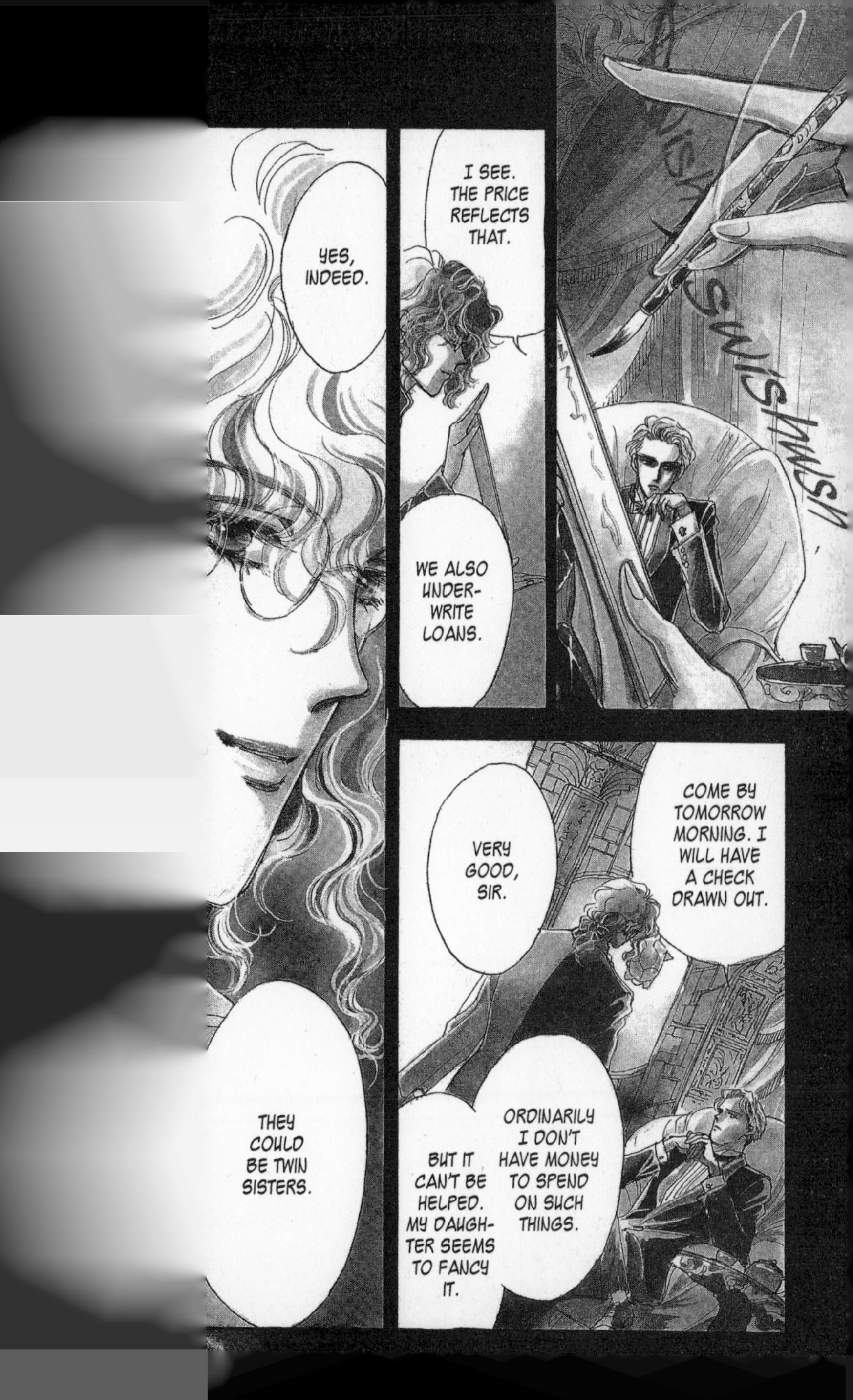
SWISH SWISH
I SEE. THE PRICE REFLECTS THAT.
WE ALSO UNDER-WRITE LOANS.
COME BY TOMORROW MORNING. I WILL HAVE A CHECK DRAWN OUT.
VERY GOOD, SIR.
ORDINARILY I DON'T HAVE MONEY TO SPEND ON SUCH THINGS.
BUT IT CAN'T BE HELPED. MY DAUGHTER SEEMS TO FANCY IT.
YES, INDEED.
THEY COULD BE TWIN SISTERS.

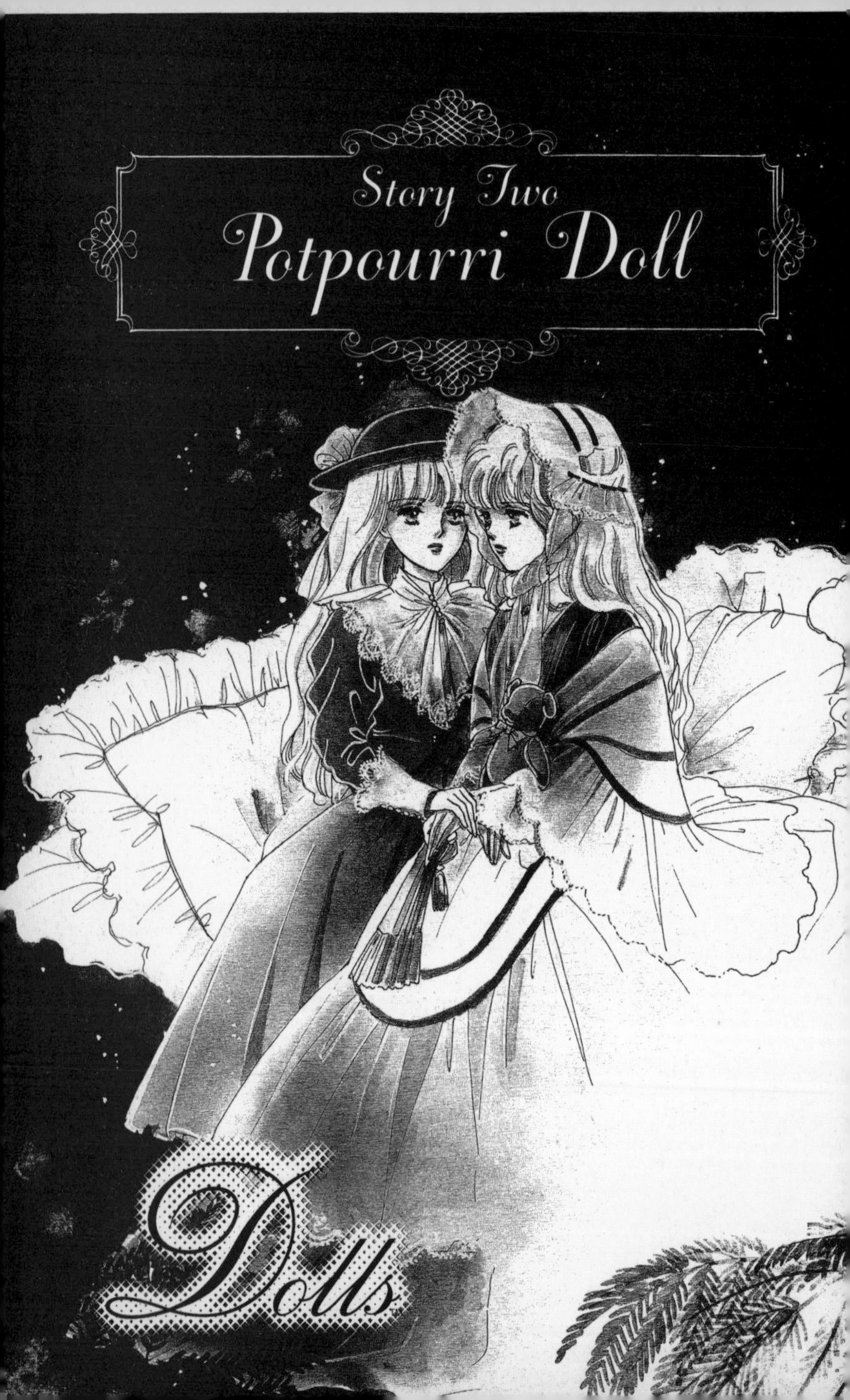
Story Two
Potpourri Doll
Dolls

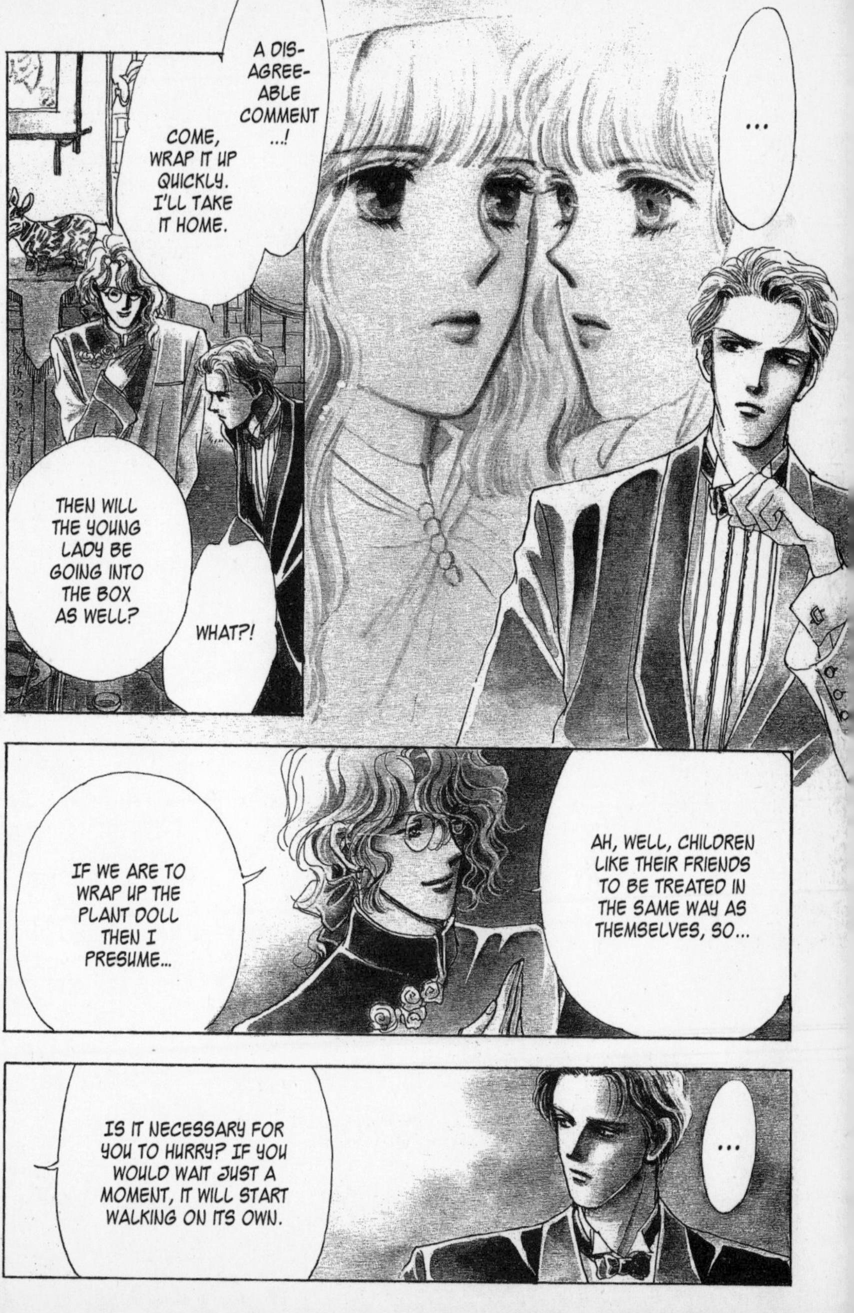
...
A DIS-AGREEABLE COMMENT ...!
COME, WRAP IT UP QUICKLY. I'LL TAKE IT HOME.
THEN WILL THE YOUNG LADY BE GOING INTO THE BOX AS WELL?
WHAT?!
AH, WELL, CHILDREN LIKE THEIR FRIENDS TO BE TREATED IN THE SAME WAY AS THEMSELVES, SO...
IF WE ARE TO WRAP UP THE PLANT DOLL THEN I PRESUME...
...
IS IT NECESSARY FOR YOU TO HURRY? IF YOU WOULD WAIT JUST A MOMENT, IT WILL START WALKING ON ITS OWN.

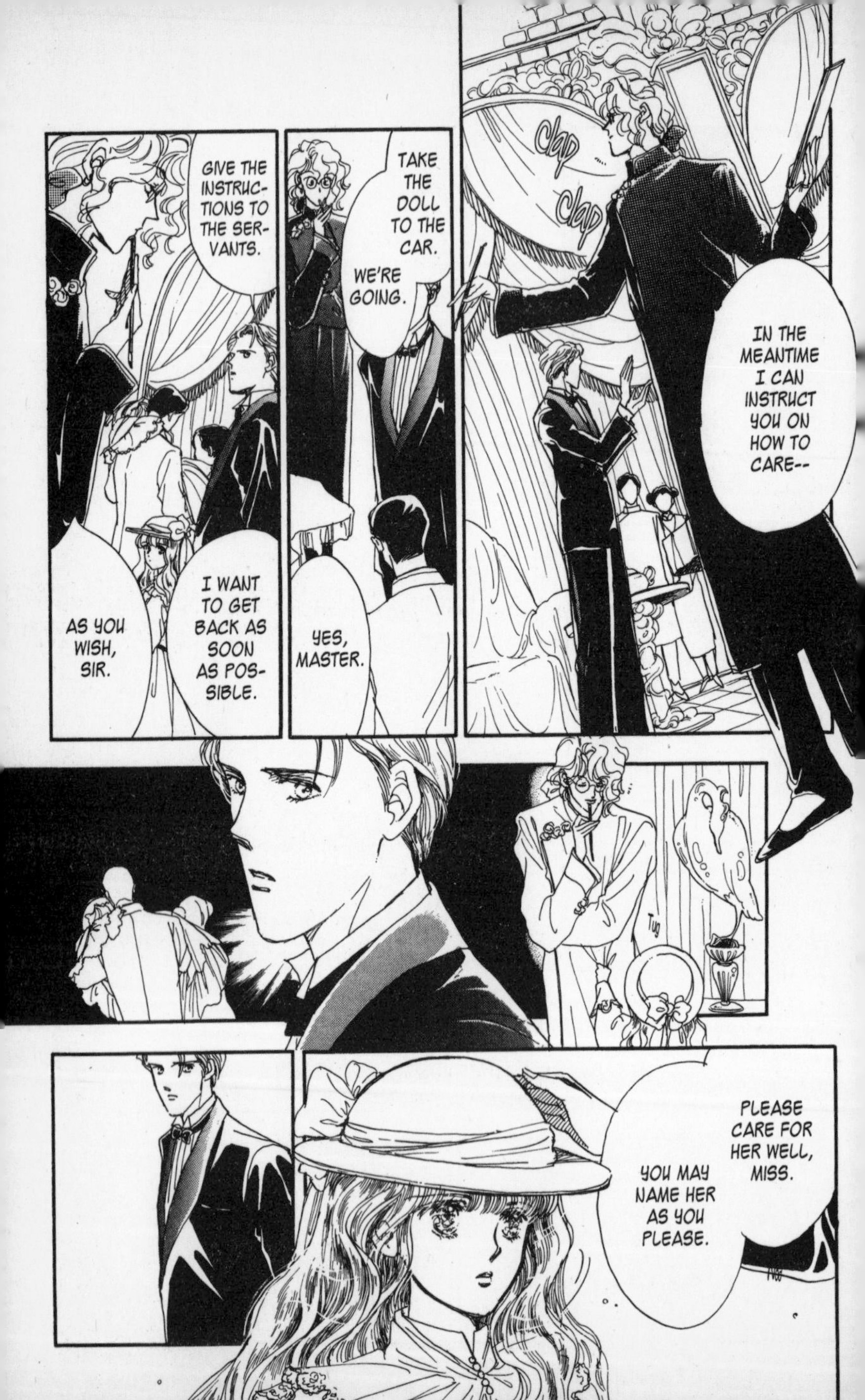
clap
clap
IN THE MEANTIME I CAN INSTRUCT YOU ON HOW TO CARE--
TAKE THE DOLL TO THE CAR.
WE'RE GOING.
YES, MASTER.
GIVE THE INSTRUCTIONS TO THE SERVANTS.
I WANT TO GET BACK AS SOON AS POSSIBLE.
AS YOU WISH, SIR.
Tug
PLEASE CARE FOR HER WELL, MISS.
YOU MAY NAME HER AS YOU PLEASE.

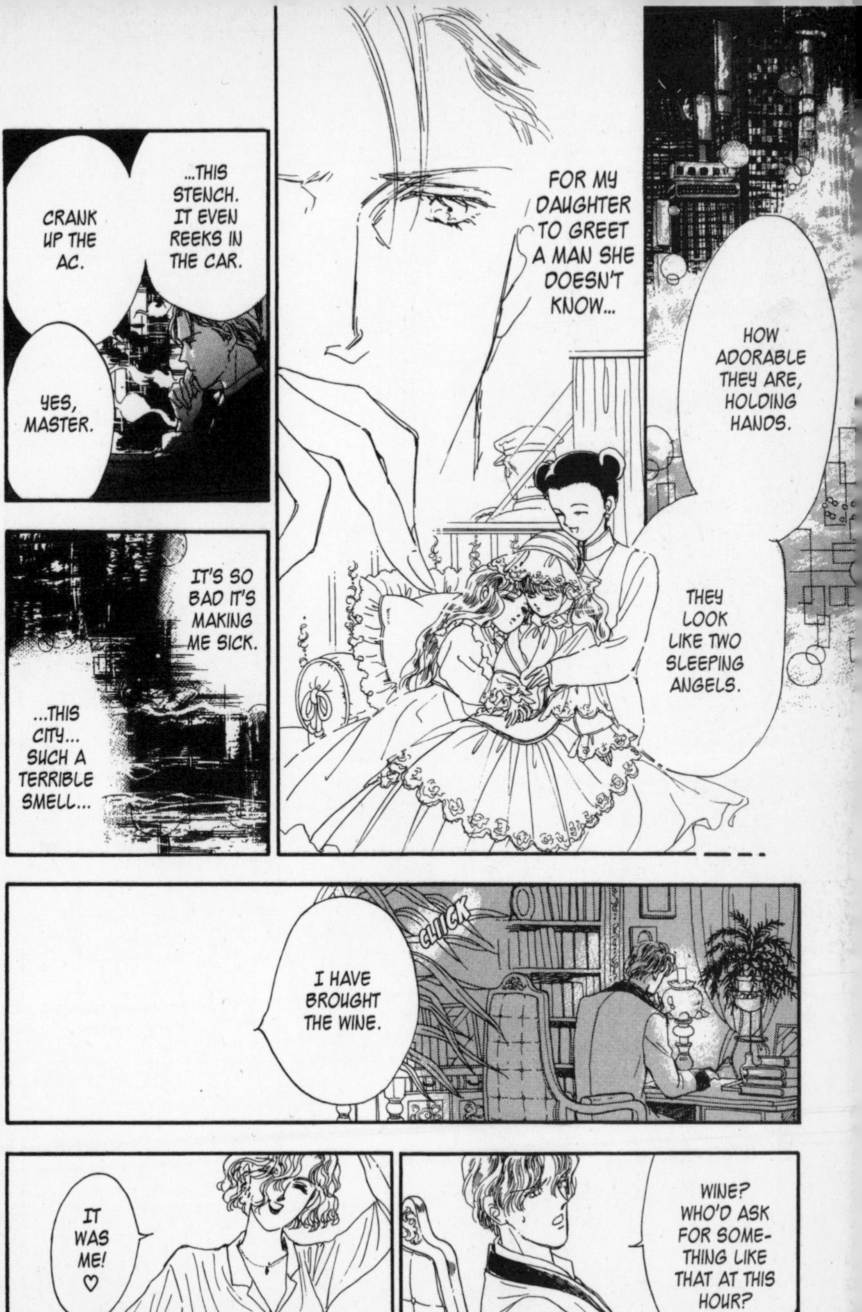
HOW ADORABLE THEY ARE, HOLDING HANDS.
THEY LOOK LIKE TWO SLEEPING ANGELS.
FOR MY DAUGHTER TO GREET A MAN SHE DOESN'T KNOW...
...THIS STENCH. IT EVEN REEKS IN THE CAR.
CRANK UP THE AC.
YES, MASTER.
IT'S SO BAD IT'S MAKING ME SICK.
...THIS CITY... SUCH A TERRIBLE SMELL...
CLICK
I HAVE BROUGHT THE WINE.
WINE? WHO'D ASK FOR SOME-THING LIKE THAT AT THIS HOUR?
IT WAS ME! ♡

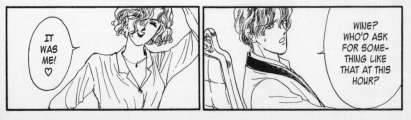

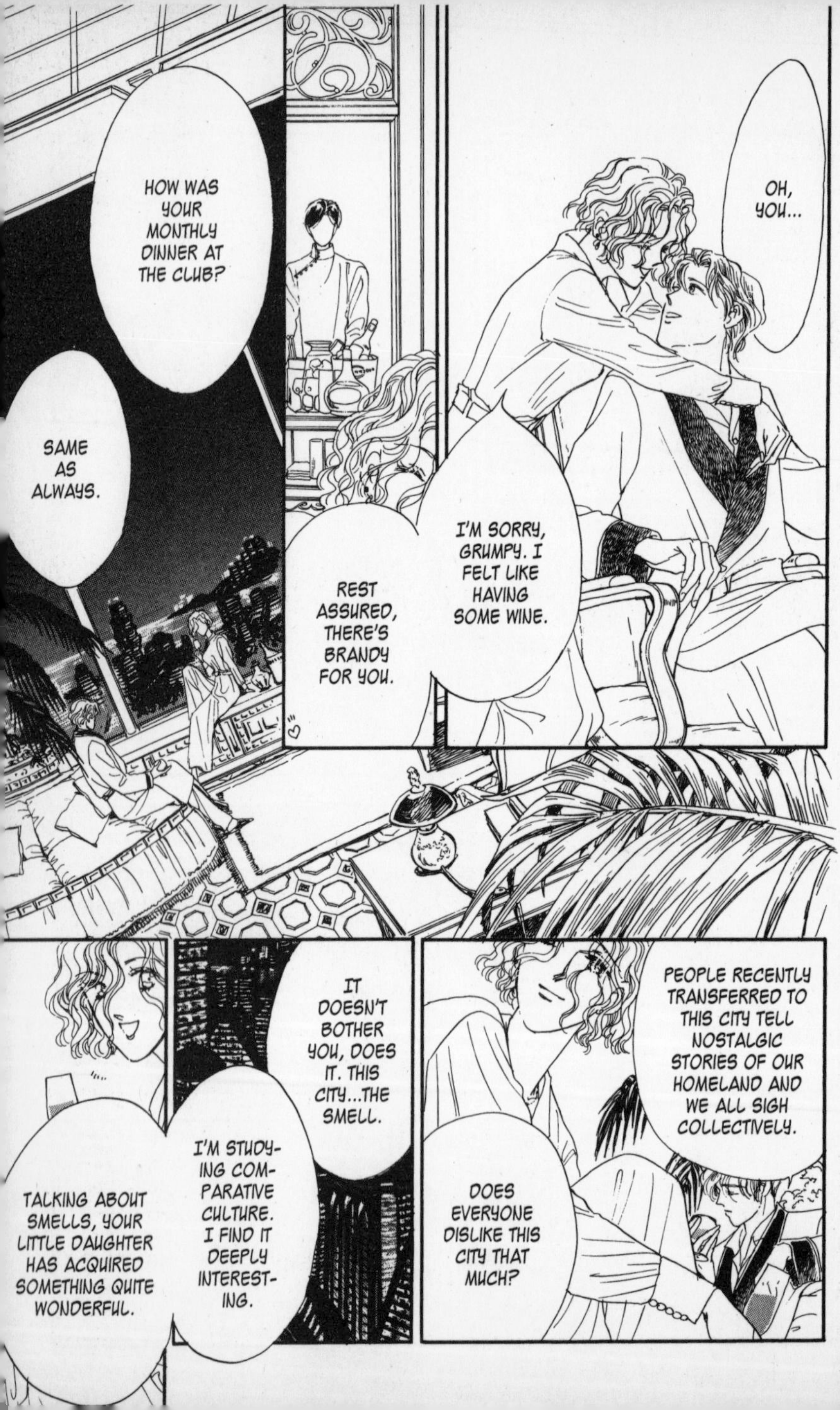
OH, YOU...
I'M SORRY, GRUMPY. I FELT LIKE HAVING SOME WINE.
REST ASSURED, THERE'S BRANDY FOR YOU.
HOW WAS YOUR MONTHLY DINNER AT THE CLUB?
SAME AS ALWAYS.
PEOPLE RECENTLY TRANSFERRED TO THIS CITY TELL NOSTALGIC STORIES OF OUR HOMELAND AND WE ALL SIGH COLLECTIVELY.
DOES EVERYONE DISLIKE THIS CITY THAT MUCH?
IT DOESN'T BOTHER YOU, DOES IT. THIS CITY...THE SMELL.
I'M STUDYING COMPARATIVE CULTURE. I FIND IT DEEPLY INTERESTING.
TALKING ABOUT SMELLS, YOUR LITTLE DAUGHTER HAS ACQUIRED SOMETHING QUITE WONDERFUL.

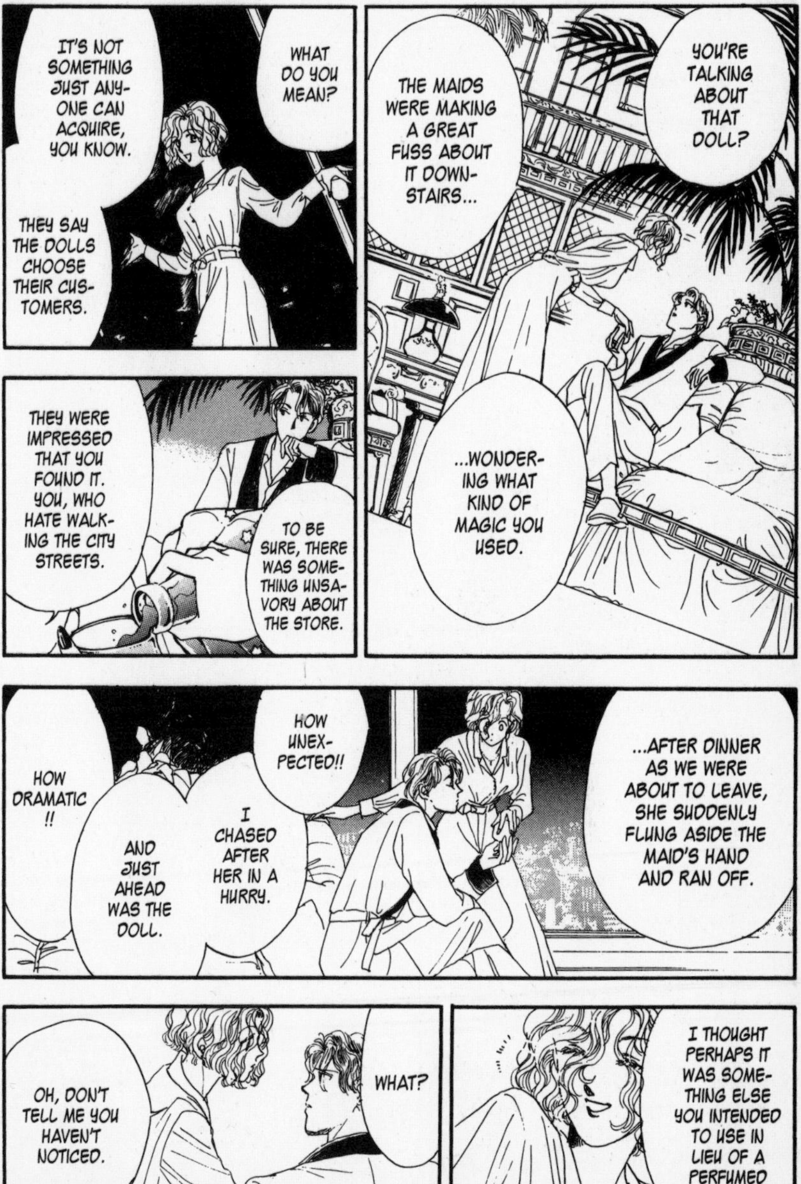
YOU'RE TALKING ABOUT THAT DOLL?
THE MAIDS WERE MAKING A GREAT FUSS ABOUT IT DOWN-STAIRS...
...WONDER-ING WHAT KIND OF MAGIC YOU USED.
WHAT DO YOU MEAN?
IT'S NOT SOMETHING JUST ANY-ONE CAN ACQUIRE, YOU KNOW.
THEY SAY THE DOLLS CHOOSE THEIR CUS-TOMERS.
THEY WERE IMPRESSED THAT YOU FOUND IT. YOU, WHO HATE WALK-ING THE CITY STREETS.
TO BE SURE, THERE WAS SOME-THING UNSA-VORY ABOUT THE STORE.
...AFTER DINNER AS WE WERE ABOUT TO LEAVE, SHE SUDDENLY FLUNG ASIDE THE MAID'S HAND AND RAN OFF.
HOW UNEX-PECTED!!
I CHASED AFTER HER IN A HURRY.
AND JUST AHEAD WAS THE DOLL.
HOW DRAMATIC !!
I THOUGHT PERHAPS IT WAS SOME-THING ELSE YOU INTENDED TO USE IN LIEU OF A PERFUMED SACHET.
WHAT?
OH, DON'T TELL ME YOU HAVEN'T NOTICED.

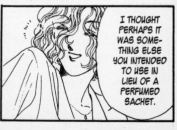

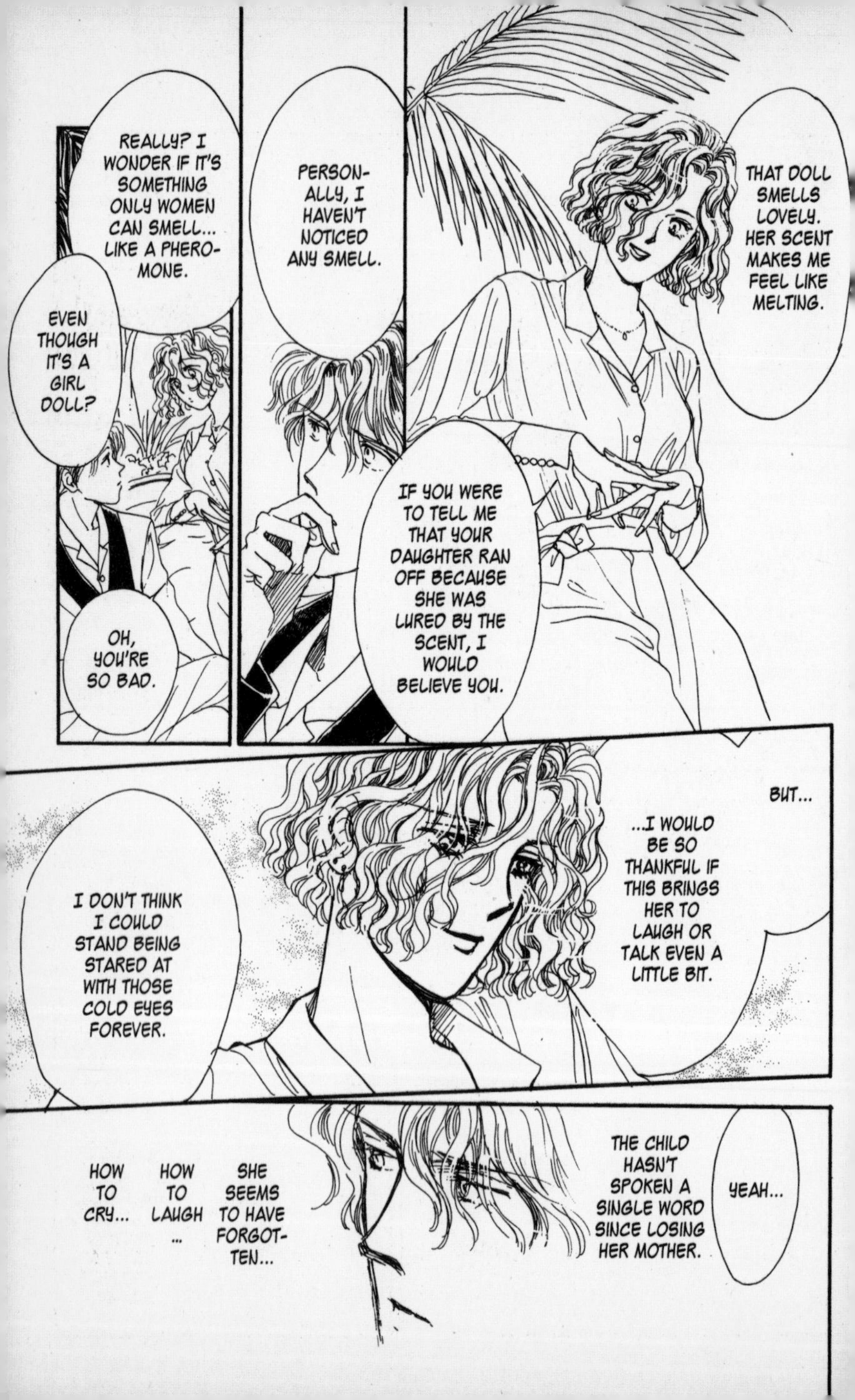
THAT DOLL SMELLS LOVELY. HER SCENT MAKES ME FEEL LIKE MELTING.
IF YOU WERE TO TELL ME THAT YOUR DAUGHTER RAN OFF BECAUSE SHE WAS LURED BY THE SCENT, I WOULD BELIEVE YOU.
PERSON-ALLY, I HAVEN'T NOTICED ANY SMELL.
REALLY? I WONDER IF IT'S SOMETHING ONLY WOMEN CAN SMELL... LIKE A PHERO-MONE.
EVEN THOUGH IT'S A GIRL DOLL?
OH, YOU'RE SO BAD.
BUT...
...I WOULD BE SO THANKFUL IF THIS BRINGS HER TO LAUGH OR TALK EVEN A LITTLE BIT.
I DON'T THINK I COULD STAND BEING STARED AT WITH THOSE COLD EYES FOREVER.
YEAH...
THE CHILD HASN'T SPOKEN A SINGLE WORD SINCE LOSING HER MOTHER.
SHE SEEMS TO HAVE FORGOT-TEN...
HOW TO LAUGH...
HOW TO CRY...

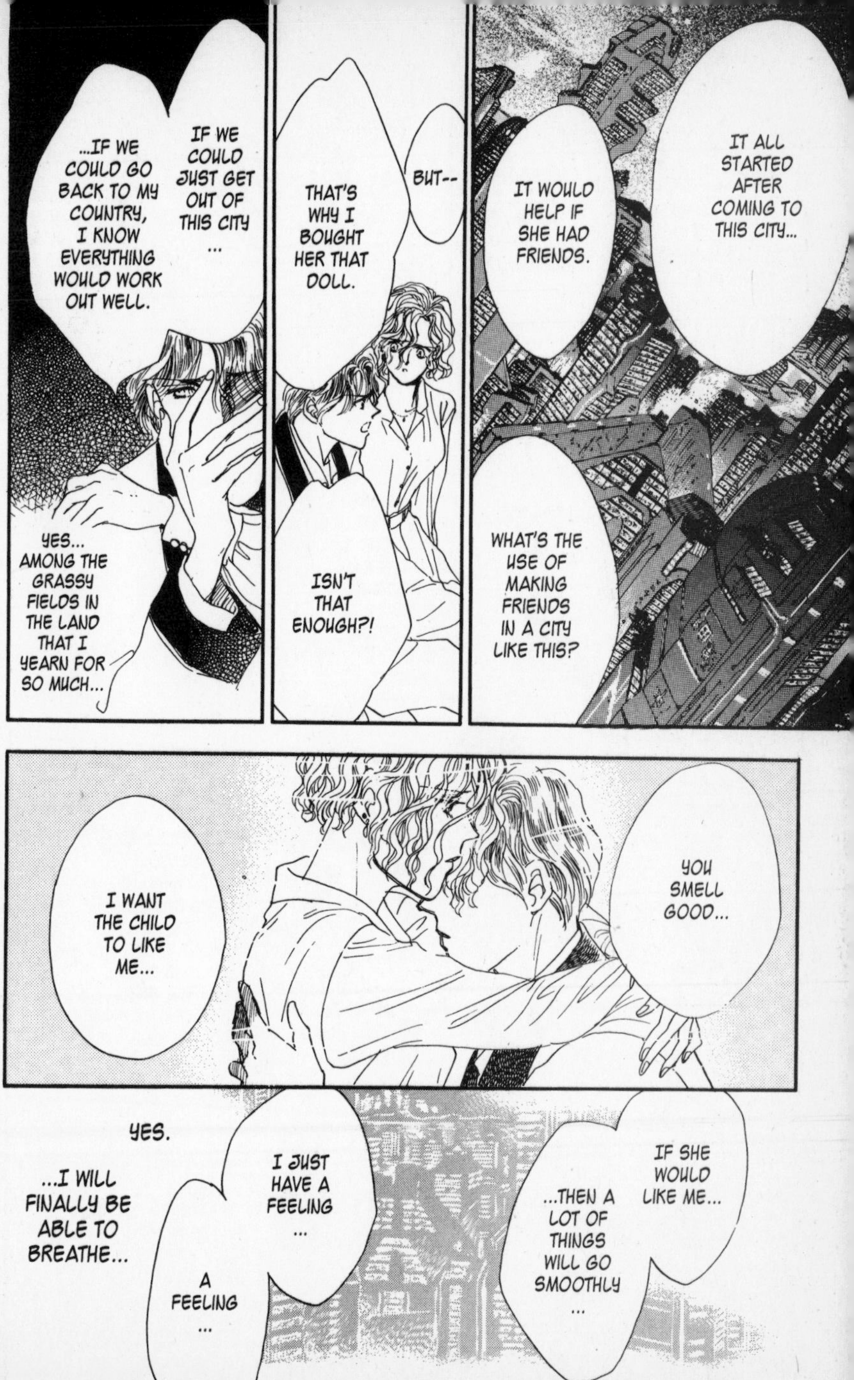
IT ALL STARTED AFTER COMING TO THIS CITY...
IT WOULD HELP IF SHE HAD FRIENDS.
WHAT'S THE USE OF MAKING FRIENDS IN A CITY LIKE THIS?
BUT--
THAT'S WHY I BOUGHT HER THAT DOLL.
ISN'T THAT ENOUGH?!
IF WE COULD JUST GET OUT OF THIS CITY ...
...IF WE COULD GO BACK TO MY COUNTRY, I KNOW EVERYTHING WOULD WORK OUT WELL.
YES... AMONG THE GRASSY FIELDS IN THE LAND THAT I YEARN FOR SO MUCH...
YOU SMELL GOOD...
I WANT THE CHILD TO LIKE ME...
IF SHE WOULD LIKE ME...
...THEN A LOT OF THINGS WILL GO SMOOTHLY ...
I JUST HAVE A FEELING ...
A FEELING ...
YES.
...I WILL FINALLY BE ABLE TO BREATHE...

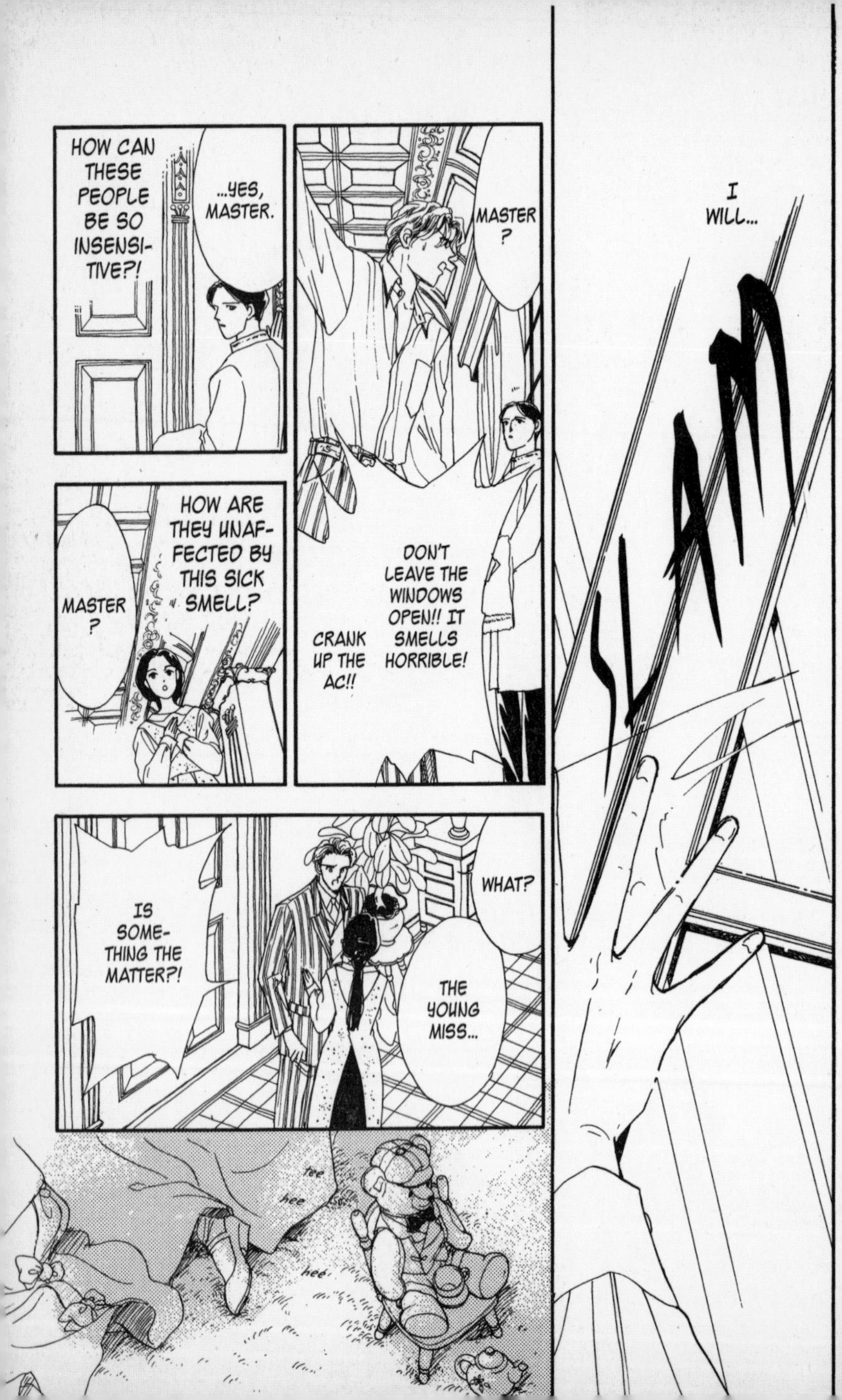
I WILL...
SLAM
MASTER?
DON'T LEAVE THE WINDOWS OPEN!! IT SMELLS HORRIBLE!
CRANK UP THE AC!!
...YES, MASTER.
HOW CAN THESE PEOPLE BE SO INSENSITIVE?!
HOW ARE THEY UNAFFECTED BY THIS SICK SMELL?
MASTER?
WHAT?
THE YOUNG MISS...
IS SOMETHING THE MATTER?!
tee hee hee

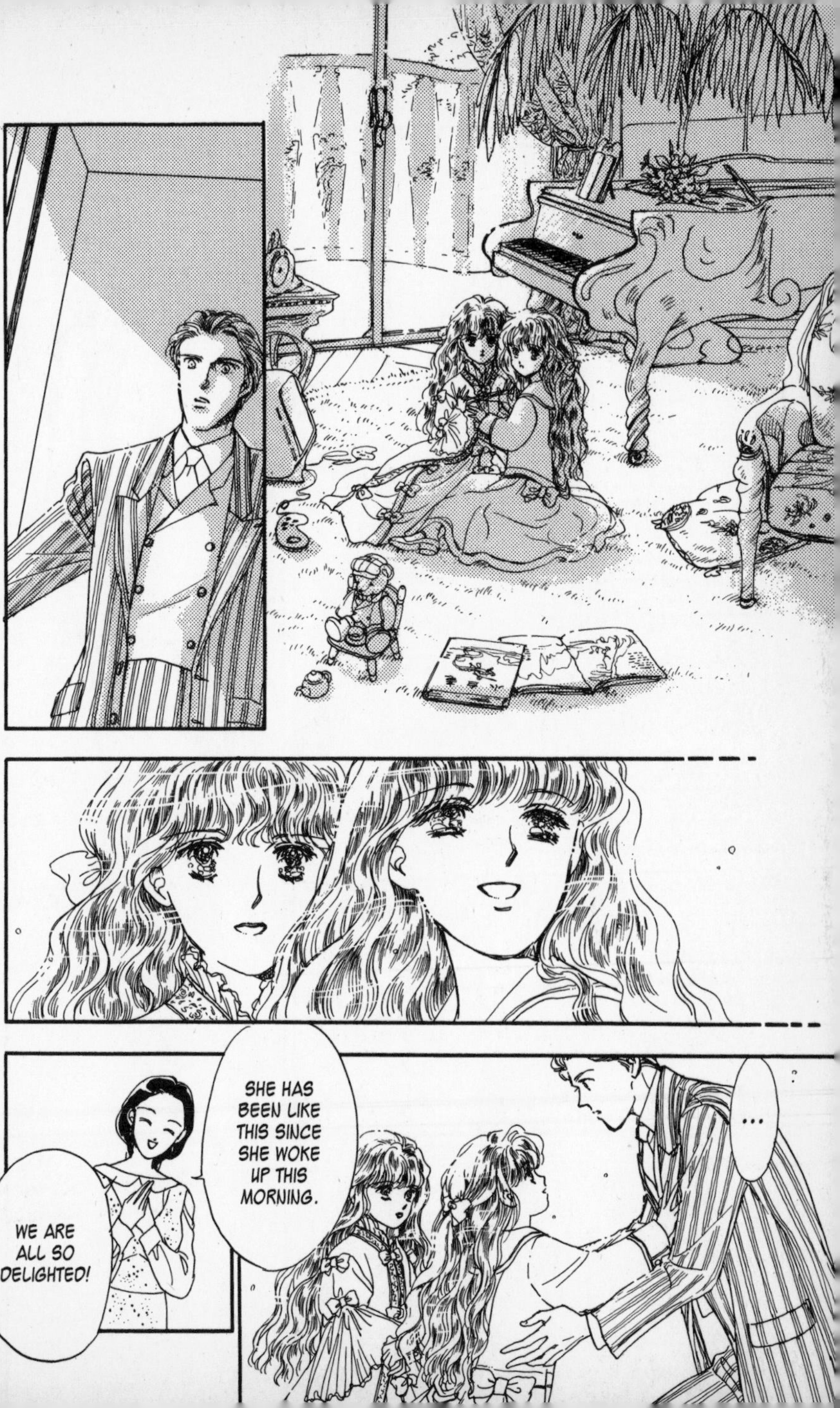
...
SHE HAS BEEN LIKE THIS SINCE SHE WOKE UP THIS MORNING.
WE ARE ALL SO DELIGHTED!

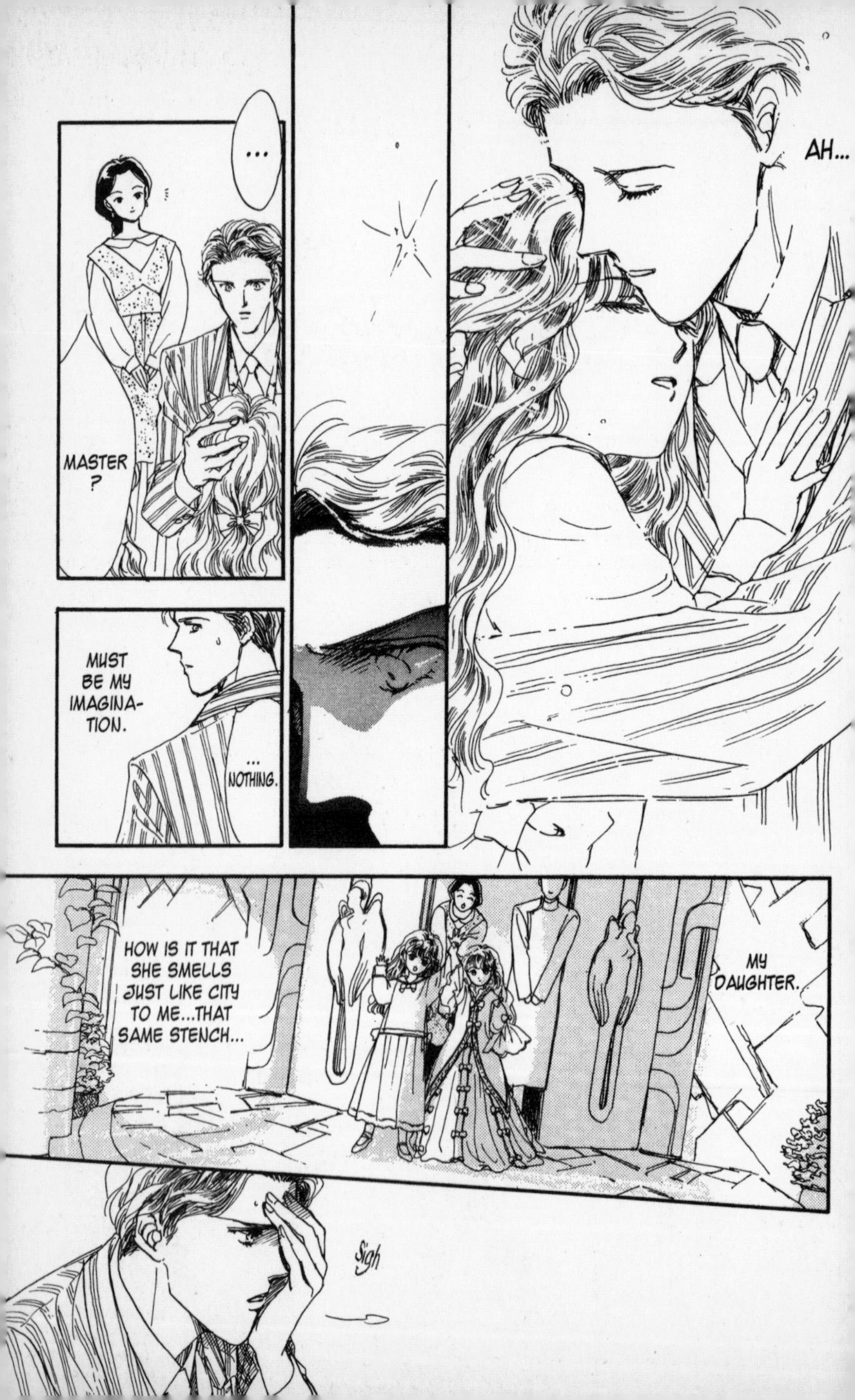
AH...
...
MASTER ?
... NOTHING.
MUST BE MY IMAGINATION.
MY DAUGHTER.
HOW IS IT THAT SHE SMELLS JUST LIKE CITY TO ME...THAT SAME STENCH...
Sigh

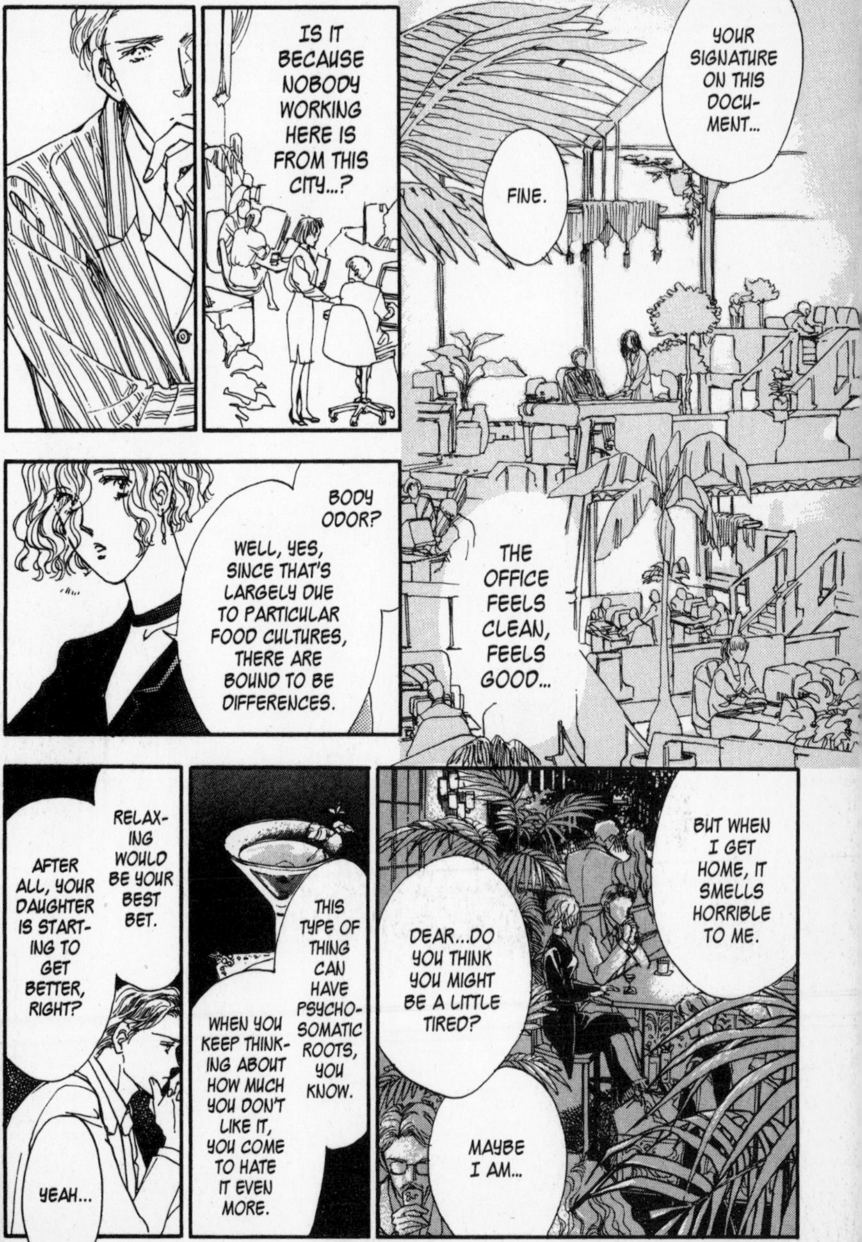
YOUR SIGNATURE ON THIS DOCUMENT...
FINE.
THE OFFICE FEELS CLEAN, FEELS GOOD...
IS IT BECAUSE NOBODY WORKING HERE IS FROM THIS CITY...?
BODY ODOR?
WELL, YES, SINCE THAT'S LARGELY DUE TO PARTICULAR FOOD CULTURES, THERE ARE BOUND TO BE DIFFERENCES.
BUT WHEN I GET HOME, IT SMELLS HORRIBLE TO ME.
DEAR...DO YOU THINK YOU MIGHT BE A LITTLE TIRED?
MAYBE I AM...
THIS TYPE OF THING CAN HAVE PSYCHOSOMATIC ROOTS, YOU KNOW.
WHEN YOU KEEP THINKING ABOUT HOW MUCH YOU DON'T LIKE IT, YOU COME TO HATE IT EVEN MORE.
RELAXING WOULD BE YOUR BEST BET.
AFTER ALL, YOUR DAUGHTER IS STARTING TO GET BETTER, RIGHT?
YEAH...

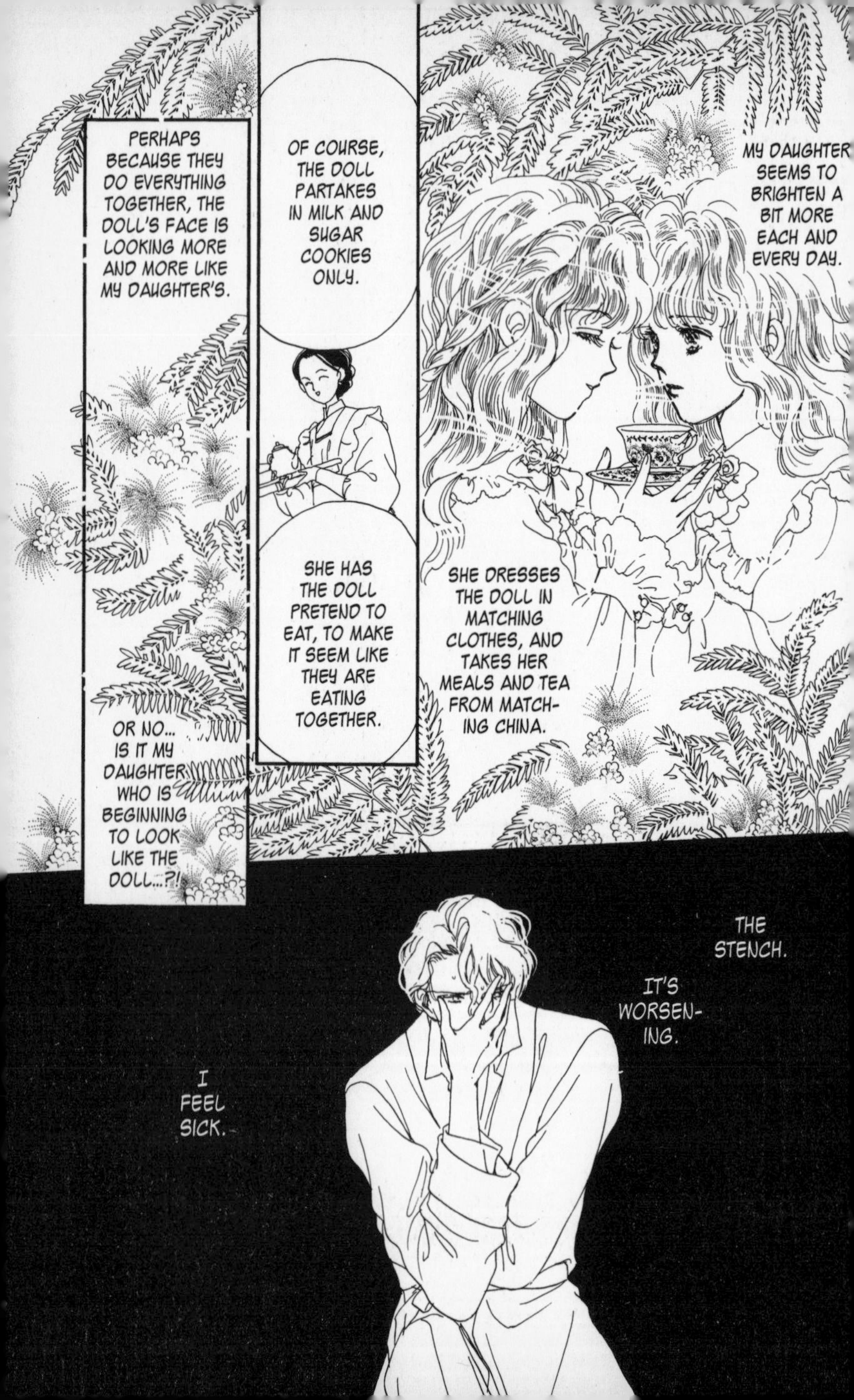
MY DAUGHTER SEEMS TO BRIGHTEN A BIT MORE EACH AND EVERY DAY.
SHE DRESSES THE DOLL IN MATCHING CLOTHES, AND TAKES HER MEALS AND TEA FROM MATCH-ING CHINA.
OF COURSE, THE DOLL PARTAKES IN MILK AND SUGAR COOKIES ONLY.
SHE HAS THE DOLL PRETEND TO EAT, TO MAKE IT SEEM LIKE THEY ARE EATING TOGETHER.
PERHAPS BECAUSE THEY DO EVERYTHING TOGETHER, THE DOLL'S FACE IS LOOKING MORE AND MORE LIKE MY DAUGHTER'S.
OR NO... IS IT MY DAUGHTER WHO IS BEGINNING TO LOOK LIKE THE DOLL...?!
THE STENCH.
IT'S WORSEN-ING.
I FEEL SICK.

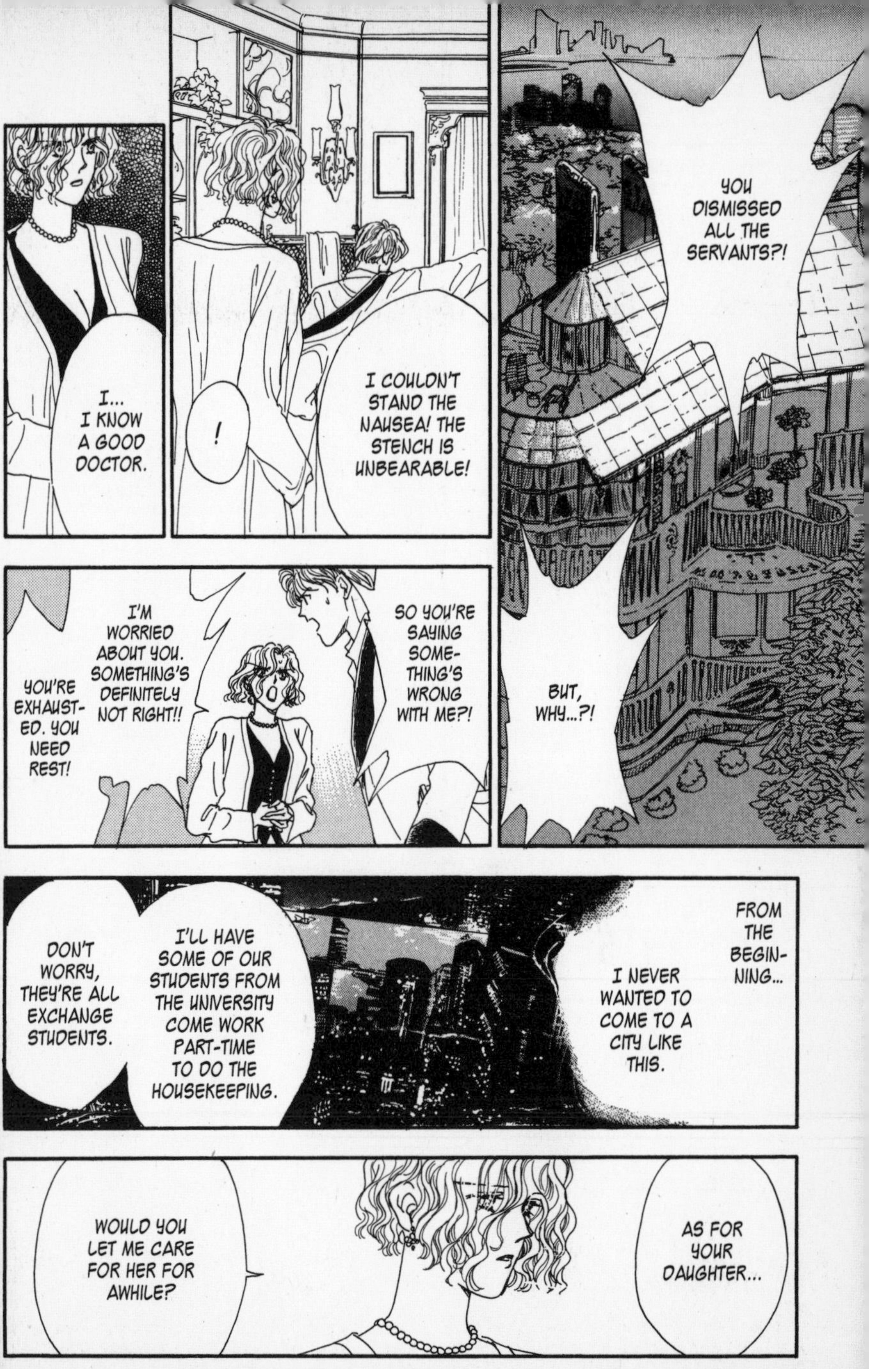
YOU DISMISSED ALL THE SERVANTS?!
BUT, WHY...?!
I COULDN'T STAND THE NAUSEA! THE STENCH IS UNBEARABLE!
!
I... I KNOW A GOOD DOCTOR.
SO YOU'RE SAYING SOME-THING'S WRONG WITH ME?!
I'M WORRIED ABOUT YOU. SOMETHING'S DEFINITELY NOT RIGHT!!
YOU'RE EXHAUST-ED. YOU NEED REST!
FROM THE BEGIN-NING...
I NEVER WANTED TO COME TO A CITY LIKE THIS.
I'LL HAVE SOME OF OUR STUDENTS FROM THE UNIVERSITY COME WORK PART-TIME TO DO THE HOUSEKEEPING.
DON'T WORRY, THEY'RE ALL EXCHANGE STUDENTS.
AS FOR YOUR DAUGHTER...
WOULD YOU LET ME CARE FOR HER FOR AWHILE?

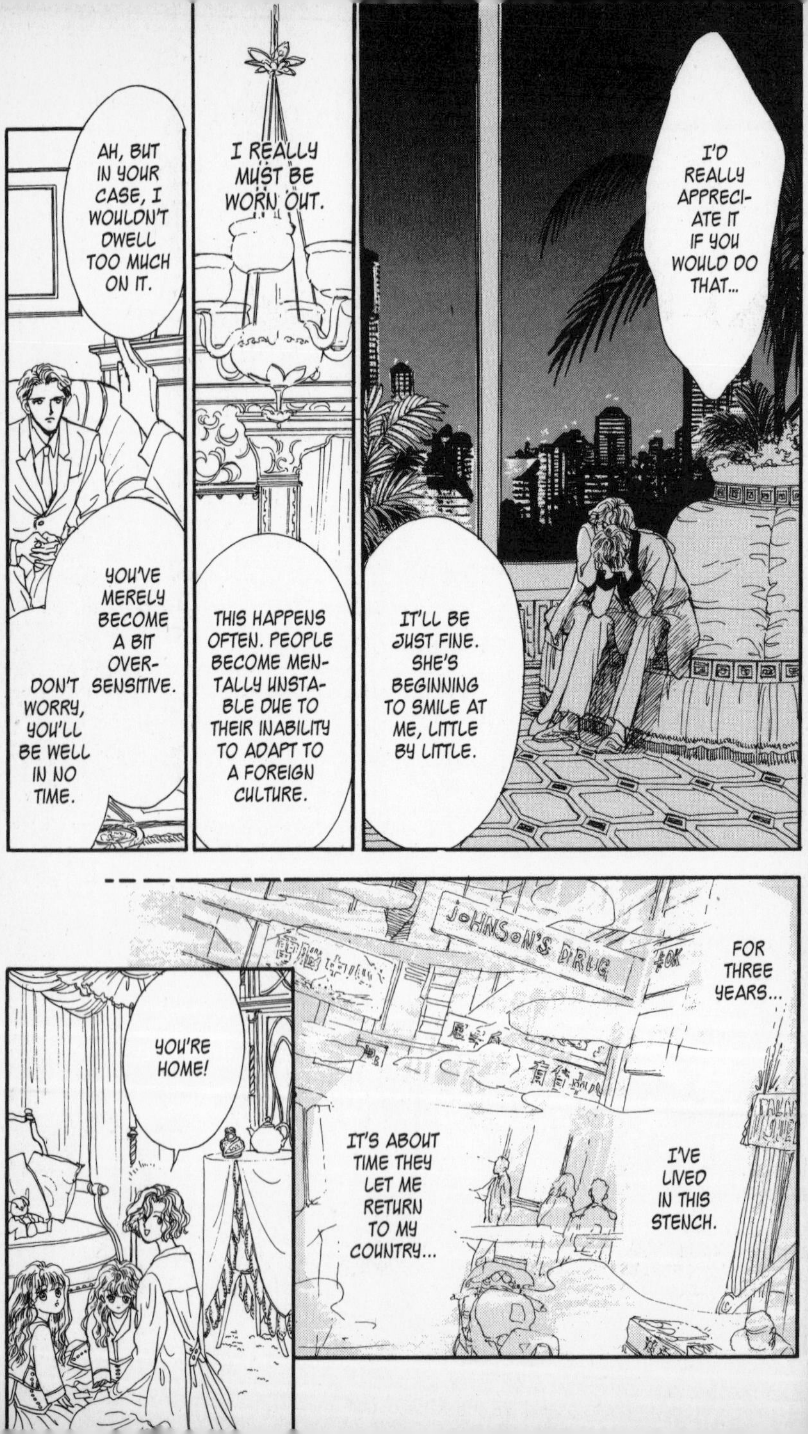
I'D REALLY APPRECIATE IT IF YOU WOULD DO THAT...
IT'LL BE JUST FINE. SHE'S BEGINNING TO SMILE AT ME, LITTLE BY LITTLE.
I REALLY MUST BE WORN OUT.
THIS HAPPENS OFTEN. PEOPLE BECOME MENTALLY UNSTABLE DUE TO THEIR INABILITY TO ADAPT TO A FOREIGN CULTURE.
AH, BUT IN YOUR CASE, I WOULDN'T DWELL TOO MUCH ON IT.
YOU'VE MERELY BECOME A BIT OVER-SENSITIVE.
DON'T WORRY, YOU'LL BE WELL IN NO TIME.
JOHNSON'S DRUG
FOR THREE YEARS...
I'VE LIVED IN THIS STENCH.
IT'S ABOUT TIME THEY LET ME RETURN TO MY COUNTRY...
YOU'RE HOME!

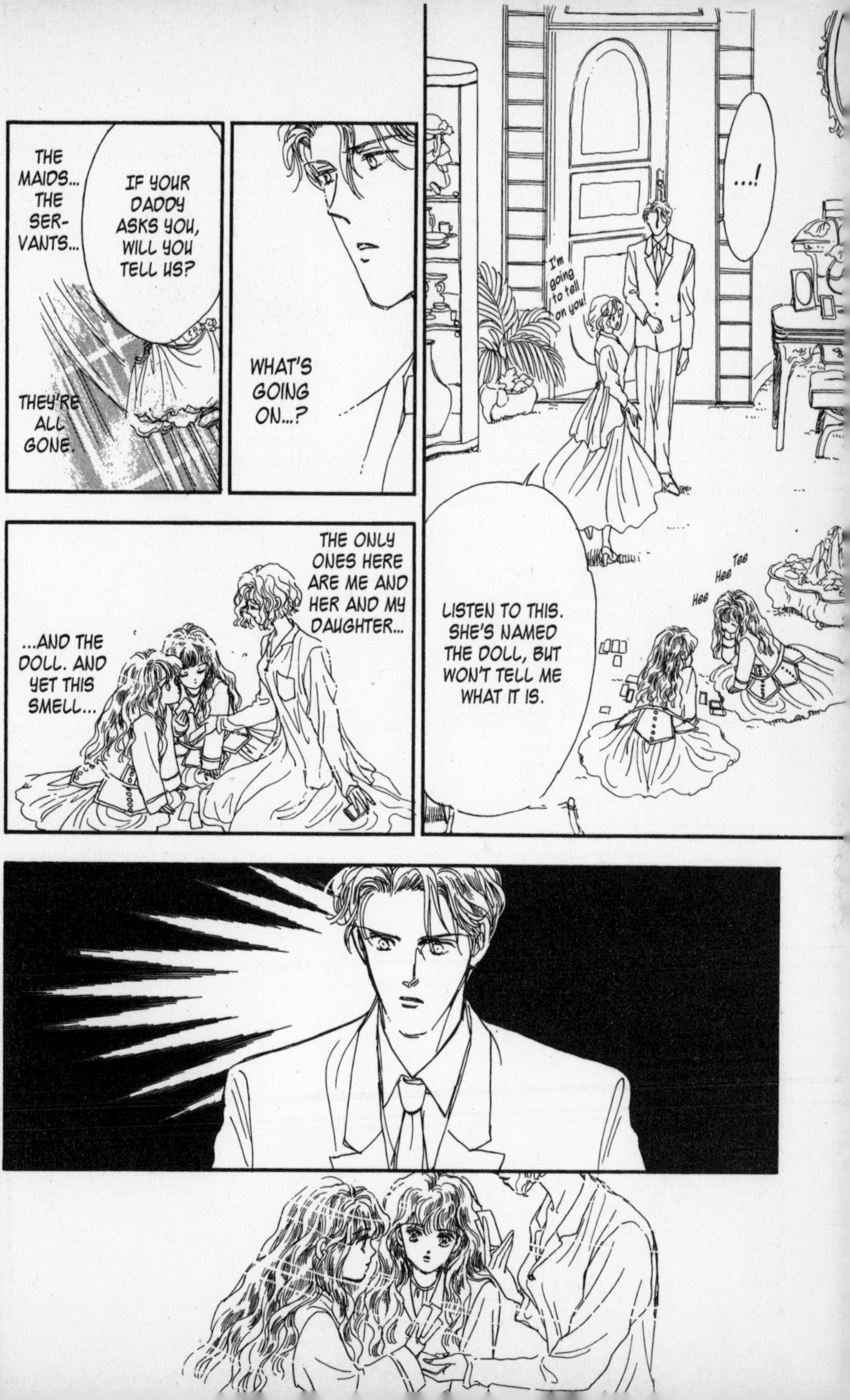
...!
I'm going to tell on you!
Tee Hee Hee
LISTEN TO THIS. SHE'S NAMED THE DOLL, BUT WON'T TELL ME WHAT IT IS.
WHAT'S GOING ON...?
IF YOUR DADDY ASKS YOU, WILL YOU TELL US?
THE MAIDS... THE SER-VANTS...
THEY'RE ALL GONE.
THE ONLY ONES HERE ARE ME AND HER AND MY DAUGHTER...
...AND THE DOLL. AND YET THIS SMELL...

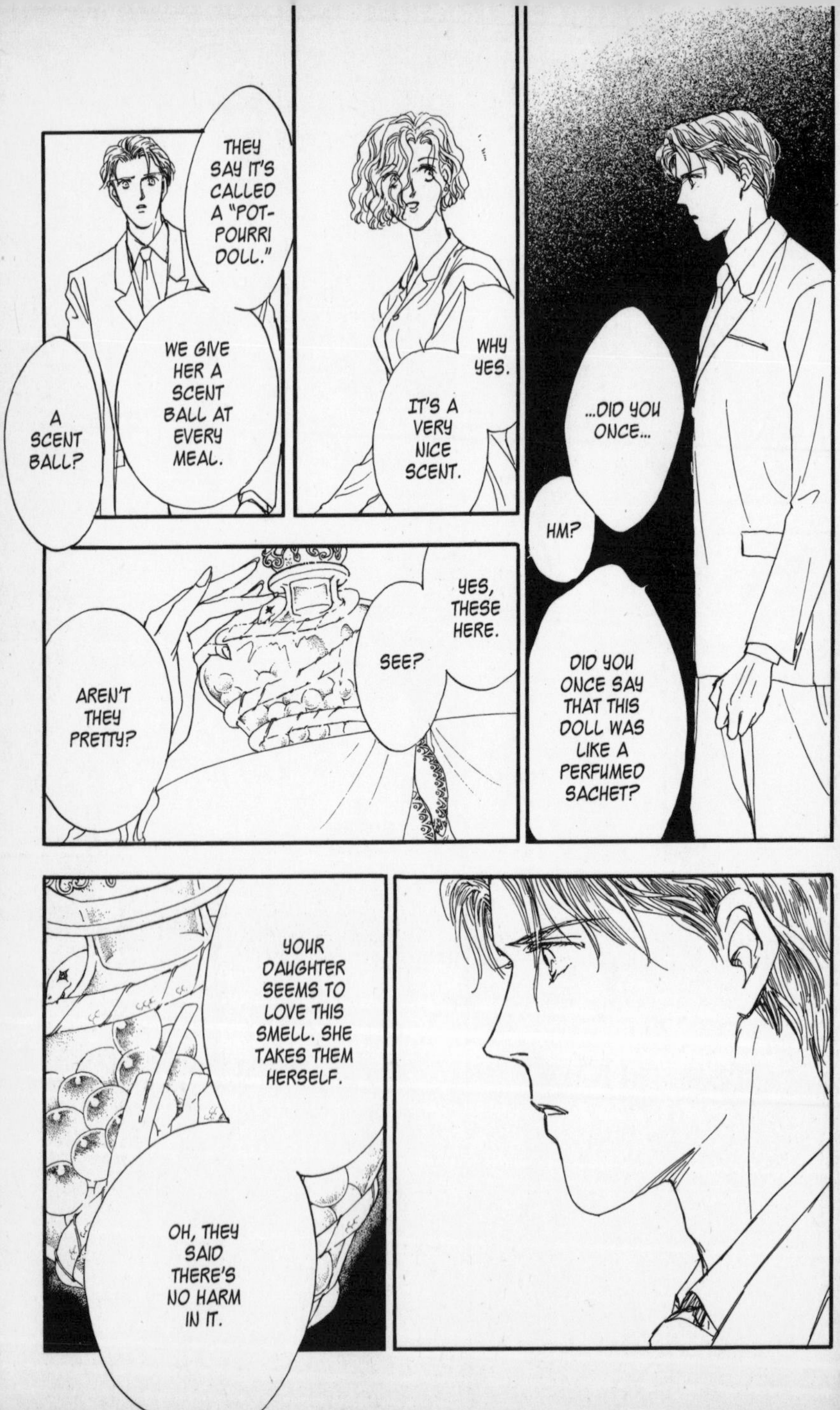
...DID YOU ONCE...
HM?
DID YOU ONCE SAY THAT THIS DOLL WAS LIKE A PERFUMED SACHET?
WHY YES.
IT'S A VERY NICE SCENT.
THEY SAY IT'S CALLED A "POT-POURRI DOLL."
WE GIVE HER A SCENT BALL AT EVERY MEAL.
A SCENT BALL?
YES, THESE HERE.
SEE?
AREN'T THEY PRETTY?
YOUR DAUGHTER SEEMS TO LOVE THIS SMELL. SHE TAKES THEM HERSELF.
OH, THEY SAID THERE'S NO HARM IN IT.

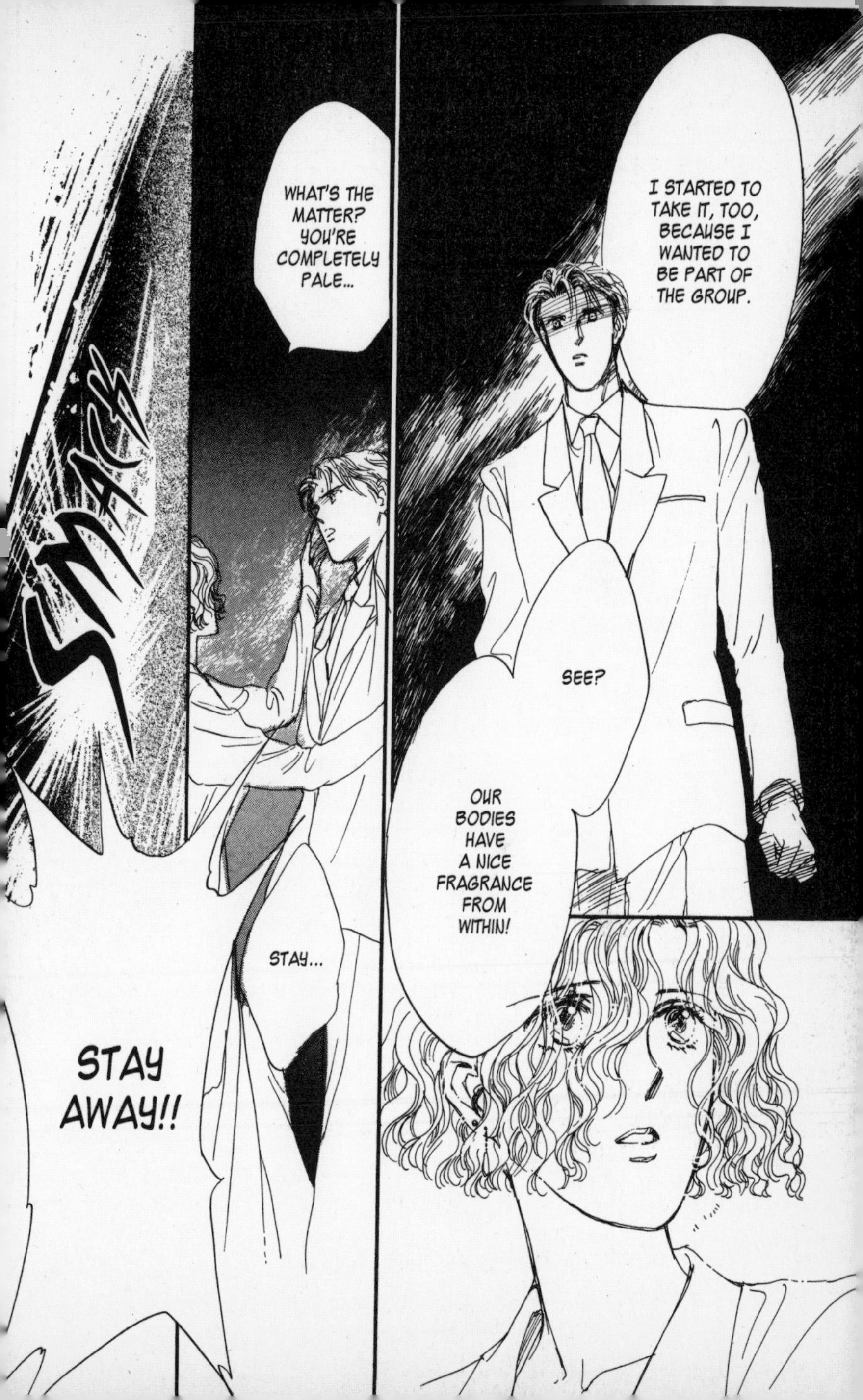
I STARTED TO TAKE IT, TOO, BECAUSE I WANTED TO BE PART OF THE GROUP.
SEE?
OUR BODIES HAVE A NICE FRAGRANCE FROM WITHIN!
WHAT'S THE MATTER? YOU'RE COMPLETELY PALE...
STAY...
SMACK
STAY AWAY!!

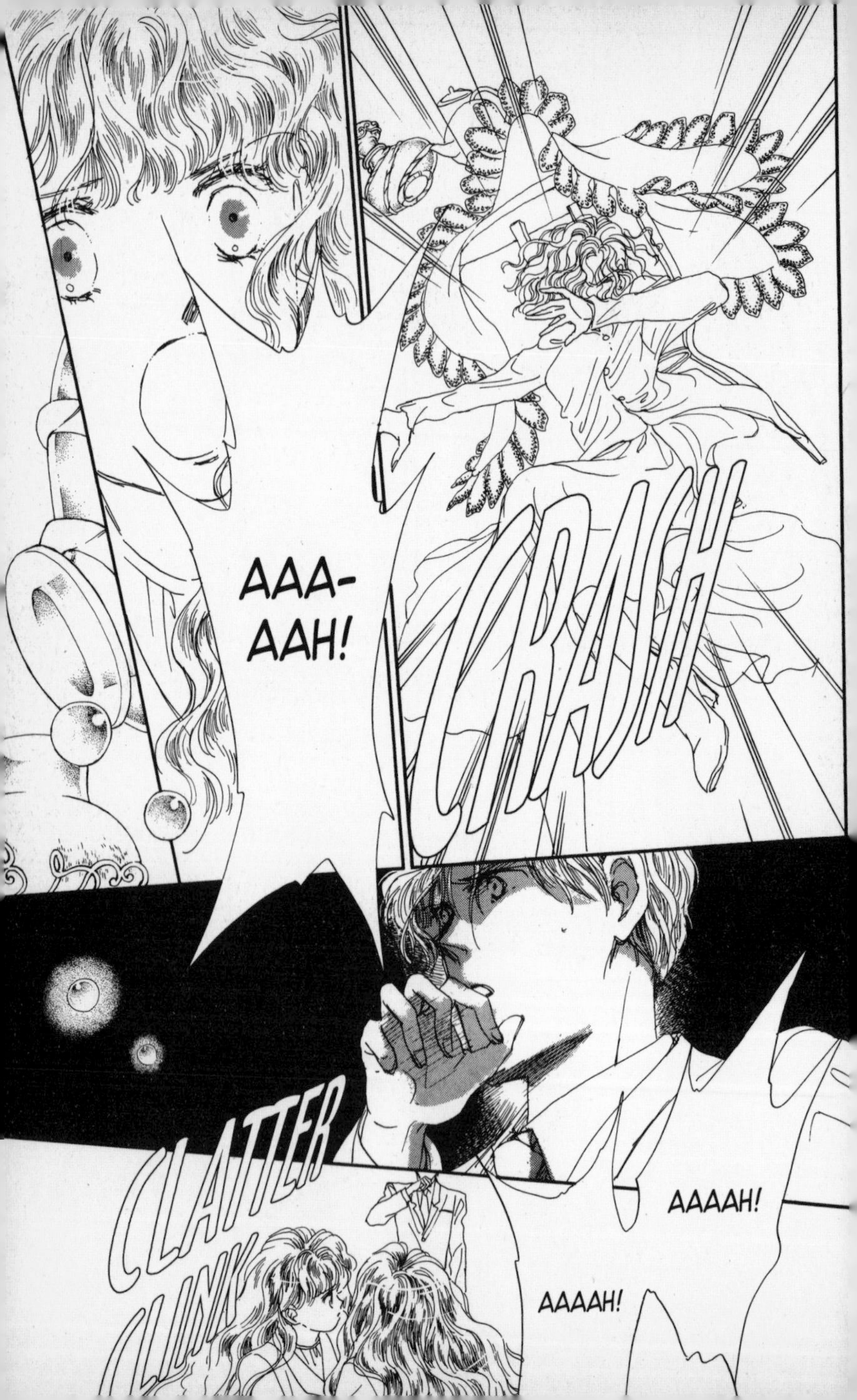
CRASH
AAA-AAH!
CLATTER
AAAAH!
AAAAH!
CLINK

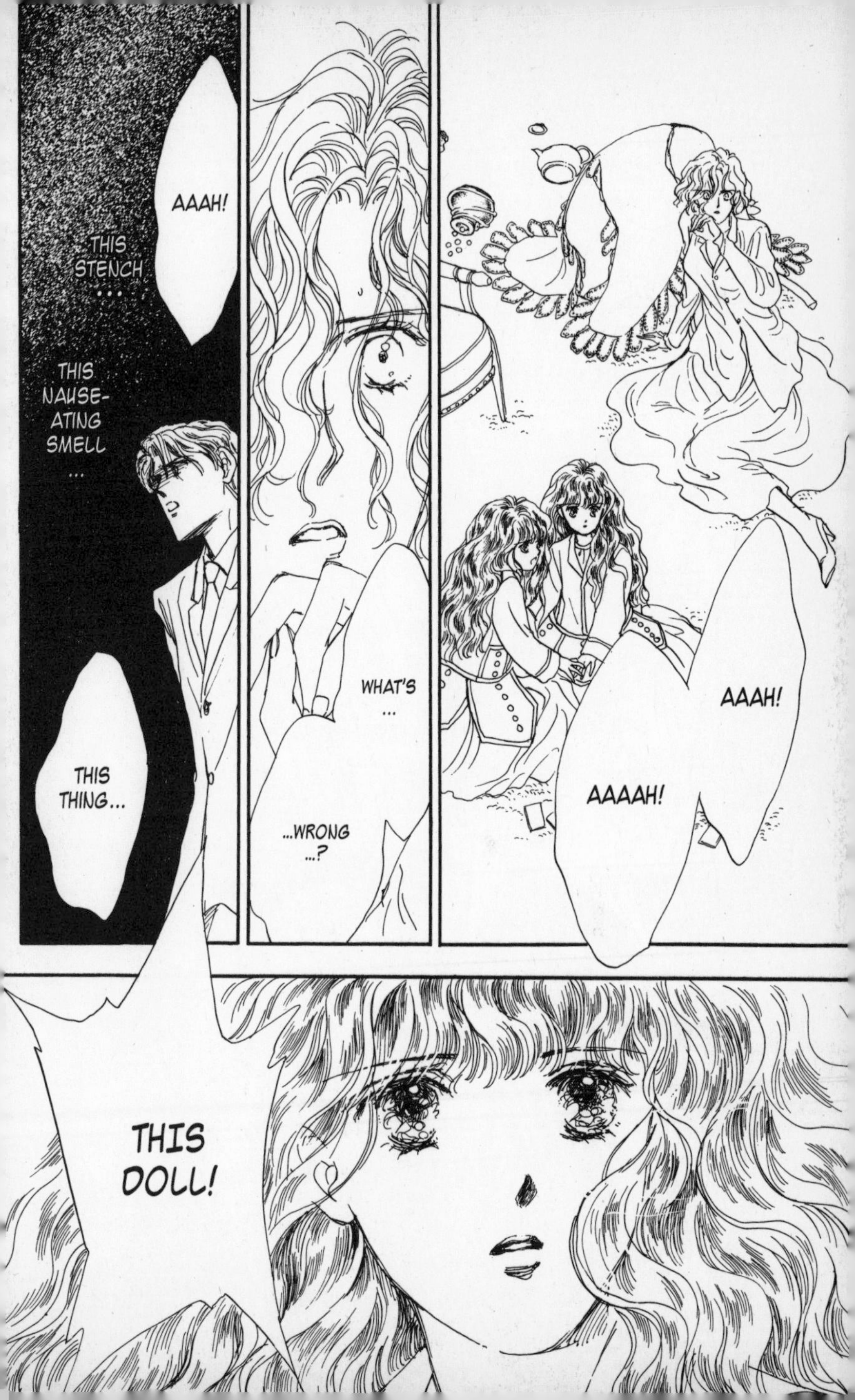
AAAH!
AAAAH!
WHAT'S ...
...WRONG ...?
AAAH!
THIS STENCH ...
THIS NAUSE-ATING SMELL ...
THIS THING...
THIS DOLL!

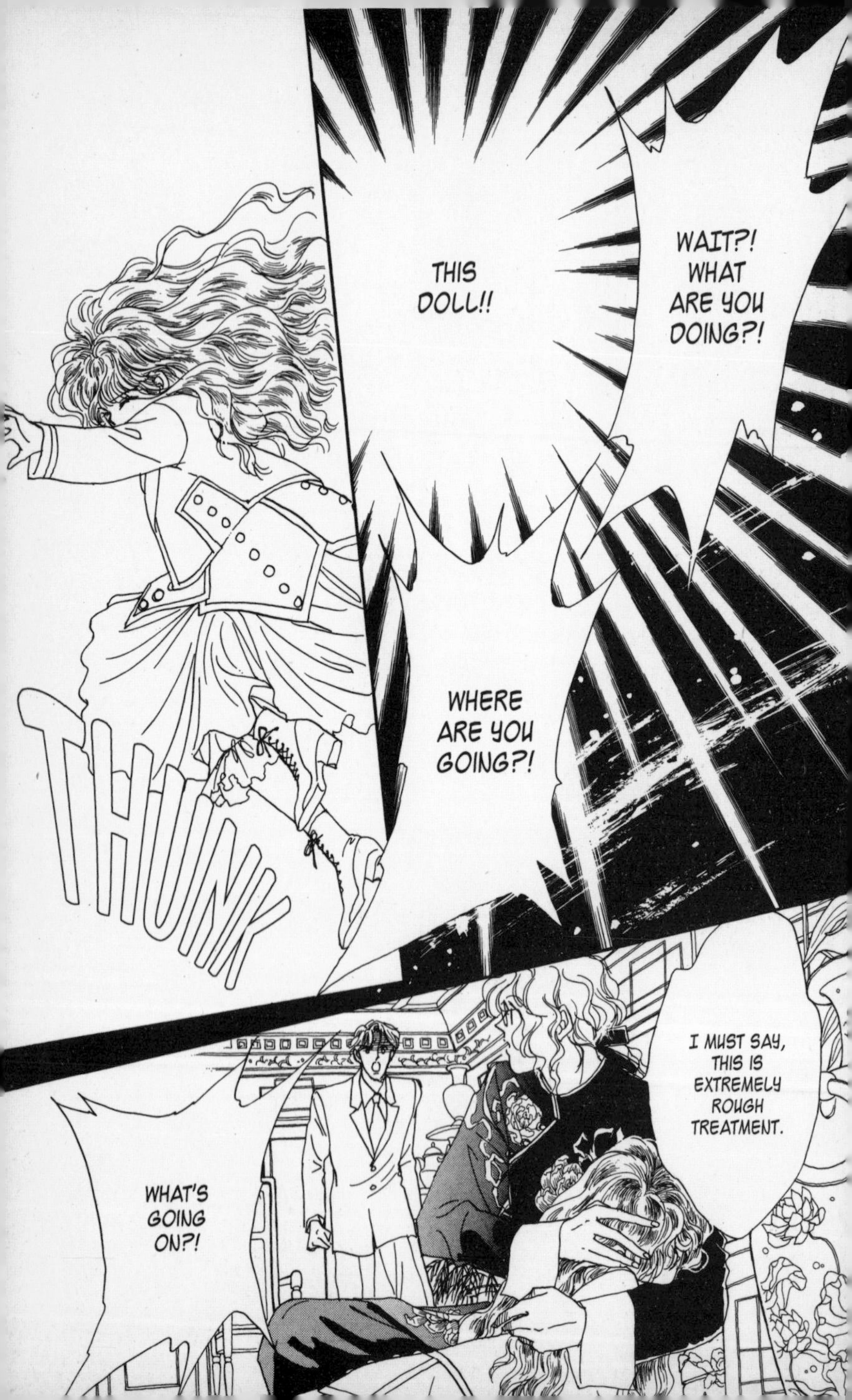
WAIT?! WHAT ARE YOU DOING?!
THIS DOLL!!
WHERE ARE YOU GOING?!
THUNK
I MUST SAY, THIS IS EXTREMELY ROUGH TREATMENT.
WHAT'S GOING ON?!

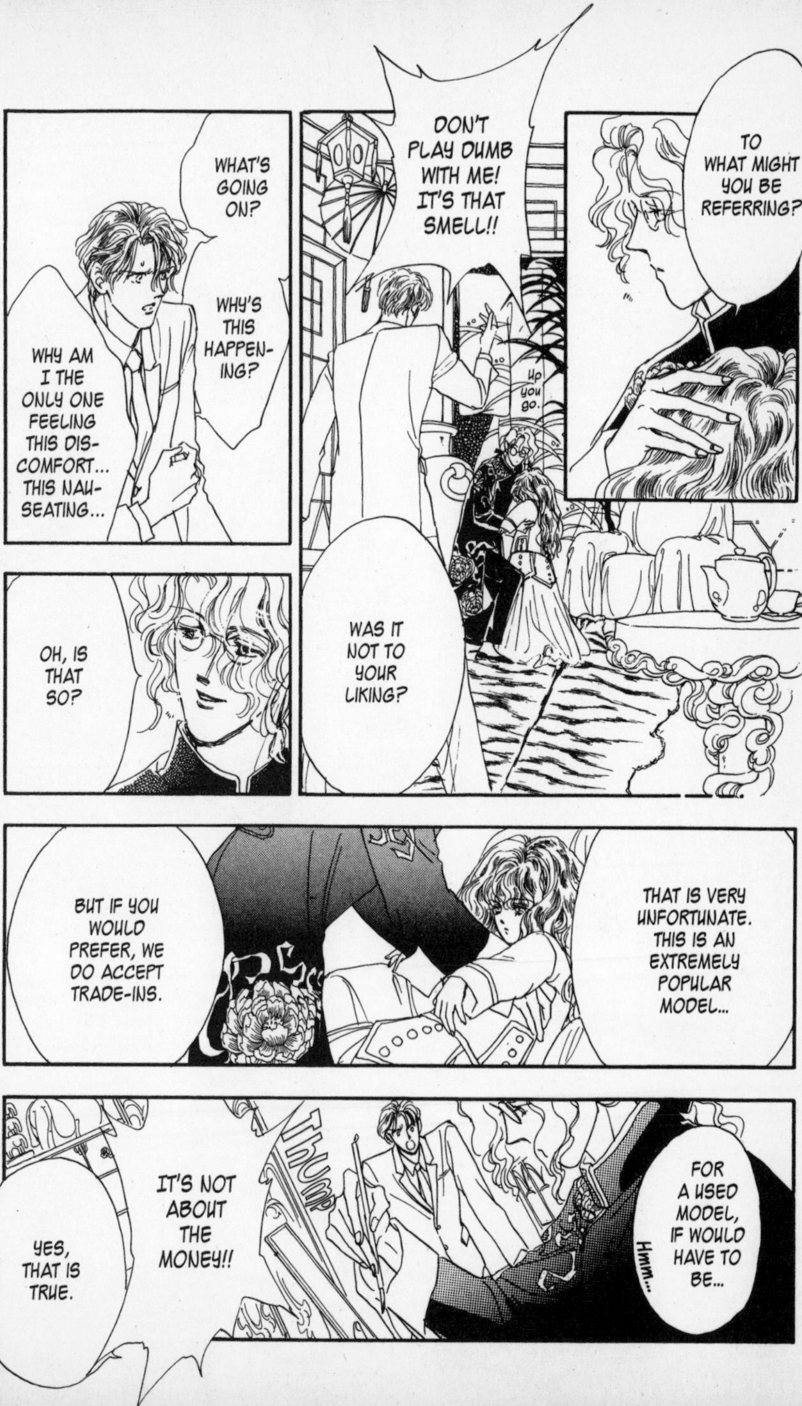
TO WHAT MIGHT YOU BE REFERRING?
DON'T PLAY DUMB WITH ME! IT'S THAT SMELL!!
Up you go.
WAS IT NOT TO YOUR LIKING?
WHAT'S GOING ON?
WHY'S THIS HAPPEN-ING?
WHY AM I THE ONLY ONE FEELING THIS DIS-COMFORT... THIS NAU-SEATING...
OH, IS THAT SO?
THAT IS VERY UNFORTUNATE. THIS IS AN EXTREMELY POPULAR MODEL...
BUT IF YOU WOULD PREFER, WE DO ACCEPT TRADE-INS.
FOR A USED MODEL, IF WOULD HAVE TO BE...
Hmm...
Thump
IT'S NOT ABOUT THE MONEY!!
YES, THAT IS TRUE.

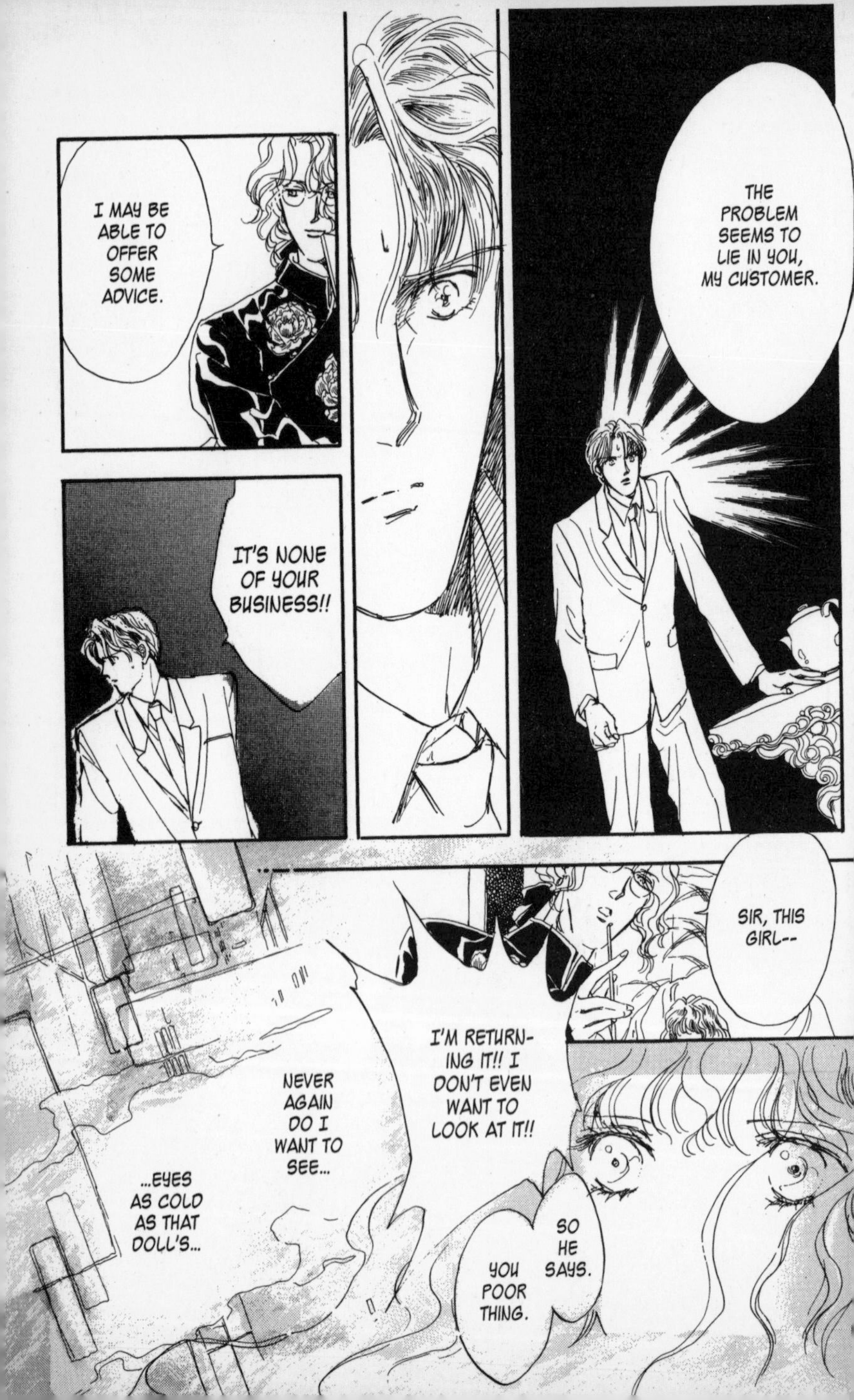
THE PROBLEM SEEMS TO LIE IN YOU, MY CUSTOMER.
I MAY BE ABLE TO OFFER SOME ADVICE.
IT'S NONE OF YOUR BUSINESS!!
SIR, THIS GIRL--
I'M RETURNING IT!! I DON'T EVEN WANT TO LOOK AT IT!!
SO HE SAYS.
YOU POOR THING.
NEVER AGAIN DO I WANT TO SEE...
...EYES AS COLD AS THAT DOLL'S...

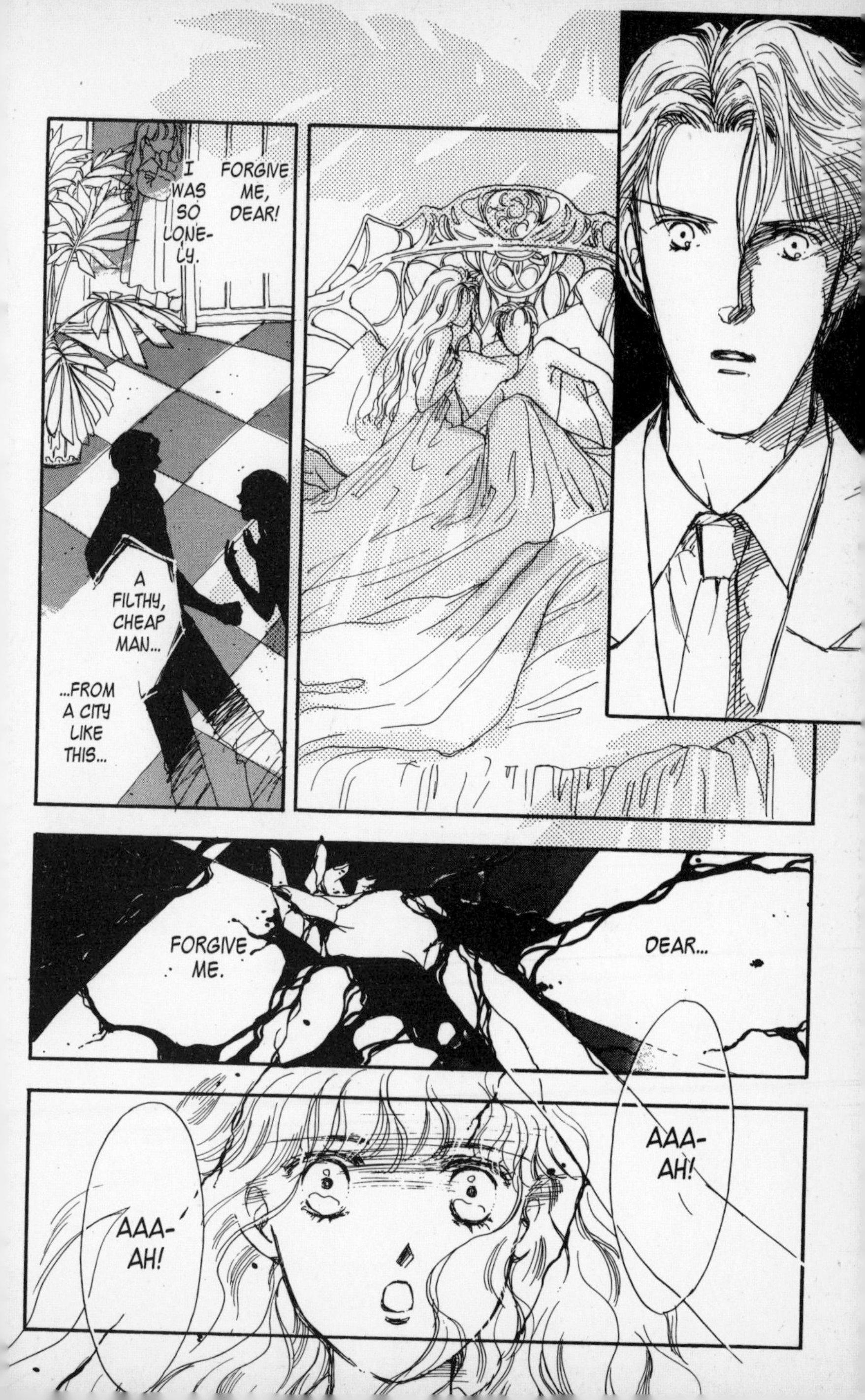
FORGIVE ME, DEAR!
I WAS SO LONE-LY.
A FILTHY, CHEAP MAN...
...FROM A CITY LIKE THIS...
DEAR...
FORGIVE ME.
AAA-AH!
AAA-AH!

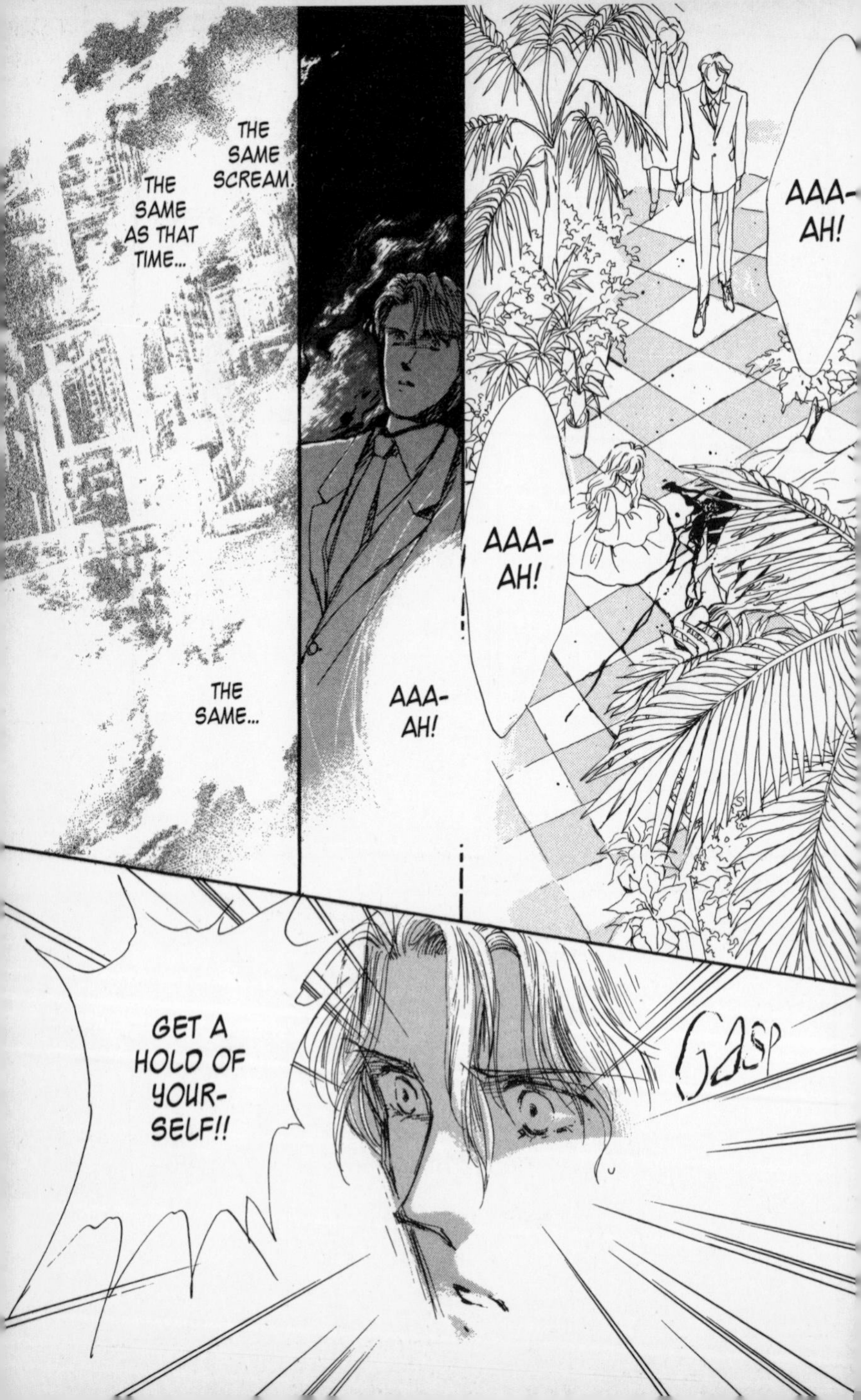
AAA-AH!
AAA-AH!
AAA-AH!
THE SAME SCREAM.
THE SAME AS THAT TIME...
THE SAME...
GET A HOLD OF YOURSELF!!
Gasp

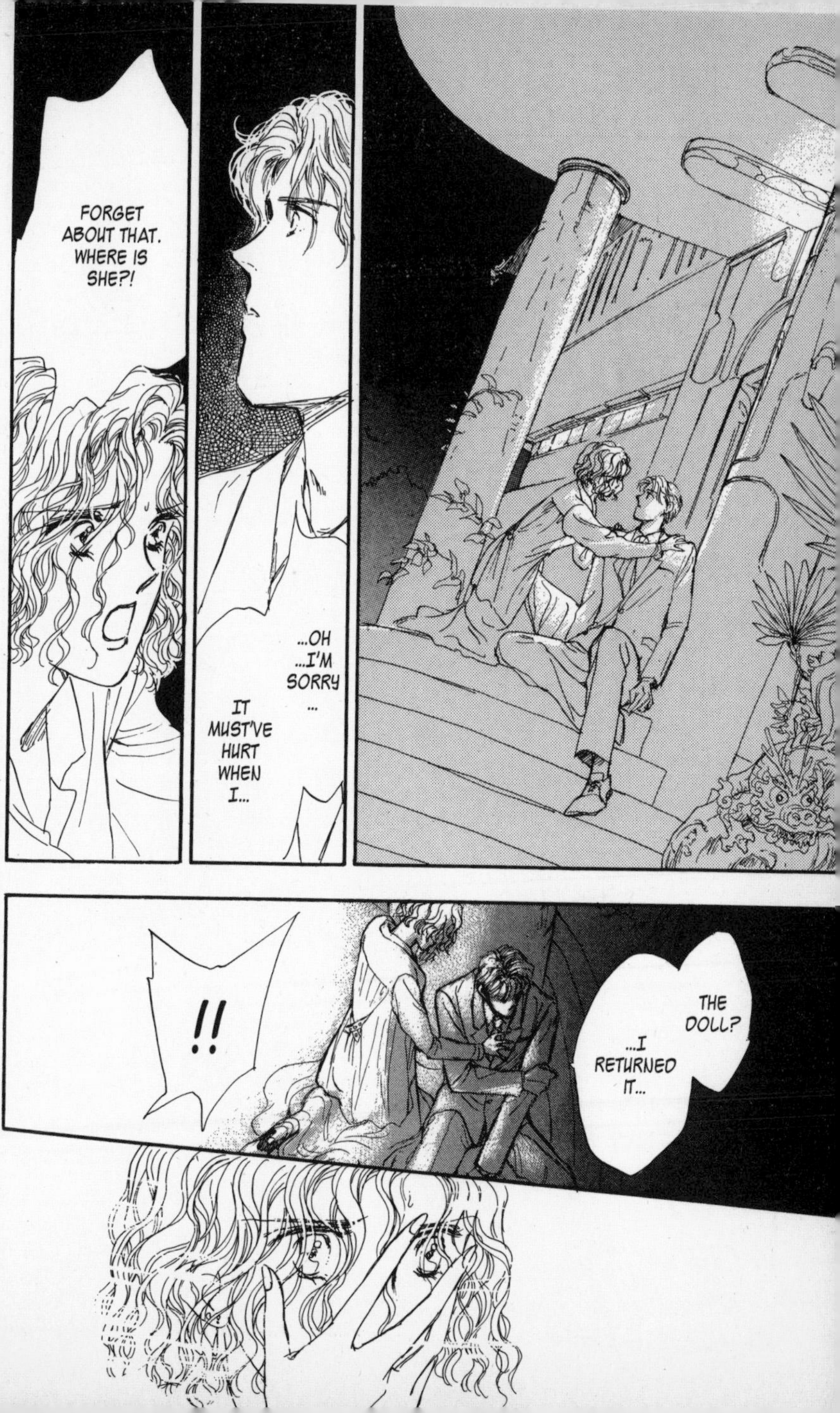
...OH ...I'M SORRY ...
IT MUST'VE HURT WHEN I...
FORGET ABOUT THAT. WHERE IS SHE?!
THE DOLL?
...I RETURNED IT...
!!

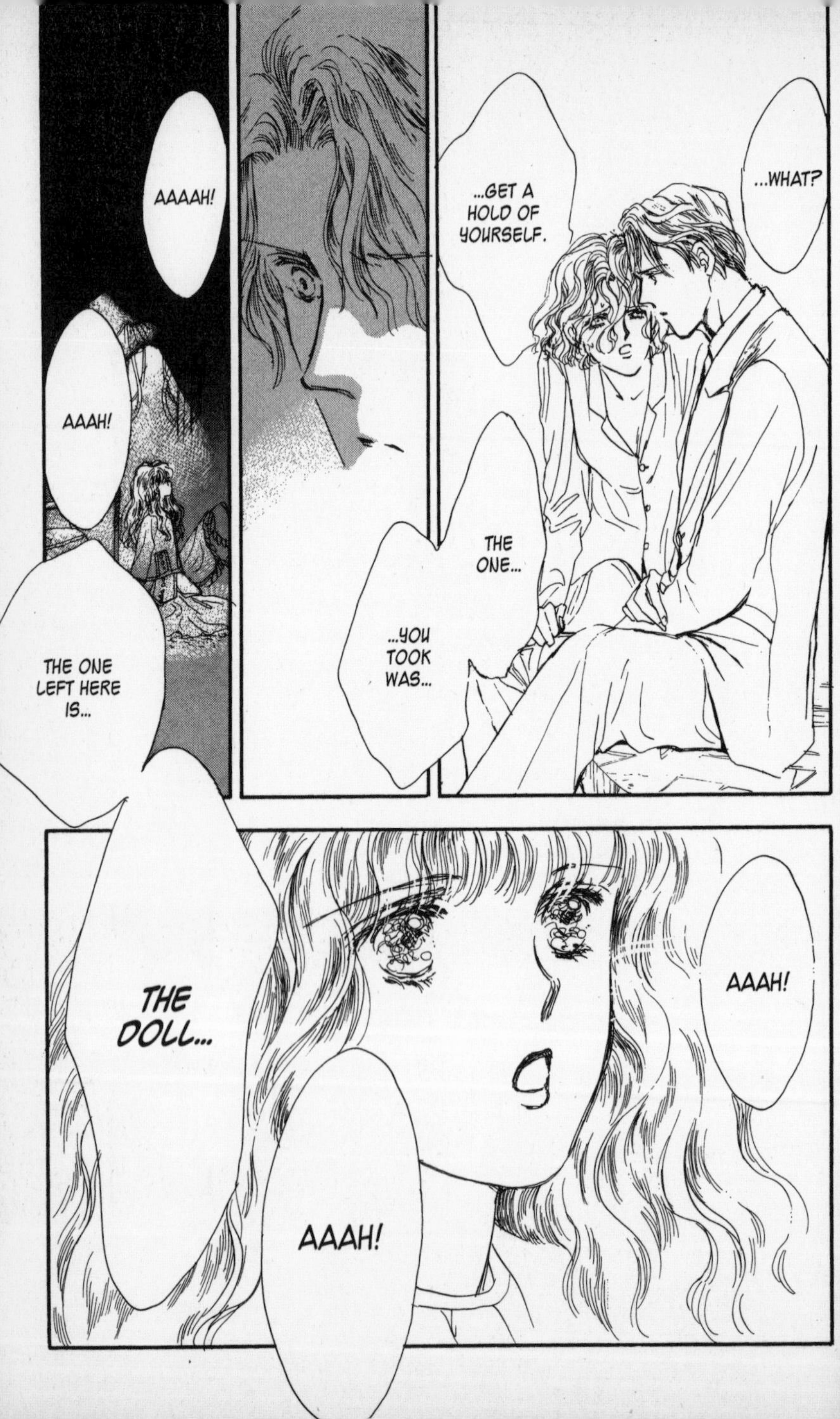
...WHAT?
...GET A HOLD OF YOURSELF.
THE ONE...
...YOU TOOK WAS...
AAAAH!
AAAH!
THE ONE LEFT HERE IS...
AAAH!
THE DOLL...
AAAH!

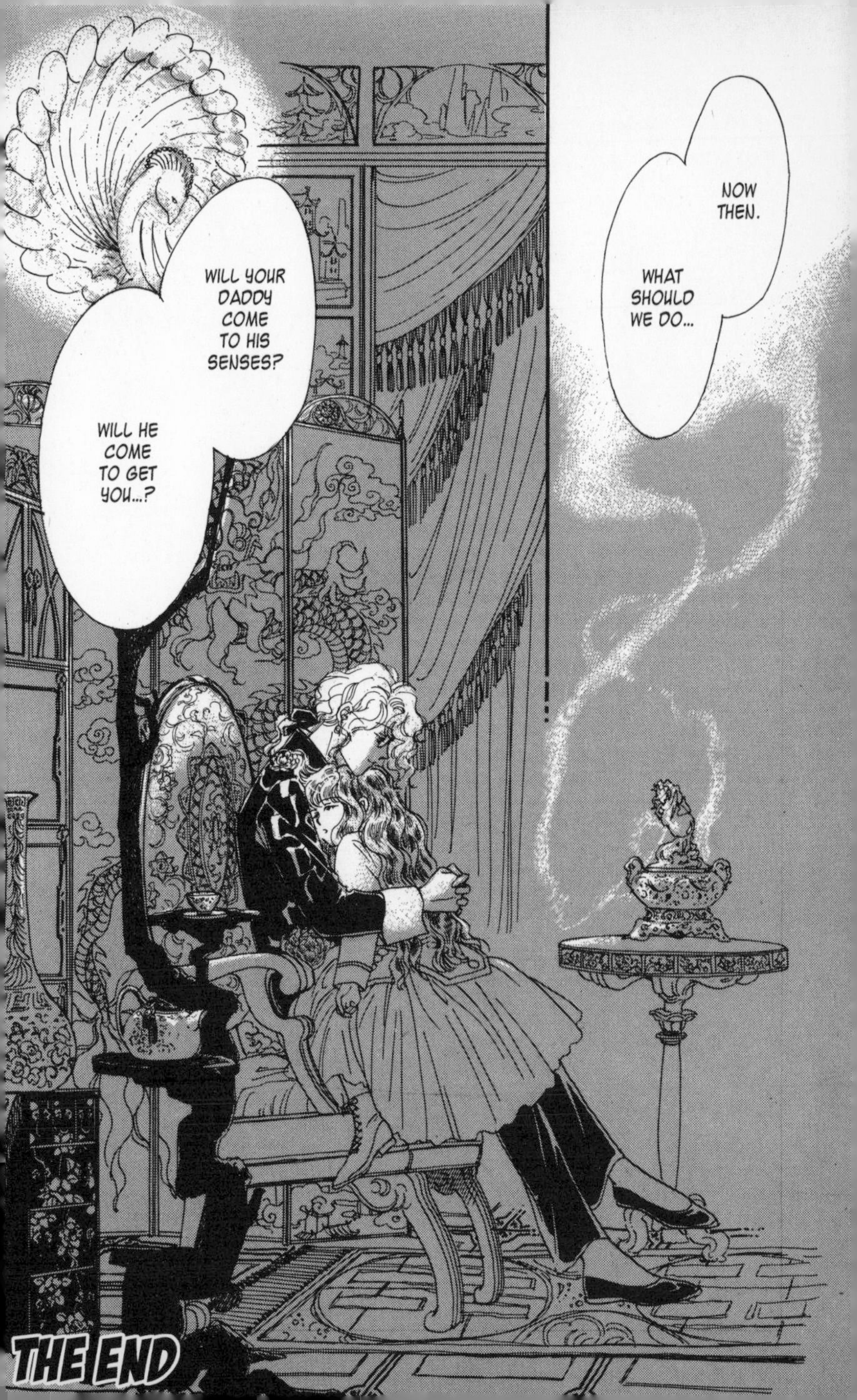
NOW THEN.
WHAT SHOULD WE DO...
WILL YOUR DADDY COME TO HIS SENSES?
WILL HE COME TO GET YOU...?
THE END

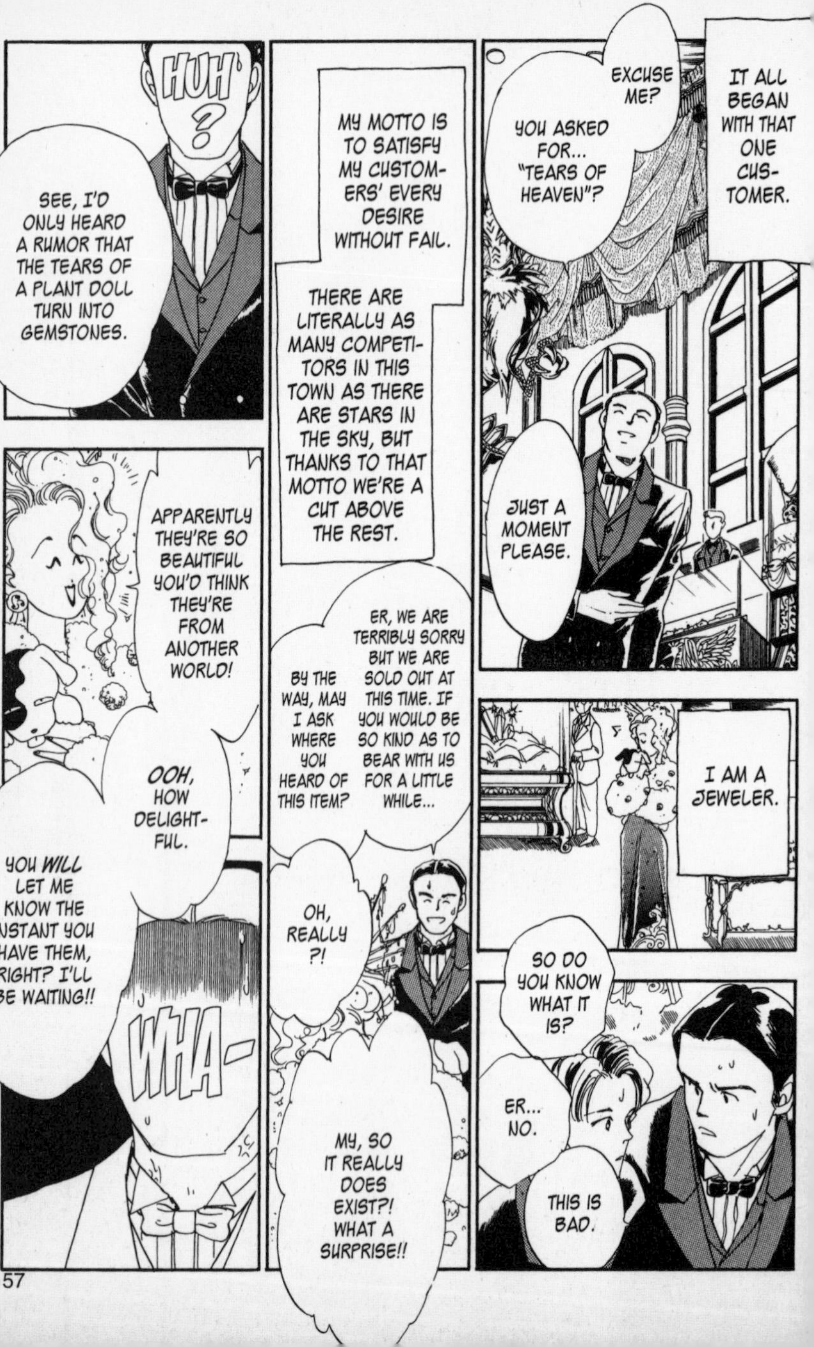
IT ALL BEGAN WITH THAT ONE CUS-TOMER.
EXCUSE ME?
YOU ASKED FOR... "TEARS OF HEAVEN"?
JUST A MOMENT PLEASE.
I AM A JEWELER.
SO DO YOU KNOW WHAT IT IS?
ER... NO.
THIS IS BAD.
MY MOTTO IS TO SATISFY MY CUSTOM-ERS' EVERY DESIRE WITHOUT FAIL.
THERE ARE LITERALLY AS MANY COMPETI-TORS IN THIS TOWN AS THERE ARE STARS IN THE SKY, BUT THANKS TO THAT MOTTO WE'RE A CUT ABOVE THE REST.
ER, WE ARE TERRIBLY SORRY BUT WE ARE SOLD OUT AT THIS TIME. IF YOU WOULD BE SO KIND AS TO BEAR WITH US FOR A LITTLE WHILE...
BY THE WAY, MAY I ASK WHERE YOU HEARD OF THIS ITEM?
OH, REALLY?!
MY, SO IT REALLY DOES EXIST?! WHAT A SURPRISE!!
HUH?
SEE, I'D ONLY HEARD A RUMOR THAT THE TEARS OF A PLANT DOLL TURN INTO GEMSTONES.
APPARENTLY THEY'RE SO BEAUTIFUL YOU'D THINK THEY'RE FROM ANOTHER WORLD!
OOH, HOW DELIGHT-FUL.
YOU WILL LET ME KNOW THE INSTANT YOU HAVE THEM, RIGHT? I'LL BE WAITING!!
WHA-

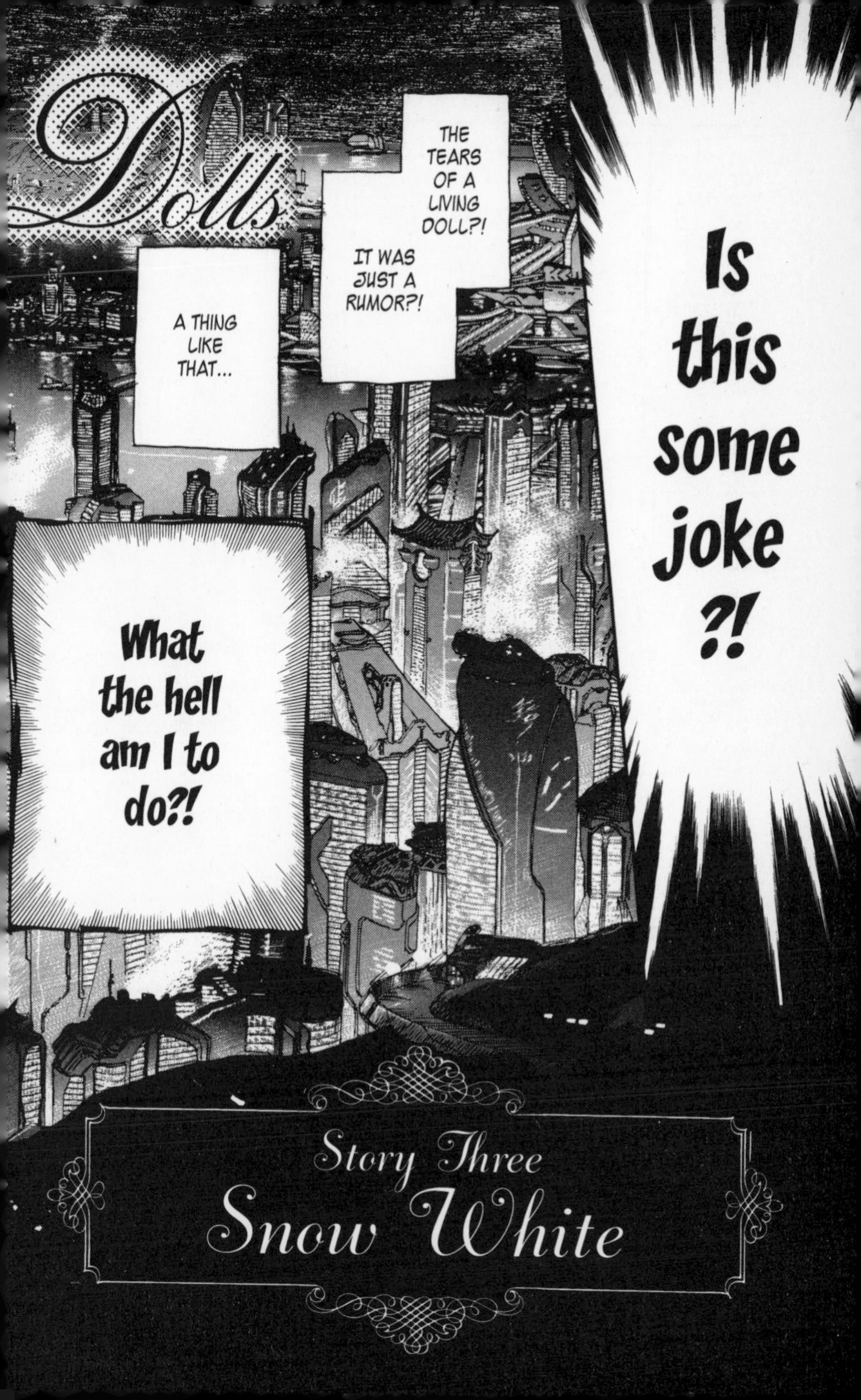
Dolls
Is this some joke?!
THE TEARS OF A LIVING DOLL?!
IT WAS JUST A RUMOR?!
A THING LIKE THAT...
What the hell am I to do?!
Story Three
Snow White

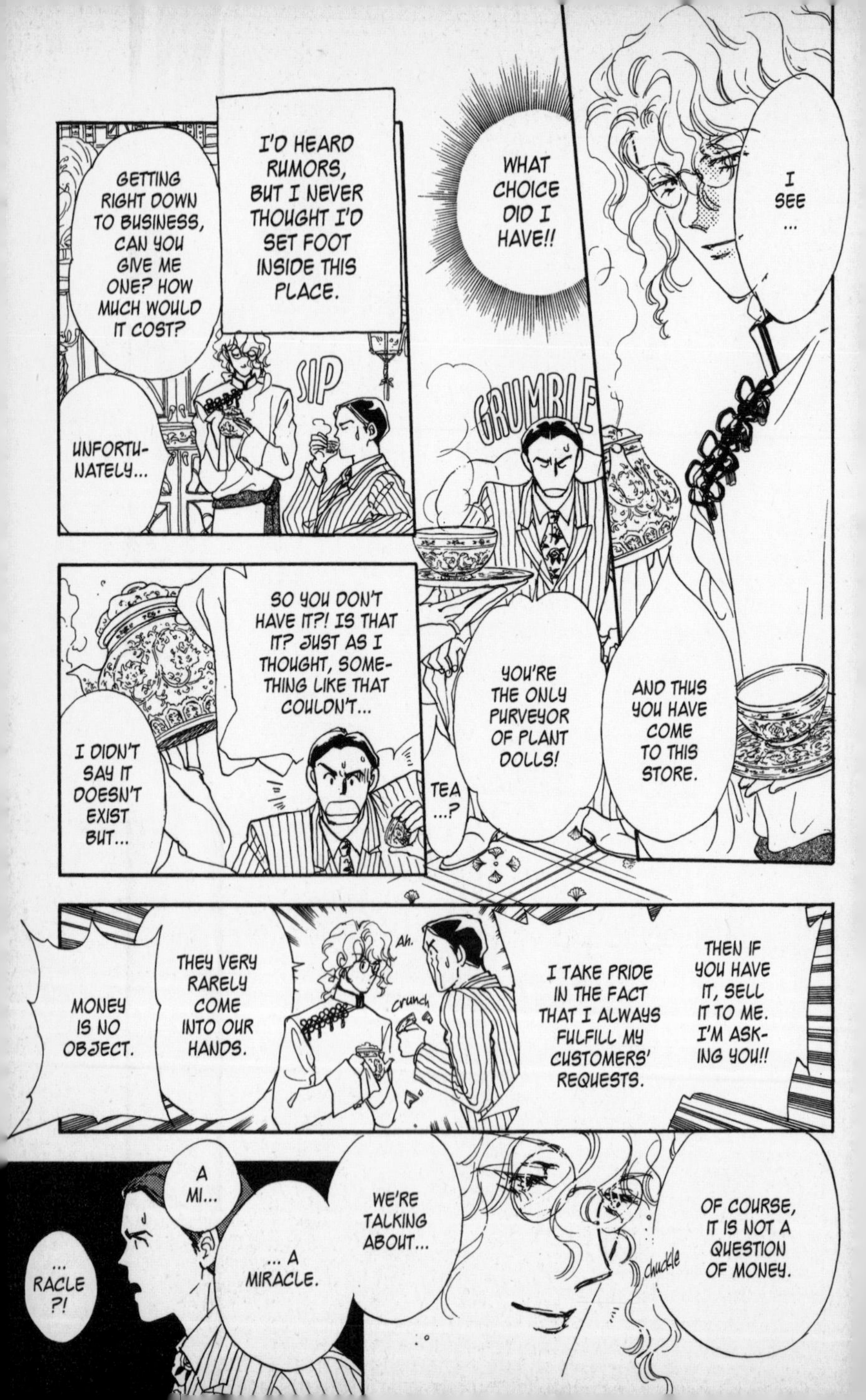
I SEE ...
AND THUS YOU HAVE COME TO THIS STORE.
WHAT CHOICE DID I HAVE!!
GRUMBLE
YOU'RE THE ONLY PURVEYOR OF PLANT DOLLS!
I'D HEARD RUMORS, BUT I NEVER THOUGHT I'D SET FOOT INSIDE THIS PLACE.
GETTING RIGHT DOWN TO BUSINESS, CAN YOU GIVE ME ONE? HOW MUCH WOULD IT COST?
SIP
UNFORTU-NATELY...
TEA ...?
SO YOU DON'T HAVE IT?! IS THAT IT? JUST AS I THOUGHT, SOME-THING LIKE THAT COULDN'T...
I DIDN'T SAY IT DOESN'T EXIST BUT...
THEN IF YOU HAVE IT, SELL IT TO ME. I'M ASK-ING YOU!!
I TAKE PRIDE IN THE FACT THAT I ALWAYS FULFILL MY CUSTOMERS' REQUESTS.
Ah.
Crunch
THEY VERY RARELY COME INTO OUR HANDS.
MONEY IS NO OBJECT.
OF COURSE, IT IS NOT A QUESTION OF MONEY.
chuckle
WE'RE TALKING ABOUT...
A MI...
... A MIRACLE.
... RACLE ?!

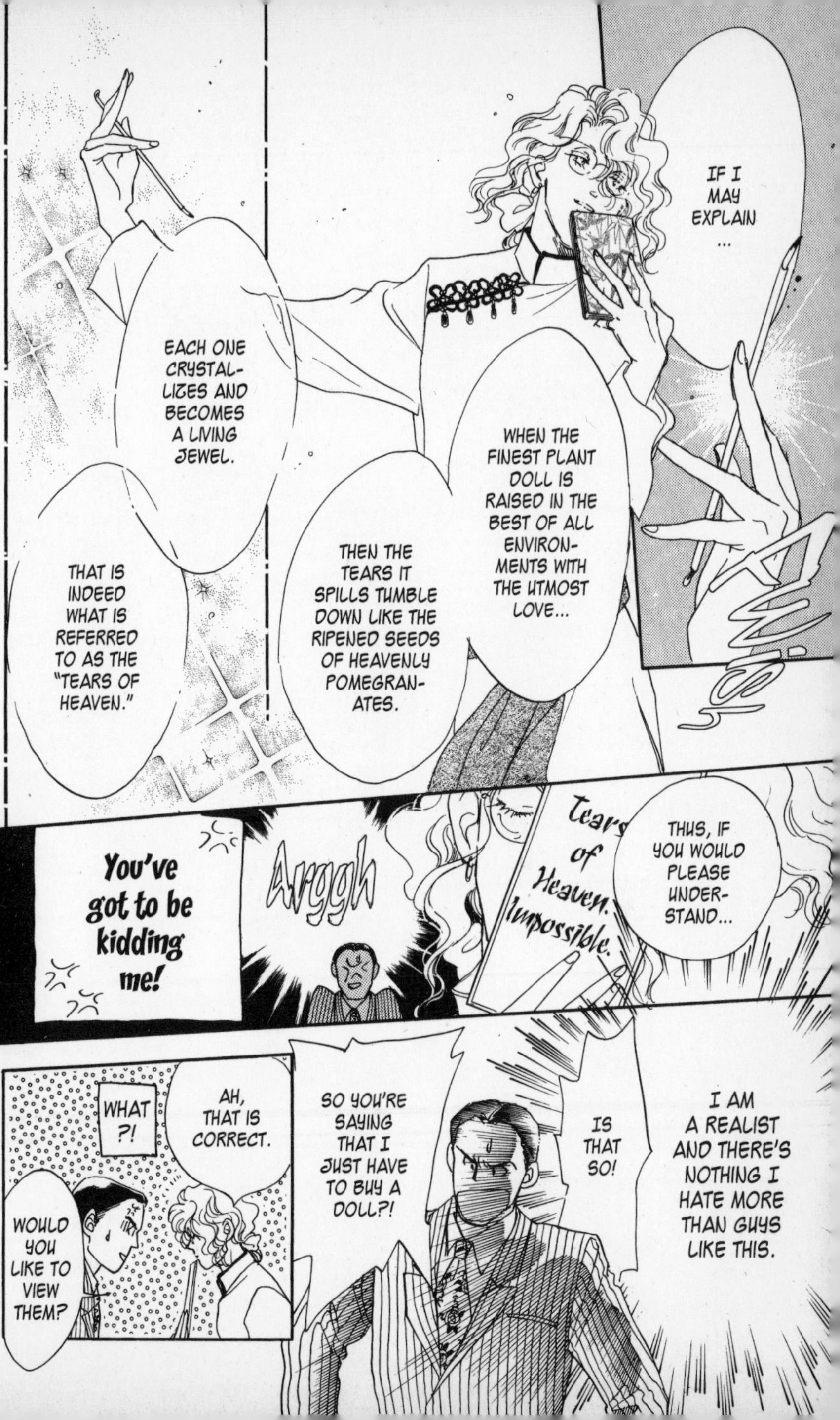
IF I MAY EXPLAIN ...
WHEN THE FINEST PLANT DOLL IS RAISED IN THE BEST OF ALL ENVIRON-MENTS WITH THE UTMOST LOVE...
THEN THE TEARS IT SPILLS TUMBLE DOWN LIKE THE RIPENED SEEDS OF HEAVENLY POMEGRAN-ATES.
EACH ONE CRYSTAL-LIZES AND BECOMES A LIVING JEWEL.
THAT IS INDEED WHAT IS REFERRED TO AS THE "TEARS OF HEAVEN."
THUS, IF YOU WOULD PLEASE UNDER-STAND...
Tears of Heaven. Impossible.
Arggh
You've got to be kidding me!
I AM A REALIST AND THERE'S NOTHING I HATE MORE THAN GUYS LIKE THIS.
IS THAT SO!
SO YOU'RE SAYING THAT I JUST HAVE TO BUY A DOLL?!
AH, THAT IS CORRECT.
WHAT?!
WOULD YOU LIKE TO VIEW THEM?

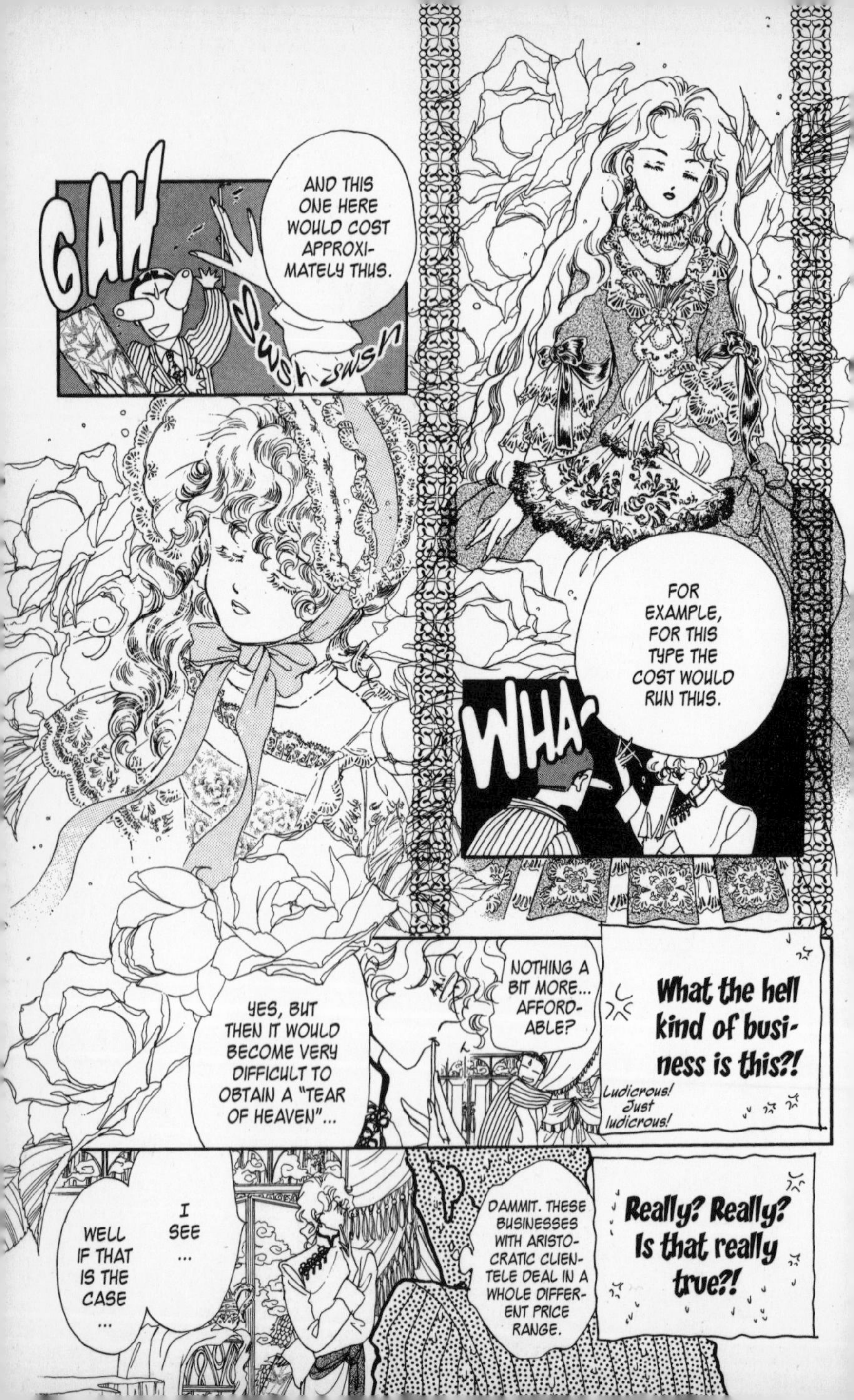
FOR EXAMPLE, FOR THIS TYPE THE COST WOULD RUN THUS.
WHA
AND THIS ONE HERE WOULD COST APPROXIMATELY THUS.
CAH
swsh swsh
What the hell kind of business is this?!
Ludicrous! Just ludicrous!
NOTHING A BIT MORE... AFFORDABLE?
YES, BUT THEN IT WOULD BECOME VERY DIFFICULT TO OBTAIN A "TEAR OF HEAVEN"...
Really? Really? Is that really true?!
DAMMIT. THESE BUSINESSES WITH ARISTOCRATIC CLIENTELE DEAL IN A WHOLE DIFFERENT PRICE RANGE.
I SEE ...
WELL IF THAT IS THE CASE ...

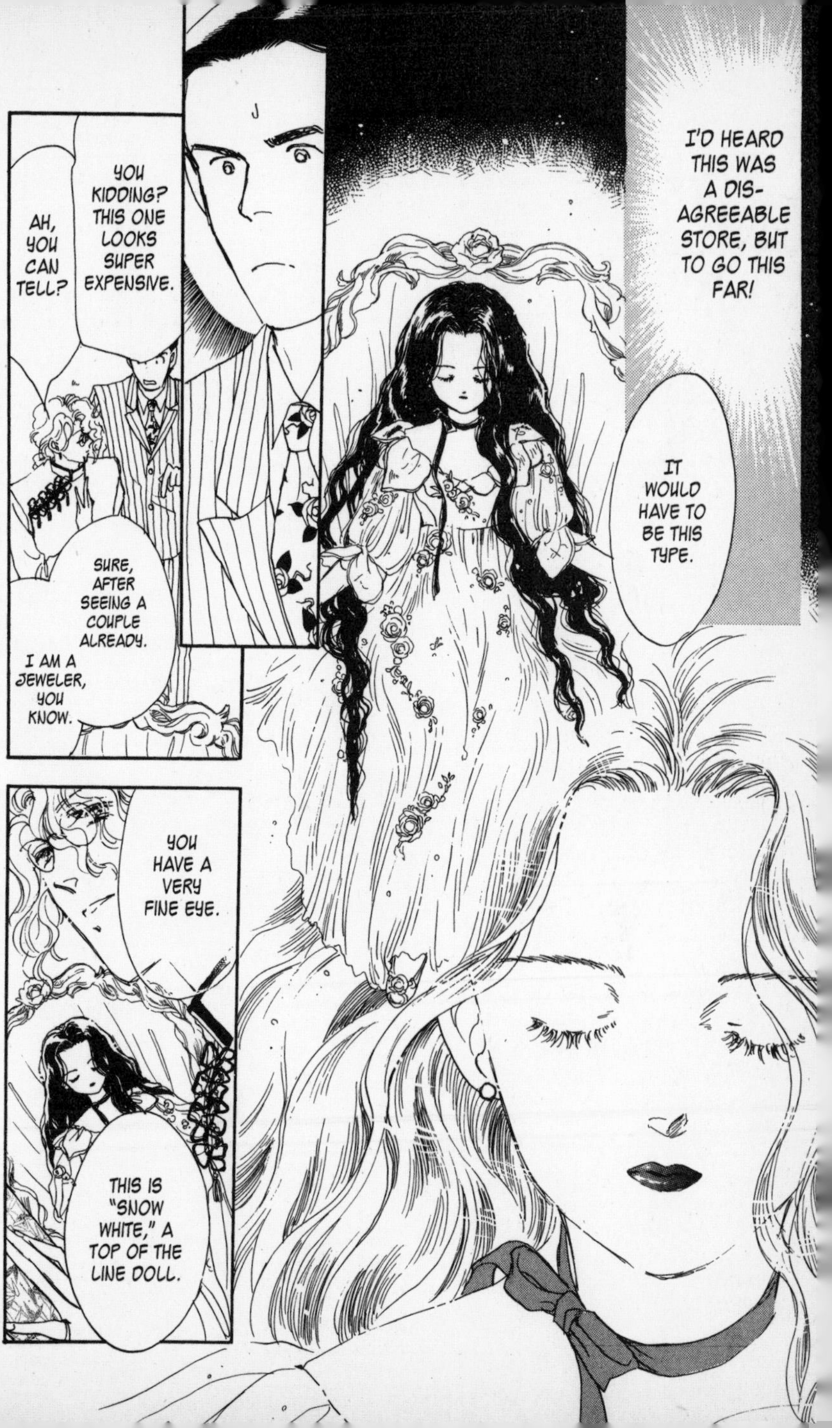
I'D HEARD THIS WAS A DIS-AGREEABLE STORE, BUT TO GO THIS FAR!
IT WOULD HAVE TO BE THIS TYPE.
YOU KIDDING? THIS ONE LOOKS SUPER EXPENSIVE.
AH, YOU CAN TELL?
SURE, AFTER SEEING A COUPLE ALREADY.
I AM A JEWELER, YOU KNOW.
YOU HAVE A VERY FINE EYE.
THIS IS "SNOW WHITE," A TOP OF THE LINE DOLL.

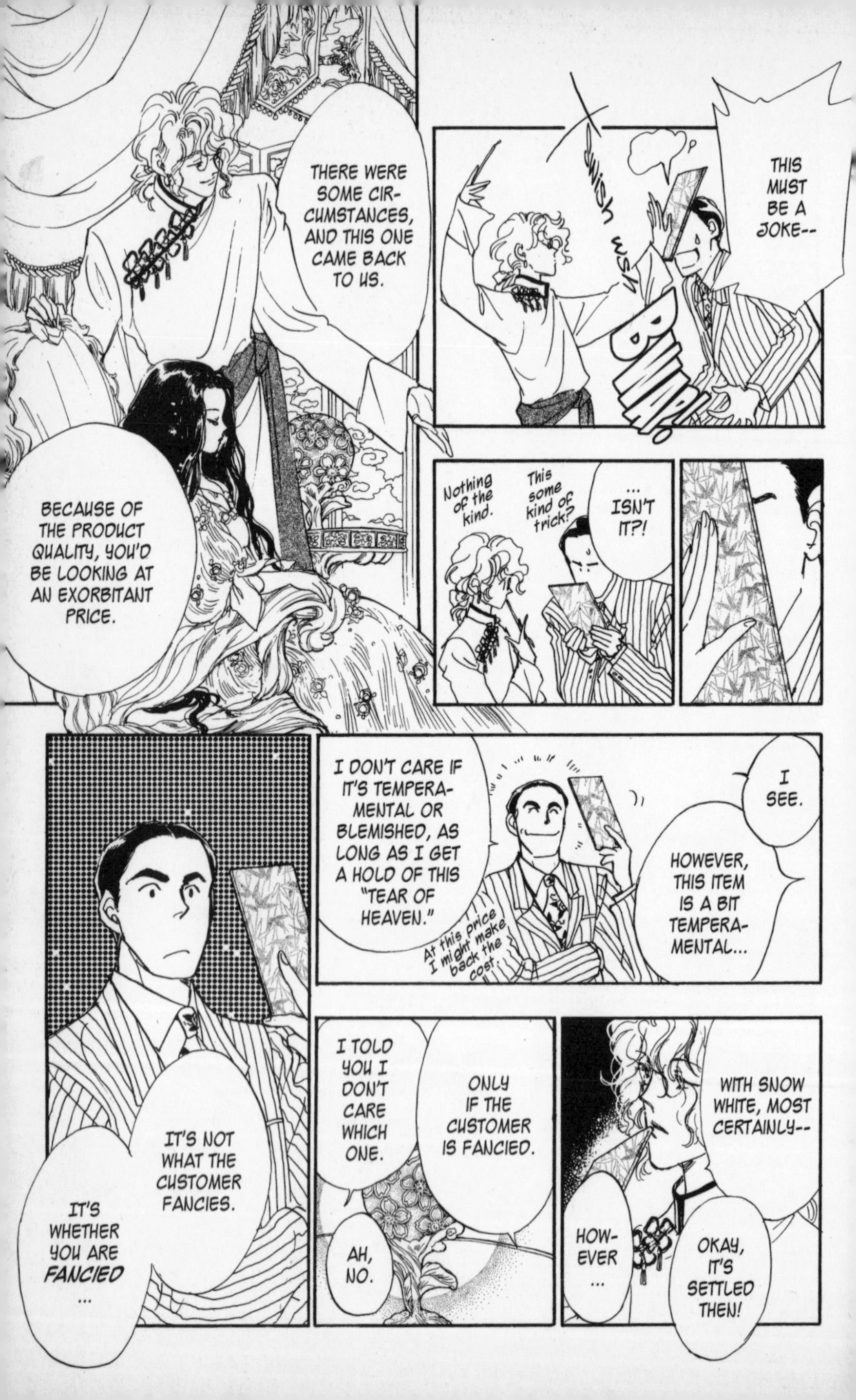
THIS MUST BE A JOKE--
Swish
BUMP!
... ISN'T IT?!
This some kind of trick?
Nothing of the kind.
THERE WERE SOME CIR-CUMSTANCES, AND THIS ONE CAME BACK TO US.
BECAUSE OF THE PRODUCT QUALITY, YOU'D BE LOOKING AT AN EXORBITANT PRICE.
I SEE.
HOWEVER, THIS ITEM IS A BIT TEMPERA-MENTAL...
I DON'T CARE IF IT'S TEMPERA-MENTAL OR BLEMISHED, AS LONG AS I GET A HOLD OF THIS "TEAR OF HEAVEN."
At this price I might make back the cost.
WITH SNOW WHITE, MOST CERTAINLY--
OKAY, IT'S SETTLED THEN!
HOW-EVER ...
ONLY IF THE CUSTOMER IS FANCIED.
I TOLD YOU I DON'T CARE WHICH ONE.
AH, NO.
IT'S NOT WHAT THE CUSTOMER FANCIES.
IT'S WHETHER YOU ARE *FANCIED* ...

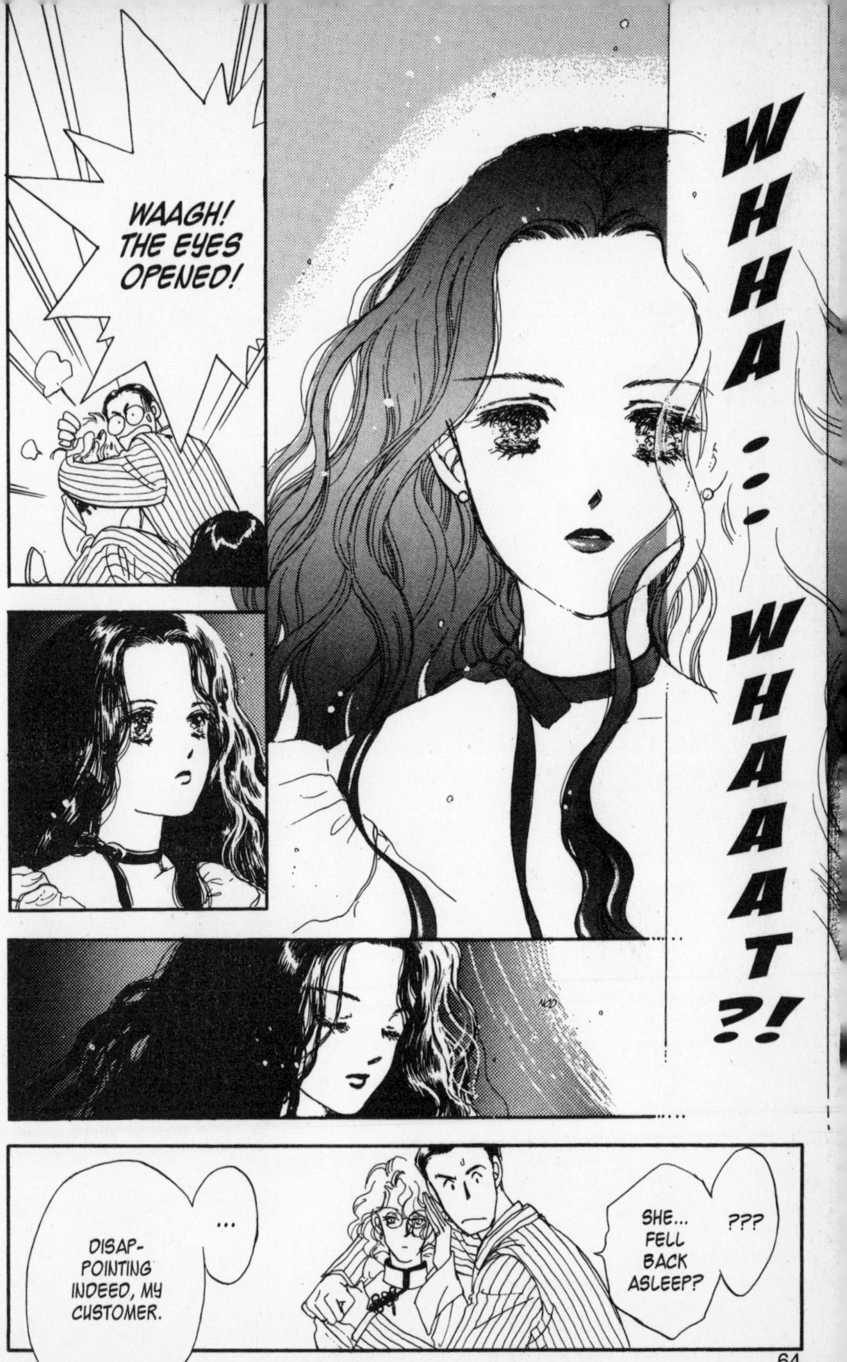
WHHA... WHHAAAT?!
WAAGH! THE EYES OPENED!
NOD
???
SHE... FELL BACK ASLEEP?
...
DISAP-POINTING INDEED, MY CUSTOMER.

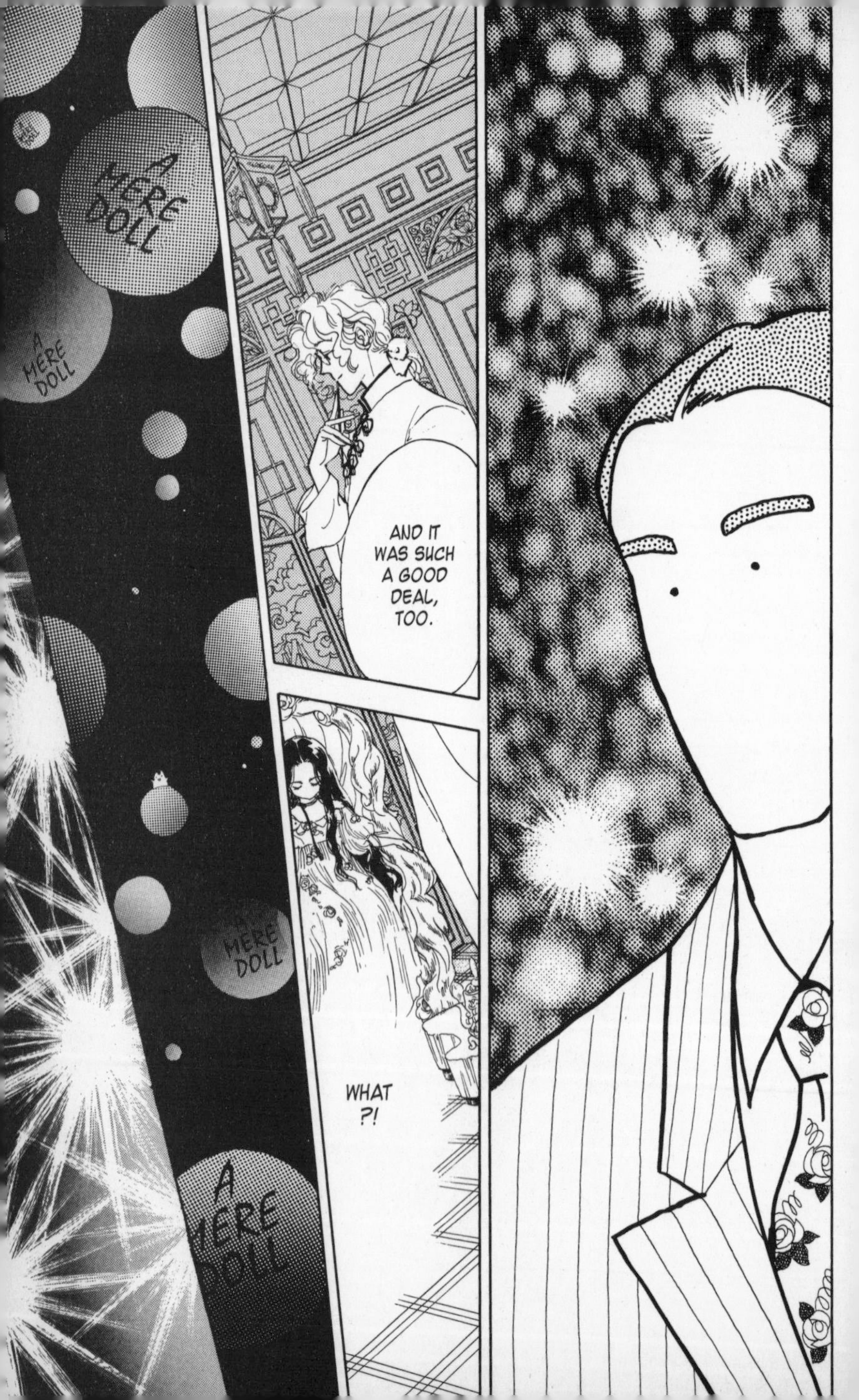
AND IT WAS SUCH A GOOD DEAL, TOO.
WHAT ?!
A MERE DOLL
A MERE DOLL
A MERE DOLL
A MERE DOLL

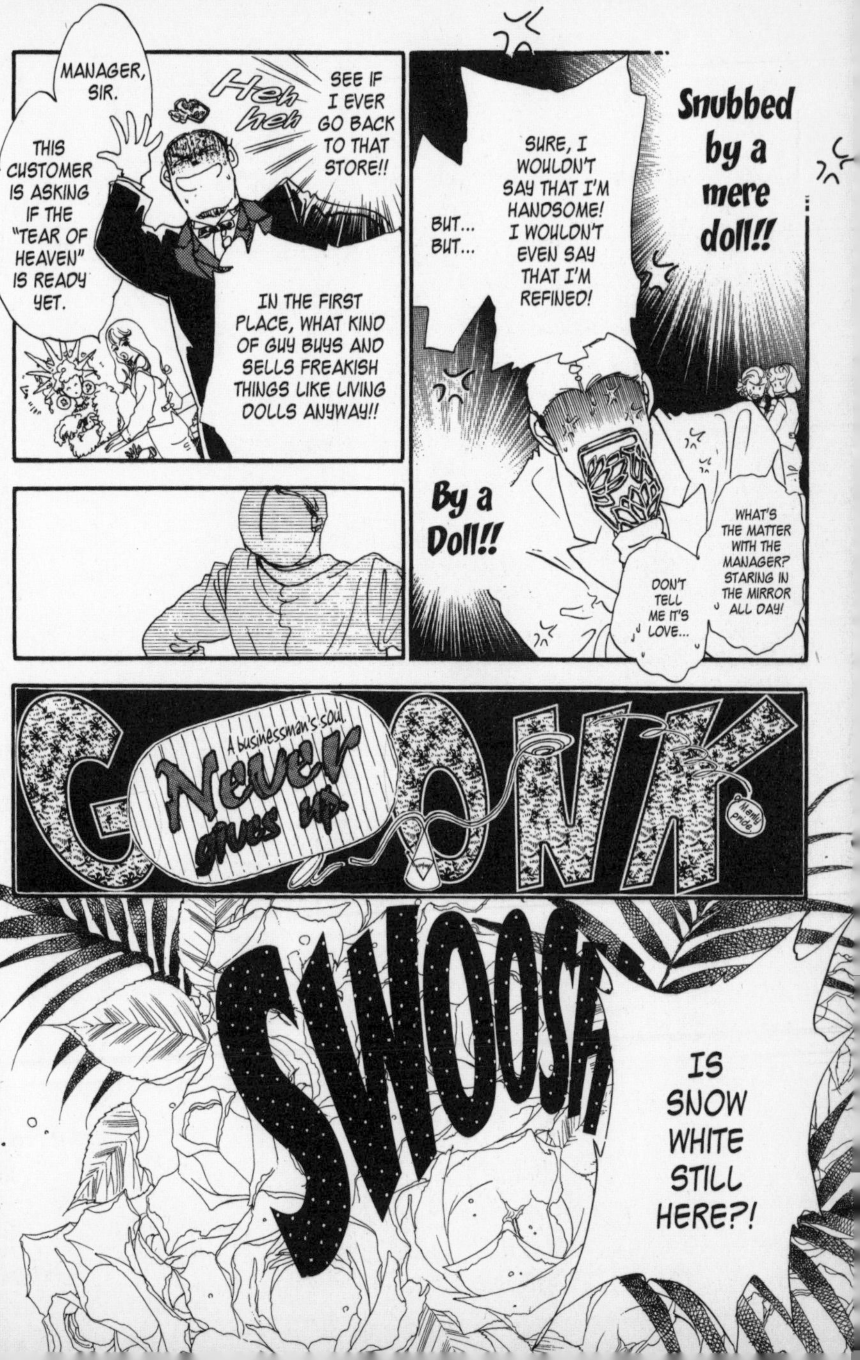
SURE, I WOULDN'T SAY THAT I'M HANDSOME! I WOULDN'T EVEN SAY THAT I'M REFINED!
BUT... BUT...
Snubbed by a mere doll!!
By a Doll!!
WHAT'S THE MATTER WITH THE MANAGER? STARING IN THE MIRROR ALL DAY!
DON'T TELL ME IT'S LOVE...
SEE IF I EVER GO BACK TO THAT STORE!!
Heh heh
IN THE FIRST PLACE, WHAT KIND OF GUY BUYS AND SELLS FREAKISH THINGS LIKE LIVING DOLLS ANYWAY!!
MANAGER, SIR.
THIS CUSTOMER IS ASKING IF THE "TEAR OF HEAVEN" IS READY YET.
GONK
A businessman's soul. Never gives up.
Manly pride.
SWOOSH
IS SNOW WHITE STILL HERE?!

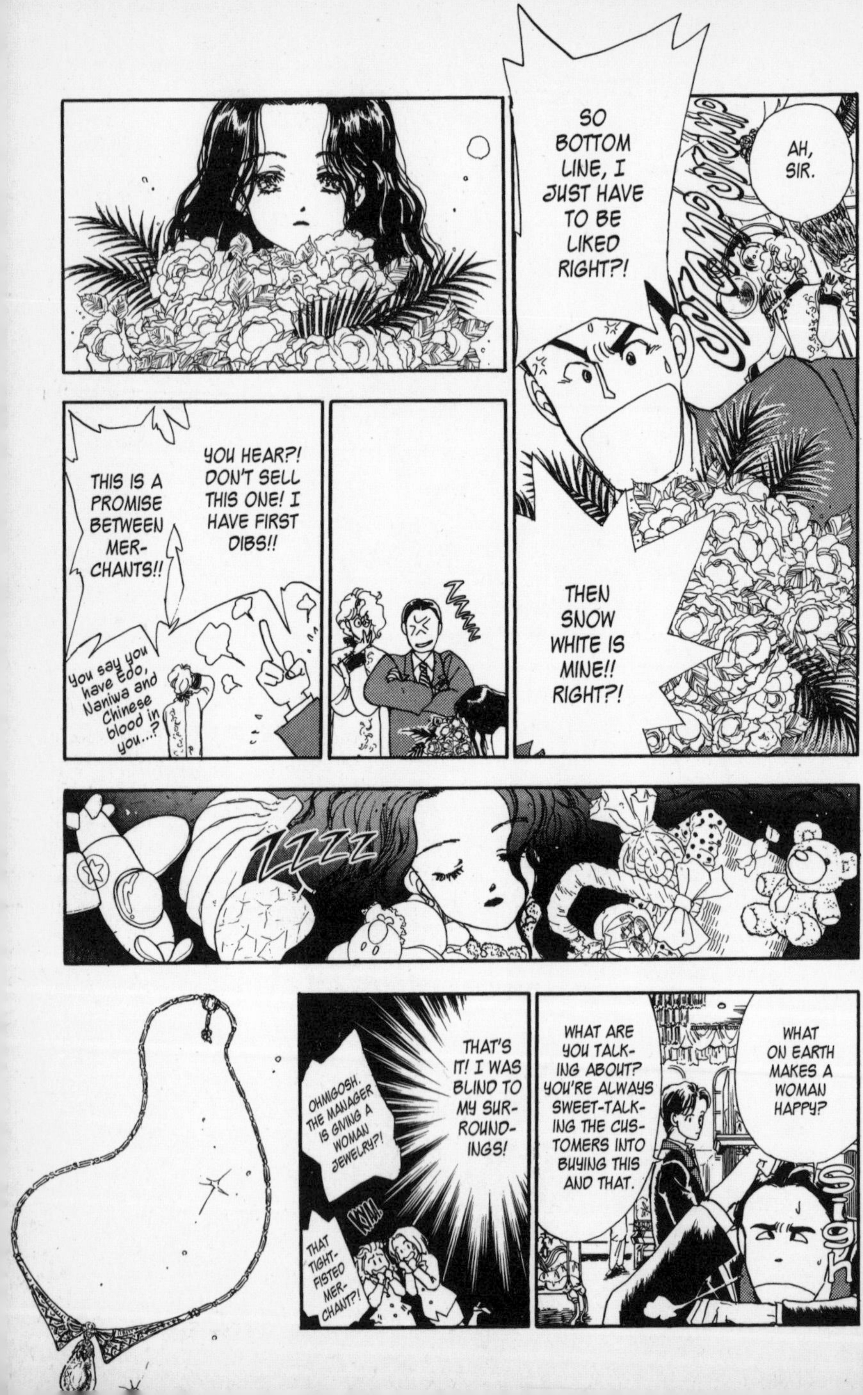
AH, SIR.
SO BOTTOM LINE, I JUST HAVE TO BE LIKED RIGHT?!
THEN SNOW WHITE IS MINE!! RIGHT?!
YOU HEAR?! DON'T SELL THIS ONE! I HAVE FIRST DIBS!!
THIS IS A PROMISE BETWEEN MER-CHANTS!!
You say you have Edo, Naniwa and Chinese blood in you...?
ZZZZ
WHAT ON EARTH MAKES A WOMAN HAPPY?
Sigh
WHAT ARE YOU TALK-ING ABOUT? YOU'RE ALWAYS SWEET-TALK-ING THE CUS-TOMERS INTO BUYING THIS AND THAT.
THAT'S IT! I WAS BLIND TO MY SUR-ROUND-INGS!
OHMIGOSH. THE MANAGER IS GIVING A WOMAN JEWELRY?!
KYA!
THAT TIGHT-FISTED MER-CHANT?!

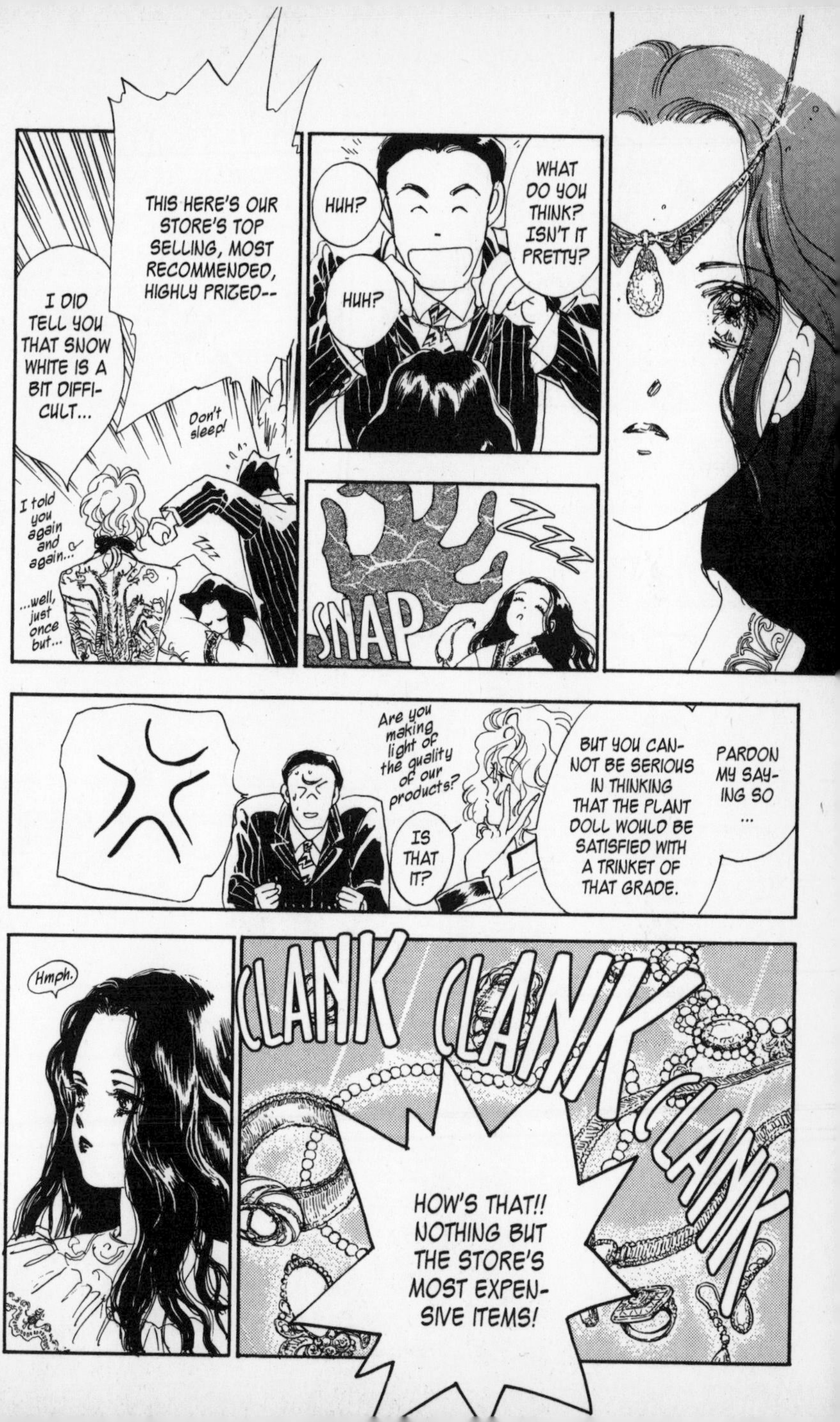
WHAT DO YOU THINK? ISN'T IT PRETTY?
HUH?
HUH?
ZZZ
SNAP
THIS HERE'S OUR STORE'S TOP SELLING, MOST RECOMMENDED, HIGHLY PRIZED--
I DID TELL YOU THAT SNOW WHITE IS A BIT DIFFI-CULT...
Don't sleep!
I told you again and again...
...well, just once but...
ZZZ
PARDON MY SAY-ING SO ...
BUT YOU CAN-NOT BE SERIOUS IN THINKING THAT THE PLANT DOLL WOULD BE SATISFIED WITH A TRINKET OF THAT GRADE.
IS THAT IT?
Are you making light of the quality of our products?
CLANK
CLANK
CLANK
CLANK
HOW'S THAT!! NOTHING BUT THE STORE'S MOST EXPEN-SIVE ITEMS!
Hmph.

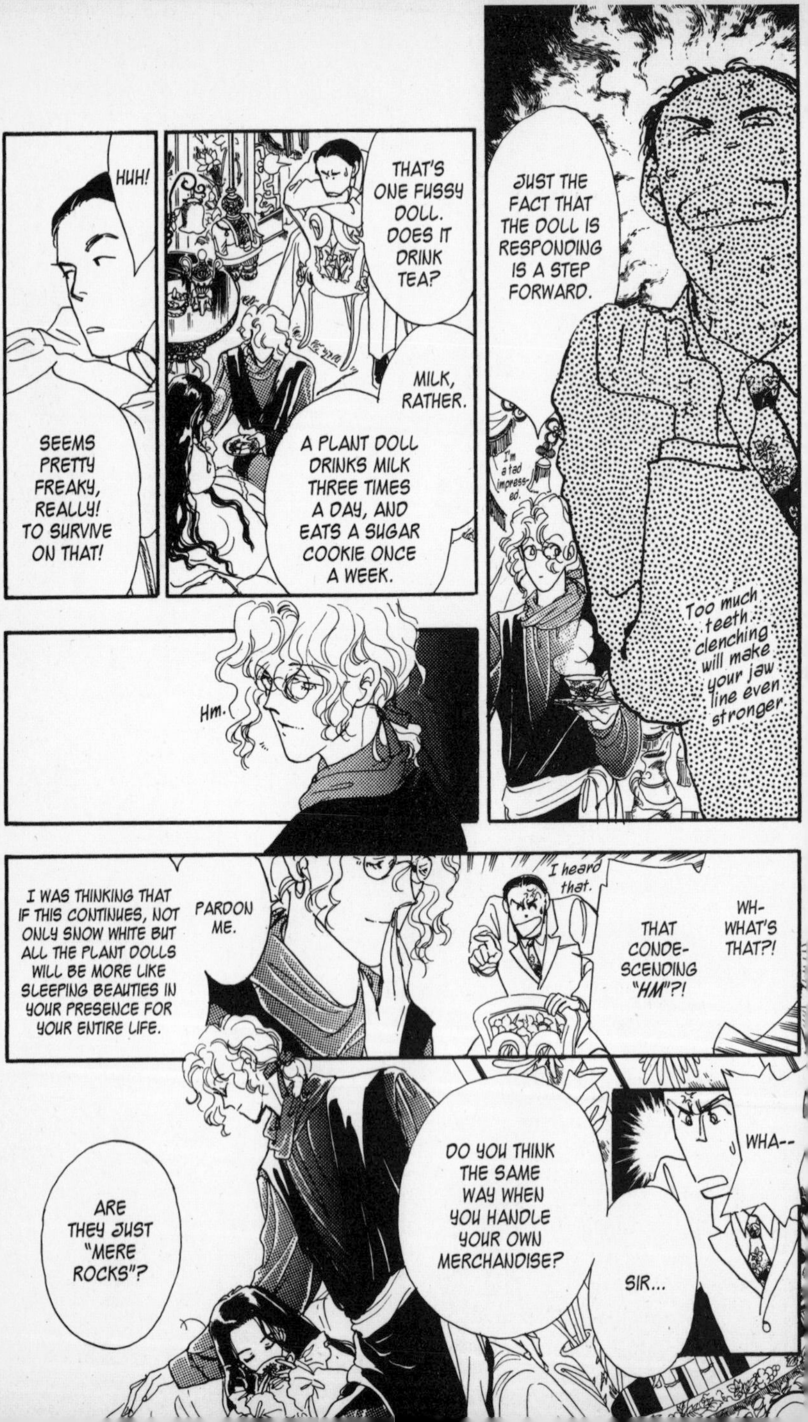
JUST THE FACT THAT THE DOLL IS RESPONDING IS A STEP FORWARD.
I'm a tad impress-ed.
Too much teeth clenching will make your jaw line even stronger.
THAT'S ONE FUSSY DOLL. DOES IT DRINK TEA?
MILK, RATHER.
A PLANT DOLL DRINKS MILK THREE TIMES A DAY, AND EATS A SUGAR COOKIE ONCE A WEEK.
HUH!
SEEMS PRETTY FREAKY, REALLY! TO SURVIVE ON THAT!
Hm.
WH- WHAT'S THAT?!
THAT CONDE-SCENDING "HM"?!
I heard that.
PARDON ME.
I WAS THINKING THAT IF THIS CONTINUES, NOT ONLY SNOW WHITE BUT ALL THE PLANT DOLLS WILL BE MORE LIKE SLEEPING BEAUTIES IN YOUR PRESENCE FOR YOUR ENTIRE LIFE.
WHA--
SIR...
DO YOU THINK THE SAME WAY WHEN YOU HANDLE YOUR OWN MERCHANDISE?
ARE THEY JUST "MERE ROCKS"?

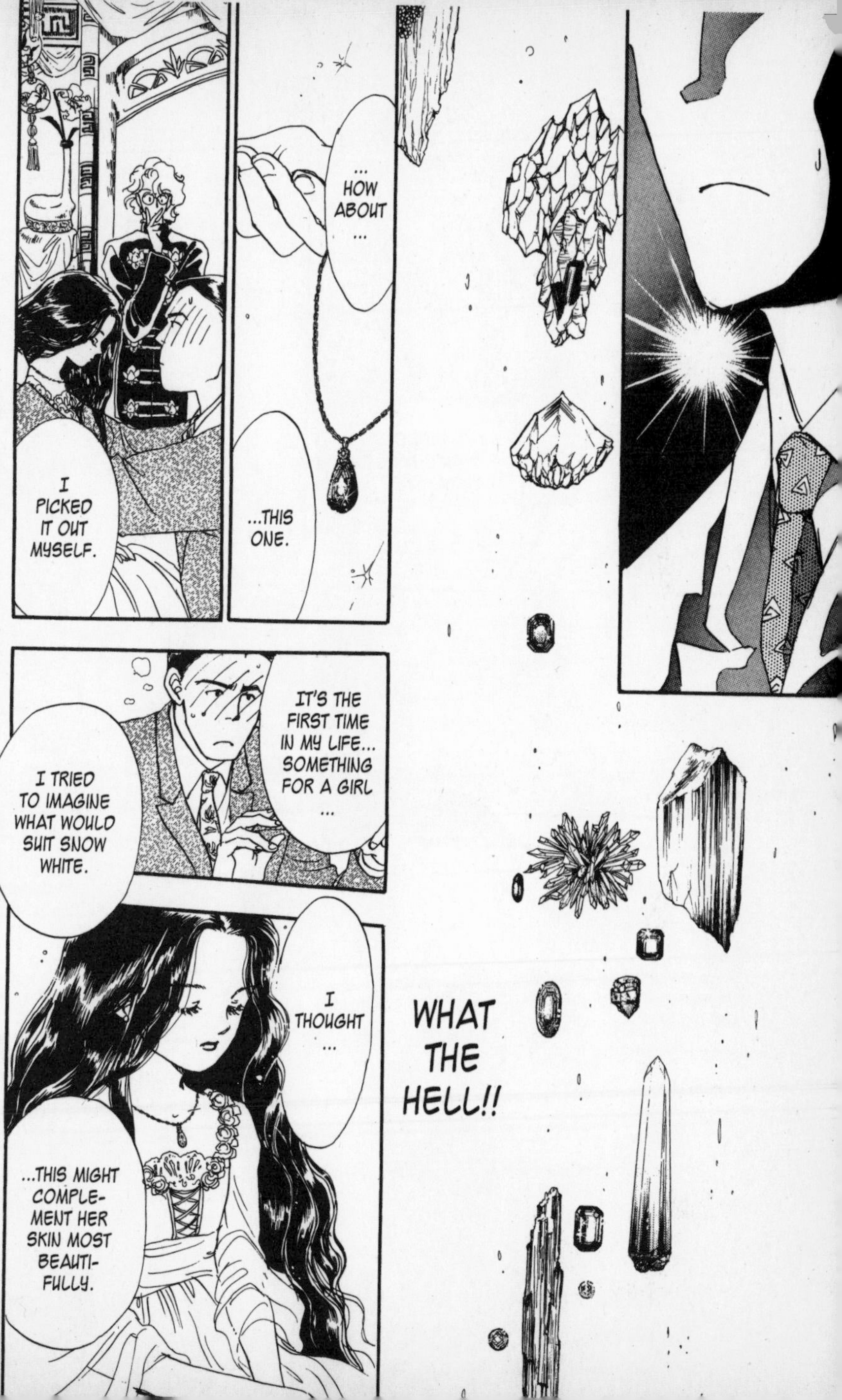
WHAT THE HELL!!
... HOW ABOUT ...
...THIS ONE.
I PICKED IT OUT MYSELF.
IT'S THE FIRST TIME IN MY LIFE... SOMETHING FOR A GIRL ...
I TRIED TO IMAGINE WHAT WOULD SUIT SNOW WHITE.
I THOUGHT ...
...THIS MIGHT COMPLEMENT HER SKIN MOST BEAUTIFULLY.

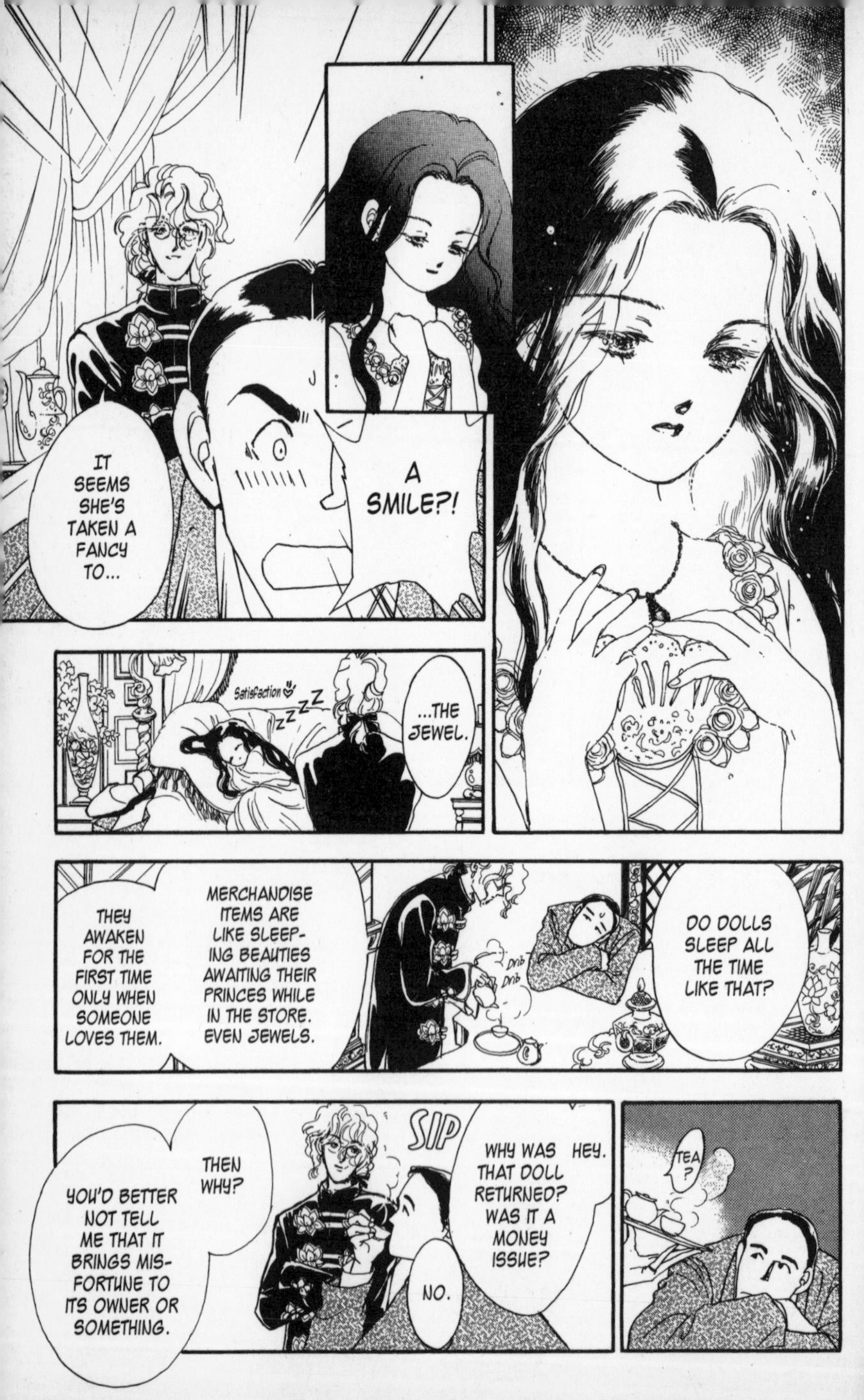
A SMILE?!
IT SEEMS SHE'S TAKEN A FANCY TO...
Satisfaction
ZZZZ
...THE JEWEL.
DO DOLLS SLEEP ALL THE TIME LIKE THAT?
Drib Drib
MERCHANDISE ITEMS ARE LIKE SLEEP-ING BEAUTIES AWAITING THEIR PRINCES WHILE IN THE STORE. EVEN JEWELS.
THEY AWAKEN FOR THE FIRST TIME ONLY WHEN SOMEONE LOVES THEM.
TEA?
HEY.
WHY WAS THAT DOLL RETURNED? WAS IT A MONEY ISSUE?
SIP
NO.
THEN WHY?
YOU'D BETTER NOT TELL ME THAT IT BRINGS MIS-FORTUNE TO ITS OWNER OR SOMETHING.

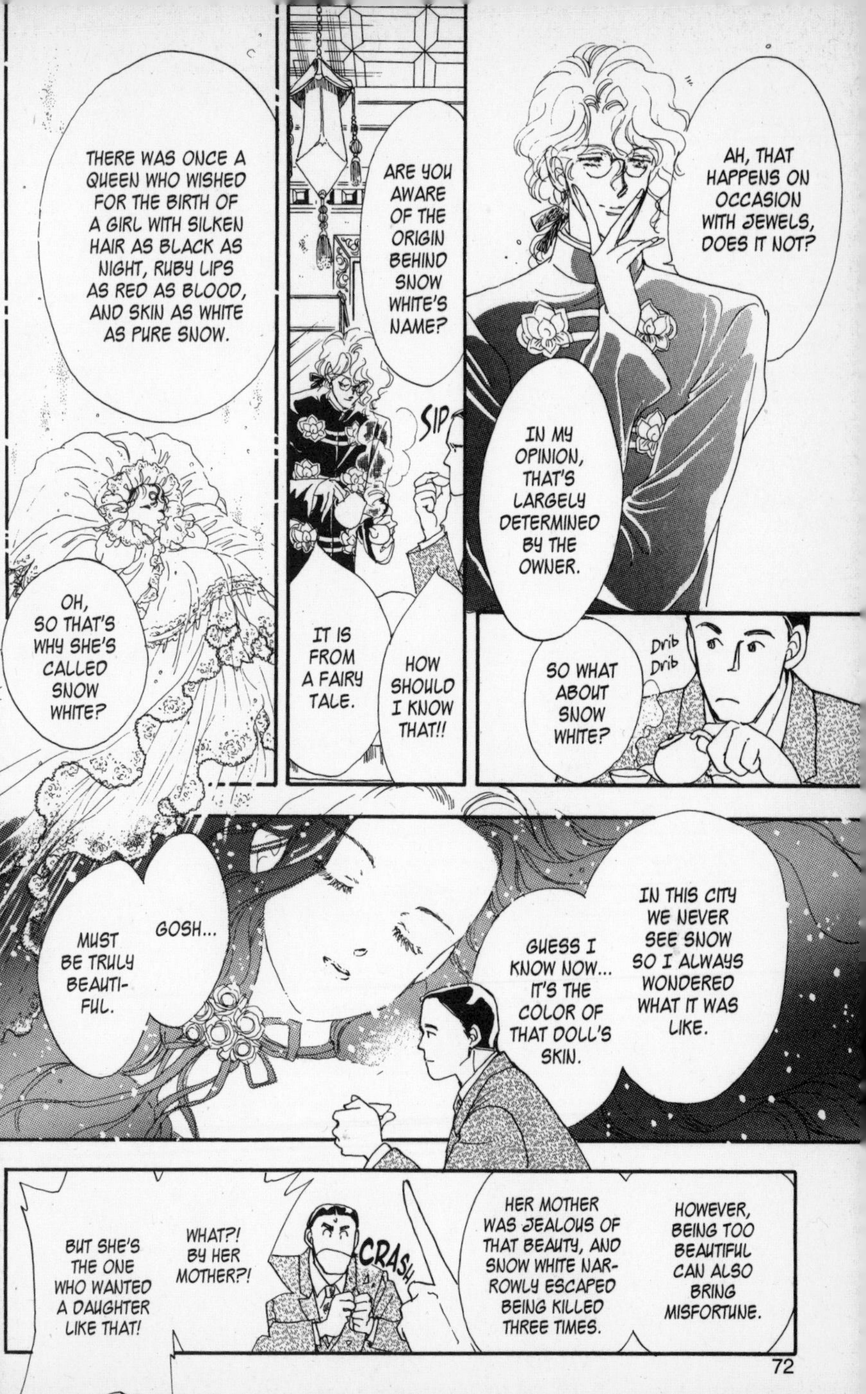
AH, THAT HAPPENS ON OCCASION WITH JEWELS, DOES IT NOT?
IN MY OPINION, THAT'S LARGELY DETERMINED BY THE OWNER.
SO WHAT ABOUT SNOW WHITE?
Drib Drib
ARE YOU AWARE OF THE ORIGIN BEHIND SNOW WHITE'S NAME?
SIP
HOW SHOULD I KNOW THAT!!
IT IS FROM A FAIRY TALE.
THERE WAS ONCE A QUEEN WHO WISHED FOR THE BIRTH OF A GIRL WITH SILKEN HAIR AS BLACK AS NIGHT, RUBY LIPS AS RED AS BLOOD, AND SKIN AS WHITE AS PURE SNOW.
OH, SO THAT'S WHY SHE'S CALLED SNOW WHITE?
IN THIS CITY WE NEVER SEE SNOW SO I ALWAYS WONDERED WHAT IT WAS LIKE.
GUESS I KNOW NOW... IT'S THE COLOR OF THAT DOLL'S SKIN.
GOSH...
MUST BE TRULY BEAUTI-FUL.
HOWEVER, BEING TOO BEAUTIFUL CAN ALSO BRING MISFORTUNE.
HER MOTHER WAS JEALOUS OF THAT BEAUTY, AND SNOW WHITE NAR-ROWLY ESCAPED BEING KILLED THREE TIMES.
CRASH
WHAT?! BY HER MOTHER?!
BUT SHE'S THE ONE WHO WANTED A DAUGHTER LIKE THAT!

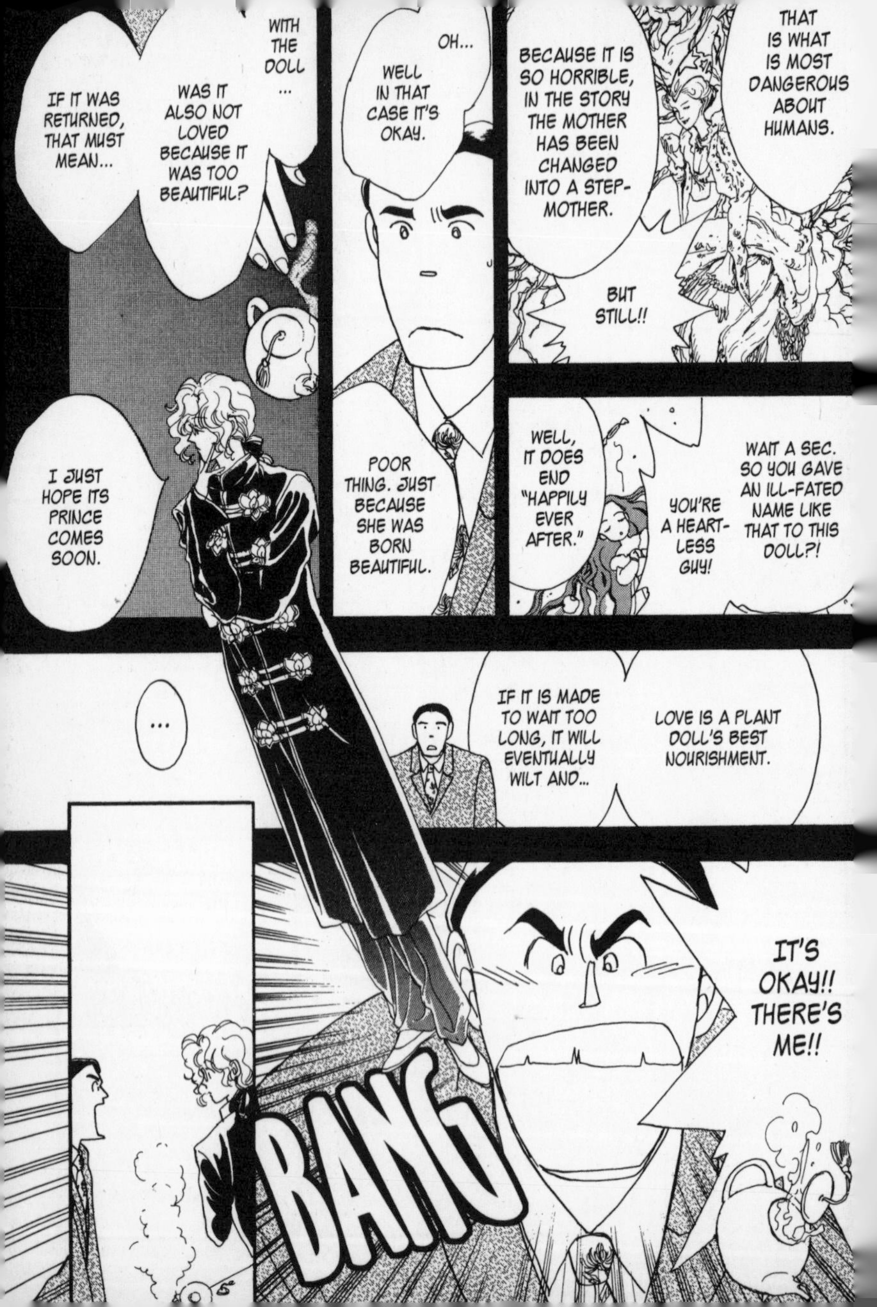
THAT IS WHAT IS MOST DANGEROUS ABOUT HUMANS.
BECAUSE IT IS SO HORRIBLE, IN THE STORY THE MOTHER HAS BEEN CHANGED INTO A STEP-MOTHER.
BUT STILL!!
WAIT A SEC. SO YOU GAVE AN ILL-FATED NAME LIKE THAT TO THIS DOLL?!
YOU'RE A HEART-LESS GUY!
WELL, IT DOES END "HAPPILY EVER AFTER."
OH...
WELL IN THAT CASE IT'S OKAY.
POOR THING. JUST BECAUSE SHE WAS BORN BEAUTIFUL.
WITH THE DOLL ...
WAS IT ALSO NOT LOVED BECAUSE IT WAS TOO BEAUTIFUL?
IF IT WAS RETURNED, THAT MUST MEAN...
I JUST HOPE ITS PRINCE COMES SOON.
LOVE IS A PLANT DOLL'S BEST NOURISHMENT.
IF IT IS MADE TO WAIT TOO LONG, IT WILL EVENTUALLY WILT AND...
...
IT'S OKAY!! THERE'S ME!!
BANG

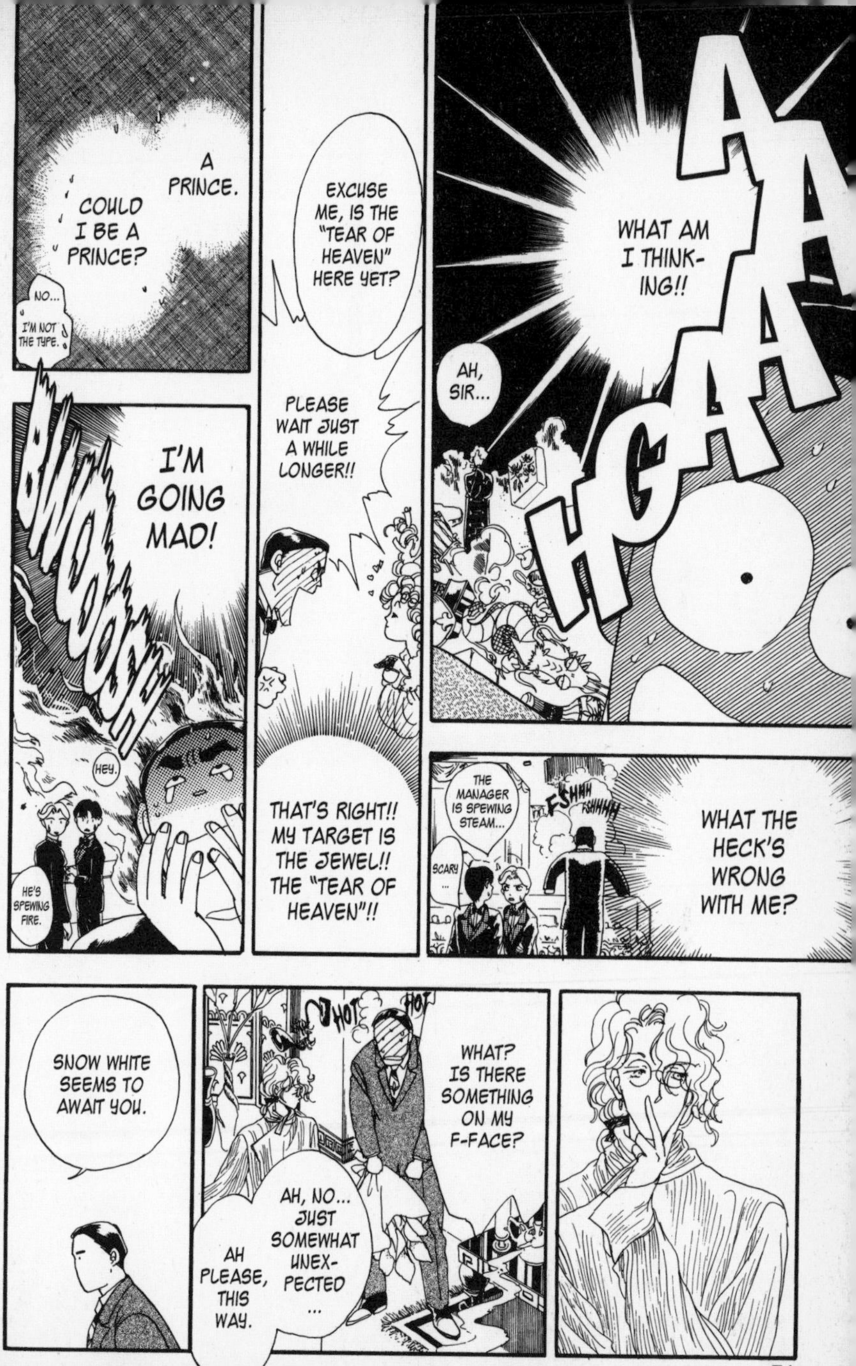
HGAAAA
WHAT AM I THINKING!!
AH, SIR...
WHAT THE HECK'S WRONG WITH ME?
FSHHH FSHHHH
THE MANAGER IS SPEWING STEAM...
SCARY ...
EXCUSE ME, IS THE "TEAR OF HEAVEN" HERE YET?
PLEASE WAIT JUST A WHILE LONGER!!
THAT'S RIGHT!! MY TARGET IS THE JEWEL!! THE "TEAR OF HEAVEN"!!
A PRINCE.
COULD I BE A PRINCE?
NO... I'M NOT THE TYPE.
I'M GOING MAD!
BWOOOSH
HEY.
HE'S SPEWING FIRE.
HOT HOT
WHAT? IS THERE SOMETHING ON MY F-FACE?
AH, NO... JUST SOMEWHAT UNEXPECTED ...
AH PLEASE, THIS WAY.
SNOW WHITE SEEMS TO AWAIT YOU.

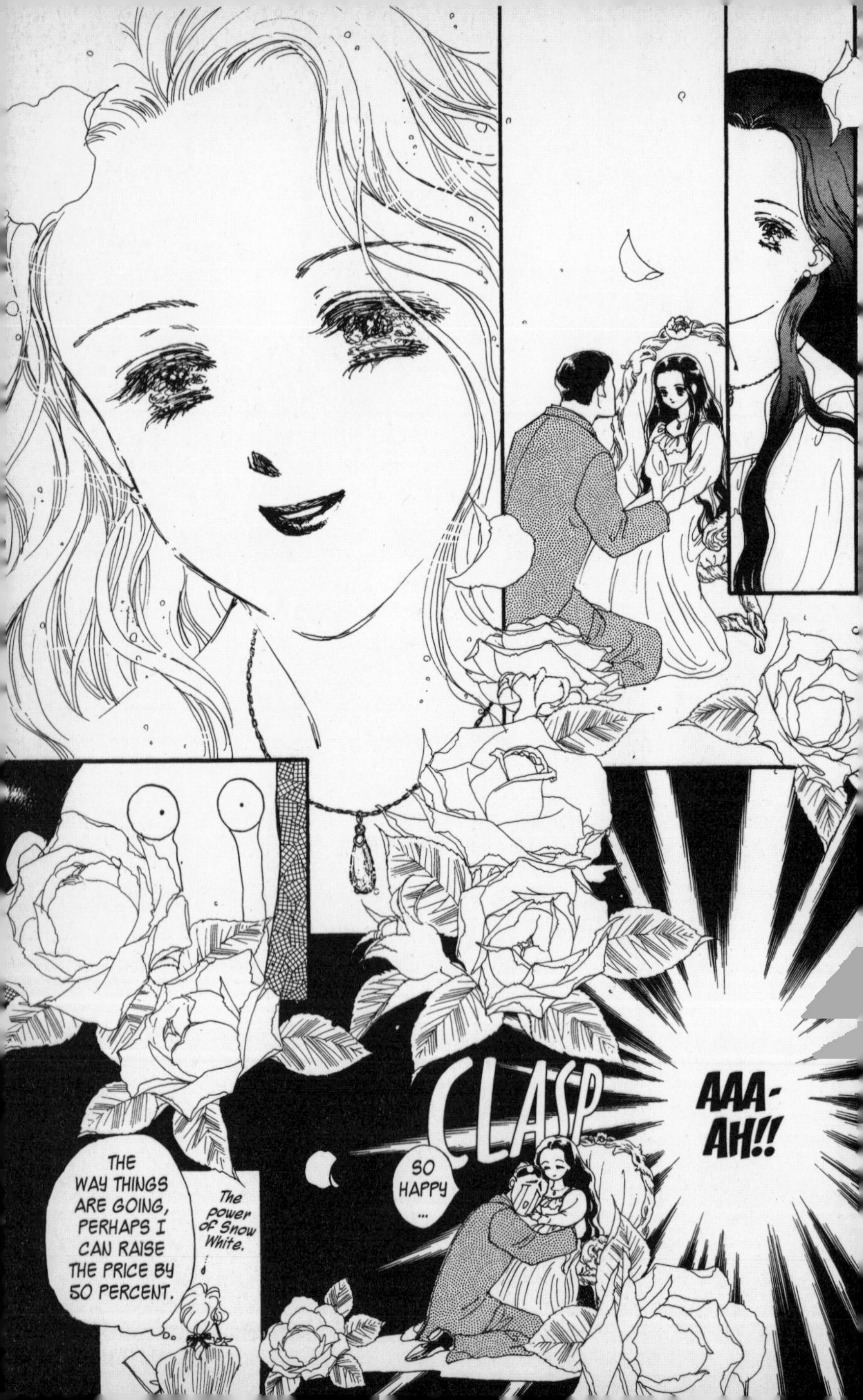
AAA-AH!!
CLASP
SO HAPPY ...
The power of Snow White.
THE WAY THINGS ARE GOING, PERHAPS I CAN RAISE THE PRICE BY 50 PERCENT.

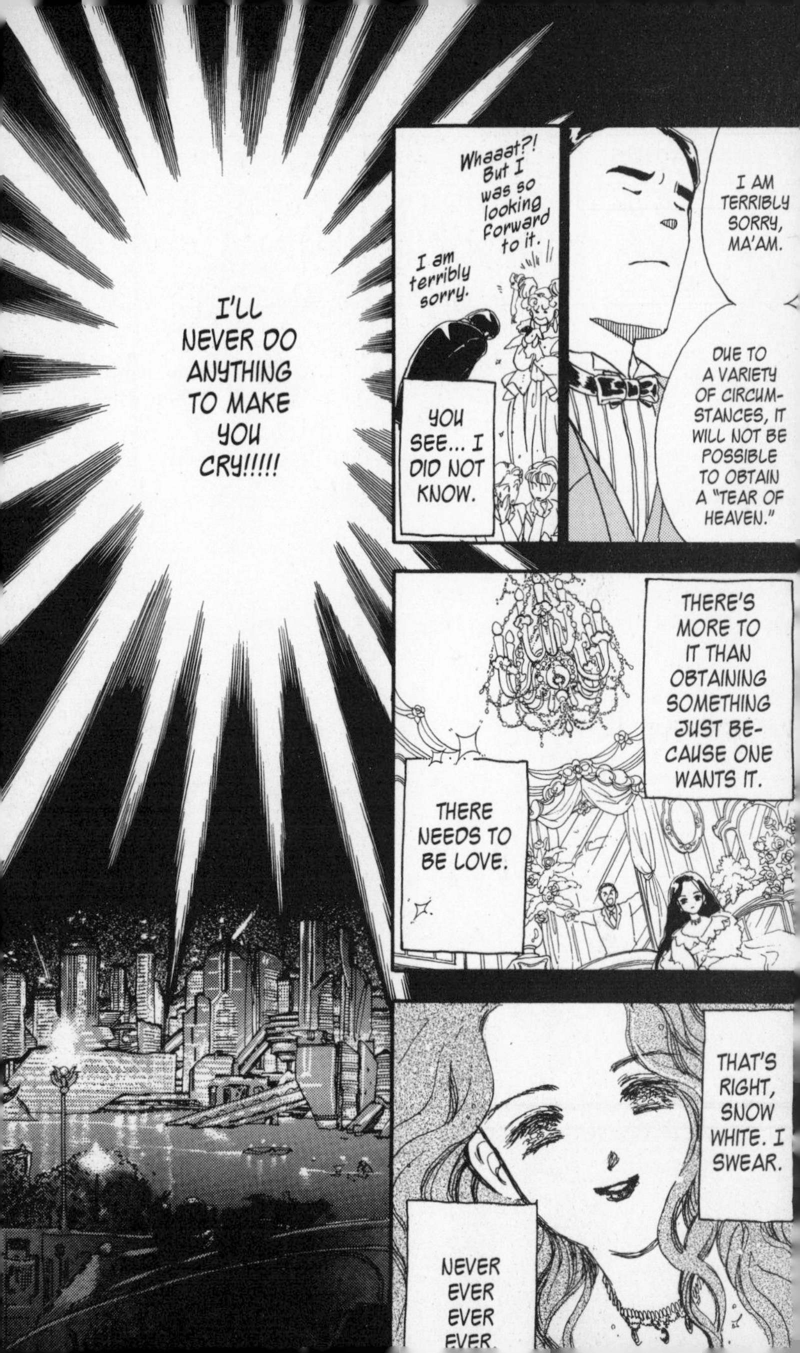
I AM TERRIBLY SORRY, MA'AM.
DUE TO A VARIETY OF CIRCUMSTANCES, IT WILL NOT BE POSSIBLE TO OBTAIN A "TEAR OF HEAVEN."
Whaaat?! But I was so looking forward to it.
I am terribly sorry.
YOU SEE... I DID NOT KNOW.
THERE'S MORE TO IT THAN OBTAINING SOMETHING JUST BECAUSE ONE WANTS IT.
THERE NEEDS TO BE LOVE.
THAT'S RIGHT, SNOW WHITE. I SWEAR.
NEVER EVER EVER EVER.
I'LL NEVER DO ANYTHING TO MAKE YOU CRY!!!!!

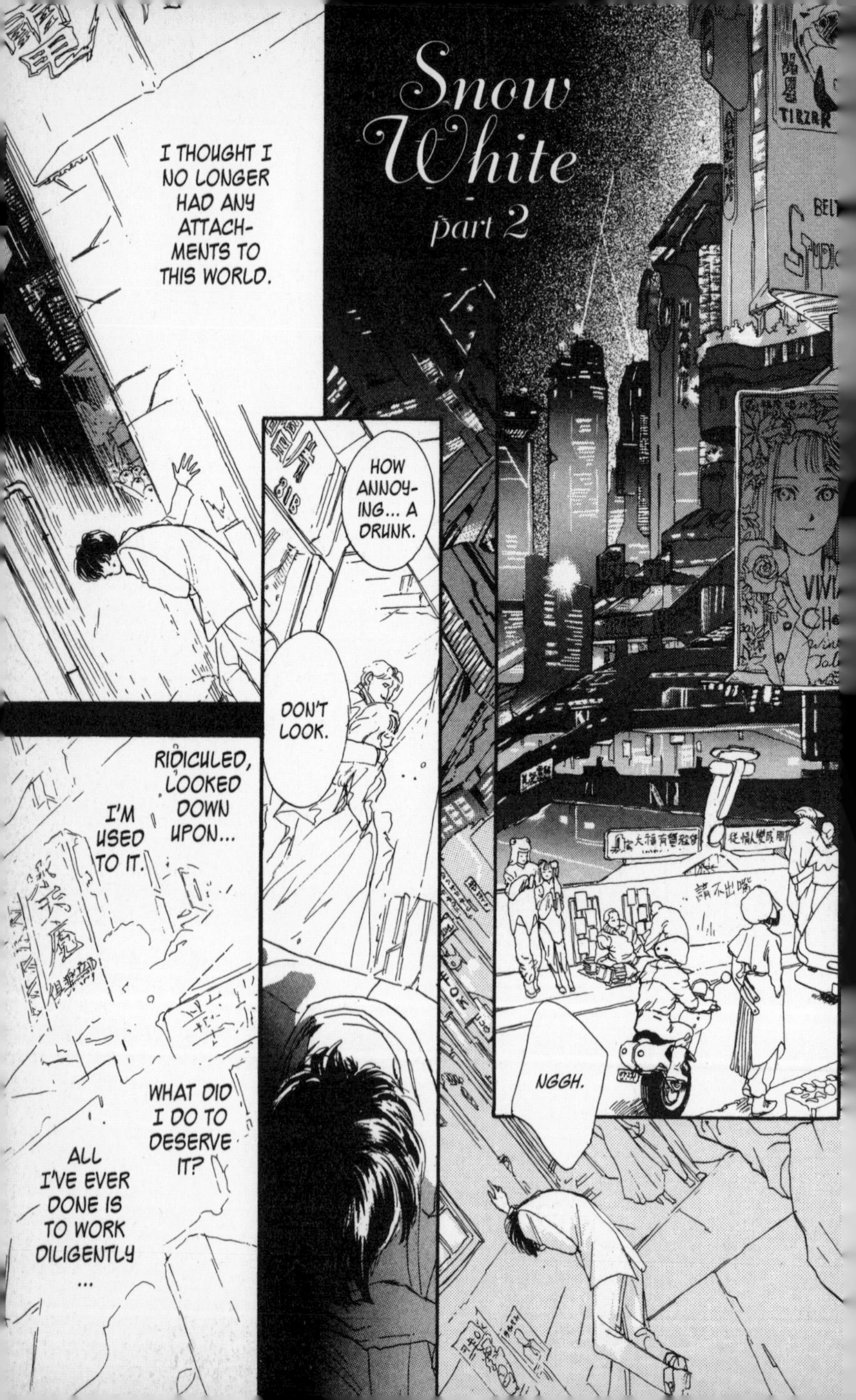
Snow White
part 2
NGGH.
HOW ANNOYING... A DRUNK.
DON'T LOOK.
I THOUGHT I NO LONGER HAD ANY ATTACHMENTS TO THIS WORLD.
RIDICULED, LOOKED DOWN UPON...
I'M USED TO IT.
WHAT DID I DO TO DESERVE IT?
ALL I'VE EVER DONE IS TO WORK DILIGENTLY...

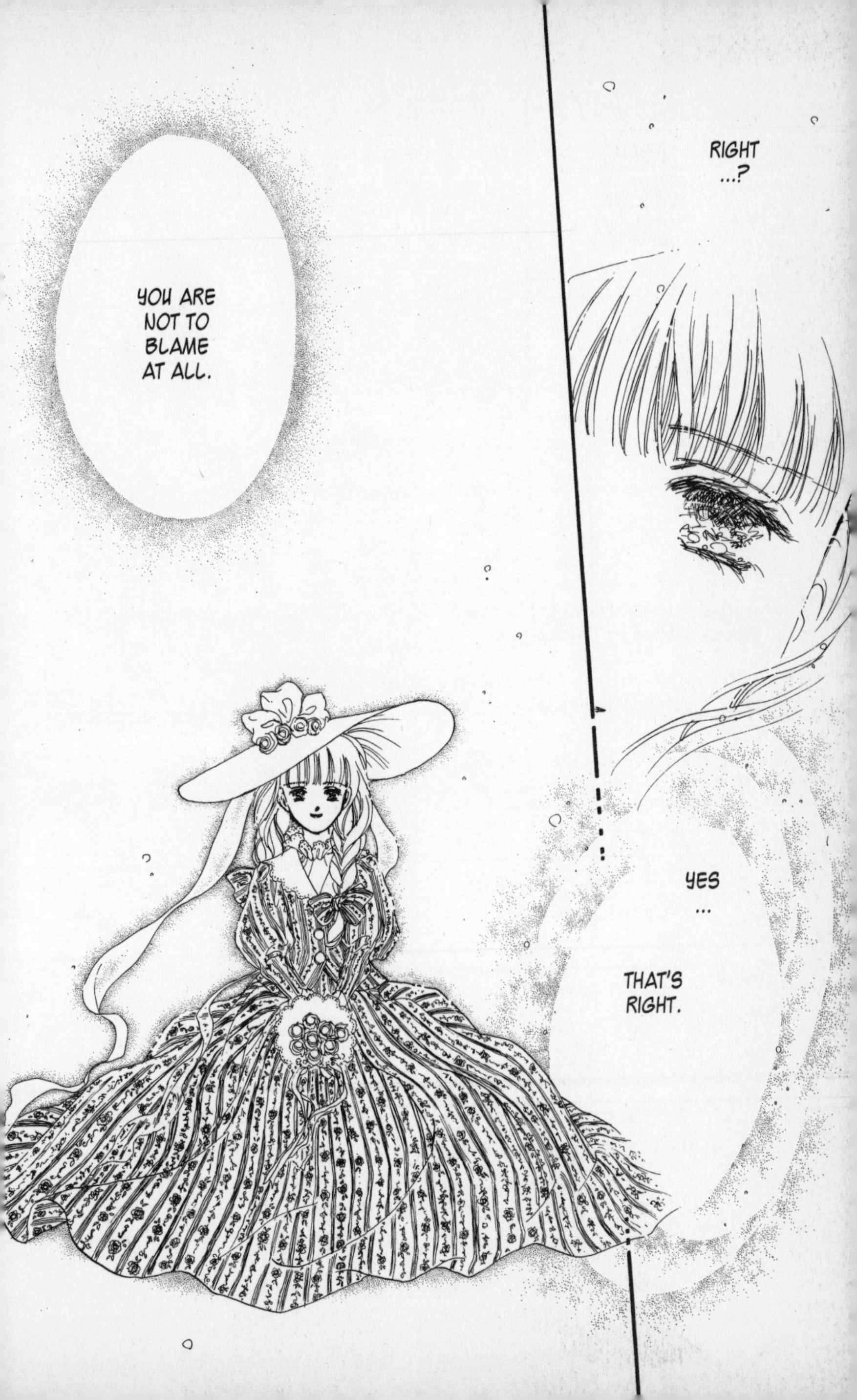
RIGHT ...?
YES ...
THAT'S RIGHT.
YOU ARE NOT TO BLAME AT ALL.

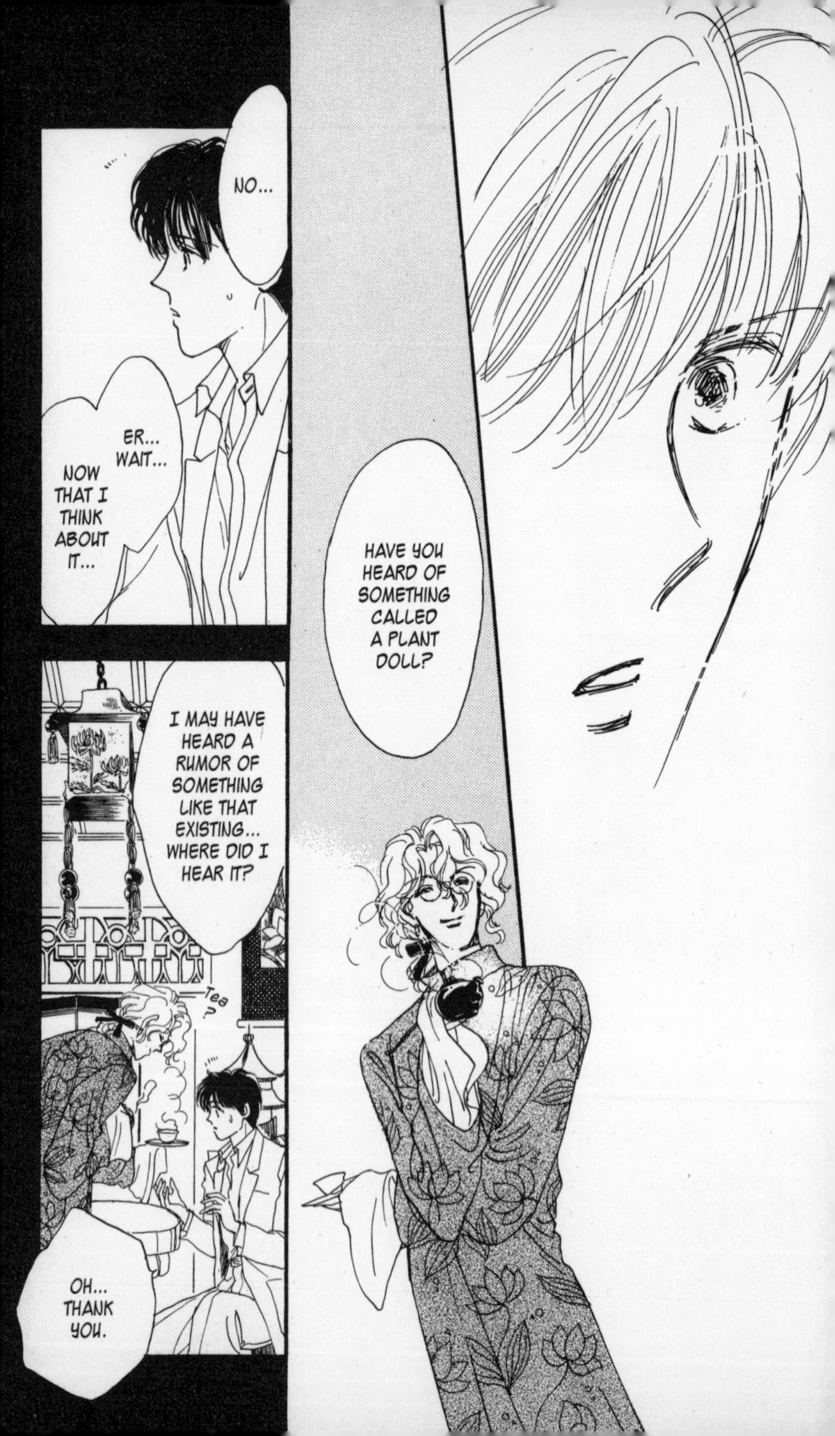
HAVE YOU HEARD OF SOMETHING CALLED A PLANT DOLL?
NO...
ER... WAIT...
NOW THAT I THINK ABOUT IT...
I MAY HAVE HEARD A RUMOR OF SOMETHING LIKE THAT EXISTING... WHERE DID I HEAR IT?
Tea?
OH... THANK YOU.

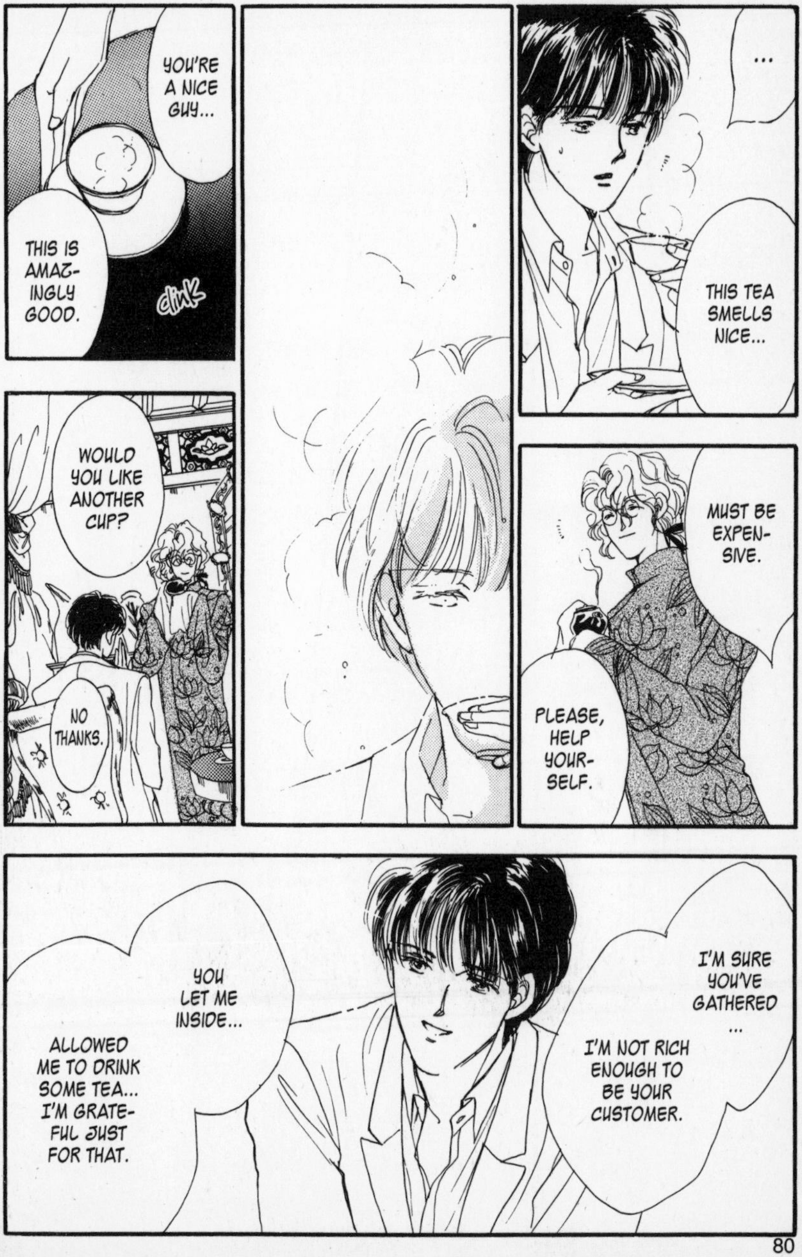
...
THIS TEA SMELLS NICE...
MUST BE EXPENSIVE.
PLEASE, HELP YOURSELF.
YOU'RE A NICE GUY...
THIS IS AMAZINGLY GOOD.
clink
WOULD YOU LIKE ANOTHER CUP?
NO THANKS.
I'M SURE YOU'VE GATHERED ...
I'M NOT RICH ENOUGH TO BE YOUR CUSTOMER.
YOU LET ME INSIDE...
ALLOWED ME TO DRINK SOME TEA... I'M GRATEFUL JUST FOR THAT.

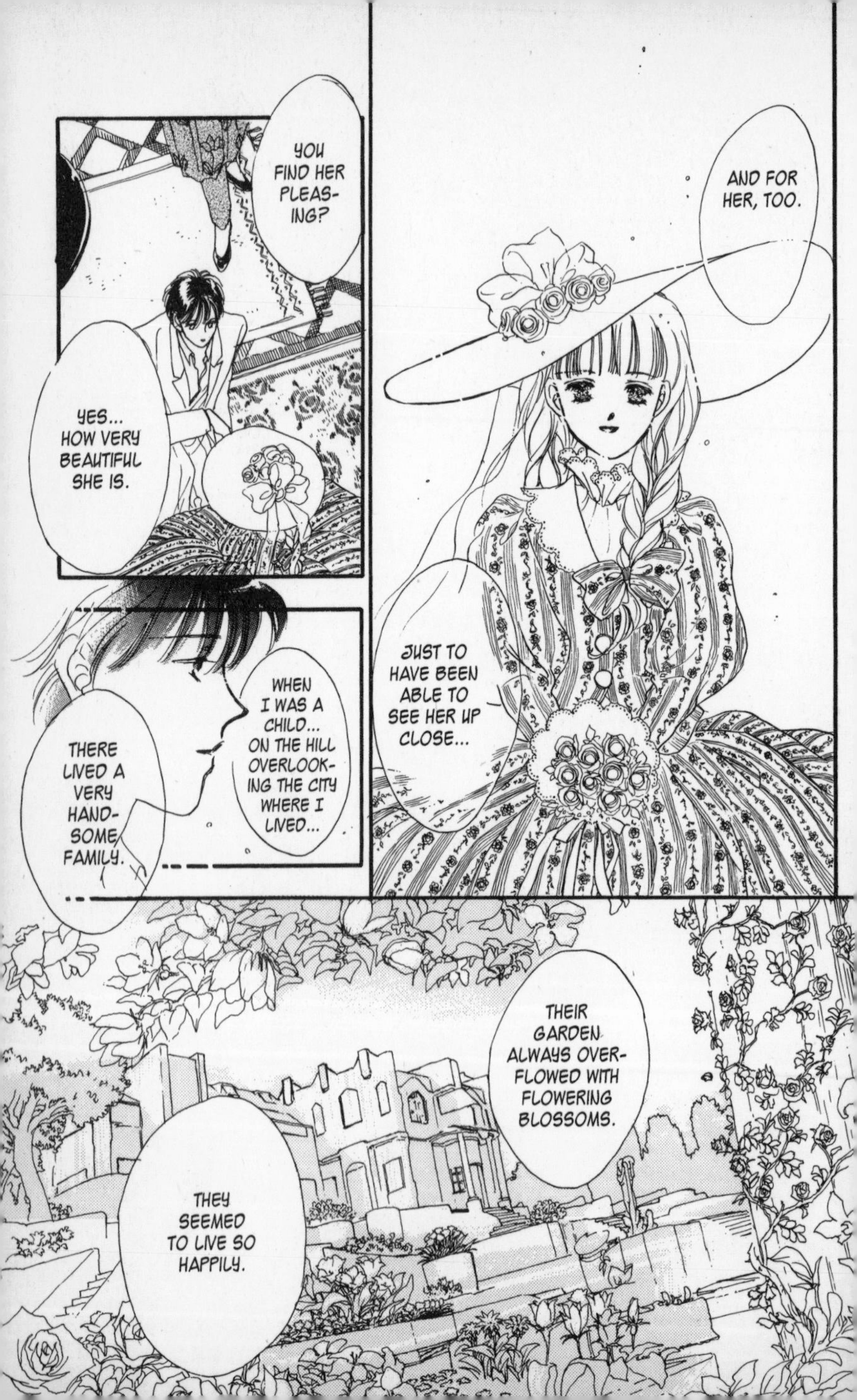
AND FOR HER, TOO.
JUST TO HAVE BEEN ABLE TO SEE HER UP CLOSE...
YOU FIND HER PLEAS-ING?
YES... HOW VERY BEAUTIFUL SHE IS.
WHEN I WAS A CHILD... ON THE HILL OVERLOOK-ING THE CITY WHERE I LIVED...
THERE LIVED A VERY HAND-SOME FAMILY.
THEIR GARDEN ALWAYS OVER-FLOWED WITH FLOWERING BLOSSOMS.
THEY SEEMED TO LIVE SO HAPPILY.

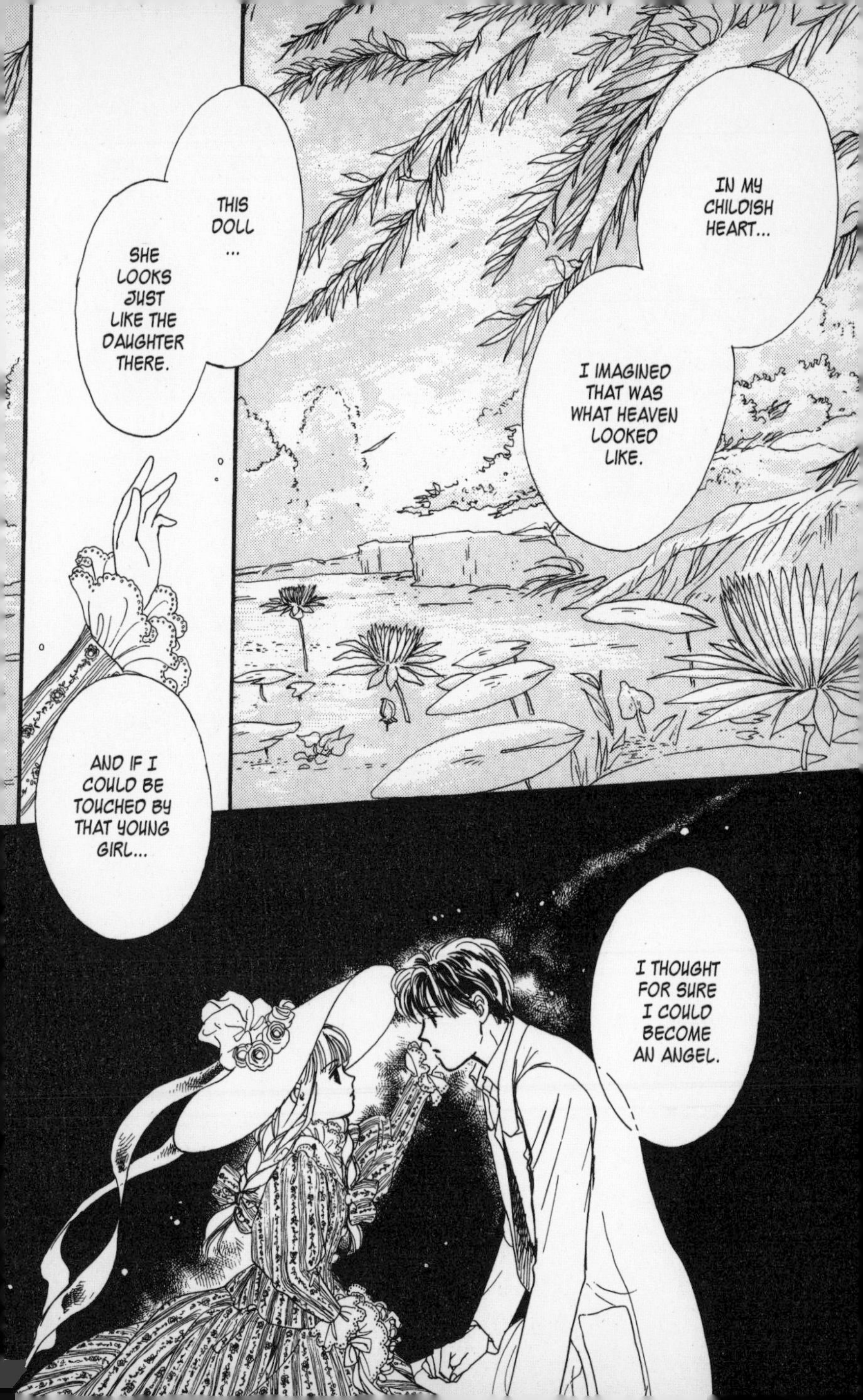
IN MY CHILDISH HEART...
I IMAGINED THAT WAS WHAT HEAVEN LOOKED LIKE.
THIS DOLL ...
SHE LOOKS JUST LIKE THE DAUGHTER THERE.
AND IF I COULD BE TOUCHED BY THAT YOUNG GIRL...
I THOUGHT FOR SURE I COULD BECOME AN ANGEL.

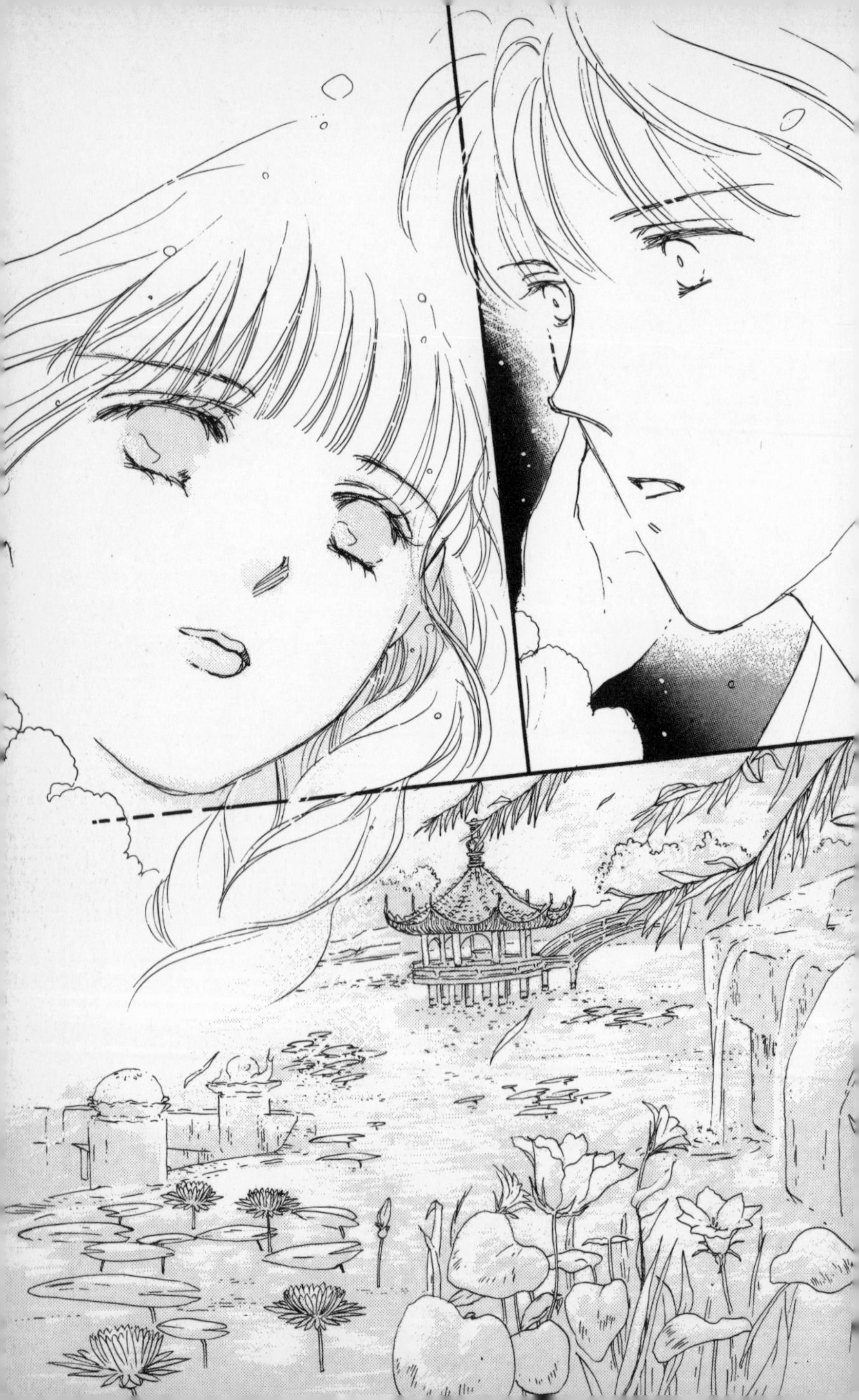

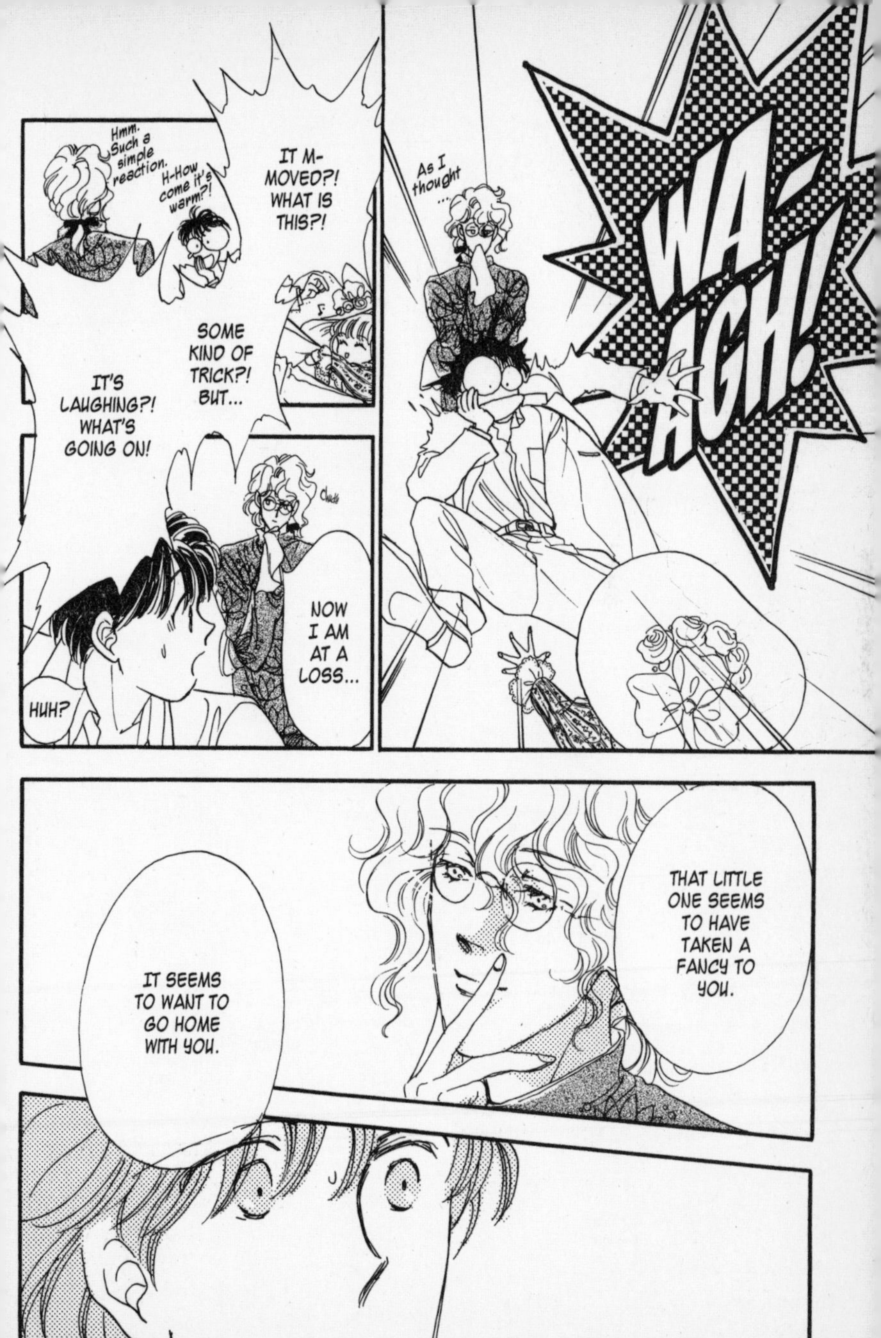
WA-AGH!
As I thought ...
IT M-MOVED?! WHAT IS THIS?!
H-How come it's warm?!
Hmm. Such a simple reaction.
SOME KIND OF TRICK?! BUT...
IT'S LAUGHING?! WHAT'S GOING ON!
NOW I AM AT A LOSS...
Chuckle
HUH?
THAT LITTLE ONE SEEMS TO HAVE TAKEN A FANCY TO YOU.
IT SEEMS TO WANT TO GO HOME WITH YOU.

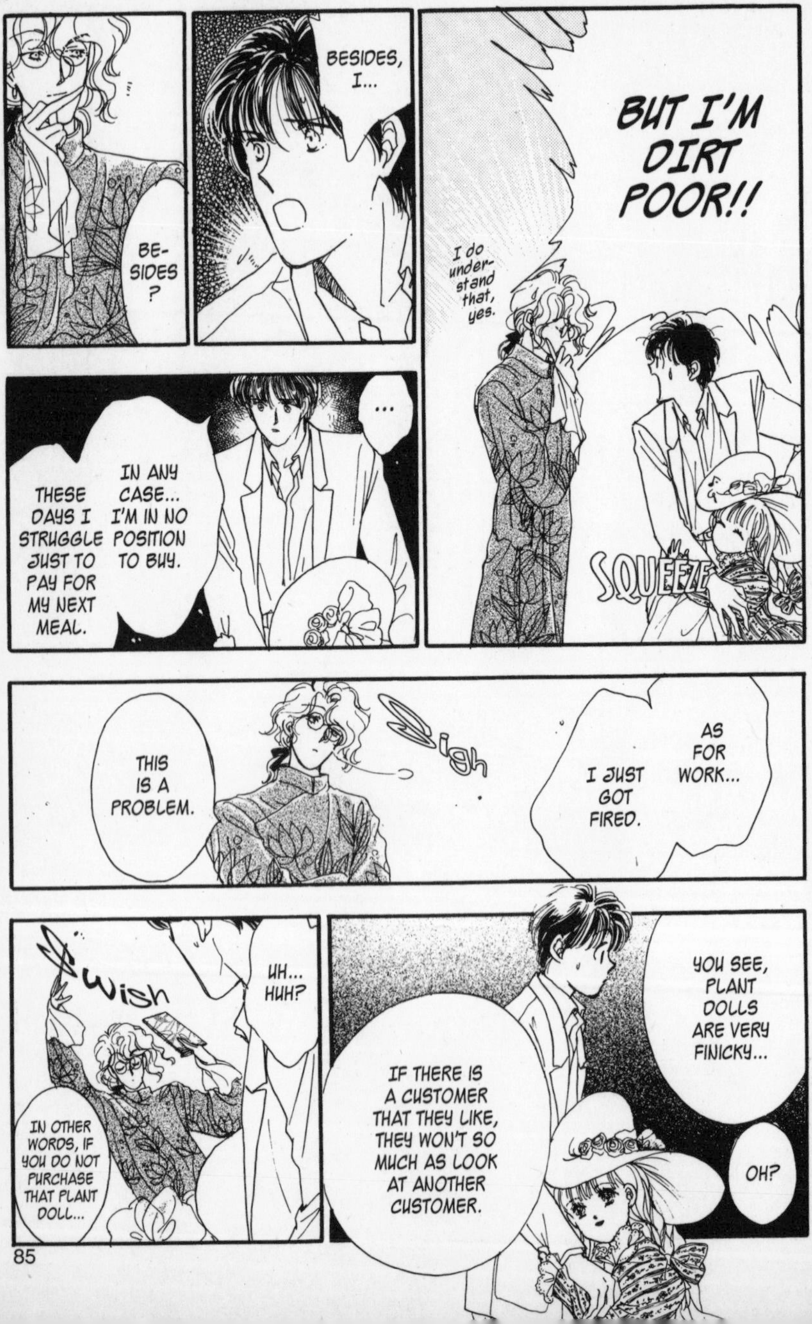
BUT I'M DIRT POOR!!
I do under-stand that, yes.
SQUEEZE
BESIDES, I...
BE-SIDES ?
...
IN ANY CASE... I'M IN NO POSITION TO BUY.
THESE DAYS I STRUGGLE JUST TO PAY FOR MY NEXT MEAL.
AS FOR WORK...
I JUST GOT FIRED.
Sigh
THIS IS A PROBLEM.
YOU SEE, PLANT DOLLS ARE VERY FINICKY...
OH?
IF THERE IS A CUSTOMER THAT THEY LIKE, THEY WON'T SO MUCH AS LOOK AT ANOTHER CUSTOMER.
UH... HUH?
Swish
IN OTHER WORDS, IF YOU DO NOT PURCHASE THAT PLANT DOLL...

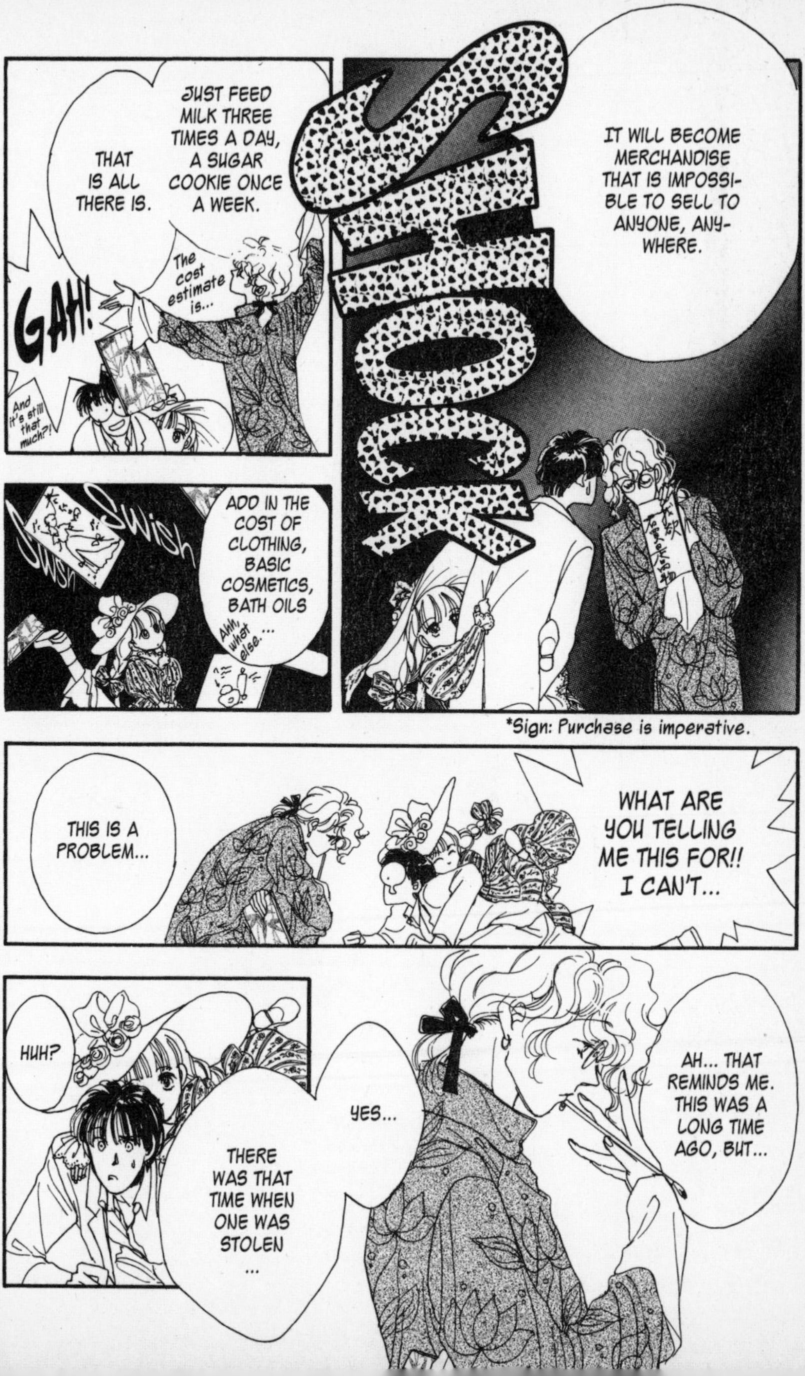
SHOCK
IT WILL BECOME MERCHANDISE THAT IS IMPOSSIBLE TO SELL TO ANYONE, ANYWHERE.
JUST FEED MILK THREE TIMES A DAY, A SUGAR COOKIE ONCE A WEEK.
THAT IS ALL THERE IS.
The cost estimate is...
GAH!
And it's still that much?!
Swish
Swish
ADD IN THE COST OF CLOTHING, BASIC COSMETICS, BATH OILS
Ahh, what else...
WHAT ARE YOU TELLING ME THIS FOR!! I CAN'T...
THIS IS A PROBLEM...
AH... THAT REMINDS ME. THIS WAS A LONG TIME AGO, BUT...
YES...
THERE WAS THAT TIME WHEN ONE WAS STOLEN ...
HUH?

*Sign: Purchase is imperative.

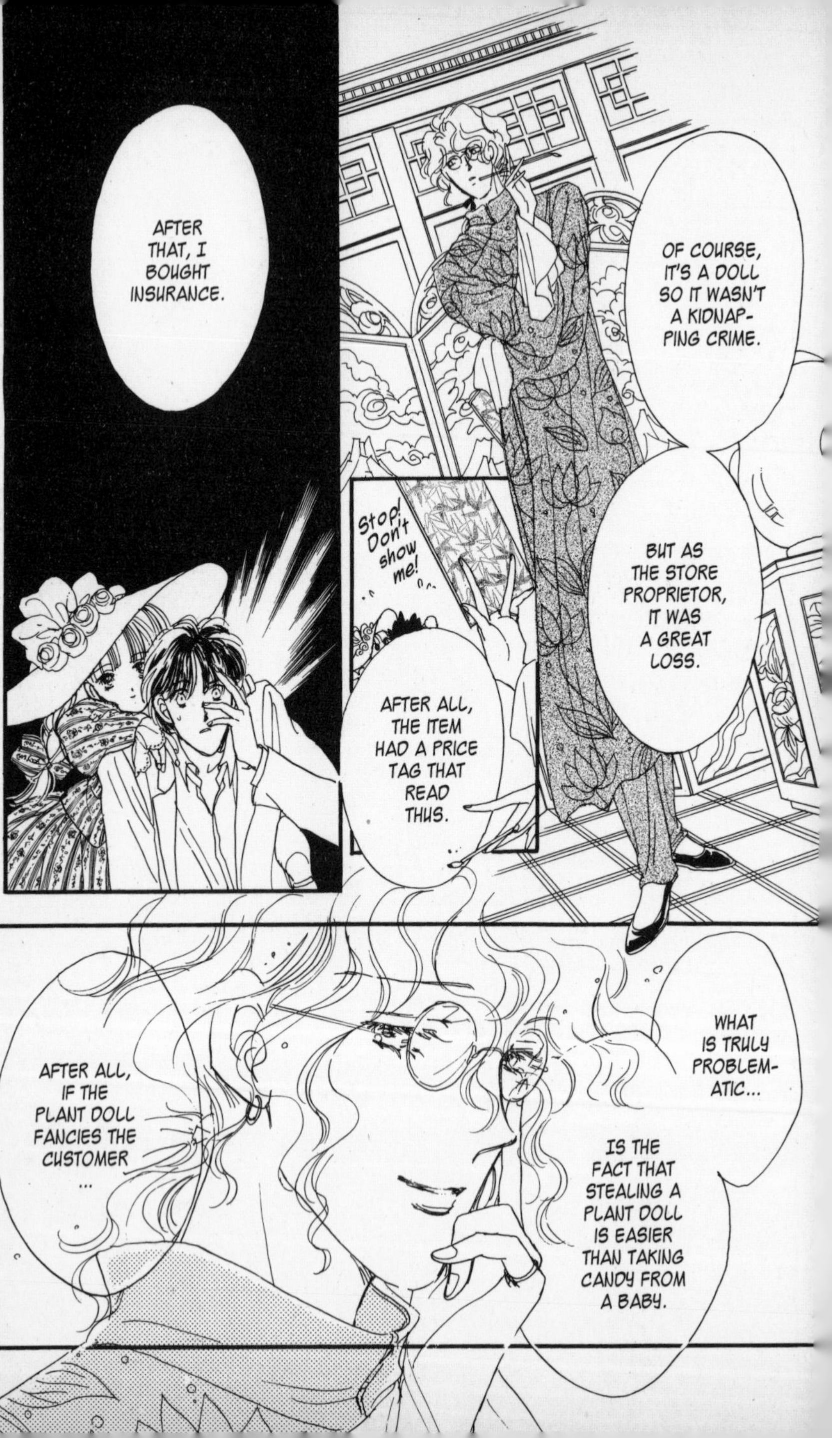
OF COURSE, IT'S A DOLL SO IT WASN'T A KIDNAP-PING CRIME.
BUT AS THE STORE PROPRIETOR, IT WAS A GREAT LOSS.
AFTER ALL, THE ITEM HAD A PRICE TAG THAT READ THUS.
Stop! Don't show me!
AFTER THAT, I BOUGHT INSURANCE.
WHAT IS TRULY PROBLEM-ATIC...
IS THE FACT THAT STEALING A PLANT DOLL IS EASIER THAN TAKING CANDY FROM A BABY.
AFTER ALL, IF THE PLANT DOLL FANCIES THE CUSTOMER ...

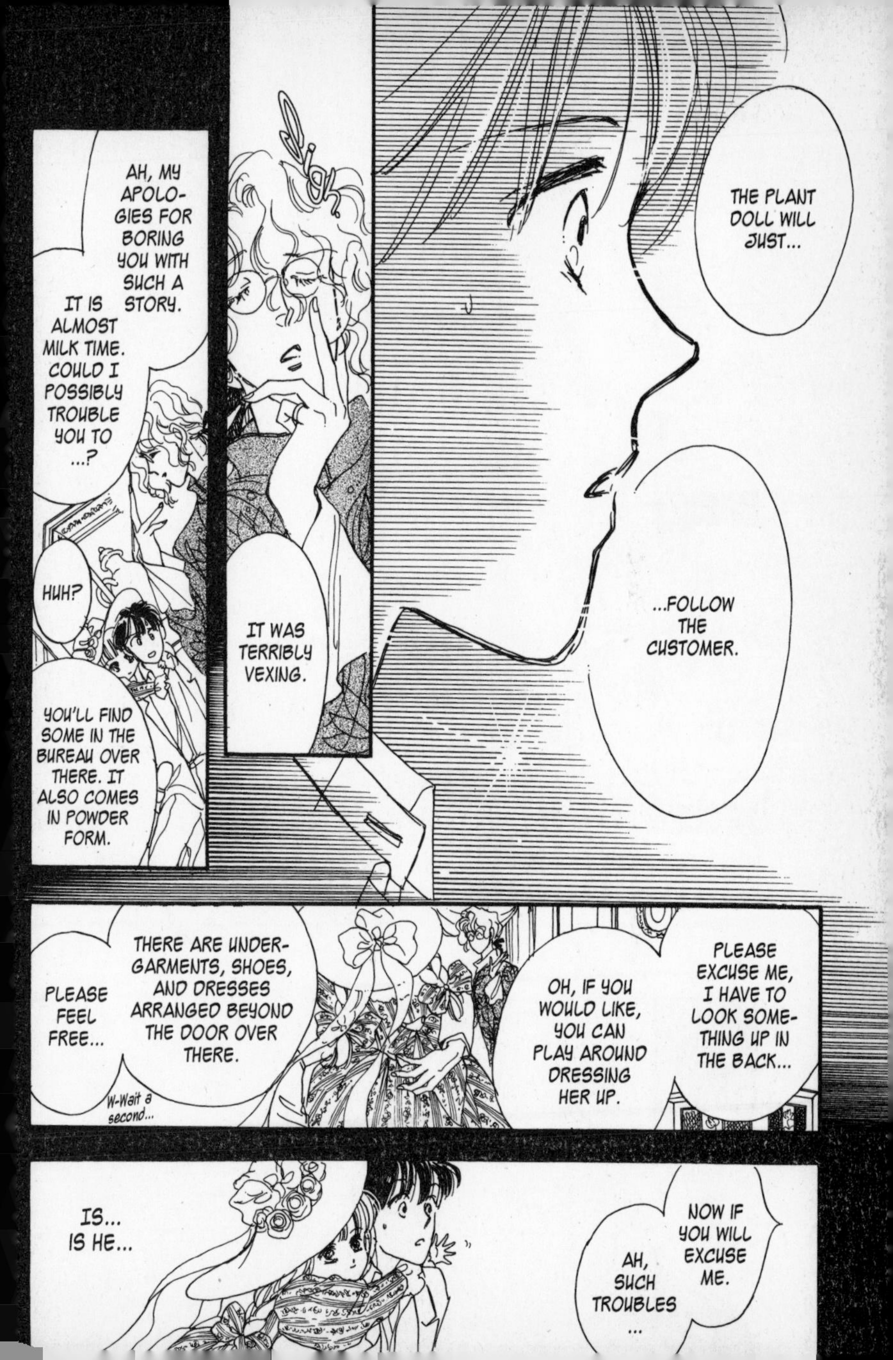
THE PLANT DOLL WILL JUST...
...FOLLOW THE CUSTOMER.
Sigh
IT WAS TERRIBLY VEXING.
AH, MY APOLOGIES FOR BORING YOU WITH SUCH A STORY.
IT IS ALMOST MILK TIME. COULD I POSSIBLY TROUBLE YOU TO ...?
HUH?
YOU'LL FIND SOME IN THE BUREAU OVER THERE. IT ALSO COMES IN POWDER FORM.
PLEASE EXCUSE ME, I HAVE TO LOOK SOMETHING UP IN THE BACK...
OH, IF YOU WOULD LIKE, YOU CAN PLAY AROUND DRESSING HER UP.
THERE ARE UNDERGARMENTS, SHOES, AND DRESSES ARRANGED BEYOND THE DOOR OVER THERE.
PLEASE FEEL FREE...
W-Wait a second...
NOW IF YOU WILL EXCUSE ME.
AH, SUCH TROUBLES ...
IS... IS HE...

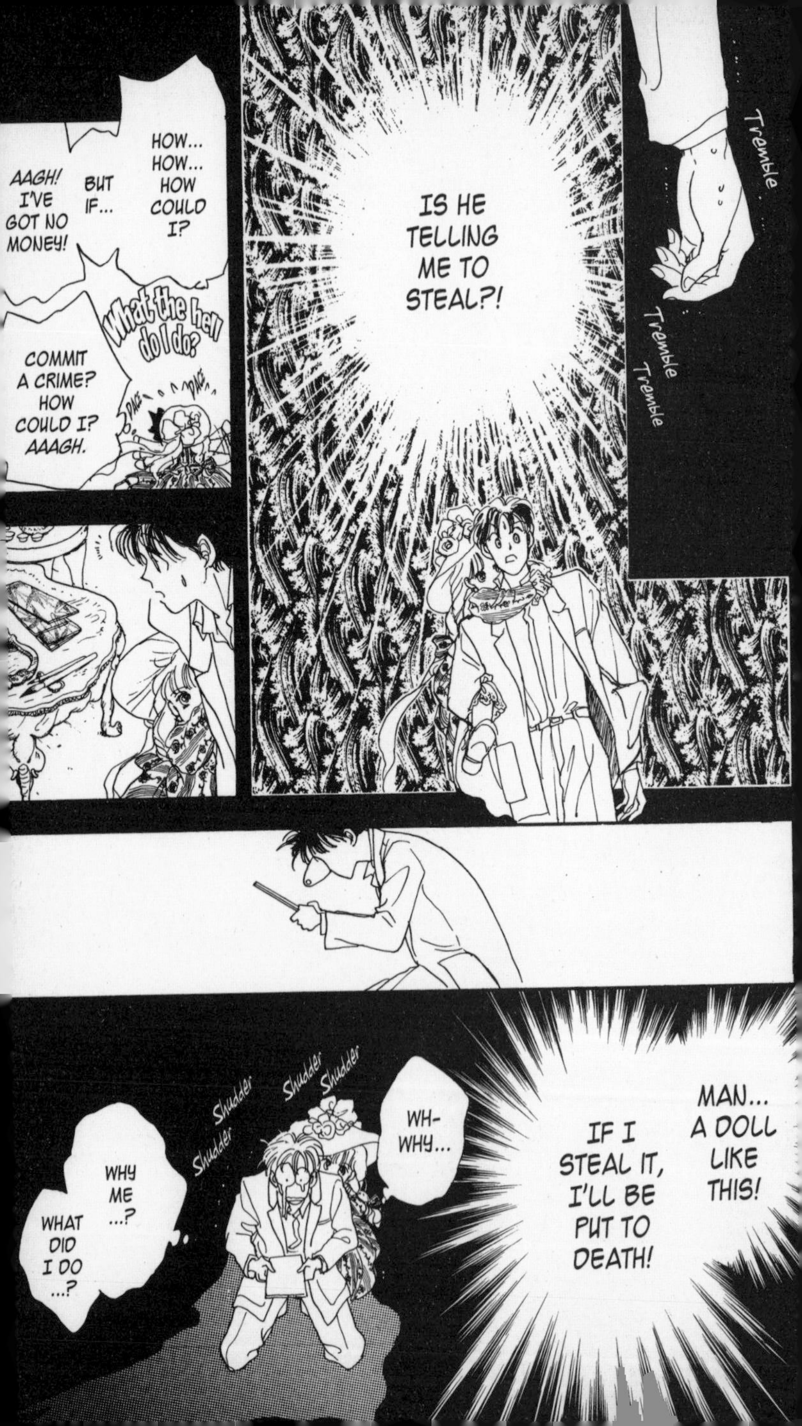
Tremble
Tremble
Tremble
IS HE TELLING ME TO STEAL?!
HOW... HOW... HOW COULD I?
BUT IF...
AAGH! I'VE GOT NO MONEY!
What the hell do I do?
PACE PACE
COMMIT A CRIME? HOW COULD I? AAAGH.
MAN... A DOLL LIKE THIS!
IF I STEAL IT, I'LL BE PUT TO DEATH!
Shudder Shudder
WH- WHY...
Shudder Shudder
WHY ME ...?
WHAT DID I DO ...?

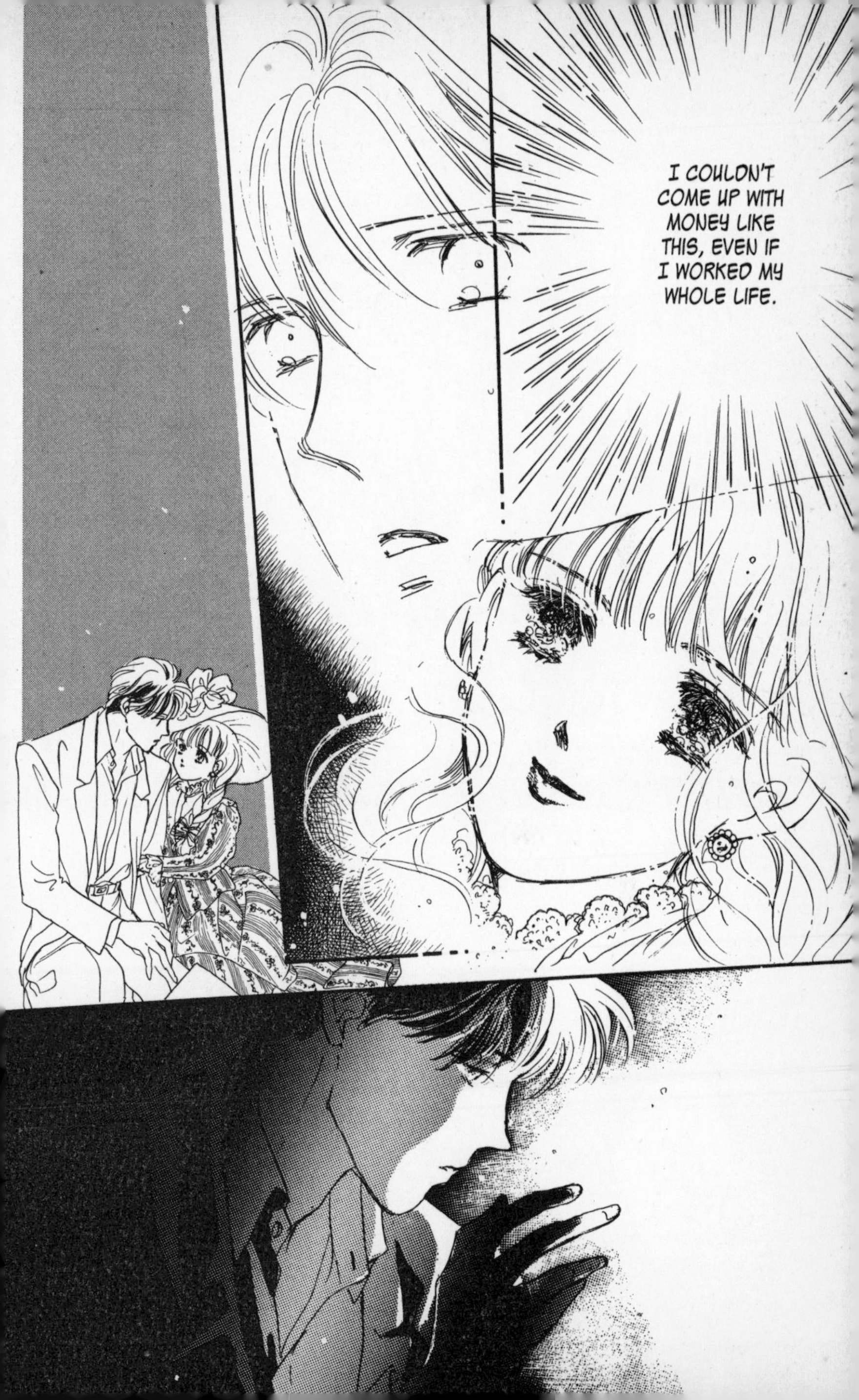
I COULDN'T COME UP WITH MONEY LIKE THIS, EVEN IF I WORKED MY WHOLE LIFE.

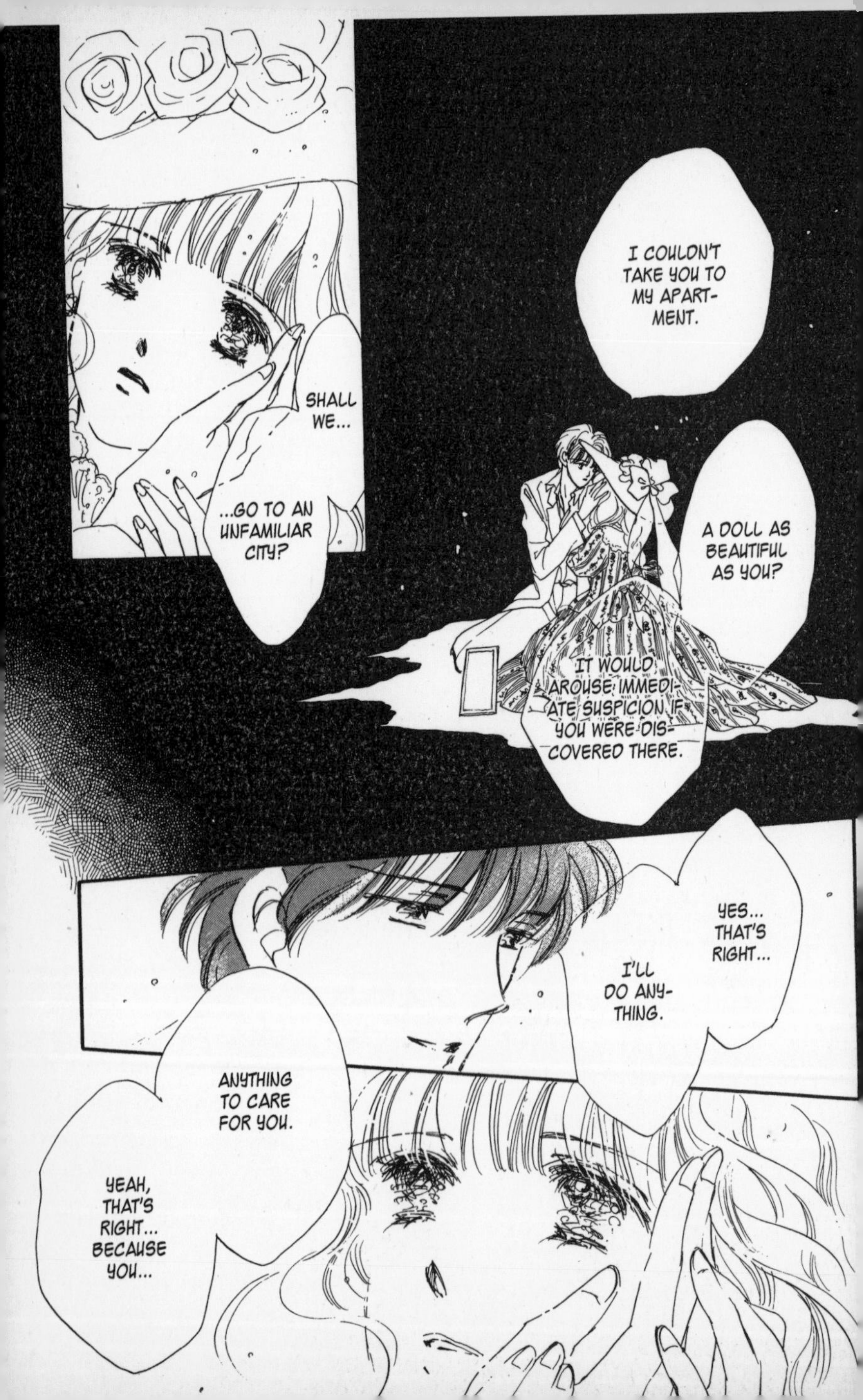
I COULDN'T TAKE YOU TO MY APART-MENT.
A DOLL AS BEAUTIFUL AS YOU?
IT WOULD AROUSE IMMEDI-ATE SUSPICION IF YOU WERE DIS-COVERED THERE.
SHALL WE...
...GO TO AN UNFAMILIAR CITY?
YES... THAT'S RIGHT...
I'LL DO ANY-THING.
ANYTHING TO CARE FOR YOU.
YEAH, THAT'S RIGHT... BECAUSE YOU...

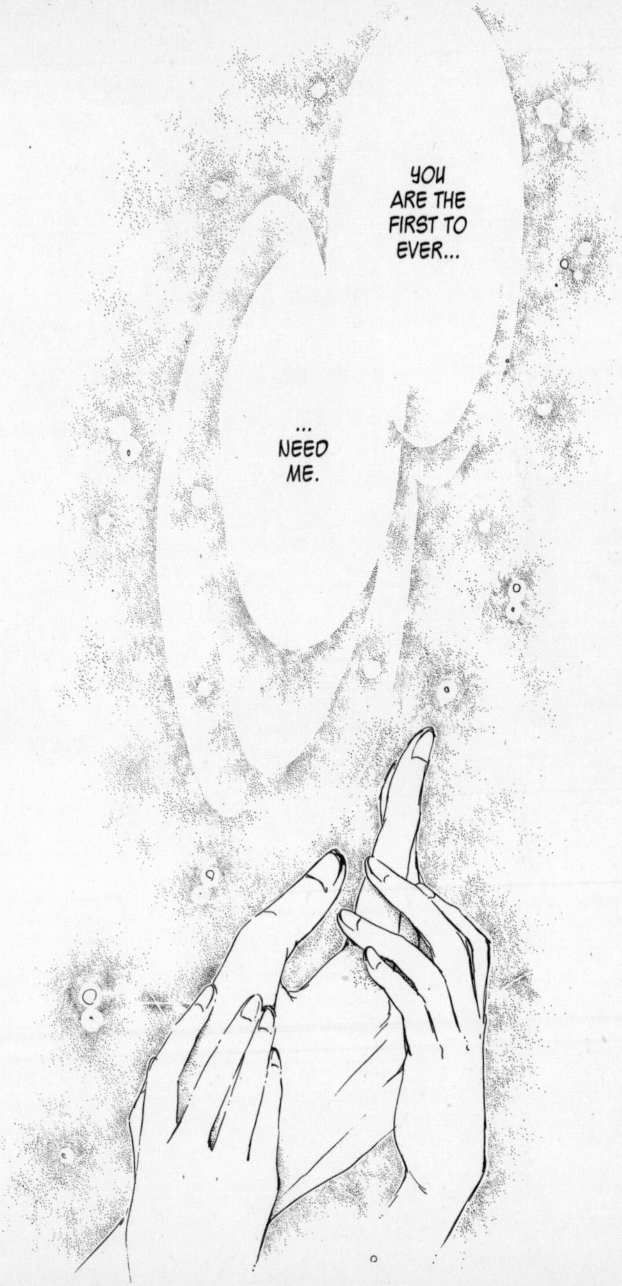
YOU ARE THE FIRST TO EVER...
... NEED ME.

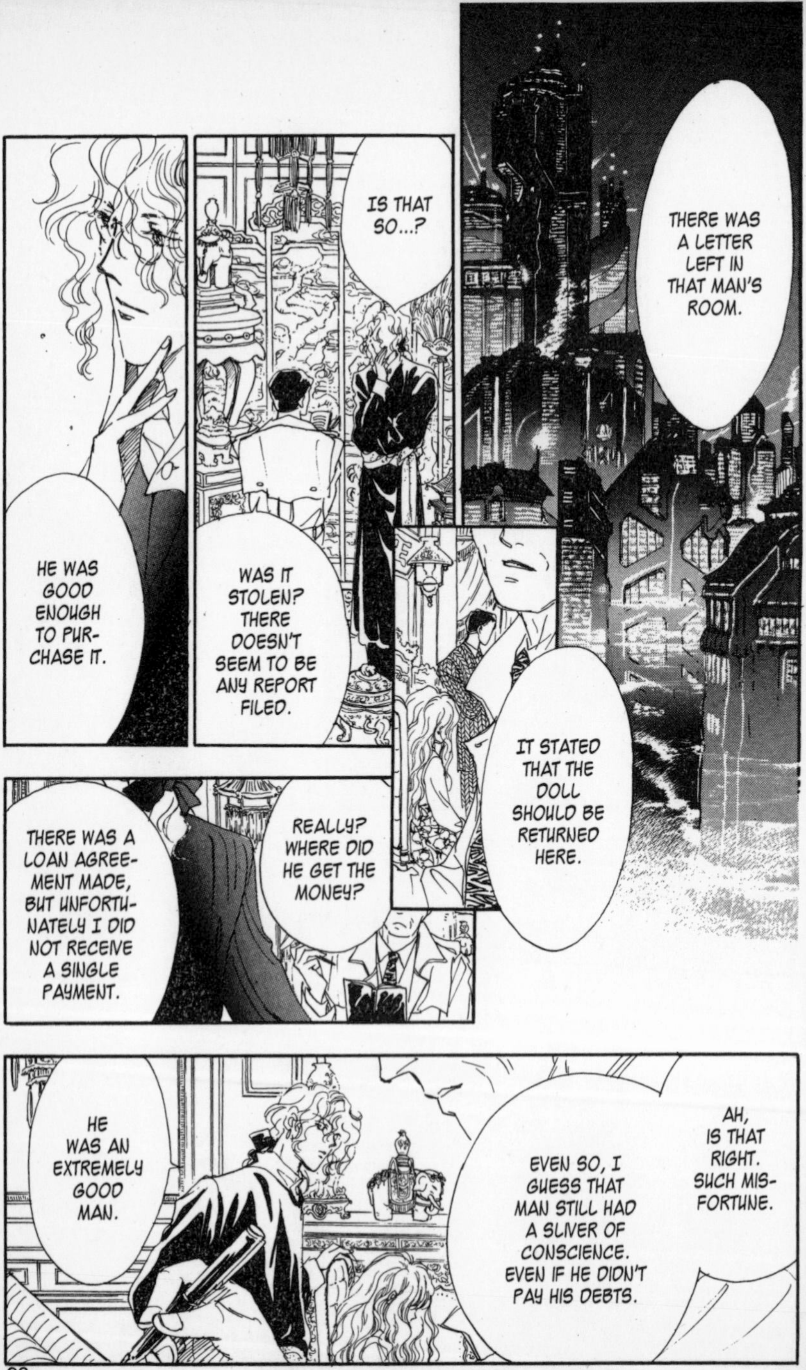
THERE WAS A LETTER LEFT IN THAT MAN'S ROOM.
IT STATED THAT THE DOLL SHOULD BE RETURNED HERE.
IS THAT SO...?
WAS IT STOLEN? THERE DOESN'T SEEM TO BE ANY REPORT FILED.
HE WAS GOOD ENOUGH TO PURCHASE IT.
REALLY? WHERE DID HE GET THE MONEY?
THERE WAS A LOAN AGREEMENT MADE, BUT UNFORTUNATELY I DID NOT RECEIVE A SINGLE PAYMENT.
AH, IS THAT RIGHT. SUCH MISFORTUNE.
EVEN SO, I GUESS THAT MAN STILL HAD A SLIVER OF CONSCIENCE. EVEN IF HE DIDN'T PAY HIS DEBTS.
HE WAS AN EXTREMELY GOOD MAN.

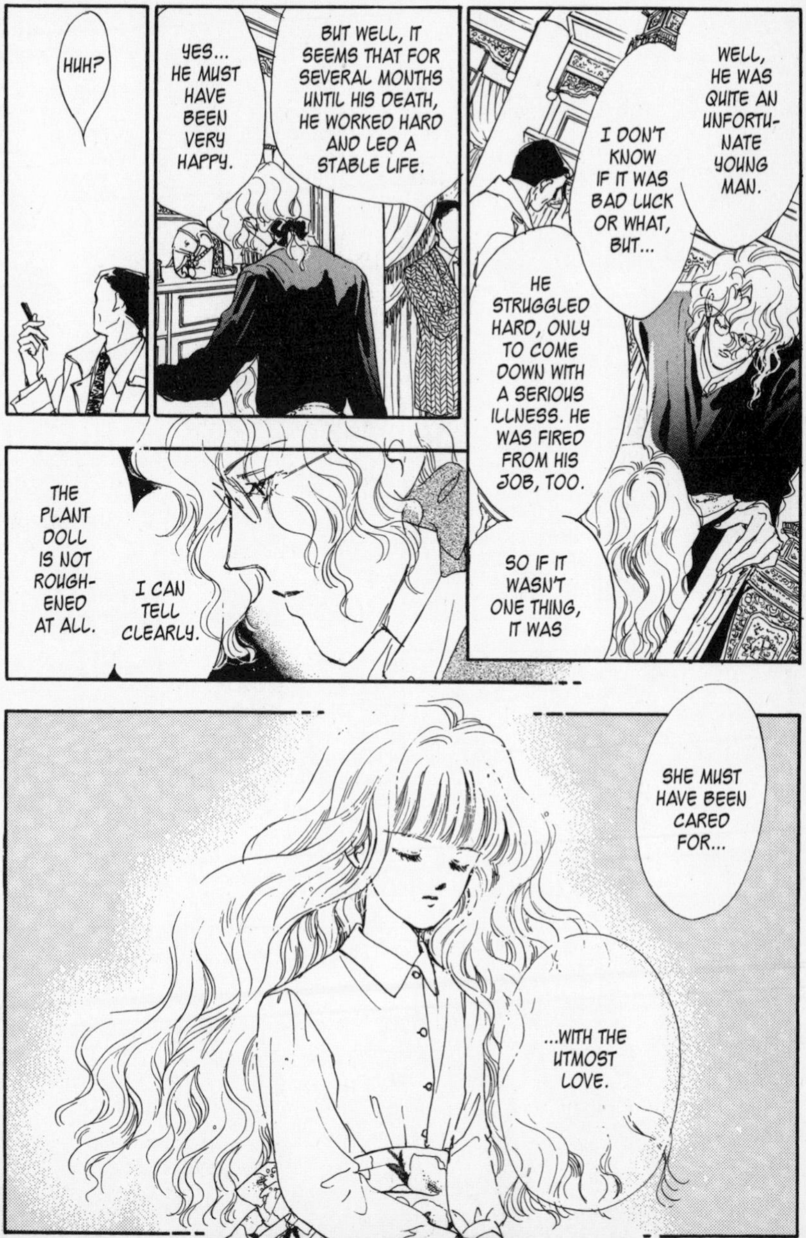
WELL, HE WAS QUITE AN UNFORTUNATE YOUNG MAN.
I DON'T KNOW IF IT WAS BAD LUCK OR WHAT, BUT...
HE STRUGGLED HARD, ONLY TO COME DOWN WITH A SERIOUS ILLNESS. HE WAS FIRED FROM HIS JOB, TOO.
SO IF IT WASN'T ONE THING, IT WAS
BUT WELL, IT SEEMS THAT FOR SEVERAL MONTHS UNTIL HIS DEATH, HE WORKED HARD AND LED A STABLE LIFE.
YES... HE MUST HAVE BEEN VERY HAPPY.
HUH?
I CAN TELL CLEARLY.
THE PLANT DOLL IS NOT ROUGHENED AT ALL.
SHE MUST HAVE BEEN CARED FOR...
...WITH THE UTMOST LOVE.

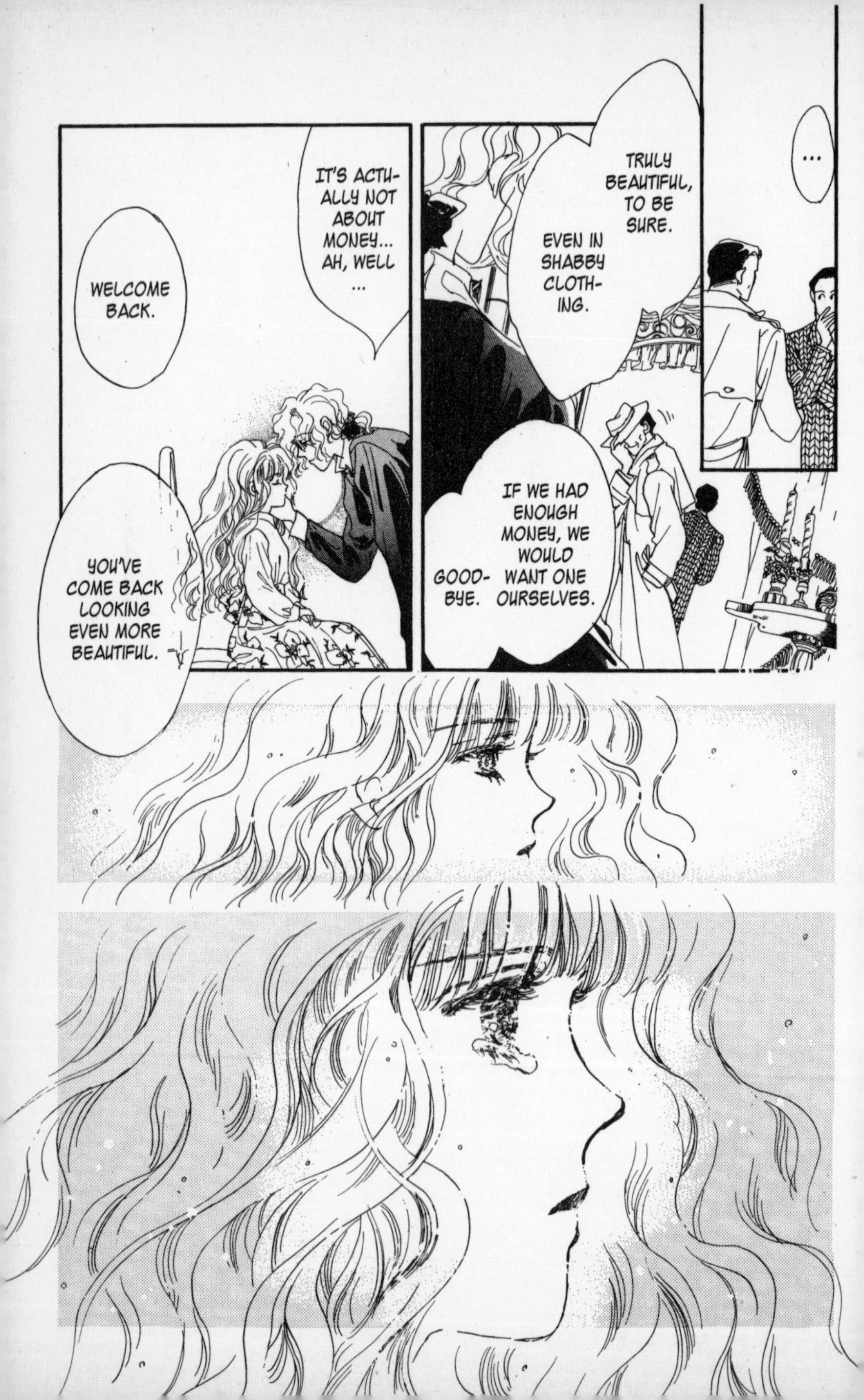
...
TRULY BEAUTIFUL, TO BE SURE.
EVEN IN SHABBY CLOTHING.
IF WE HAD ENOUGH MONEY, WE WOULD WANT ONE OURSELVES.
GOOD-BYE.
IT'S ACTU-ALLY NOT ABOUT MONEY... AH, WELL ...
WELCOME BACK.
YOU'VE COME BACK LOOKING EVEN MORE BEAUTIFUL.

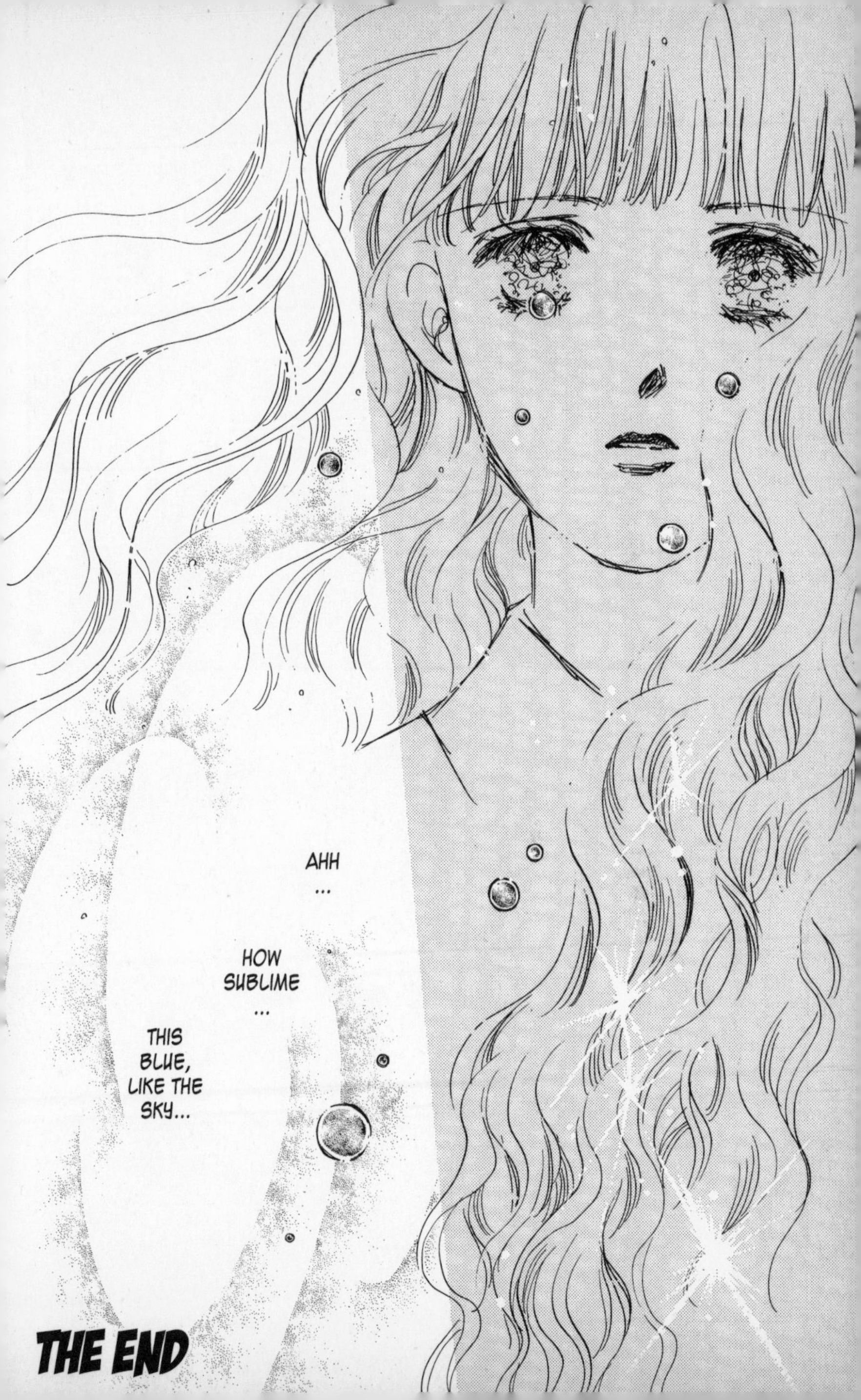
AHH ...
HOW SUBLIME ...
THIS BLUE, LIKE THE SKY...
THE END

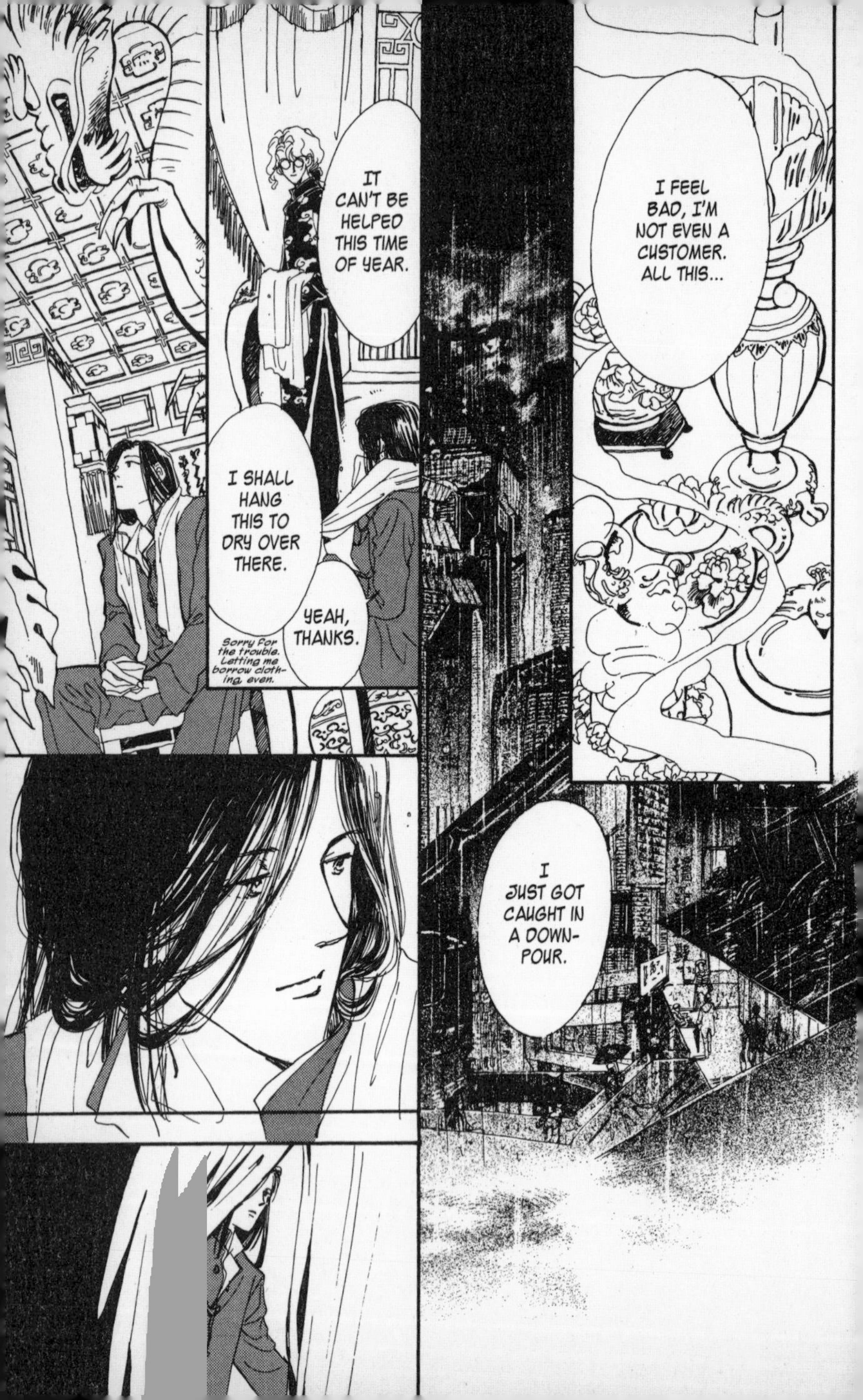
I FEEL BAD, I'M NOT EVEN A CUSTOMER. ALL THIS...
I JUST GOT CAUGHT IN A DOWN-POUR.
IT CAN'T BE HELPED THIS TIME OF YEAR.
I SHALL HANG THIS TO DRY OVER THERE.
YEAH, THANKS.
Sorry for the trouble. Letting me borrow clothing, even.

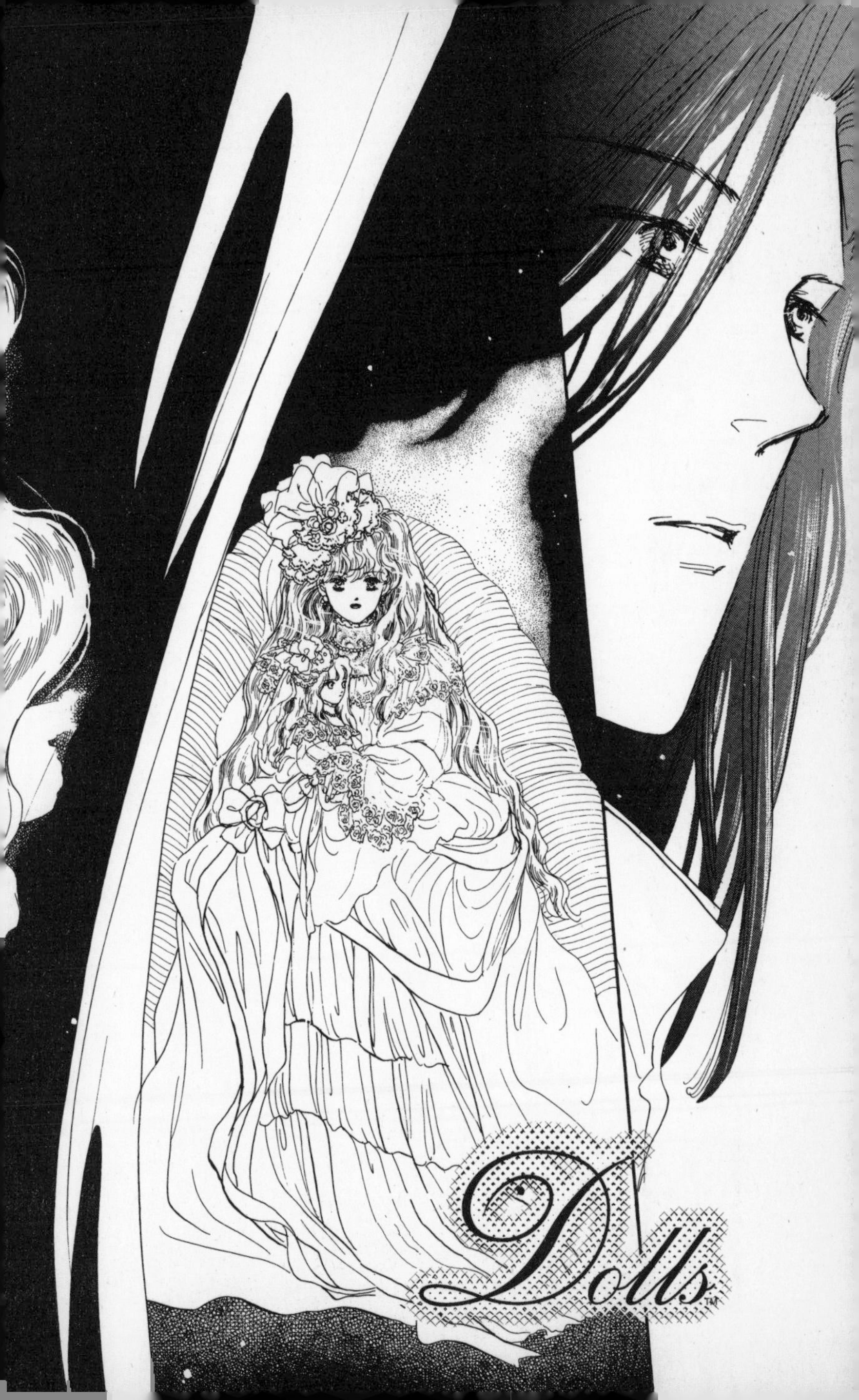
Dolls™

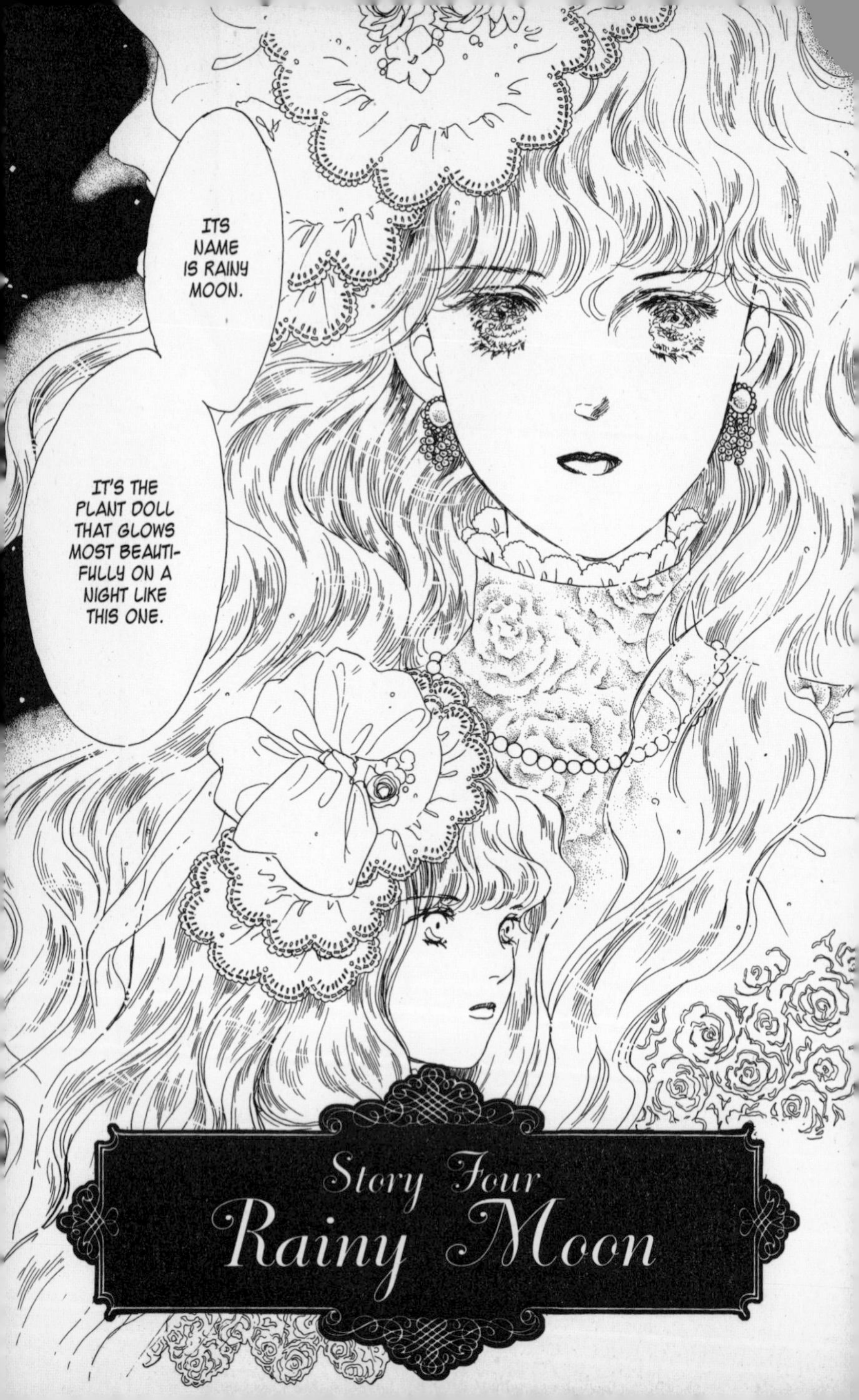
ITS NAME IS RAINY MOON.
IT'S THE PLANT DOLL THAT GLOWS MOST BEAUTIFULLY ON A NIGHT LIKE THIS ONE.
Story Four
Rainy Moon

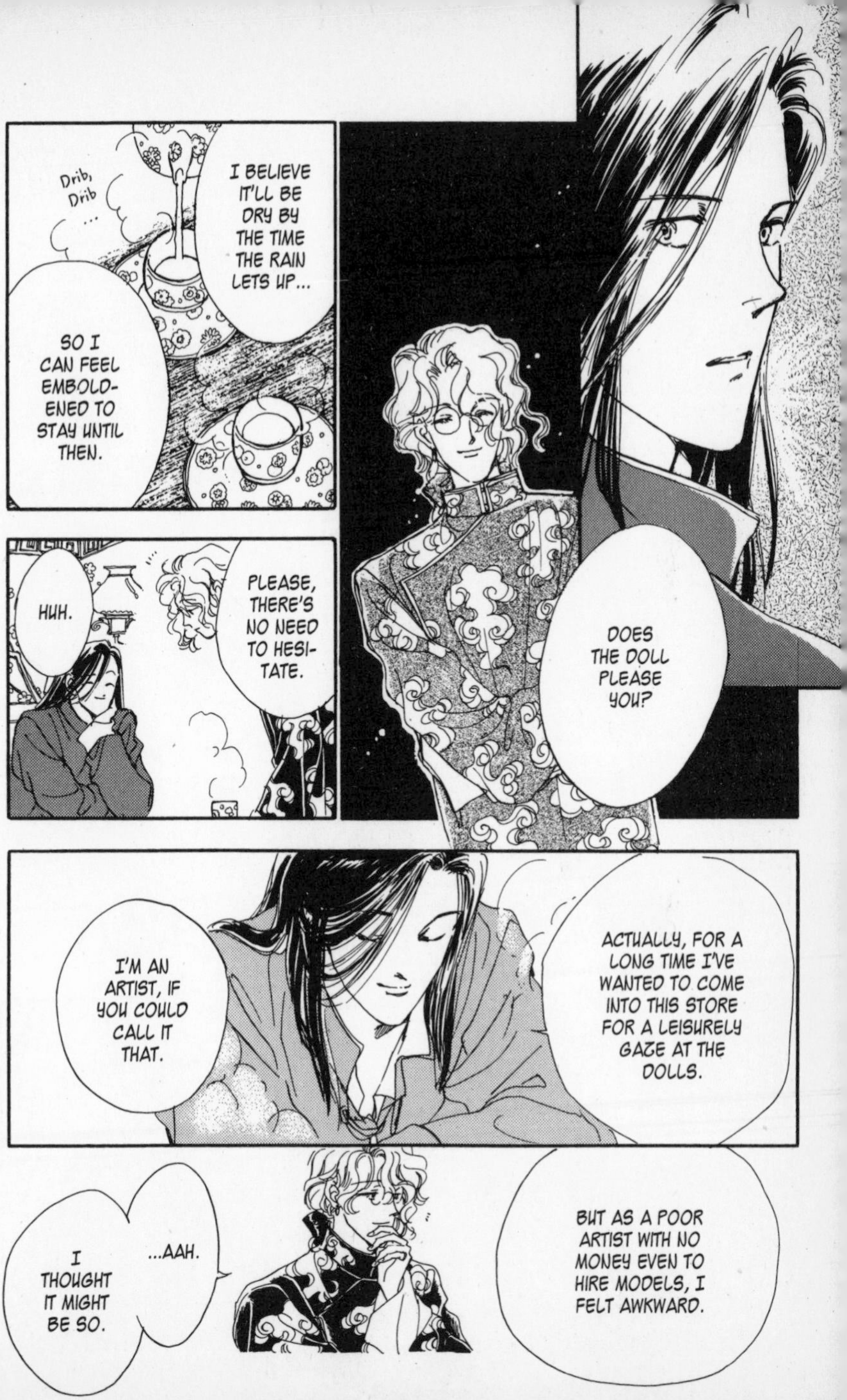
DOES THE DOLL PLEASE YOU?
I BELIEVE IT'LL BE DRY BY THE TIME THE RAIN LETS UP...
Drib, Drib ...
SO I CAN FEEL EMBOLD-ENED TO STAY UNTIL THEN.
PLEASE, THERE'S NO NEED TO HESI-TATE.
HUH.
ACTUALLY, FOR A LONG TIME I'VE WANTED TO COME INTO THIS STORE FOR A LEISURELY GAZE AT THE DOLLS.
I'M AN ARTIST, IF YOU COULD CALL IT THAT.
BUT AS A POOR ARTIST WITH NO MONEY EVEN TO HIRE MODELS, I FELT AWKWARD.
...AAH.
I THOUGHT IT MIGHT BE SO.

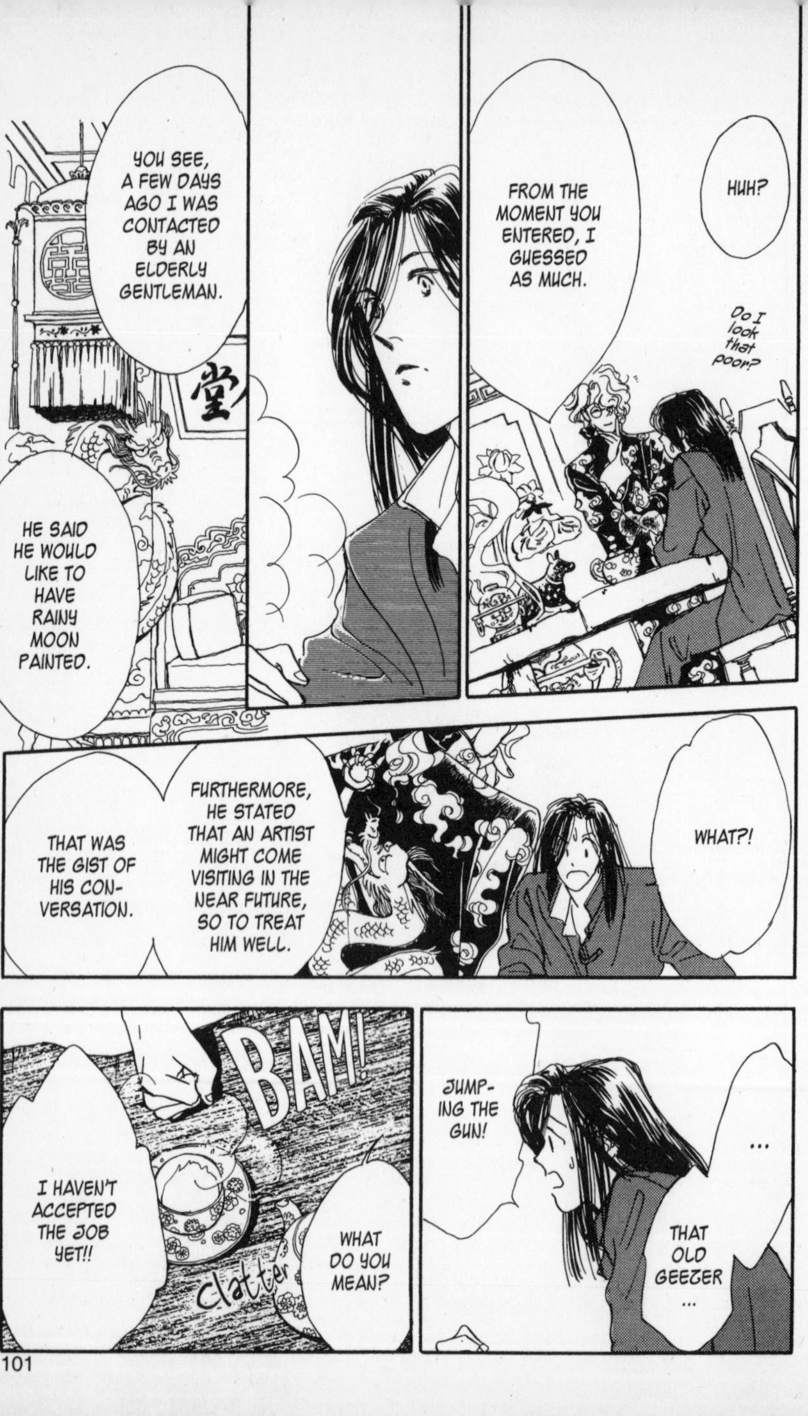
FROM THE MOMENT YOU ENTERED, I GUESSED AS MUCH.
HUH?
Do I look that poor?
YOU SEE, A FEW DAYS AGO I WAS CONTACTED BY AN ELDERLY GENTLEMAN.
HE SAID HE WOULD LIKE TO HAVE RAINY MOON PAINTED.
WHAT?!
FURTHERMORE, HE STATED THAT AN ARTIST MIGHT COME VISITING IN THE NEAR FUTURE, SO TO TREAT HIM WELL.
THAT WAS THE GIST OF HIS CON-VERSATION.
...
THAT OLD GEEZER ...
JUMP-ING THE GUN!
BAM!
I HAVEN'T ACCEPTED THE JOB YET!!
Clatter
WHAT DO YOU MEAN?

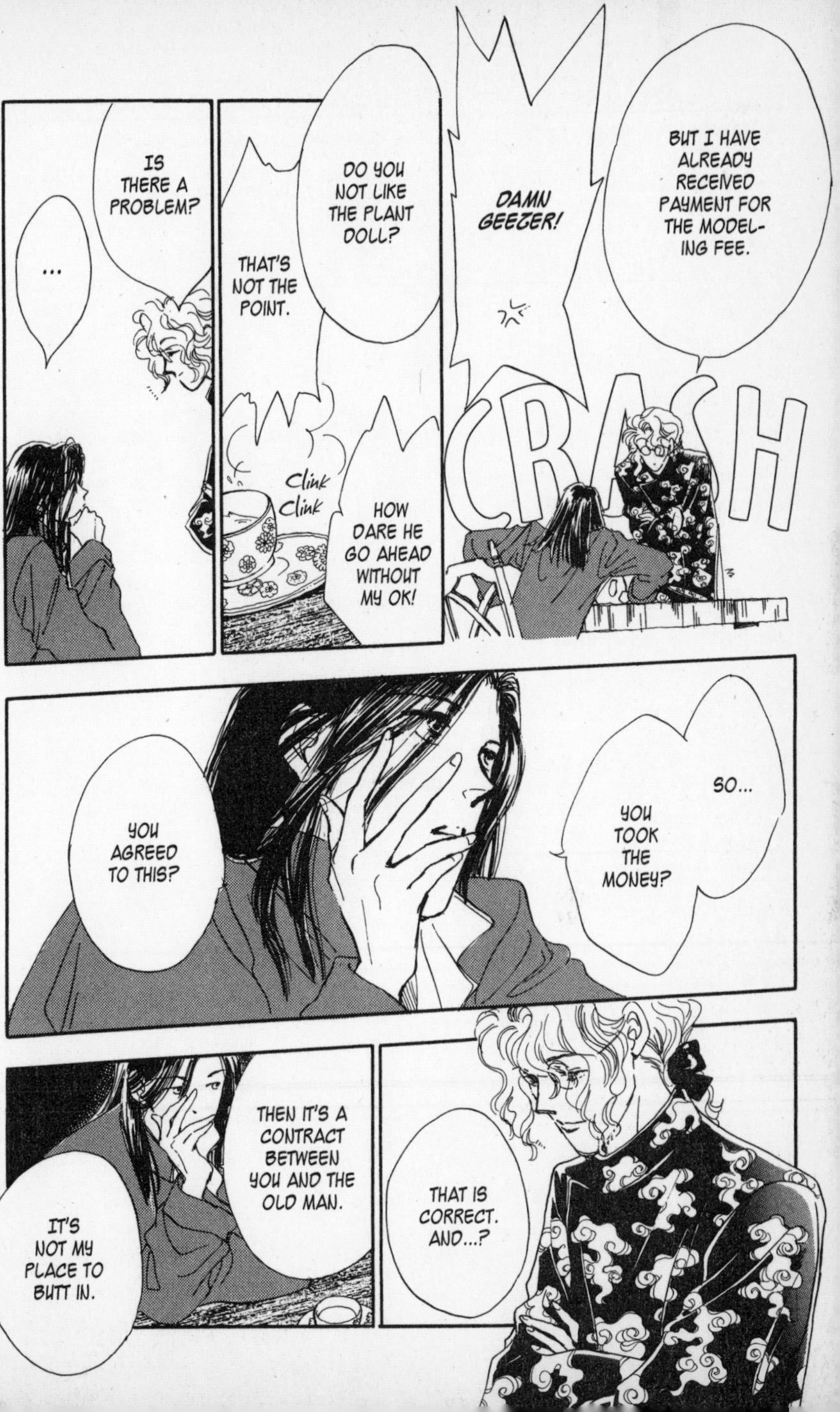

BUT I HAVE ALREADY RECEIVED PAYMENT FOR THE MODEL-ING FEE.
DAMN GEEZER!
CRASH
DO YOU NOT LIKE THE PLANT DOLL?
THAT'S NOT THE POINT.
Clink Clink
HOW DARE HE GO AHEAD WITHOUT MY OK!
IS THERE A PROBLEM?
...
SO...
YOU TOOK THE MONEY?
YOU AGREED TO THIS?
THAT IS CORRECT. AND...?
THEN IT'S A CONTRACT BETWEEN YOU AND THE OLD MAN.
IT'S NOT MY PLACE TO BUTT IN.

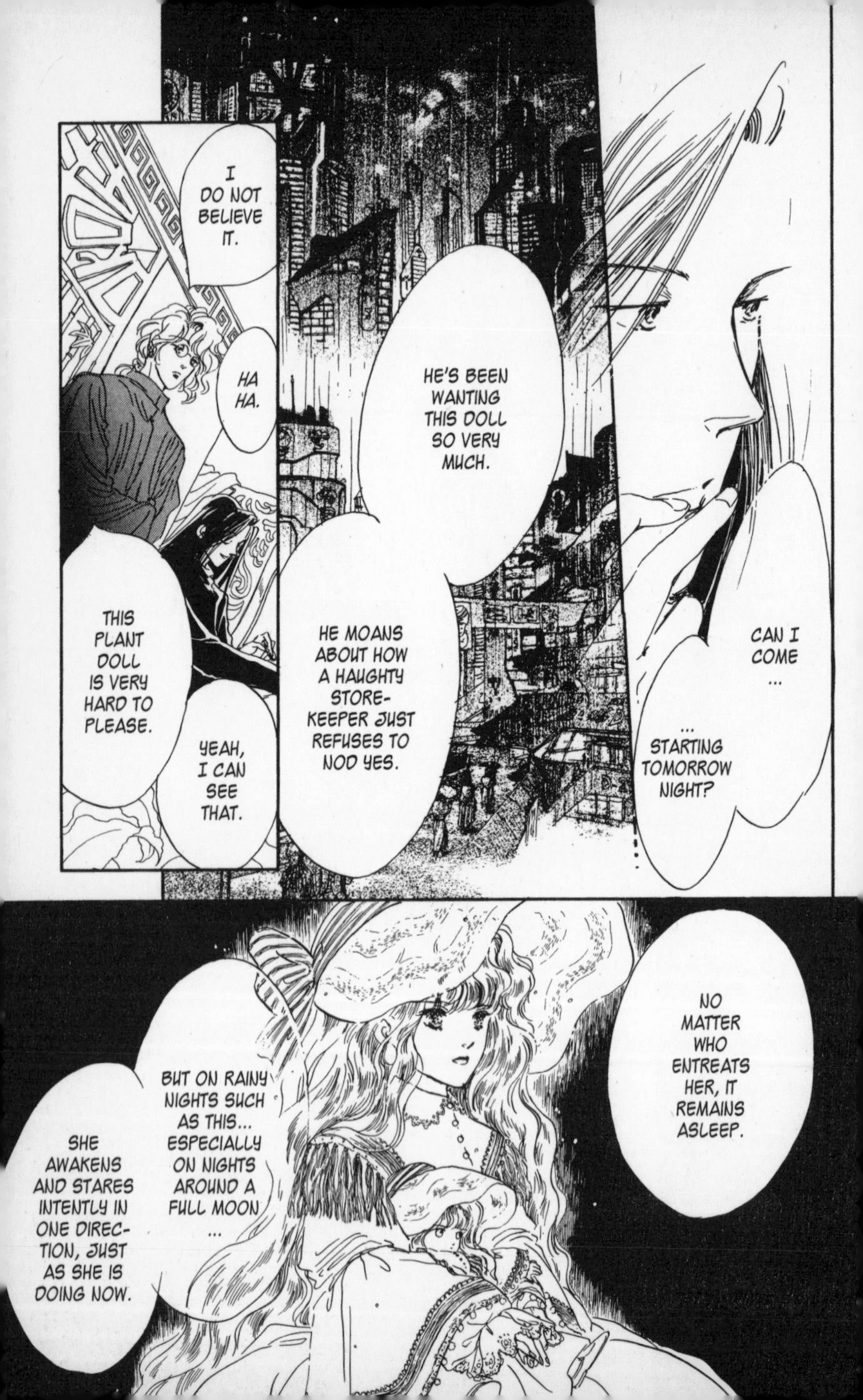
CAN I COME ...
... STARTING TOMORROW NIGHT?
HE'S BEEN WANTING THIS DOLL SO VERY MUCH.
HE MOANS ABOUT HOW A HAUGHTY STORE-KEEPER JUST REFUSES TO NOD YES.
I DO NOT BELIEVE IT.
HA HA.
THIS PLANT DOLL IS VERY HARD TO PLEASE.
YEAH, I CAN SEE THAT.
NO MATTER WHO ENTREATS HER, IT REMAINS ASLEEP.
BUT ON RAINY NIGHTS SUCH AS THIS... ESPECIALLY ON NIGHTS AROUND A FULL MOON ...
SHE AWAKENS AND STARES INTENTLY IN ONE DIRECTION, JUST AS SHE IS DOING NOW.

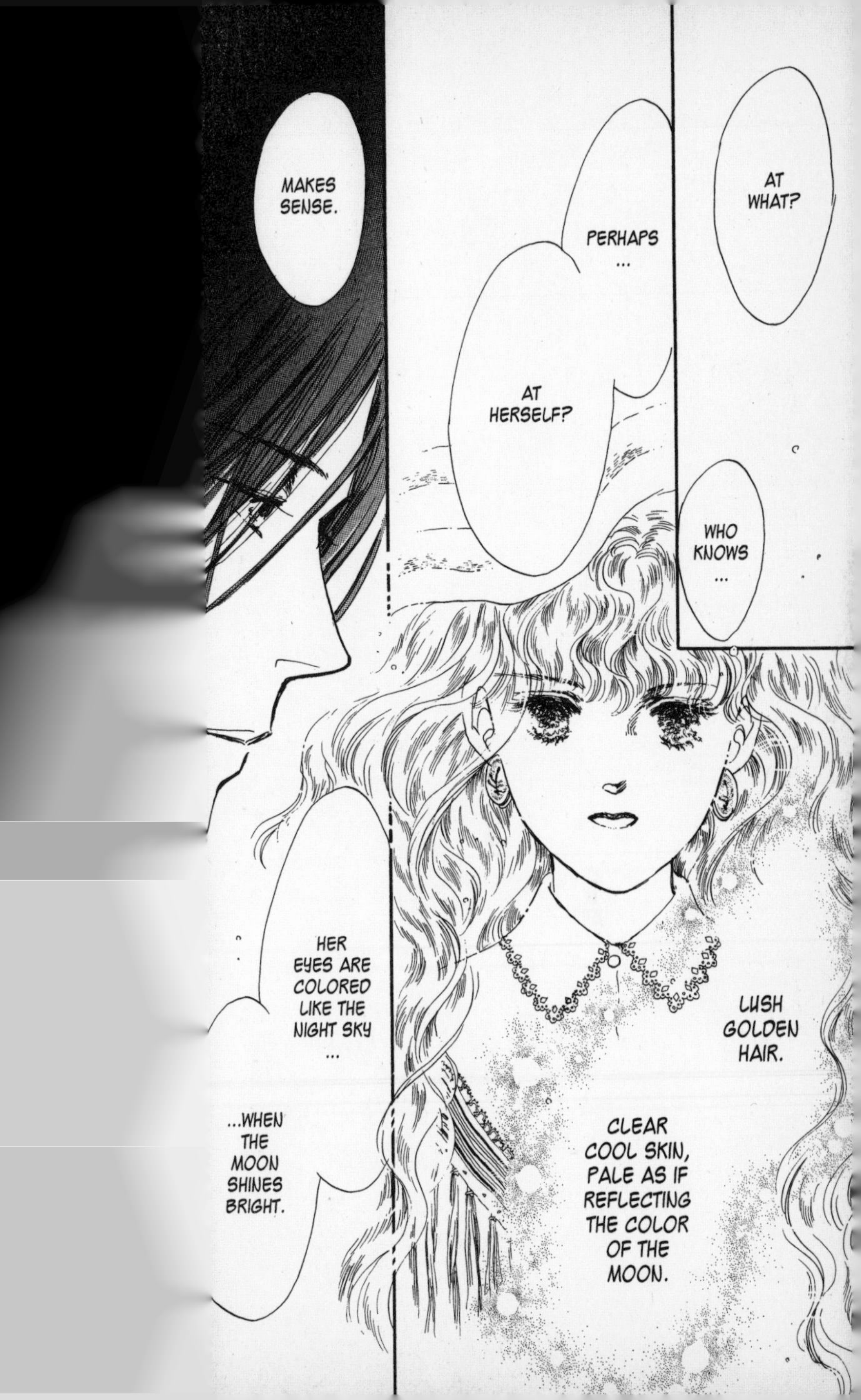
AT WHAT?
WHO KNOWS ...
PERHAPS ...
AT HERSELF?
MAKES SENSE.
LUSH GOLDEN HAIR.
CLEAR COOL SKIN, PALE AS IF REFLECTING THE COLOR OF THE MOON.
HER EYES ARE COLORED LIKE THE NIGHT SKY ...
...WHEN THE MOON SHINES BRIGHT.

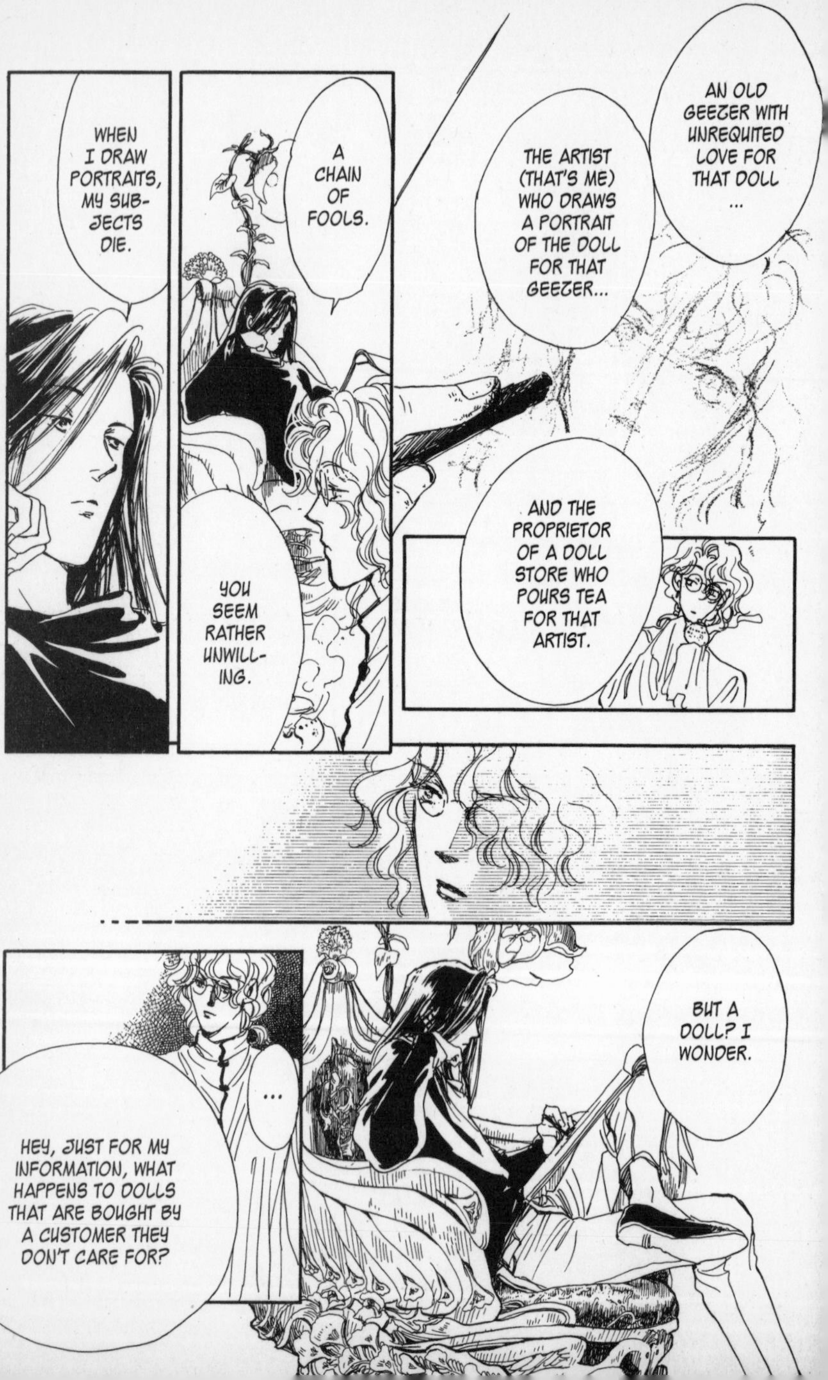
AN OLD GEEZER WITH UNREQUITED LOVE FOR THAT DOLL ...
THE ARTIST (THAT'S ME) WHO DRAWS A PORTRAIT OF THE DOLL FOR THAT GEEZER...
AND THE PROPRIETOR OF A DOLL STORE WHO POURS TEA FOR THAT ARTIST.
A CHAIN OF FOOLS.
YOU SEEM RATHER UNWILL-ING.
WHEN I DRAW PORTRAITS, MY SUB-JECTS DIE.
BUT A DOLL? I WONDER.
...
HEY, JUST FOR MY INFORMATION, WHAT HAPPENS TO DOLLS THAT ARE BOUGHT BY A CUSTOMER THEY DON'T CARE FOR?

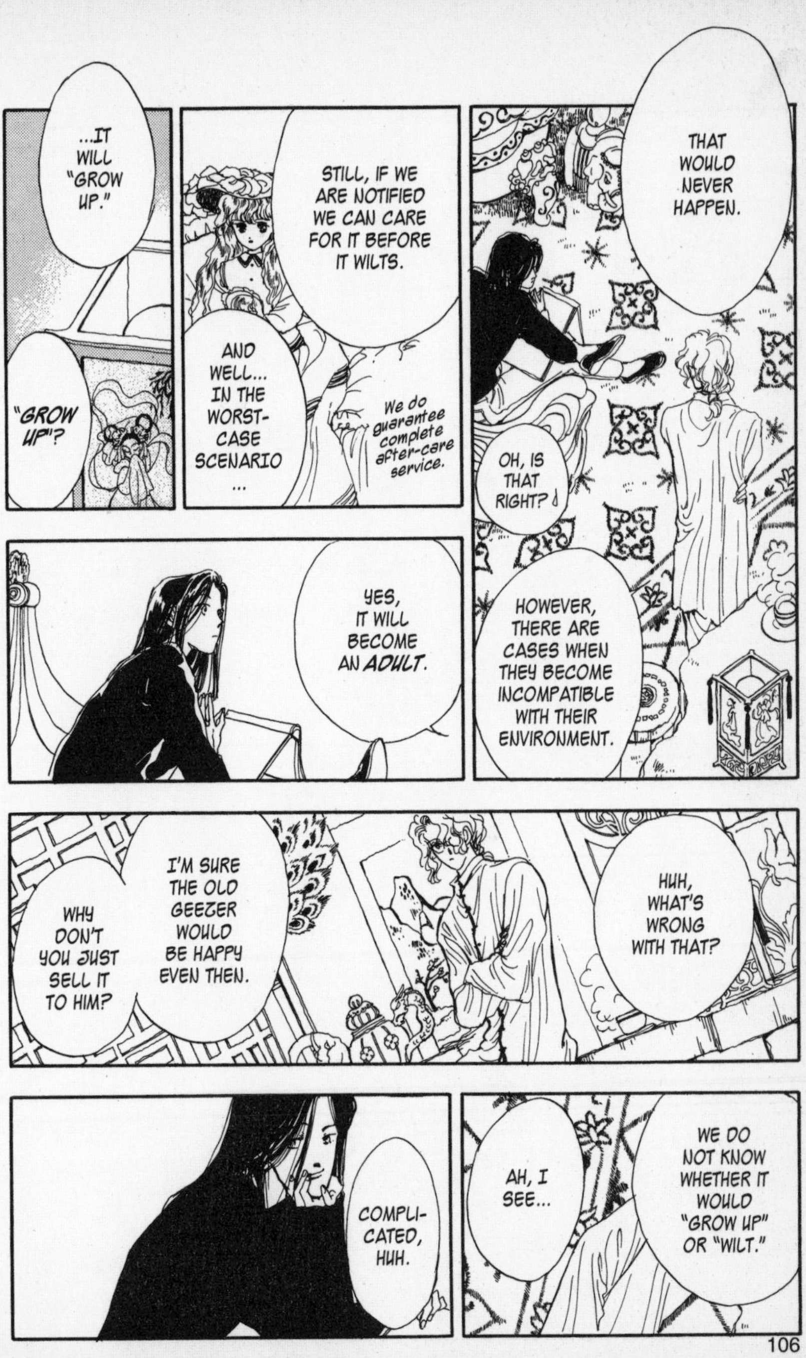
THAT WOULD NEVER HAPPEN.
OH, IS THAT RIGHT? ♪
HOWEVER, THERE ARE CASES WHEN THEY BECOME INCOMPATIBLE WITH THEIR ENVIRONMENT.
STILL, IF WE ARE NOTIFIED WE CAN CARE FOR IT BEFORE IT WILTS.
We do guarantee complete after-care service.
AND WELL... IN THE WORST-CASE SCENARIO ...
...IT WILL "GROW UP."
"GROW UP"?
YES, IT WILL BECOME AN *ADULT*.
HUH, WHAT'S WRONG WITH THAT?
I'M SURE THE OLD GEEZER WOULD BE HAPPY EVEN THEN.
WHY DON'T YOU JUST SELL IT TO HIM?
WE DO NOT KNOW WHETHER IT WOULD "GROW UP" OR "WILT."
AH, I SEE...
COMPLI-CATED, HUH.

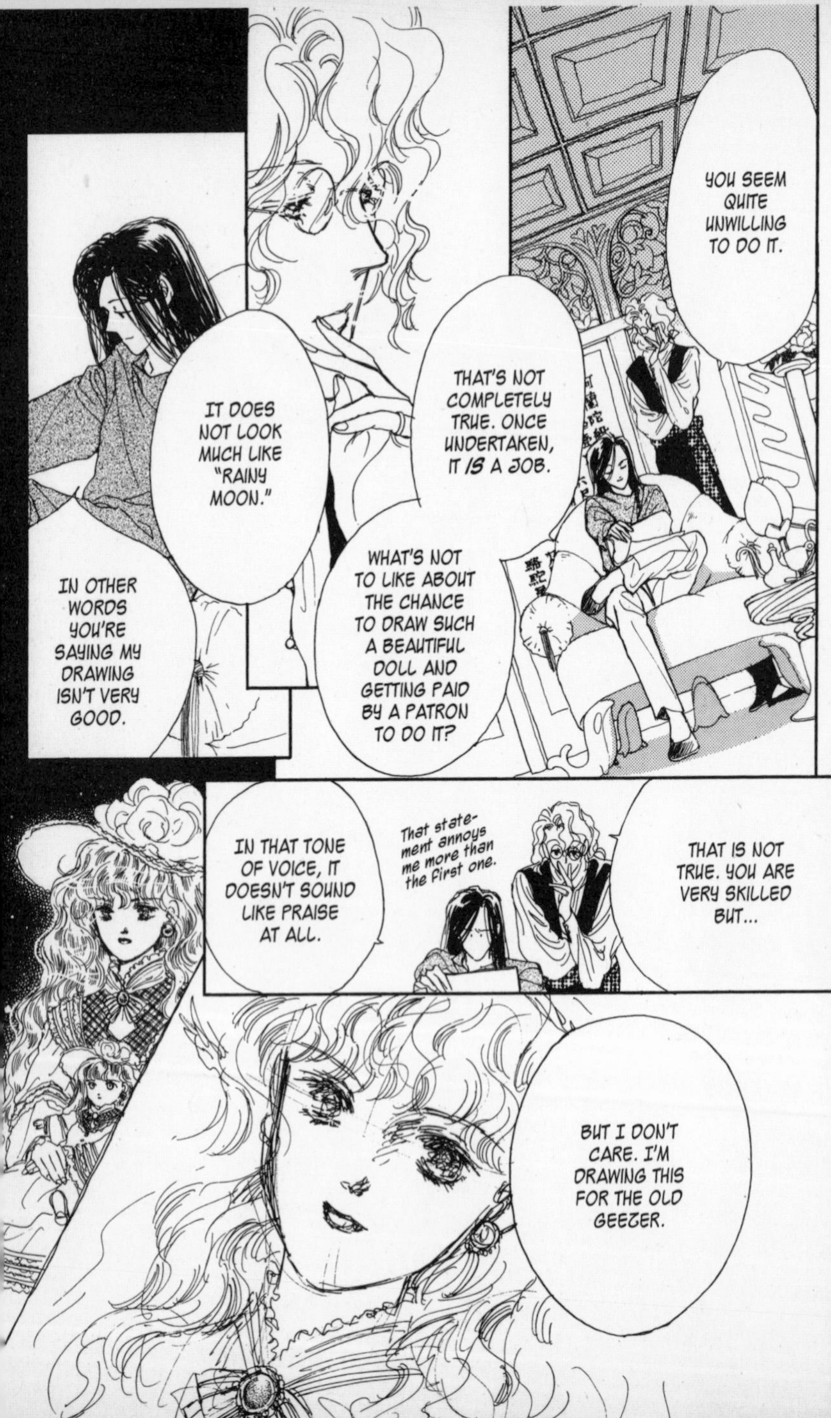
YOU SEEM QUITE UNWILLING TO DO IT.
THAT'S NOT COMPLETELY TRUE. ONCE UNDERTAKEN, IT *IS* A JOB.
WHAT'S NOT TO LIKE ABOUT THE CHANCE TO DRAW SUCH A BEAUTIFUL DOLL AND GETTING PAID BY A PATRON TO DO IT?
IT DOES NOT LOOK MUCH LIKE "RAINY MOON."
IN OTHER WORDS YOU'RE SAYING MY DRAWING ISN'T VERY GOOD.
THAT IS NOT TRUE. YOU ARE VERY SKILLED BUT...
That statement annoys me more than the first one.
IN THAT TONE OF VOICE, IT DOESN'T SOUND LIKE PRAISE AT ALL.
BUT I DON'T CARE. I'M DRAWING THIS FOR THE OLD GEEZER.

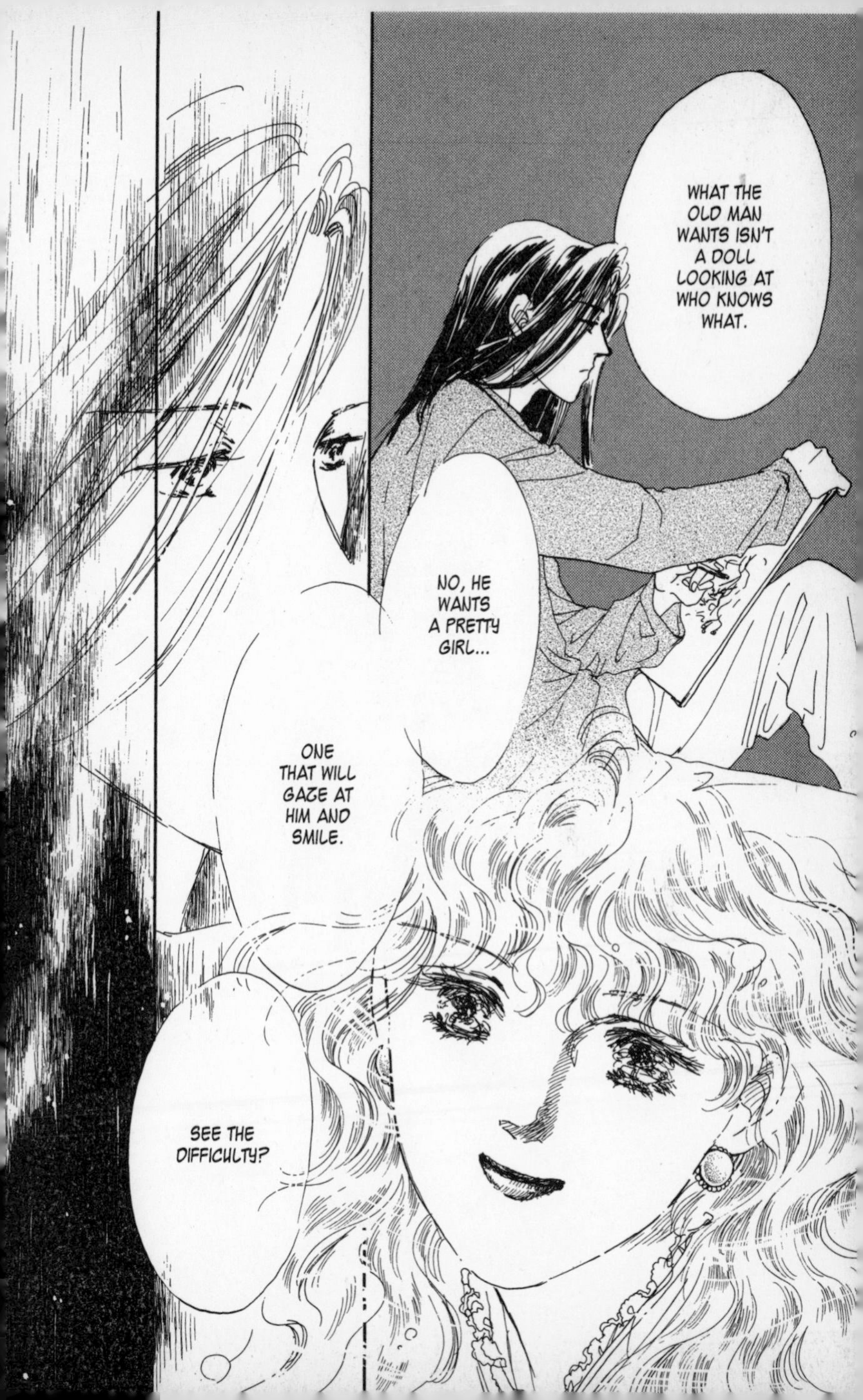
WHAT THE OLD MAN WANTS ISN'T A DOLL LOOKING AT WHO KNOWS WHAT.
NO, HE WANTS A PRETTY GIRL...
ONE THAT WILL GAZE AT HIM AND SMILE.
SEE THE DIFFICULTY?

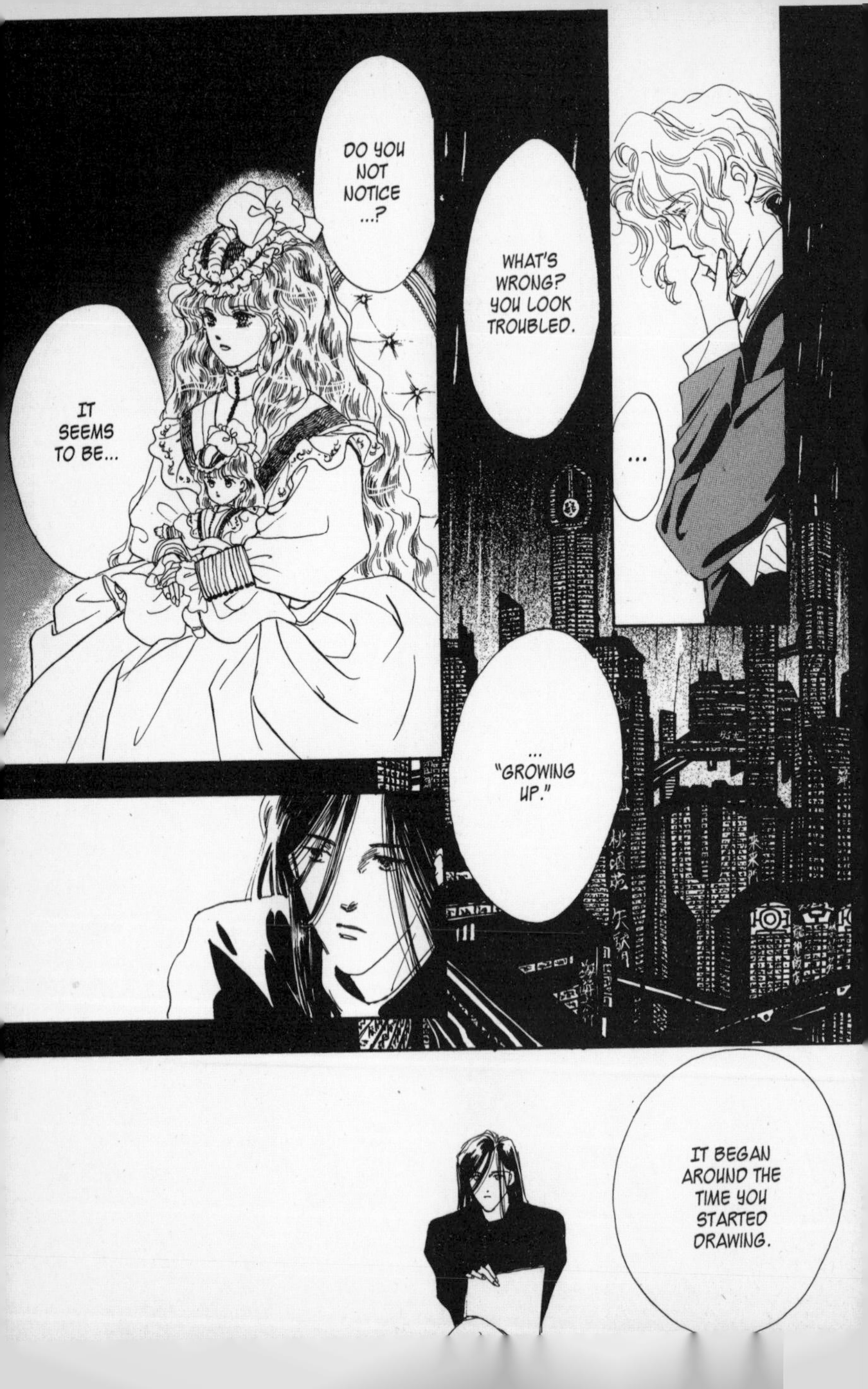
WHAT'S WRONG? YOU LOOK TROUBLED.
...
DO YOU NOT NOTICE ...?
IT SEEMS TO BE...
... "GROWING UP."
IT BEGAN AROUND THE TIME YOU STARTED DRAWING.

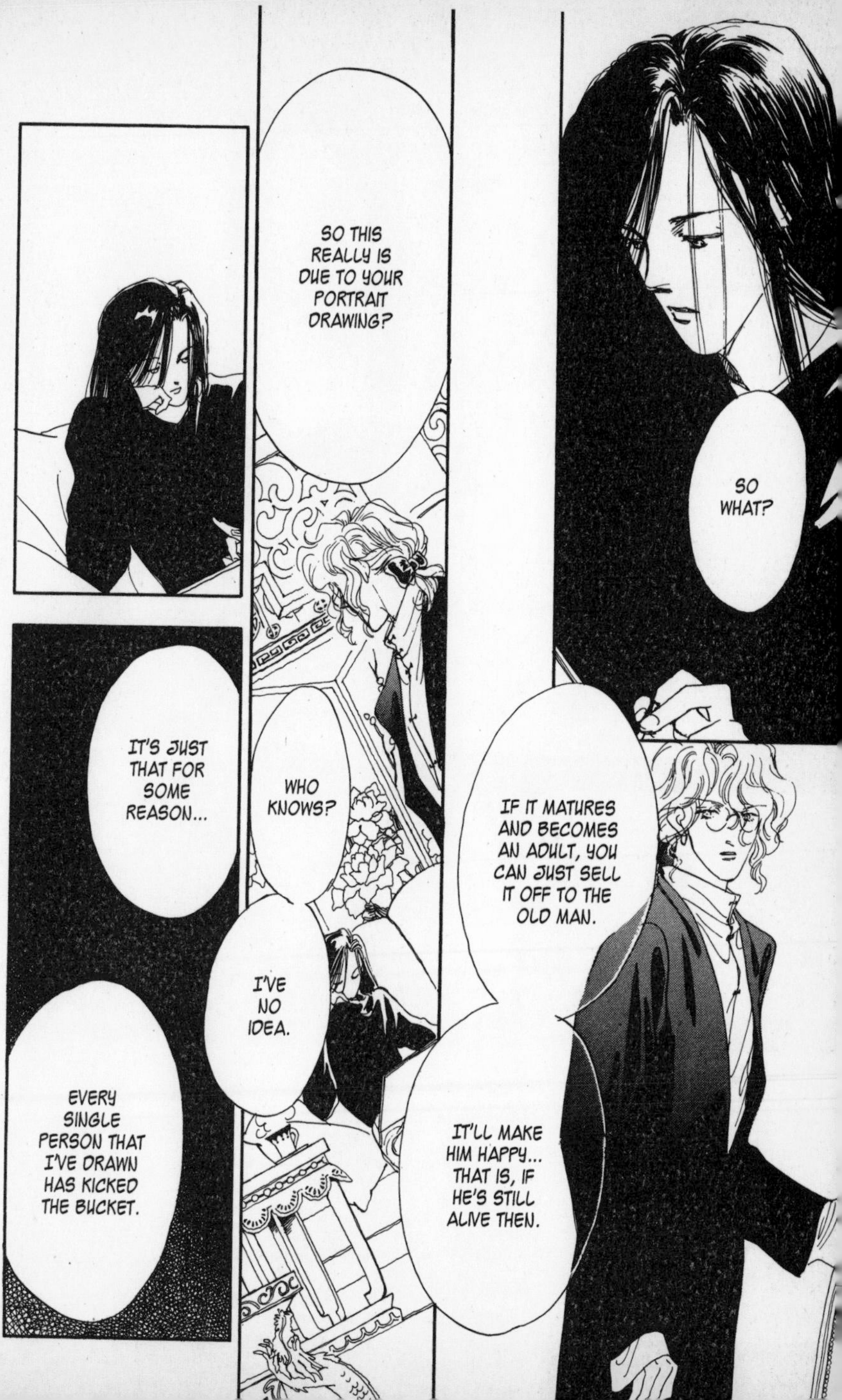
SO WHAT?
IF IT MATURES AND BECOMES AN ADULT, YOU CAN JUST SELL IT OFF TO THE OLD MAN.
IT'LL MAKE HIM HAPPY... THAT IS, IF HE'S STILL ALIVE THEN.
SO THIS REALLY IS DUE TO YOUR PORTRAIT DRAWING?
WHO KNOWS?
I'VE NO IDEA.
IT'S JUST THAT FOR SOME REASON...
EVERY SINGLE PERSON THAT I'VE DRAWN HAS KICKED THE BUCKET.

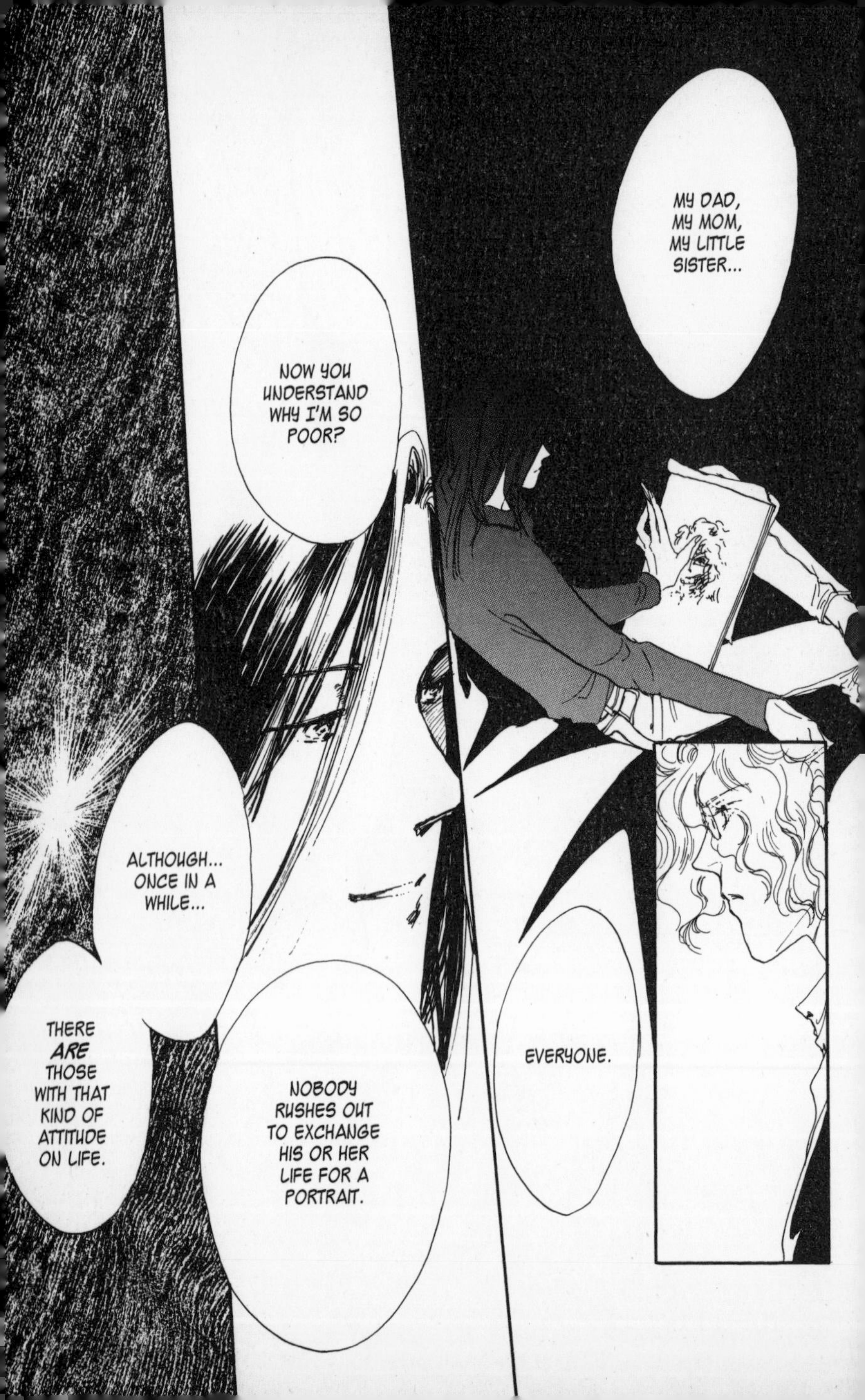
MY DAD, MY MOM, MY LITTLE SISTER...
EVERYONE.
NOW YOU UNDERSTAND WHY I'M SO POOR?
NOBODY RUSHES OUT TO EXCHANGE HIS OR HER LIFE FOR A PORTRAIT.
ALTHOUGH... ONCE IN A WHILE...
THERE *ARE* THOSE WITH THAT KIND OF ATTITUDE ON LIFE.

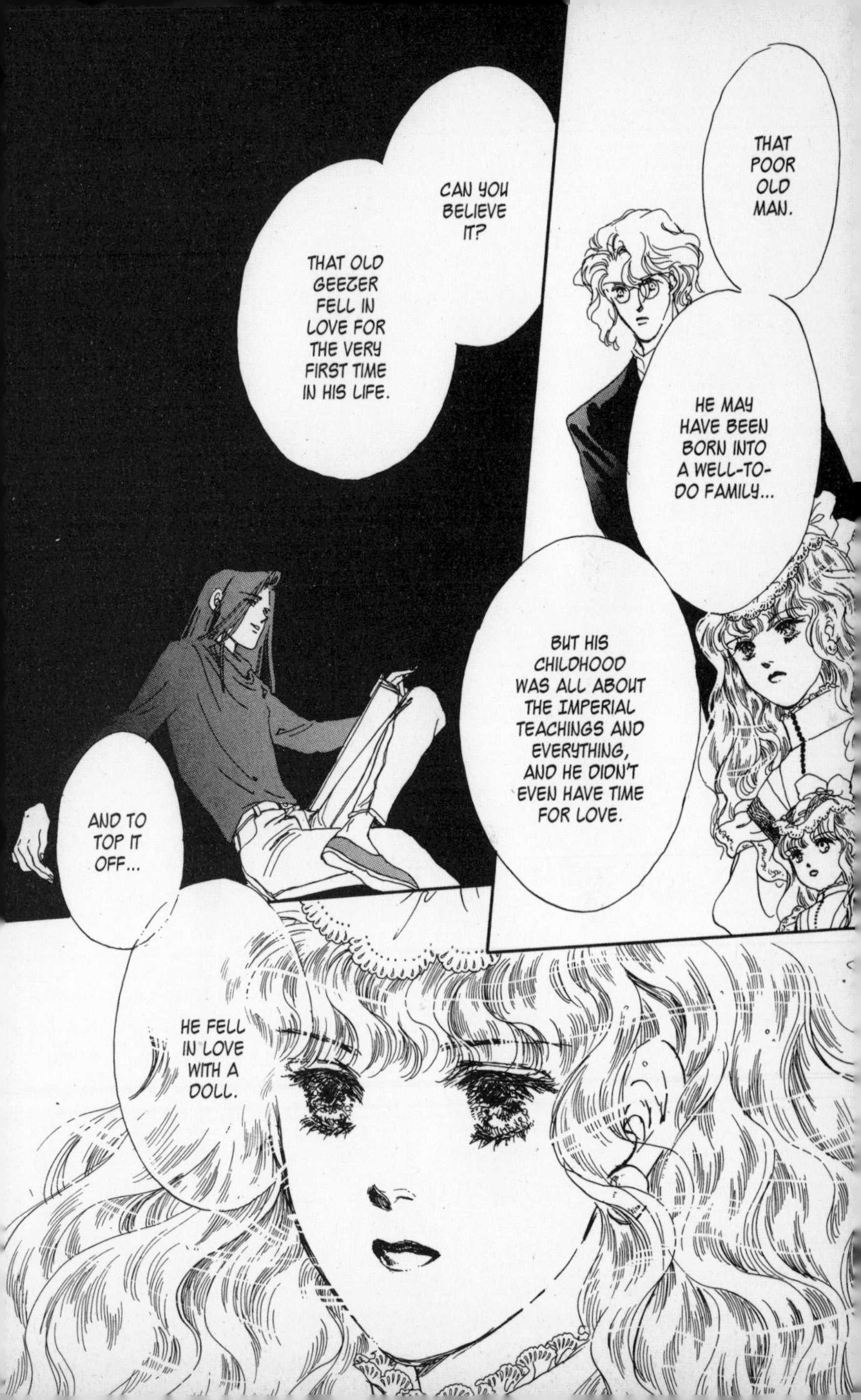
THAT POOR OLD MAN.
HE MAY HAVE BEEN BORN INTO A WELL-TO-DO FAMILY...
BUT HIS CHILDHOOD WAS ALL ABOUT THE IMPERIAL TEACHINGS AND EVERYTHING, AND HE DIDN'T EVEN HAVE TIME FOR LOVE.
CAN YOU BELIEVE IT?
THAT OLD GEEZER FELL IN LOVE FOR THE VERY FIRST TIME IN HIS LIFE.
AND TO TOP IT OFF...
HE FELL IN LOVE WITH A DOLL.

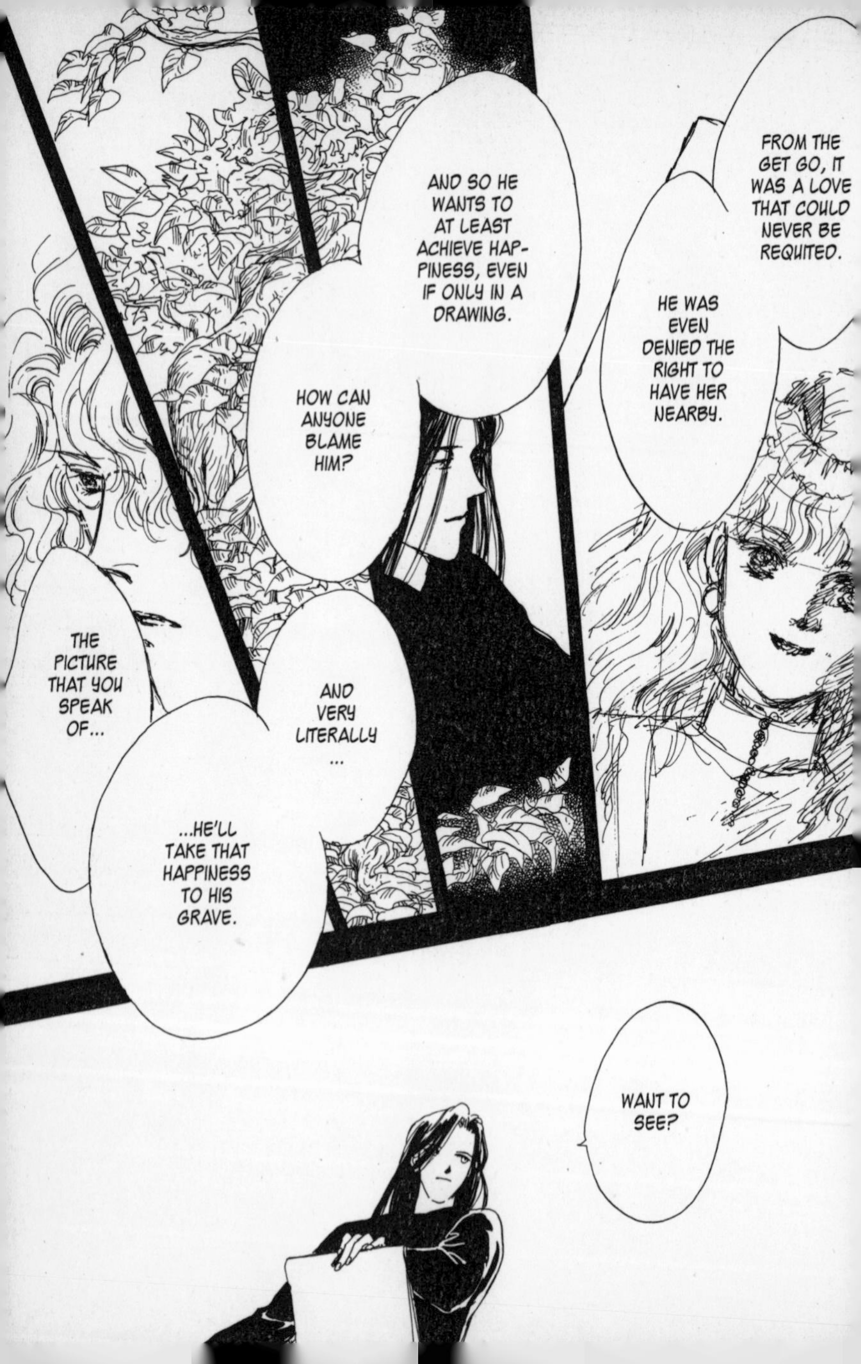
FROM THE GET GO, IT WAS A LOVE THAT COULD NEVER BE REQUITED.
HE WAS EVEN DENIED THE RIGHT TO HAVE HER NEARBY.
AND SO HE WANTS TO AT LEAST ACHIEVE HAP-PINESS, EVEN IF ONLY IN A DRAWING.
HOW CAN ANYONE BLAME HIM?
AND VERY LITERALLY ...
...HE'LL TAKE THAT HAPPINESS TO HIS GRAVE.
THE PICTURE THAT YOU SPEAK OF...
WANT TO SEE?

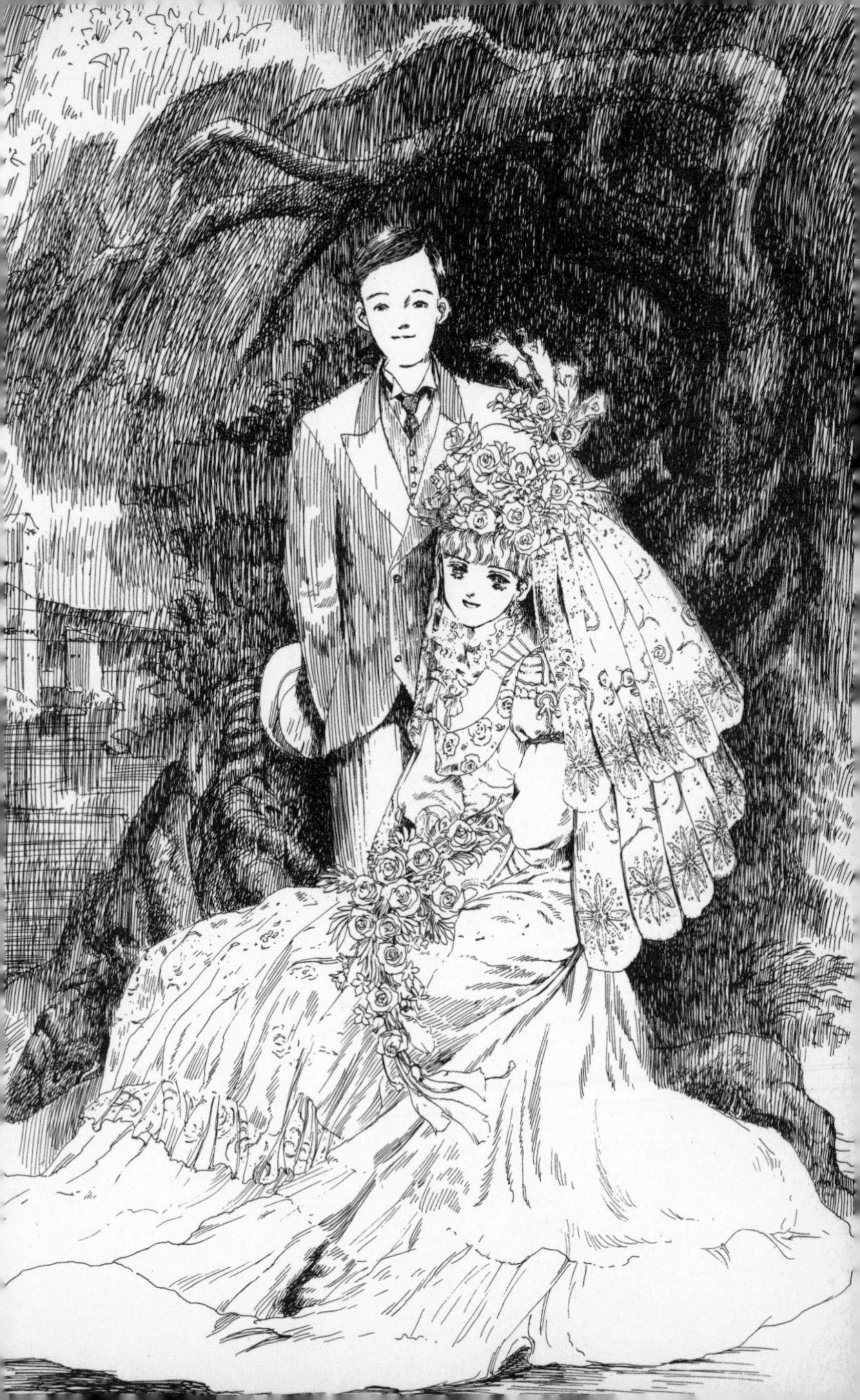

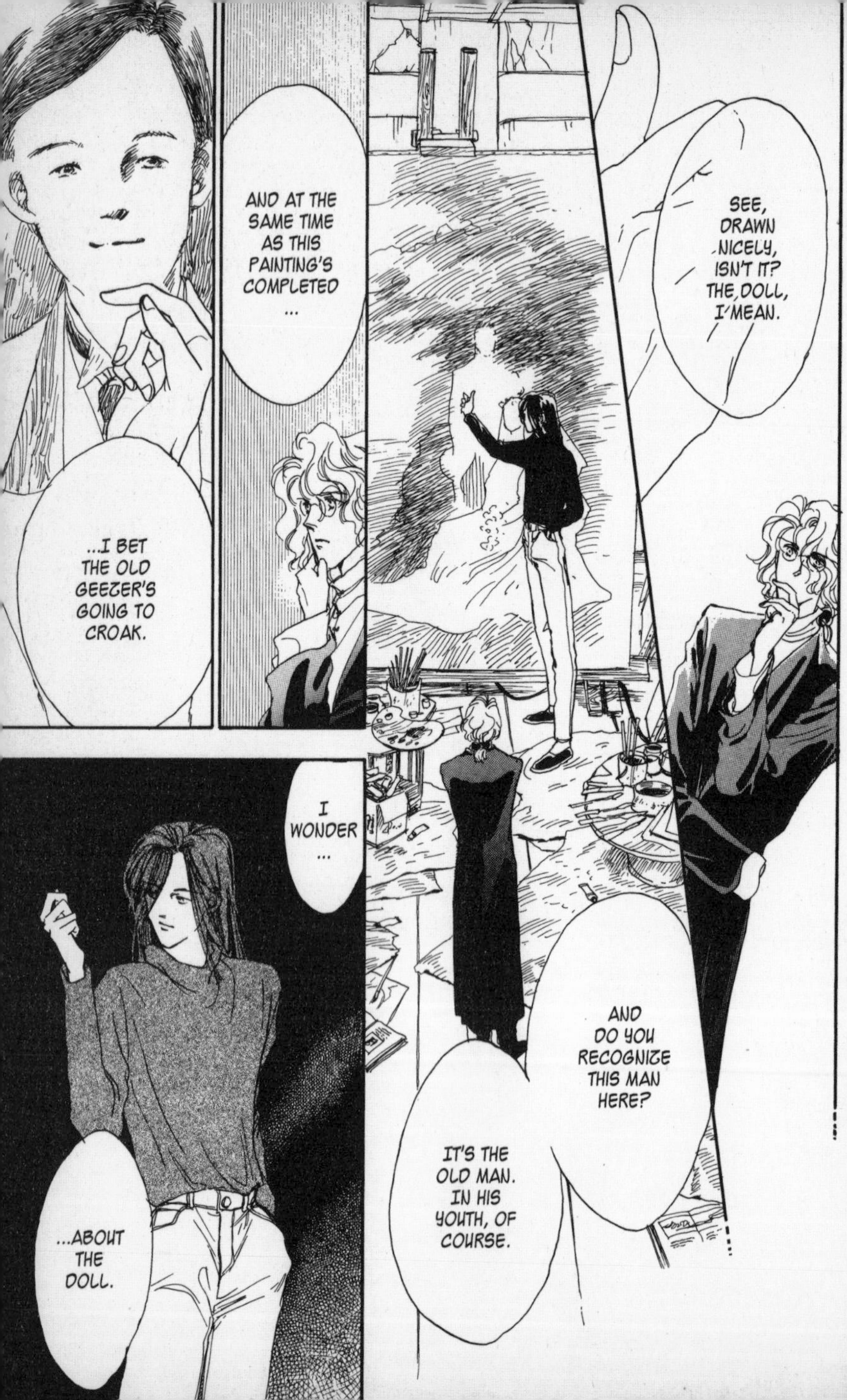
SEE, DRAWN NICELY, ISN'T IT? THE DOLL, I MEAN.
AND DO YOU RECOGNIZE THIS MAN HERE?
IT'S THE OLD MAN. IN HIS YOUTH, OF COURSE.
AND AT THE SAME TIME AS THIS PAINTING'S COMPLETED ...
...I BET THE OLD GEEZER'S GOING TO CROAK.
I WONDER ...
...ABOUT THE DOLL.

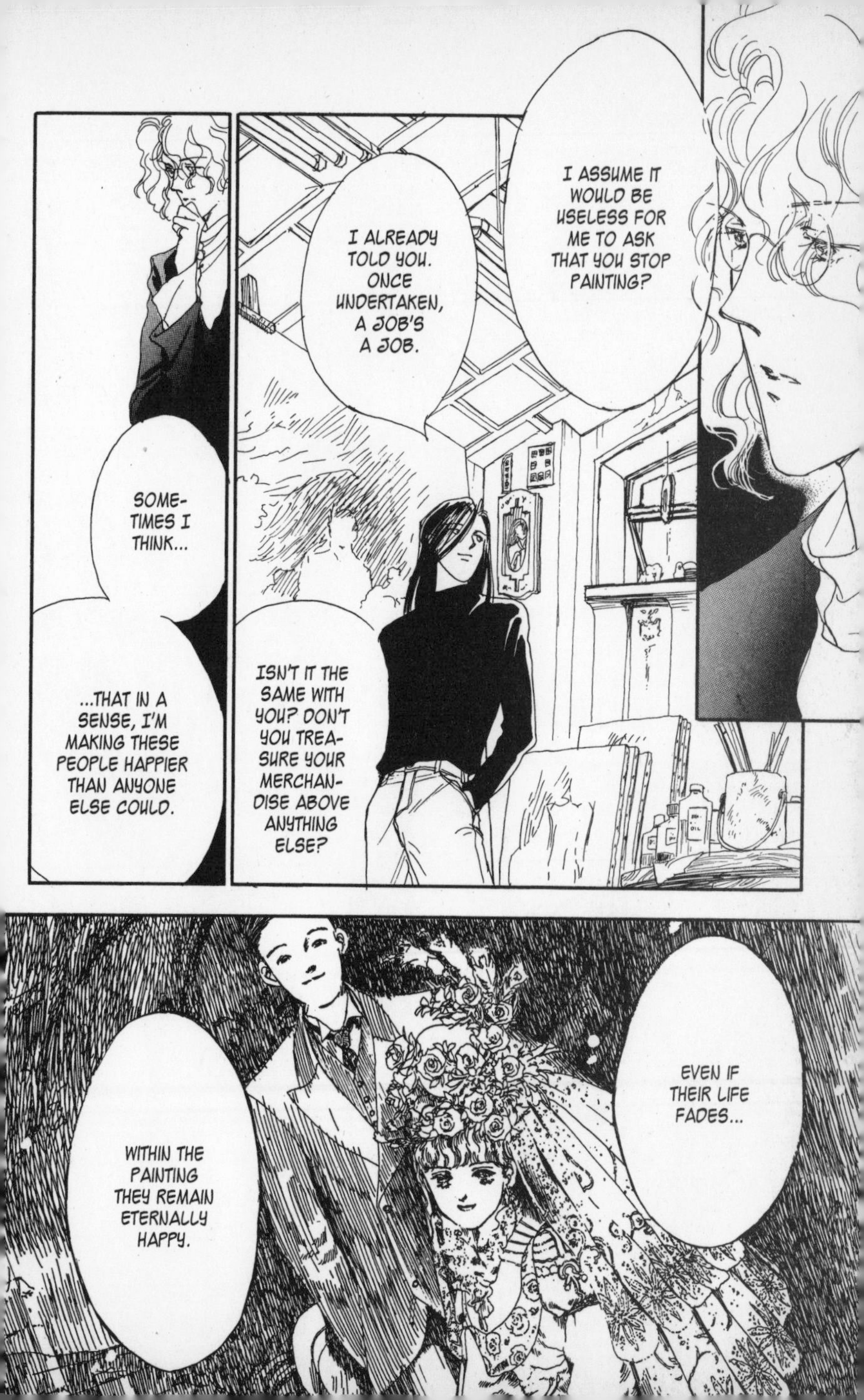
I ASSUME IT WOULD BE USELESS FOR ME TO ASK THAT YOU STOP PAINTING?
I ALREADY TOLD YOU. ONCE UNDERTAKEN, A JOB'S A JOB.
ISN'T IT THE SAME WITH YOU? DON'T YOU TREA-SURE YOUR MERCHAN-DISE ABOVE ANYTHING ELSE?
SOME-TIMES I THINK...
...THAT IN A SENSE, I'M MAKING THESE PEOPLE HAPPIER THAN ANYONE ELSE COULD.
EVEN IF THEIR LIFE FADES...
WITHIN THE PAINTING THEY REMAIN ETERNALLY HAPPY.

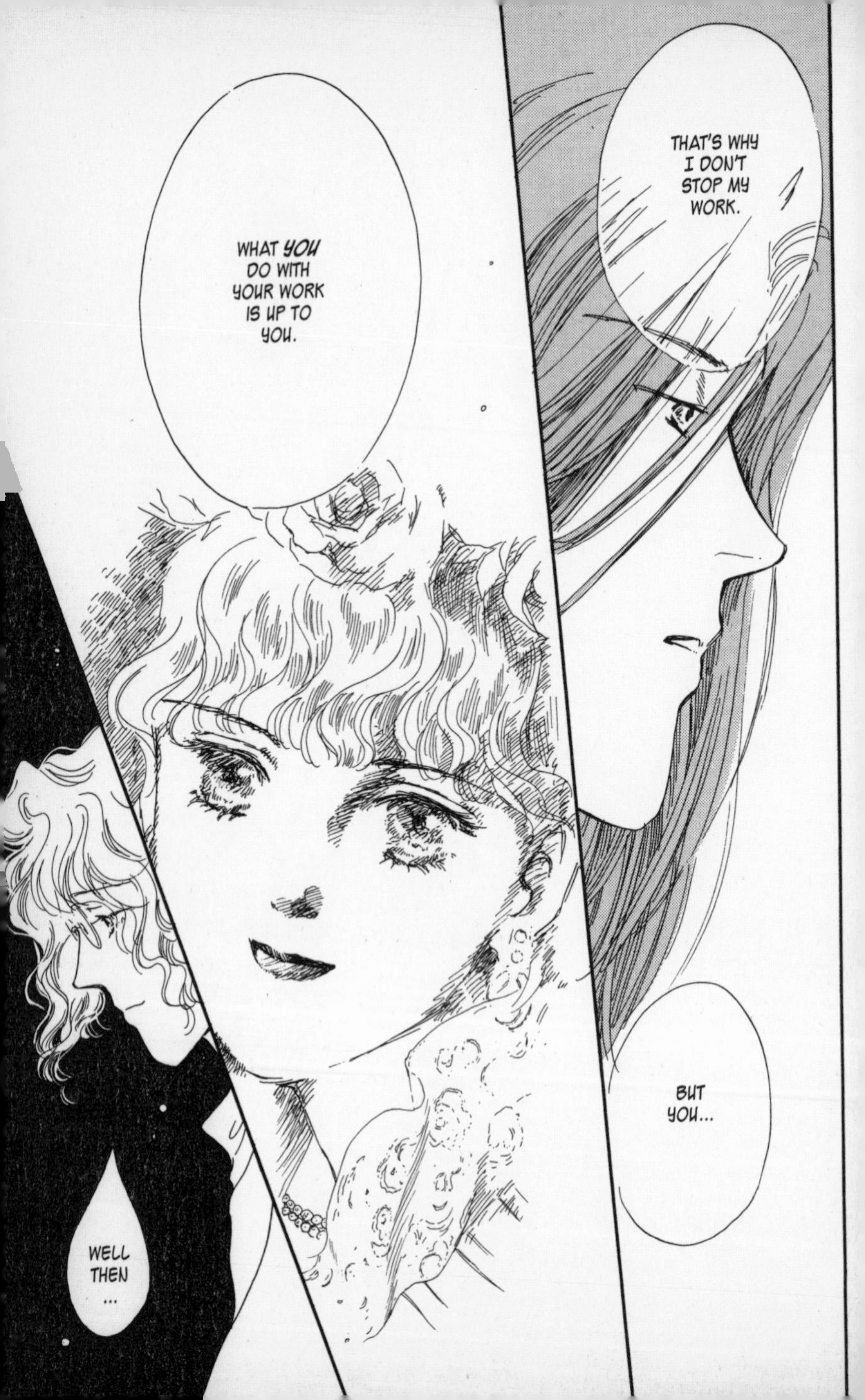
THAT'S WHY I DON'T STOP MY WORK.
BUT YOU...
WHAT *YOU* DO WITH YOUR WORK IS UP TO YOU.
WELL THEN ...

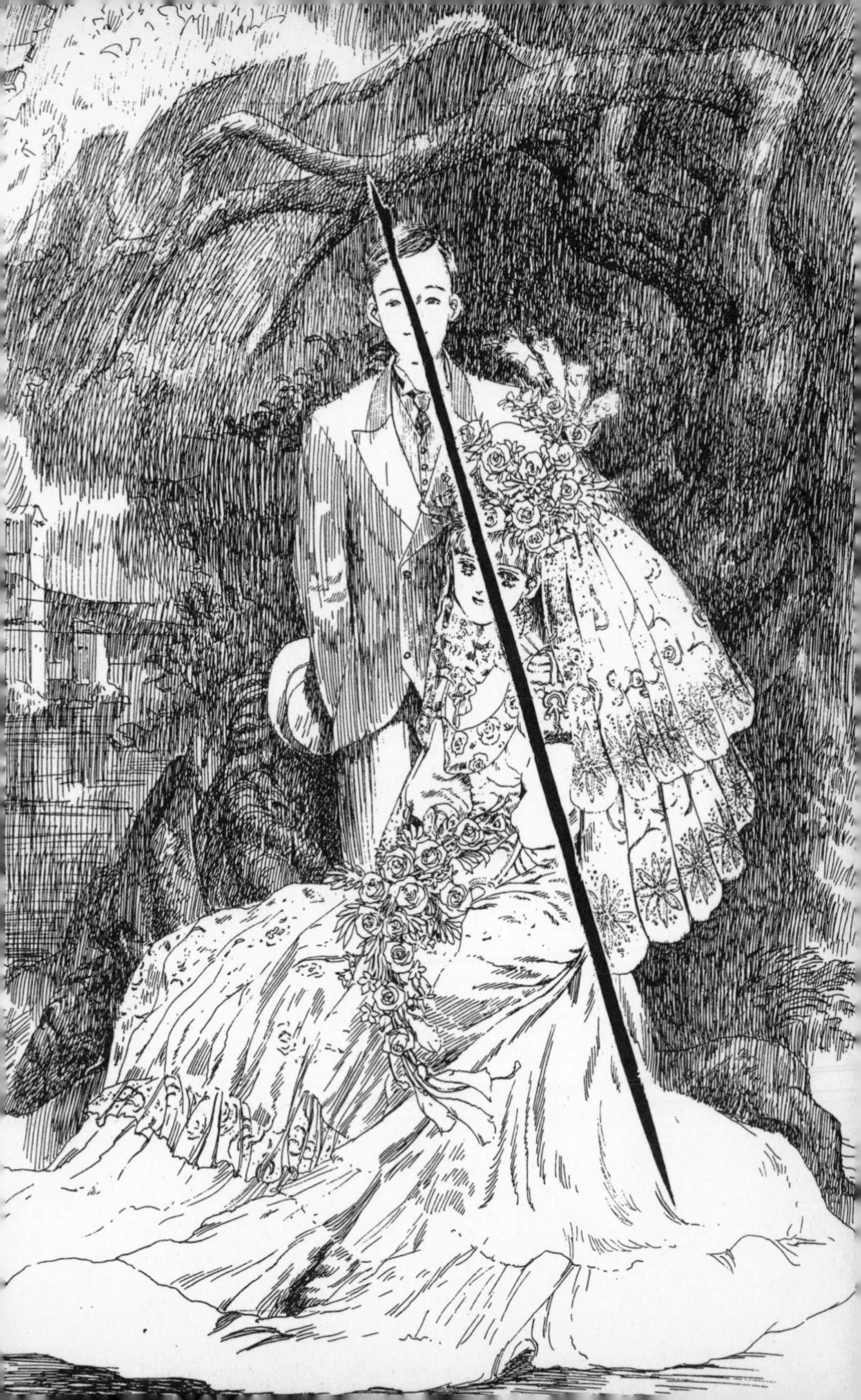

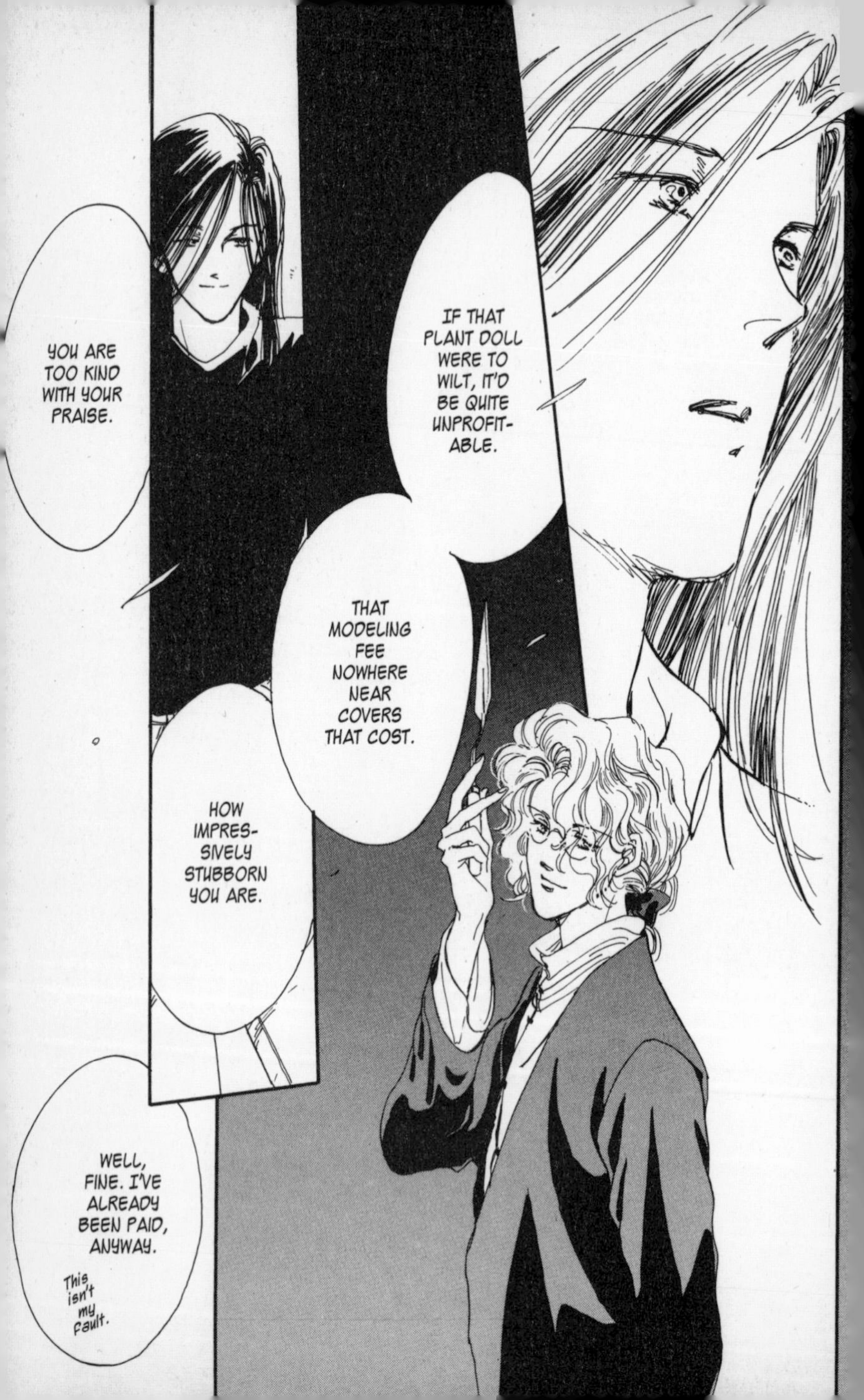
IF THAT PLANT DOLL WERE TO WILT, IT'D BE QUITE UNPROFIT-ABLE.
THAT MODELING FEE NOWHERE NEAR COVERS THAT COST.
HOW IMPRES-SIVELY STUBBORN YOU ARE.
YOU ARE TOO KIND WITH YOUR PRAISE.
WELL, FINE. I'VE ALREADY BEEN PAID, ANYWAY.
This isn't my fault.

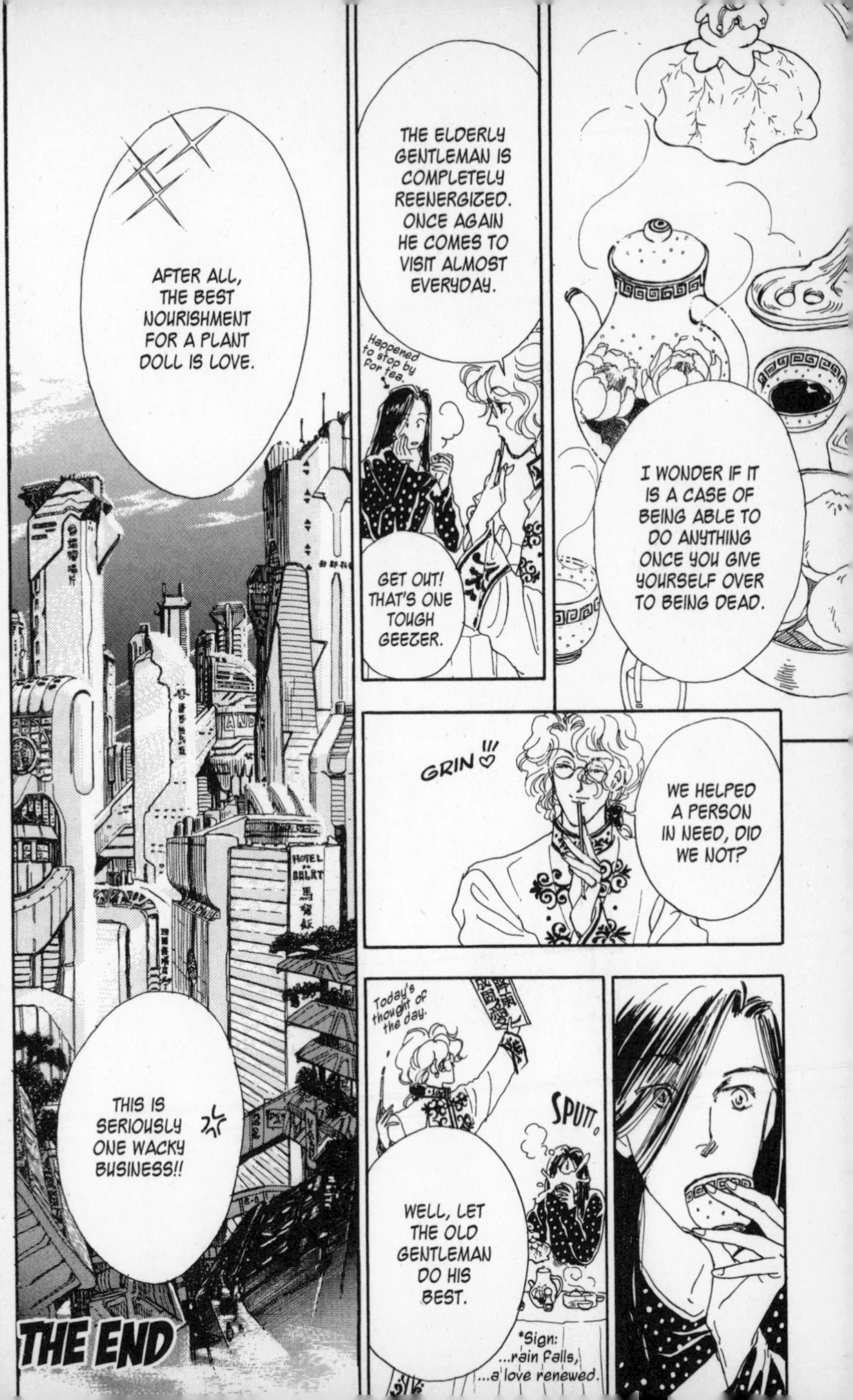
I WONDER IF IT IS A CASE OF BEING ABLE TO DO ANYTHING ONCE YOU GIVE YOURSELF OVER TO BEING DEAD.
THE ELDERLY GENTLEMAN IS COMPLETELY REENERGIZED. ONCE AGAIN HE COMES TO VISIT ALMOST EVERYDAY.
Happened to stop by for tea.
GET OUT! THAT'S ONE TOUGH GEEZER.
GRIN
WE HELPED A PERSON IN NEED, DID WE NOT?
Today's thought of the day.
SPUTT.
WELL, LET THE OLD GENTLEMAN DO HIS BEST.
*Sign: ...rain falls, ...a love renewed.
AFTER ALL, THE BEST NOURISHMENT FOR A PLANT DOLL IS LOVE.
THIS IS SERIOUSLY ONE WACKY BUSINESS!!
THE END

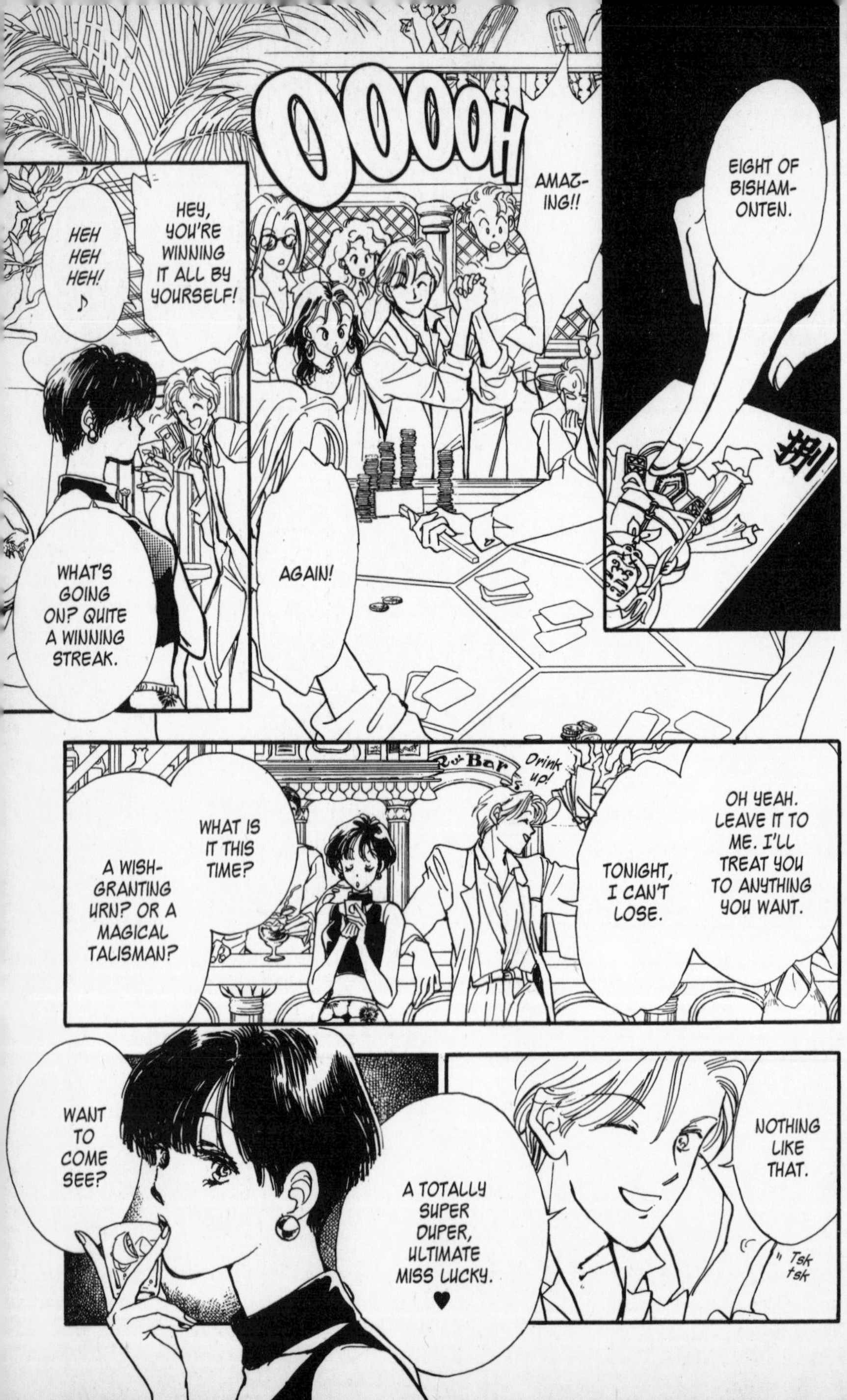
EIGHT OF BISHAM-ONTEN.
捌
OOOOH
AMAZ-ING!!
AGAIN!
HEY, YOU'RE WINNING IT ALL BY YOURSELF!
HEH HEH HEH! ♪
WHAT'S GOING ON? QUITE A WINNING STREAK.
OH YEAH. LEAVE IT TO ME. I'LL TREAT YOU TO ANYTHING YOU WANT.
TONIGHT, I CAN'T LOSE.
Drink up!
Bar
WHAT IS IT THIS TIME?
A WISH-GRANTING URN? OR A MAGICAL TALISMAN?
NOTHING LIKE THAT.
Tsk tsk
A TOTALLY SUPER DUPER, ULTIMATE MISS LUCKY. ♥
WANT TO COME SEE?

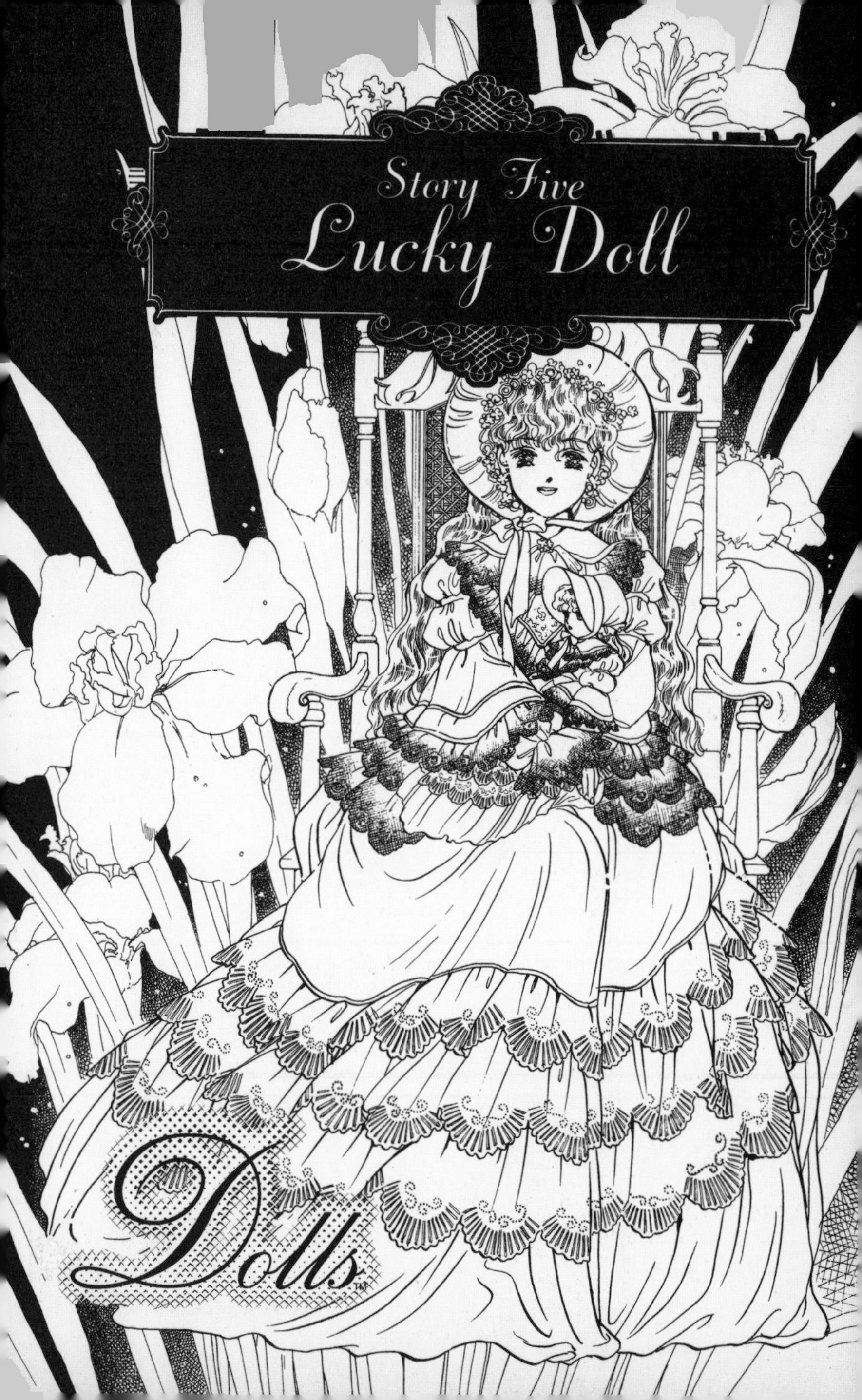
Story Five
Lucky Doll
Dolls™

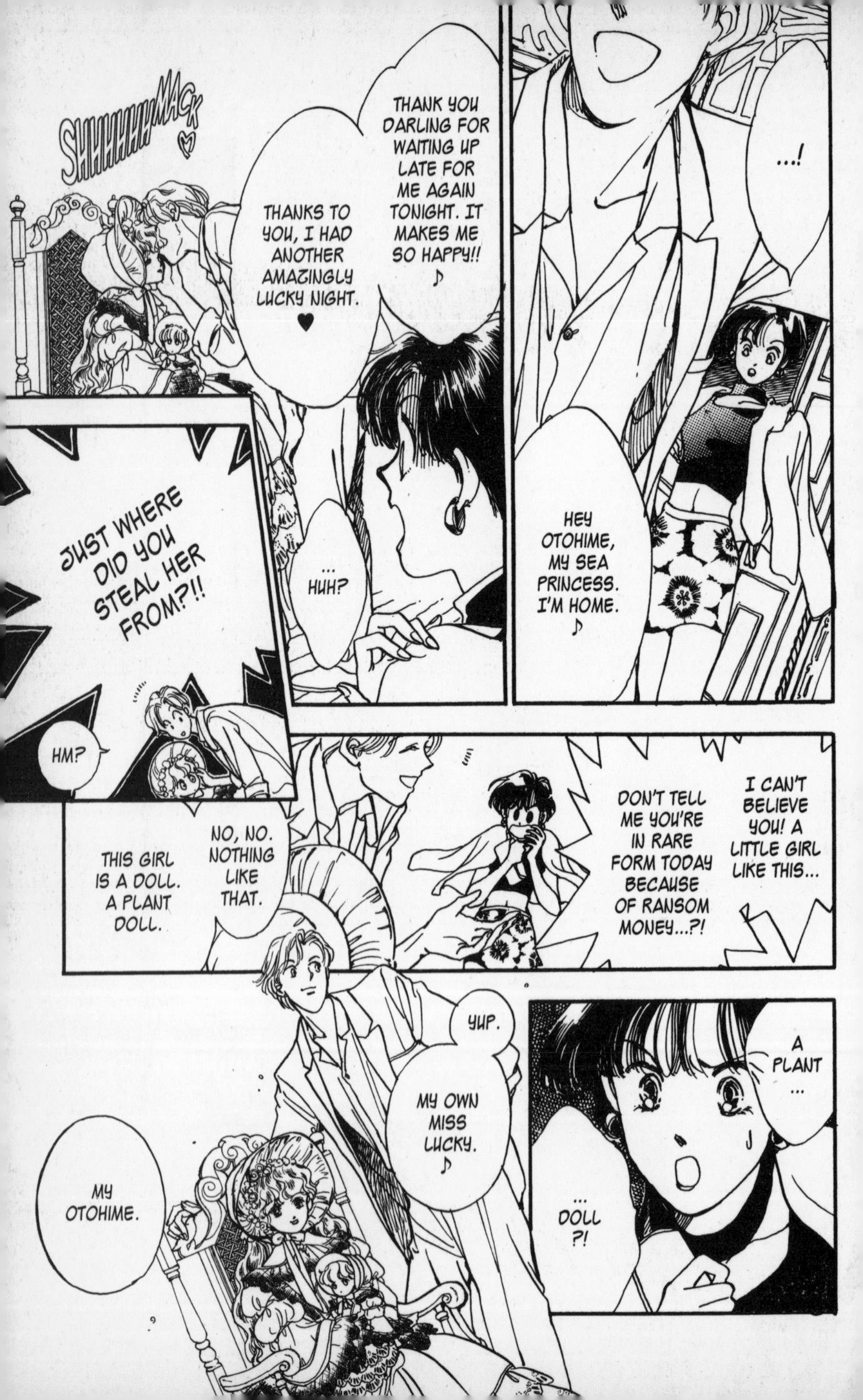
...!
HEY OTOHIME, MY SEA PRINCESS. I'M HOME. ♪
THANK YOU DARLING FOR WAITING UP LATE FOR ME AGAIN TONIGHT. IT MAKES ME SO HAPPY!! ♪
THANKS TO YOU, I HAD ANOTHER AMAZINGLY LUCKY NIGHT. ♥
... HUH?
SHHHHHHMACK ♡
JUST WHERE DID YOU STEAL HER FROM?!!
HM?
I CAN'T BELIEVE YOU! A LITTLE GIRL LIKE THIS...
DON'T TELL ME YOU'RE IN RARE FORM TODAY BECAUSE OF RANSOM MONEY...?!
NO, NO. NOTHING LIKE THAT.
THIS GIRL IS A DOLL. A PLANT DOLL.
A PLANT ...
... DOLL ?!
YUP.
MY OWN MISS LUCKY. ♪
MY OTOHIME.

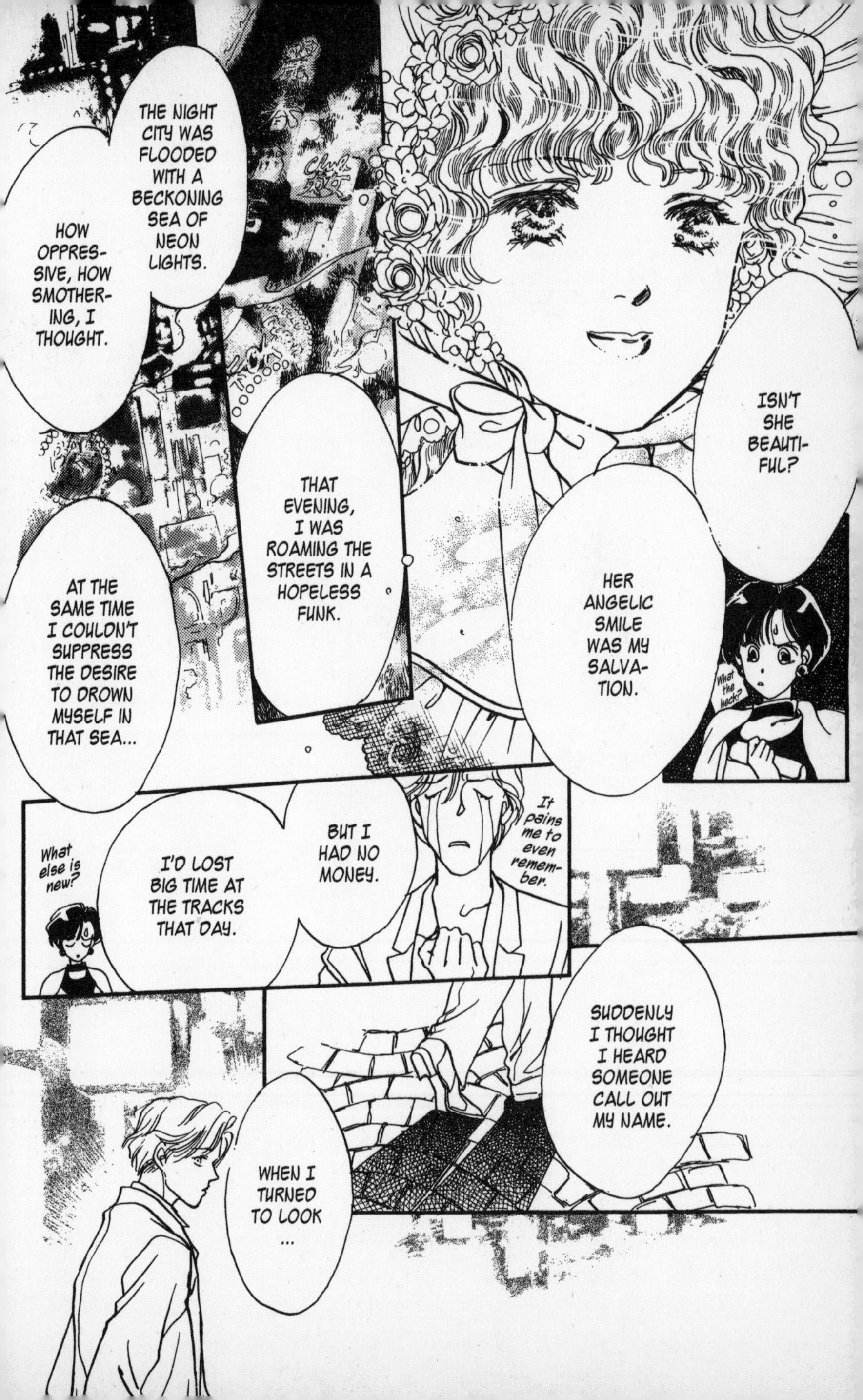
ISN'T SHE BEAUTIFUL?
HER ANGELIC SMILE WAS MY SALVATION.
What the heck?
THAT EVENING, I WAS ROAMING THE STREETS IN A HOPELESS FUNK.
THE NIGHT CITY WAS FLOODED WITH A BECKONING SEA OF NEON LIGHTS.
HOW OPPRESSIVE, HOW SMOTHERING, I THOUGHT.
AT THE SAME TIME I COULDN'T SUPPRESS THE DESIRE TO DROWN MYSELF IN THAT SEA...
It pains me to even remember.
BUT I HAD NO MONEY.
I'D LOST BIG TIME AT THE TRACKS THAT DAY.
What else is new?
SUDDENLY I THOUGHT I HEARD SOMEONE CALL OUT MY NAME.
WHEN I TURNED TO LOOK ...

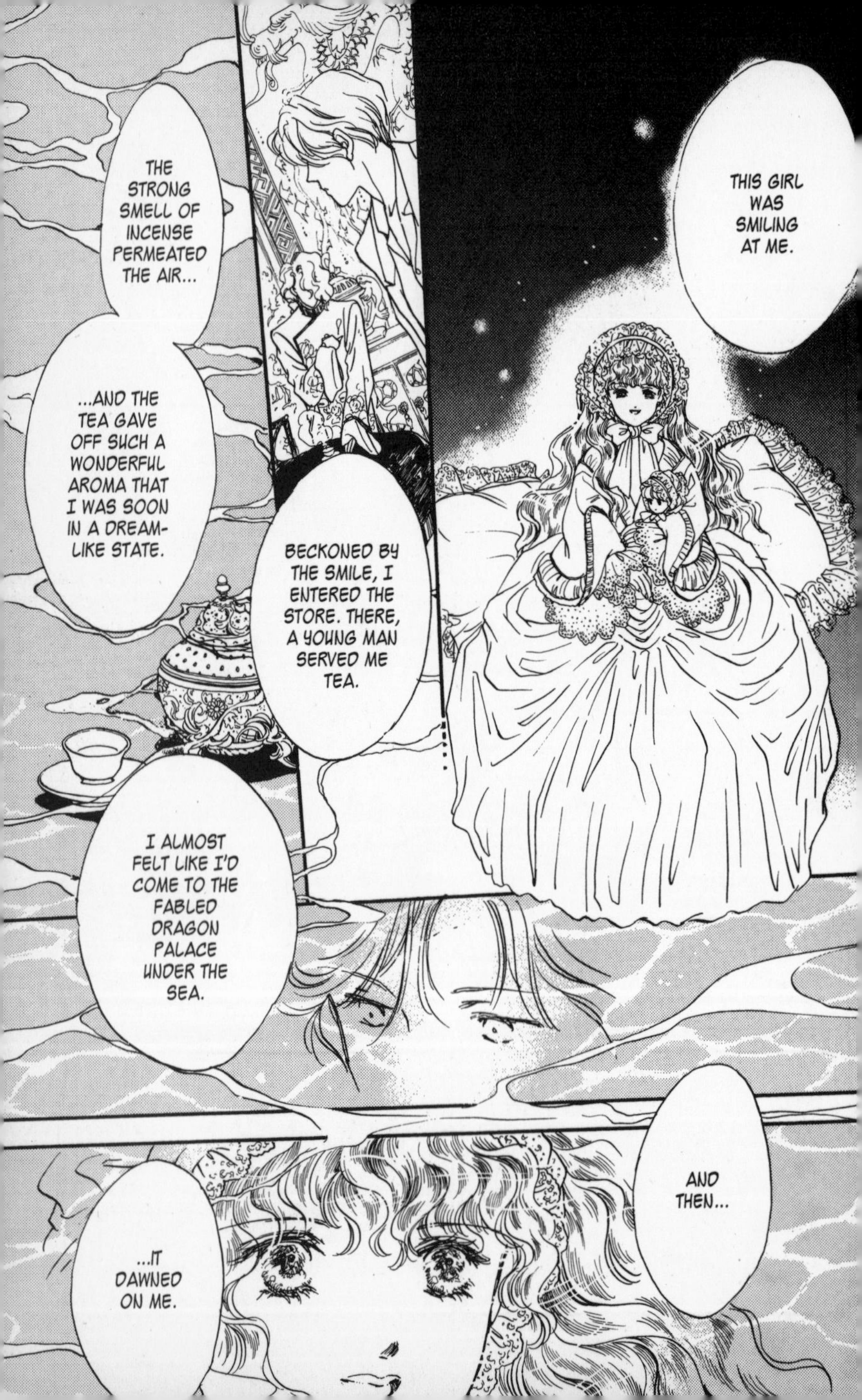
THIS GIRL WAS SMILING AT ME.
BECKONED BY THE SMILE, I ENTERED THE STORE. THERE, A YOUNG MAN SERVED ME TEA.
THE STRONG SMELL OF INCENSE PERMEATED THE AIR...
...AND THE TEA GAVE OFF SUCH A WONDERFUL AROMA THAT I WAS SOON IN A DREAM-LIKE STATE.
I ALMOST FELT LIKE I'D COME TO THE FABLED DRAGON PALACE UNDER THE SEA.
AND THEN...
...IT DAWNED ON ME.

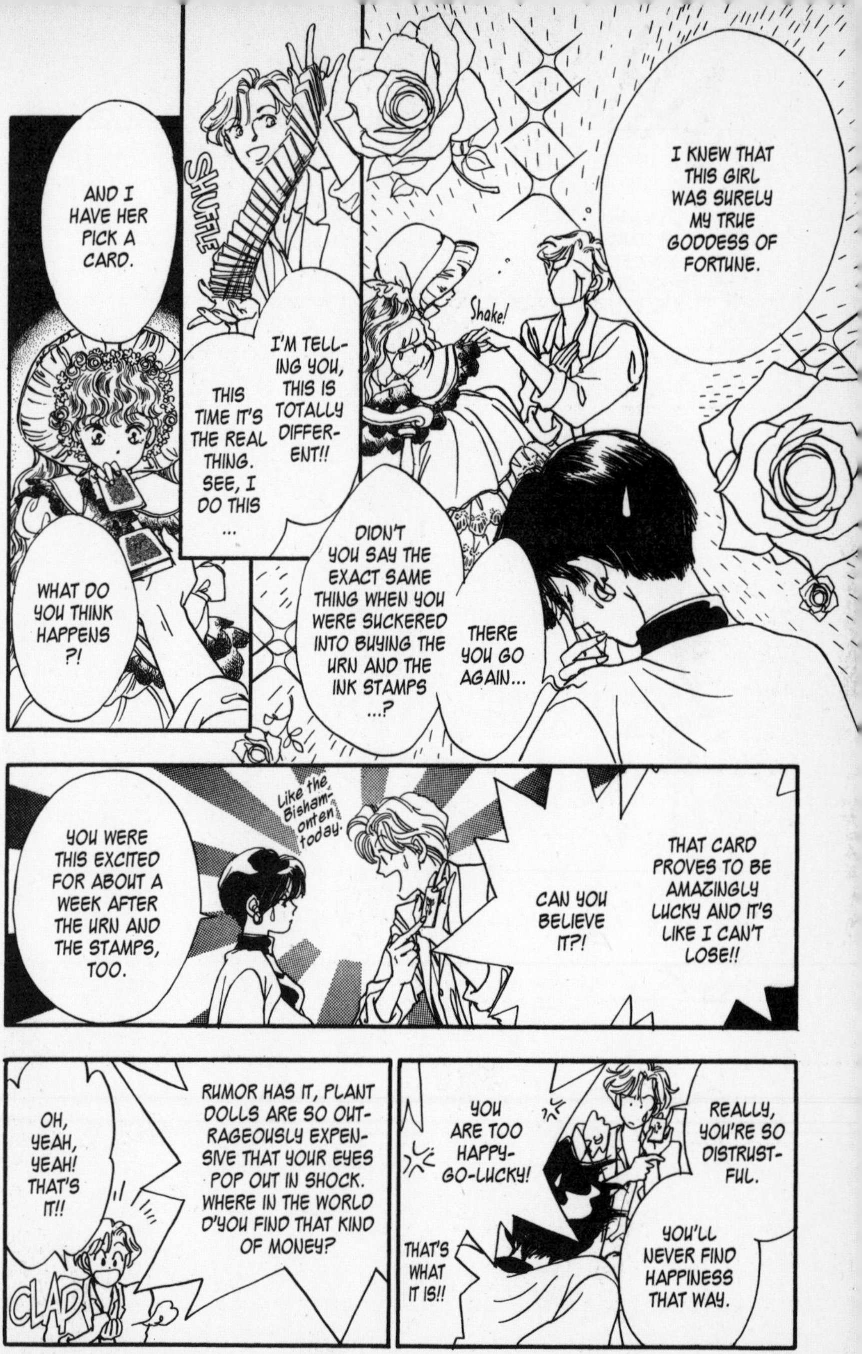
I KNEW THAT THIS GIRL WAS SURELY MY TRUE GODDESS OF FORTUNE.
Shake!
THERE YOU GO AGAIN...
DIDN'T YOU SAY THE EXACT SAME THING WHEN YOU WERE SUCKERED INTO BUYING THE URN AND THE INK STAMPS ...?
I'M TELLING YOU, THIS IS TOTALLY DIFFERENT!!
THIS TIME IT'S THE REAL THING. SEE, I DO THIS ...
SHUFFLE
AND I HAVE HER PICK A CARD.
WHAT DO YOU THINK HAPPENS ?!
THAT CARD PROVES TO BE AMAZINGLY LUCKY AND IT'S LIKE I CAN'T LOSE!!
CAN YOU BELIEVE IT?!
Like the Bishamonten today.
YOU WERE THIS EXCITED FOR ABOUT A WEEK AFTER THE URN AND THE STAMPS, TOO.
REALLY, YOU'RE SO DISTRUST-FUL.
YOU ARE TOO HAPPY-GO-LUCKY!
YOU'LL NEVER FIND HAPPINESS THAT WAY.
THAT'S WHAT IT IS!!
RUMOR HAS IT, PLANT DOLLS ARE SO OUTRAGEOUSLY EXPENSIVE THAT YOUR EYES POP OUT IN SHOCK. WHERE IN THE WORLD D'YOU FIND THAT KIND OF MONEY?
OH, YEAH, YEAH! THAT'S IT!!
CLAP

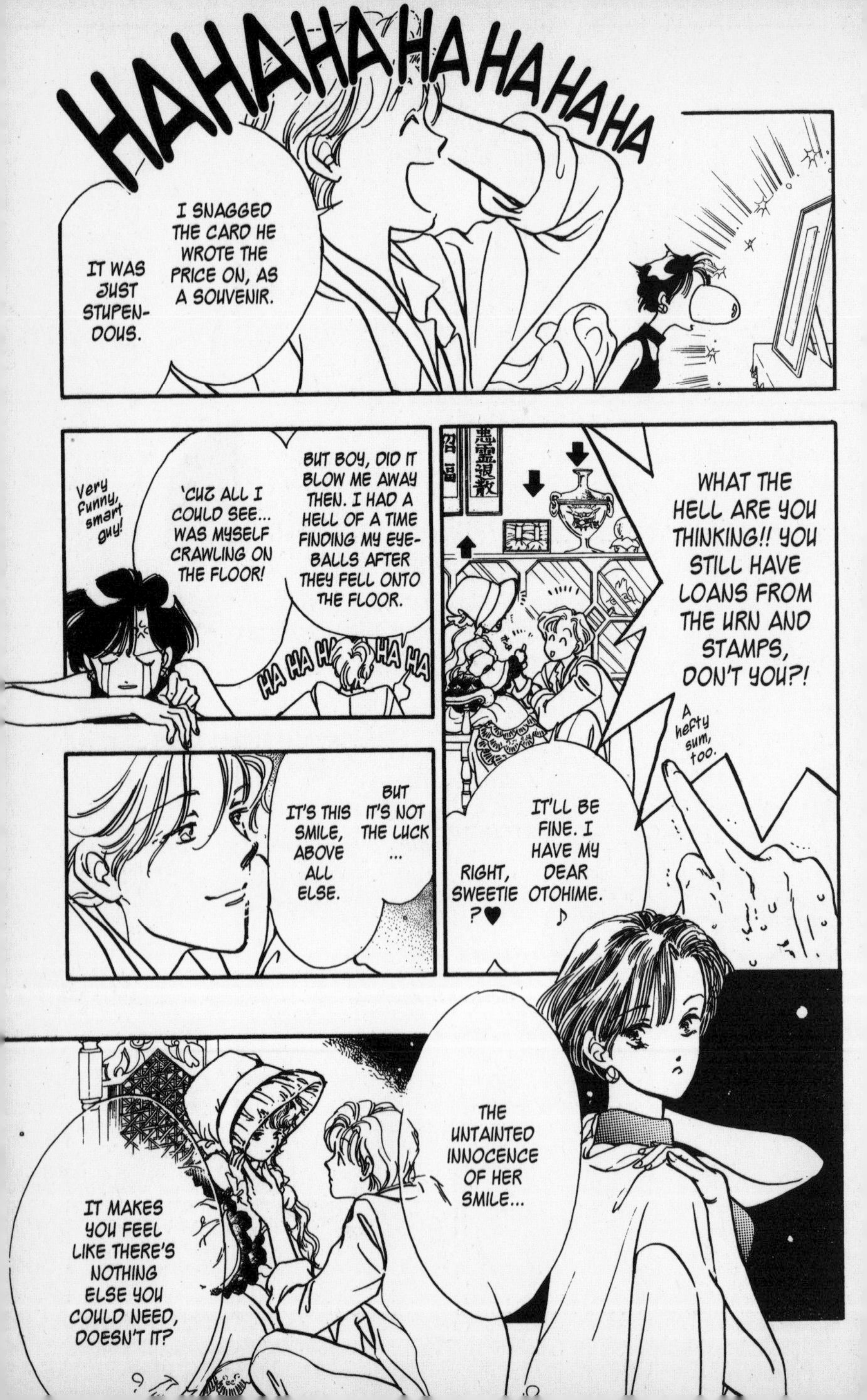
HAHAHAHAHAHAHAHAHA
I SNAGGED THE CARD HE WROTE THE PRICE ON, AS A SOUVENIR.
IT WAS JUST STUPENDOUS.
WHAT THE HELL ARE YOU THINKING!! YOU STILL HAVE LOANS FROM THE URN AND STAMPS, DON'T YOU?!
A hefty sum, too.
IT'LL BE FINE. I HAVE MY DEAR OTOHIME. ♪
RIGHT, SWEETIE?♥
BUT BOY, DID IT BLOW ME AWAY THEN. I HAD A HELL OF A TIME FINDING MY EYE-BALLS AFTER THEY FELL ONTO THE FLOOR.
'CUZ ALL I COULD SEE... WAS MYSELF CRAWLING ON THE FLOOR!
HA HA HA HA HA
Very funny, smart guy!
BUT IT'S NOT THE LUCK ...
IT'S THIS SMILE, ABOVE ALL ELSE.
THE UNTAINTED INNOCENCE OF HER SMILE...
IT MAKES YOU FEEL LIKE THERE'S NOTHING ELSE YOU COULD NEED, DOESN'T IT?

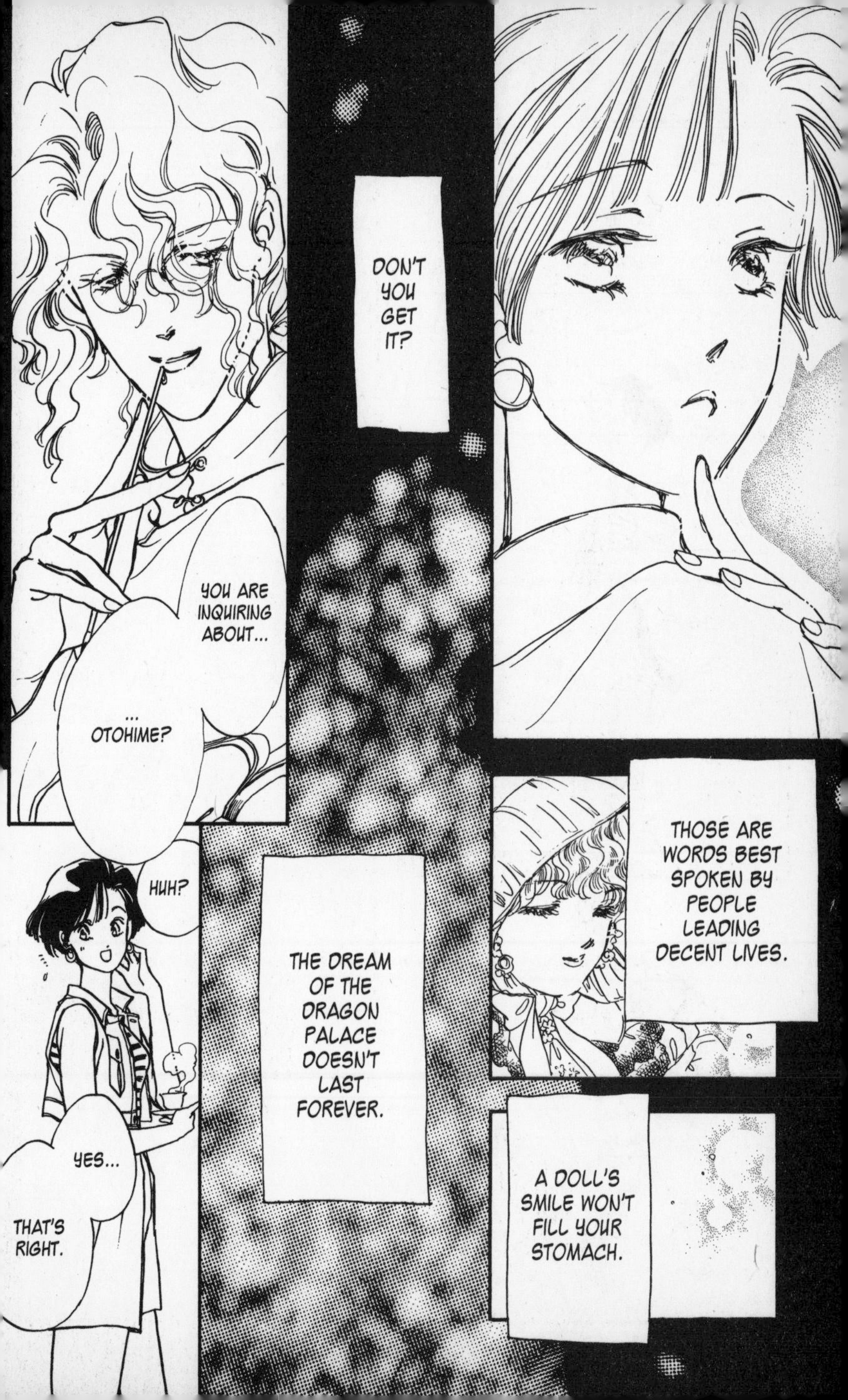
DON'T YOU GET IT?
YOU ARE INQUIRING ABOUT...
... OTOHIME?
THOSE ARE WORDS BEST SPOKEN BY PEOPLE LEADING DECENT LIVES.
A DOLL'S SMILE WON'T FILL YOUR STOMACH.
THE DREAM OF THE DRAGON PALACE DOESN'T LAST FOREVER.
HUH?
YES...
THAT'S RIGHT.

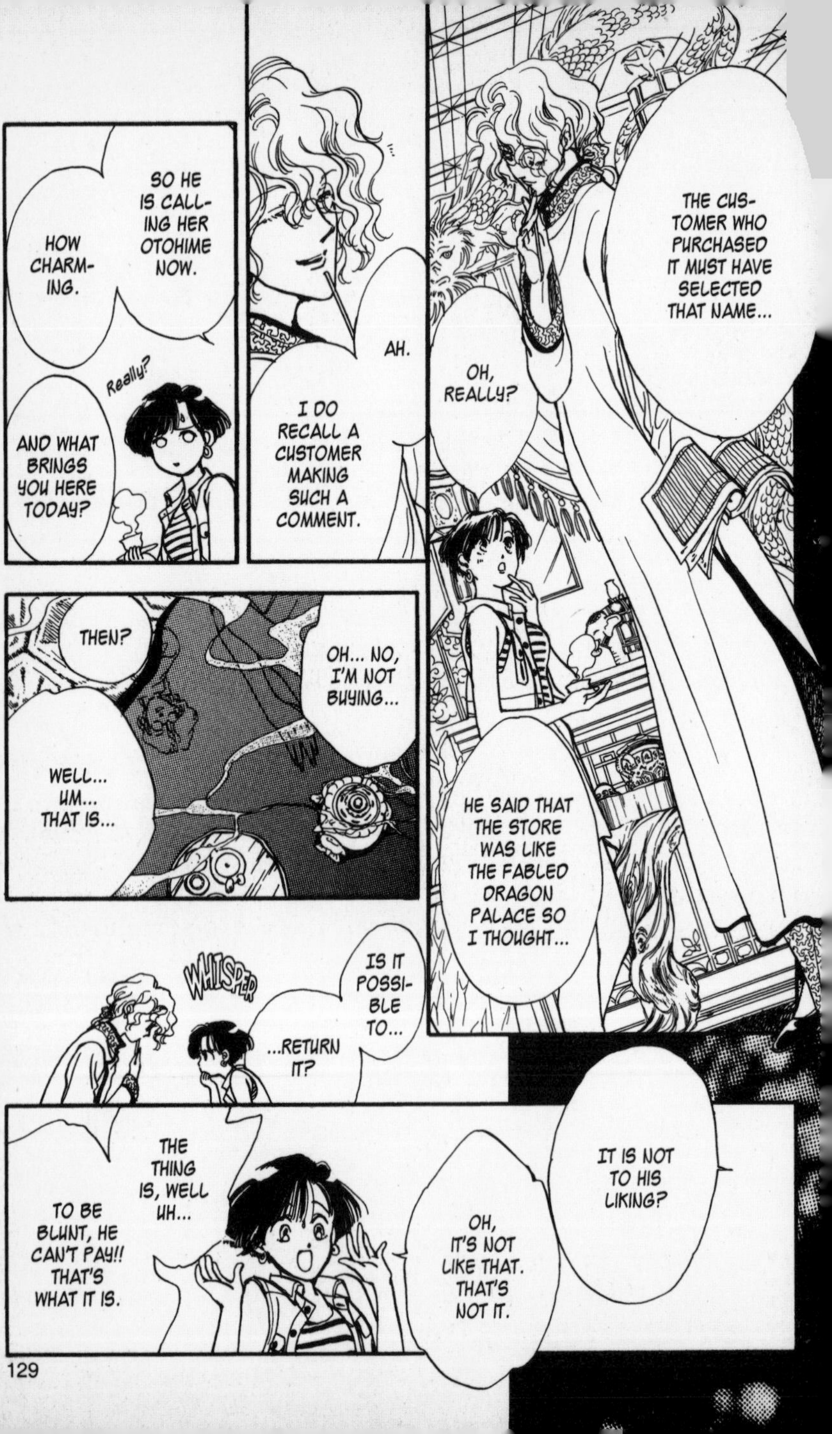
THE CUSTOMER WHO PURCHASED IT MUST HAVE SELECTED THAT NAME...
OH, REALLY?
HE SAID THAT THE STORE WAS LIKE THE FABLED DRAGON PALACE SO I THOUGHT...
AH.
I DO RECALL A CUSTOMER MAKING SUCH A COMMENT.
SO HE IS CALLING HER OTOHIME NOW.
HOW CHARMING.
Really?
AND WHAT BRINGS YOU HERE TODAY?
OH... NO, I'M NOT BUYING...
THEN?
WELL... UM... THAT IS...
IS IT POSSIBLE TO...
WHISPER
...RETURN IT?
IT IS NOT TO HIS LIKING?
OH, IT'S NOT LIKE THAT. THAT'S NOT IT.
THE THING IS, WELL UH...
TO BE BLUNT, HE CAN'T PAY!! THAT'S WHAT IT IS.

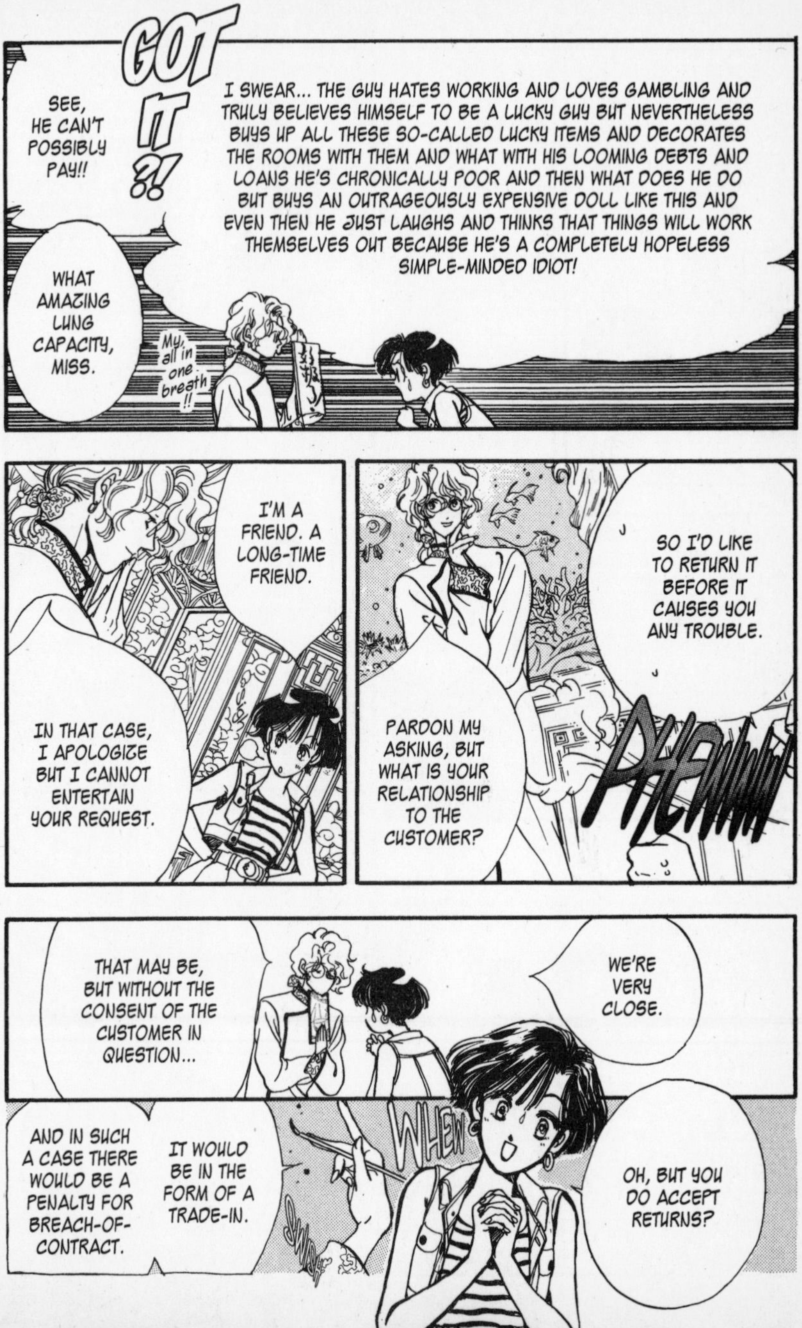
I SWEAR... THE GUY HATES WORKING AND LOVES GAMBLING AND TRULY BELIEVES HIMSELF TO BE A LUCKY GUY BUT NEVERTHELESS BUYS UP ALL THESE SO-CALLED LUCKY ITEMS AND DECORATES THE ROOMS WITH THEM AND WHAT WITH HIS LOOMING DEBTS AND LOANS HE'S CHRONICALLY POOR AND THEN WHAT DOES HE DO BUT BUYS AN OUTRAGEOUSLY EXPENSIVE DOLL LIKE THIS AND EVEN THEN HE JUST LAUGHS AND THINKS THAT THINGS WILL WORK THEMSELVES OUT BECAUSE HE'S A COMPLETELY HOPELESS SIMPLE-MINDED IDIOT!
GOT IT ?!
SEE, HE CAN'T POSSIBLY PAY!!
My, all in one breath!!
WHAT AMAZING LUNG CAPACITY, MISS.
SO I'D LIKE TO RETURN IT BEFORE IT CAUSES YOU ANY TROUBLE.
PARDON MY ASKING, BUT WHAT IS YOUR RELATIONSHIP TO THE CUSTOMER?
I'M A FRIEND. A LONG-TIME FRIEND.
IN THAT CASE, I APOLOGIZE BUT I CANNOT ENTERTAIN YOUR REQUEST.
WE'RE VERY CLOSE.
THAT MAY BE, BUT WITHOUT THE CONSENT OF THE CUSTOMER IN QUESTION...
OH, BUT YOU DO ACCEPT RETURNS?
WHEW
IT WOULD BE IN THE FORM OF A TRADE-IN.
AND IN SUCH A CASE THERE WOULD BE A PENALTY FOR BREACH-OF-CONTRACT.
SWISH

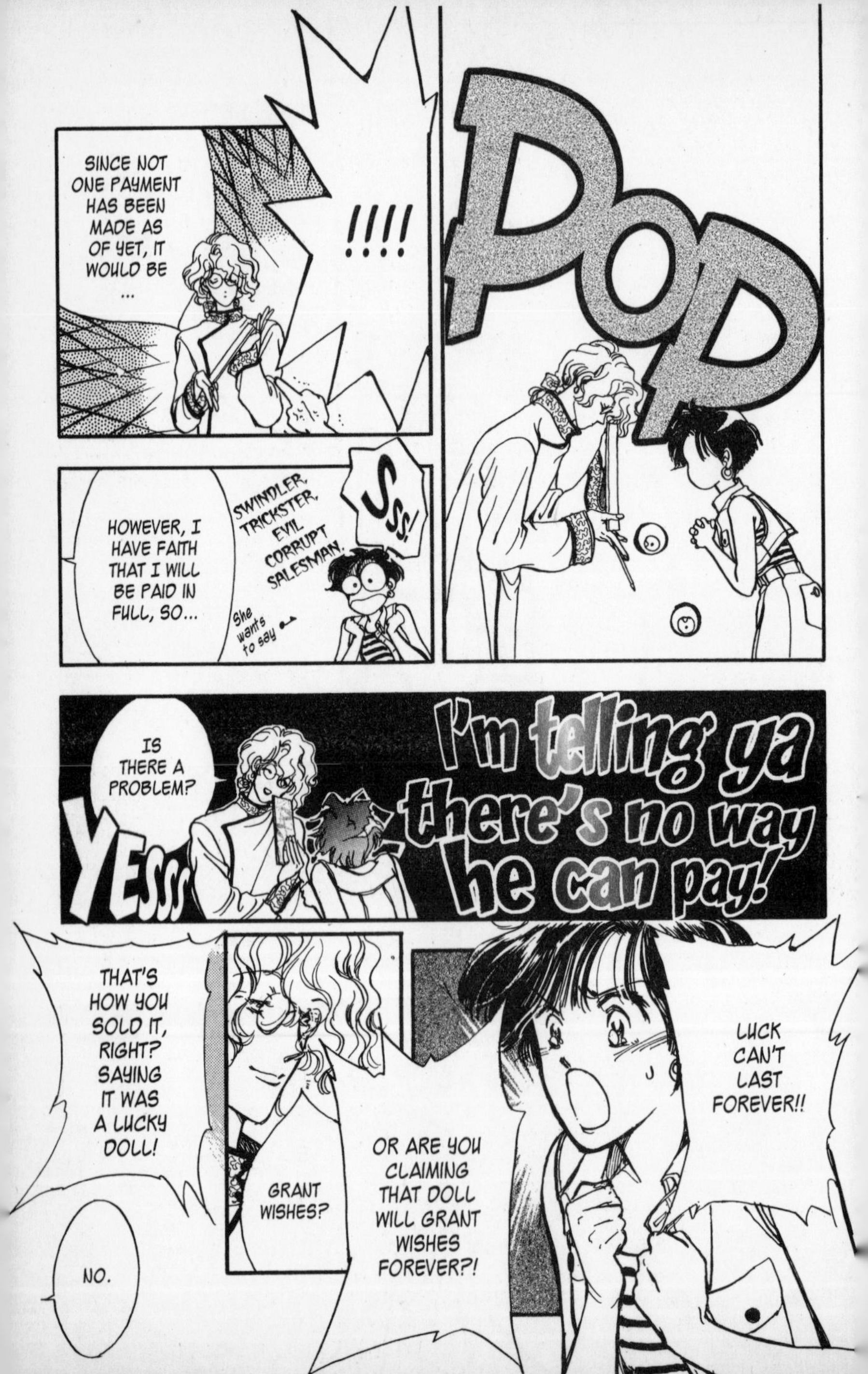
POP
SINCE NOT ONE PAYMENT HAS BEEN MADE AS OF YET, IT WOULD BE ...
!!!!
Sss!
SWINDLER, TRICKSTER, EVIL CORRUPT SALESMAN.
She wants to say
HOWEVER, I HAVE FAITH THAT I WILL BE PAID IN FULL, SO...
I'm telling ya there's no way he can pay!
IS THERE A PROBLEM?
YESsss
LUCK CAN'T LAST FOREVER!!
OR ARE YOU CLAIMING THAT DOLL WILL GRANT WISHES FOREVER?!
THAT'S HOW YOU SOLD IT, RIGHT? SAYING IT WAS A LUCKY DOLL!
GRANT WISHES?
NO.

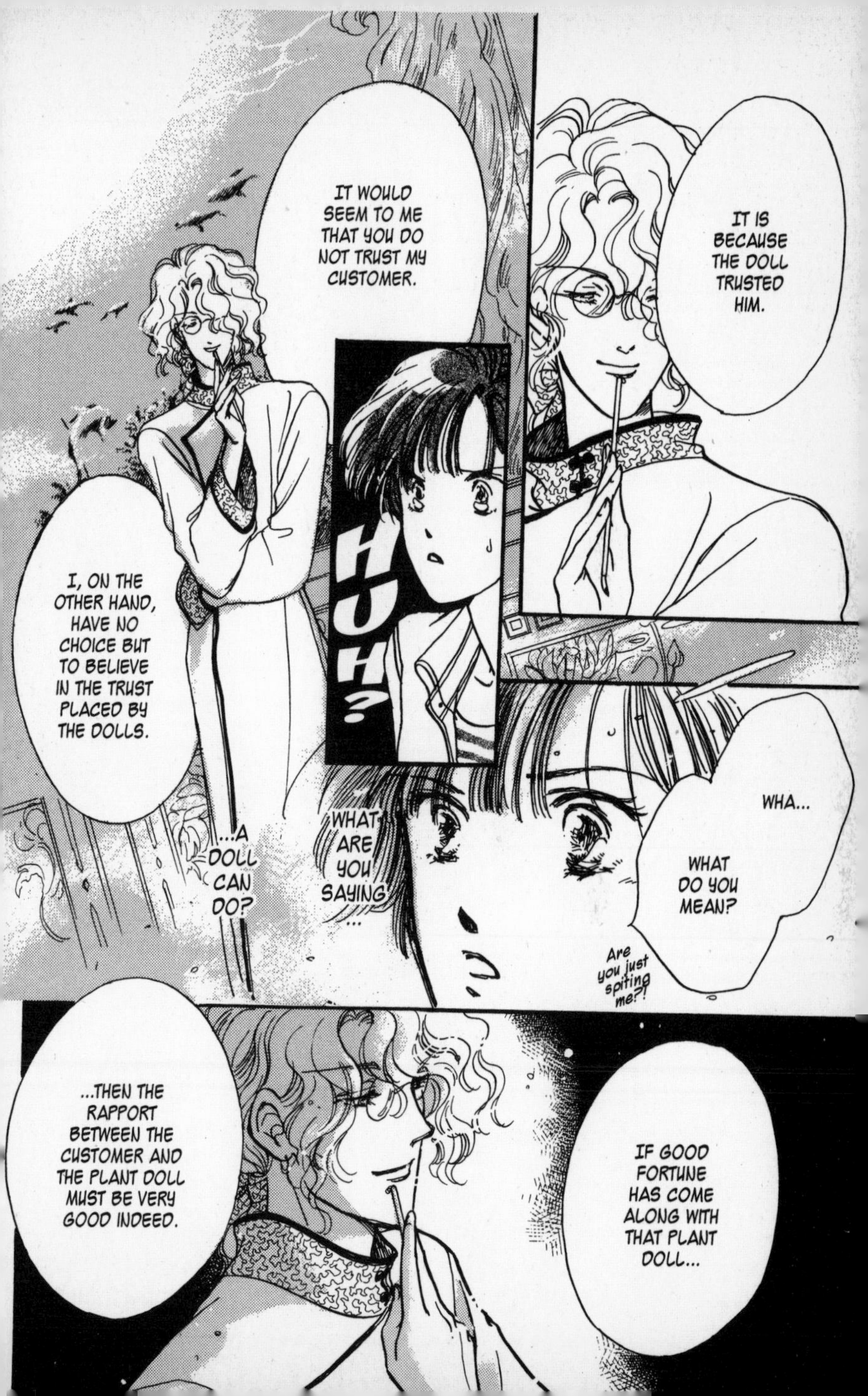
IT IS BECAUSE THE DOLL TRUSTED HIM.
IT WOULD SEEM TO ME THAT YOU DO NOT TRUST MY CUSTOMER.
HUH?
WHA...
WHAT DO YOU MEAN?
Are you just spiting me?!
WHAT ARE YOU SAYING...
...A DOLL CAN DO?
I, ON THE OTHER HAND, HAVE NO CHOICE BUT TO BELIEVE IN THE TRUST PLACED BY THE DOLLS.
IF GOOD FORTUNE HAS COME ALONG WITH THAT PLANT DOLL...
...THEN THE RAPPORT BETWEEN THE CUSTOMER AND THE PLANT DOLL MUST BE VERY GOOD INDEED.

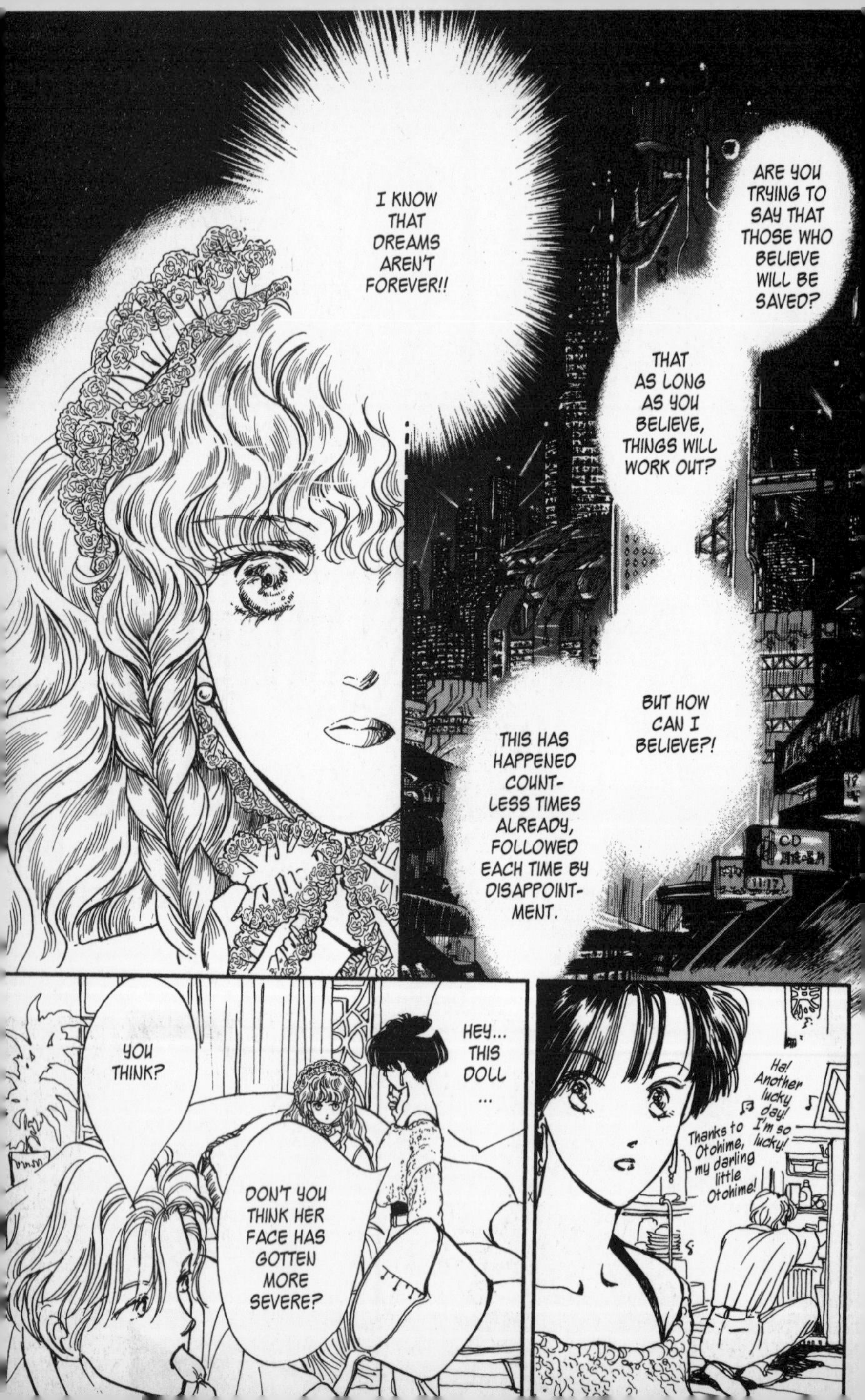
ARE YOU TRYING TO SAY THAT THOSE WHO BELIEVE WILL BE SAVED?
THAT AS LONG AS YOU BELIEVE, THINGS WILL WORK OUT?
BUT HOW CAN I BELIEVE?!
THIS HAS HAPPENED COUNT-LESS TIMES ALREADY, FOLLOWED EACH TIME BY DISAPPOINT-MENT.
I KNOW THAT DREAMS AREN'T FOREVER!!
Ha! Another lucky day! I'm so lucky!
Thanks to Otohime, my darling little Otohime!
HEY... THIS DOLL ...
DON'T YOU THINK HER FACE HAS GOTTEN MORE SEVERE?
YOU THINK?

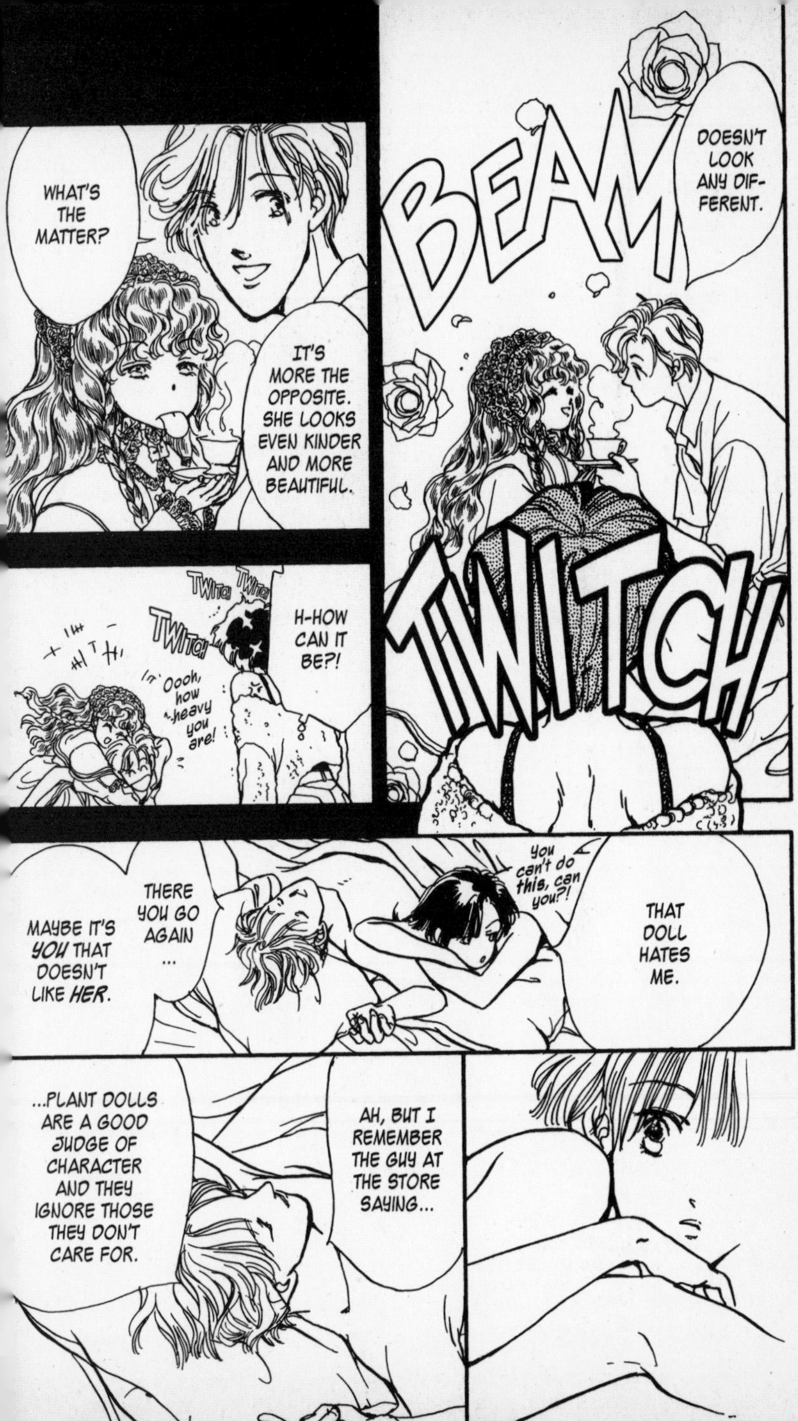
DOESN'T LOOK ANY DIF-FERENT.
BEAM
TWITCH
WHAT'S THE MATTER?
IT'S MORE THE OPPOSITE. SHE LOOKS EVEN KINDER AND MORE BEAUTIFUL.
H-HOW CAN IT BE?!
TWITCH
TWITCH
TWITCH
Oooh, how heavy you are!
THAT DOLL HATES ME.
You can't do this, can you?!
THERE YOU GO AGAIN ...
MAYBE IT'S *YOU* THAT DOESN'T LIKE *HER*.
AH, BUT I REMEMBER THE GUY AT THE STORE SAYING...
...PLANT DOLLS ARE A GOOD JUDGE OF CHARACTER AND THEY IGNORE THOSE THEY DON'T CARE FOR.

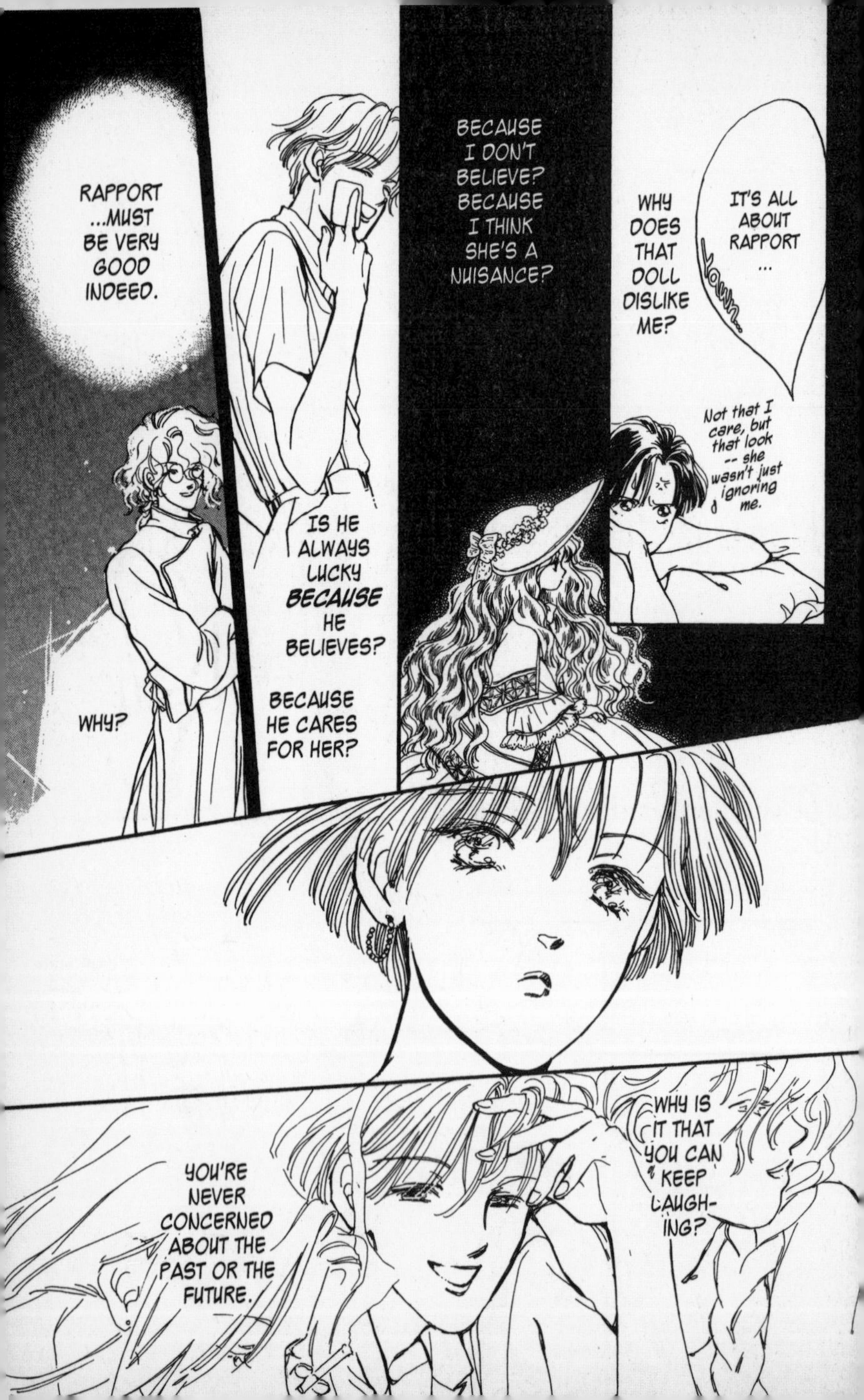
IT'S ALL ABOUT RAPPORT ...
Yawn...
WHY DOES THAT DOLL DISLIKE ME?
Not that I care, but that look -- she wasn't just ignoring me.
BECAUSE I DON'T BELIEVE? BECAUSE I THINK SHE'S A NUISANCE?
IS HE ALWAYS LUCKY *BECAUSE* HE BELIEVES?
BECAUSE HE CARES FOR HER?
RAPPORT ...MUST BE VERY GOOD INDEED.
WHY?
WHY IS IT THAT YOU CAN KEEP LAUGHING?
YOU'RE NEVER CONCERNED ABOUT THE PAST OR THE FUTURE.

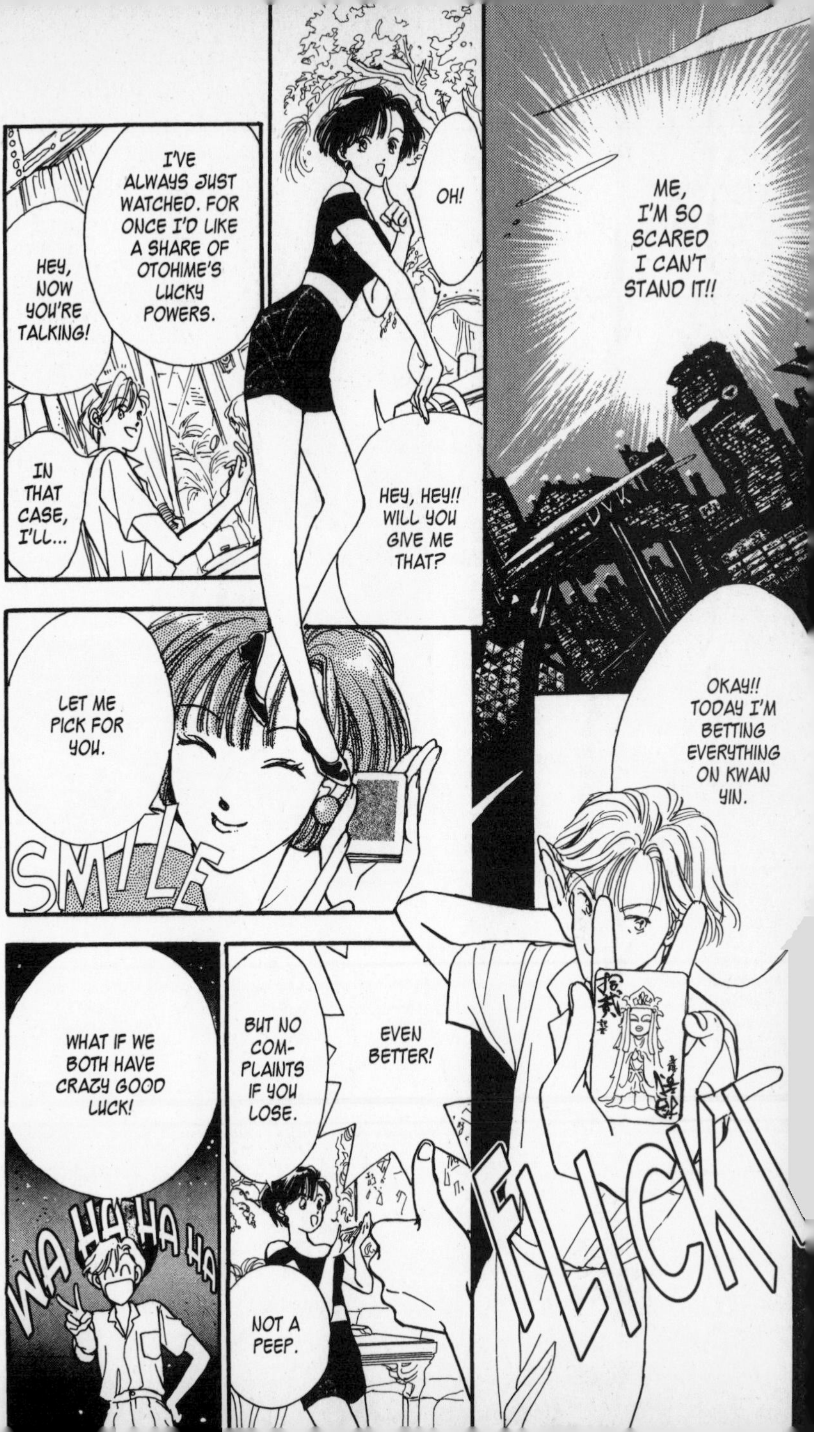
ME, I'M SO SCARED I CAN'T STAND IT!!
OH!
HEY, HEY!! WILL YOU GIVE ME THAT?
I'VE ALWAYS JUST WATCHED. FOR ONCE I'D LIKE A SHARE OF OTOHIME'S LUCKY POWERS.
HEY, NOW YOU'RE TALKING!
IN THAT CASE, I'LL...
OKAY!! TODAY I'M BETTING EVERYTHING ON KWAN YIN.
FLICK
LET ME PICK FOR YOU.
SMILE
EVEN BETTER!
BUT NO COMPLAINTS IF YOU LOSE.
NOT A PEEP.
WHAT IF WE BOTH HAVE CRAZY GOOD LUCK!
WA HA HA HA HA

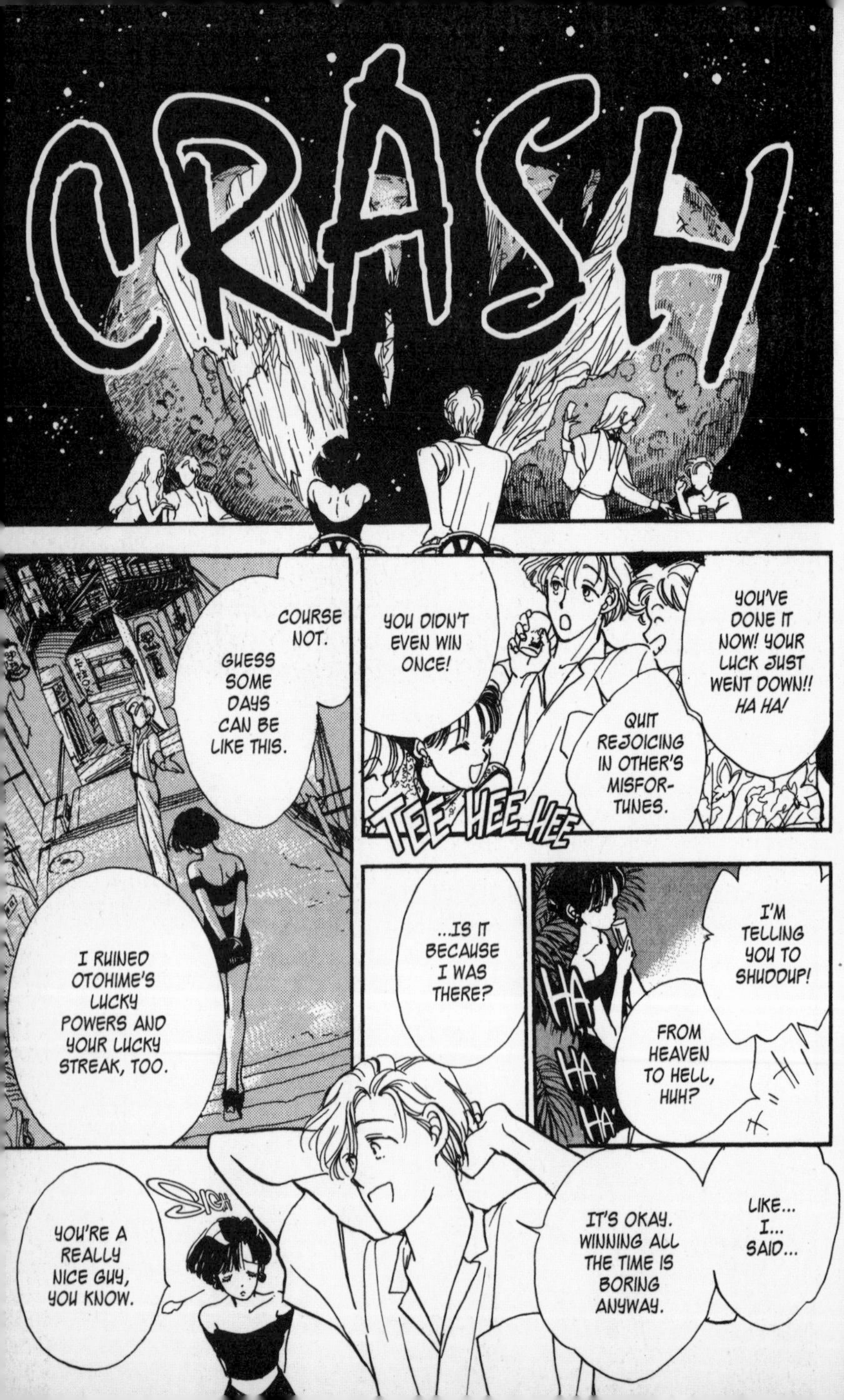
CRASH
YOU'VE DONE IT NOW! YOUR LUCK JUST WENT DOWN!! HA HA!
YOU DIDN'T EVEN WIN ONCE!
QUIT REJOICING IN OTHER'S MISFOR-TUNES.
TEE HEE HEE
I'M TELLING YOU TO SHUDDUP!
FROM HEAVEN TO HELL, HUH?
HA HA HA
...IS IT BECAUSE I WAS THERE?
COURSE NOT.
GUESS SOME DAYS CAN BE LIKE THIS.
I RUINED OTOHIME'S LUCKY POWERS AND YOUR LUCKY STREAK, TOO.
LIKE... I... SAID...
IT'S OKAY. WINNING ALL THE TIME IS BORING ANYWAY.
SIGH
YOU'RE A REALLY NICE GUY, YOU KNOW.

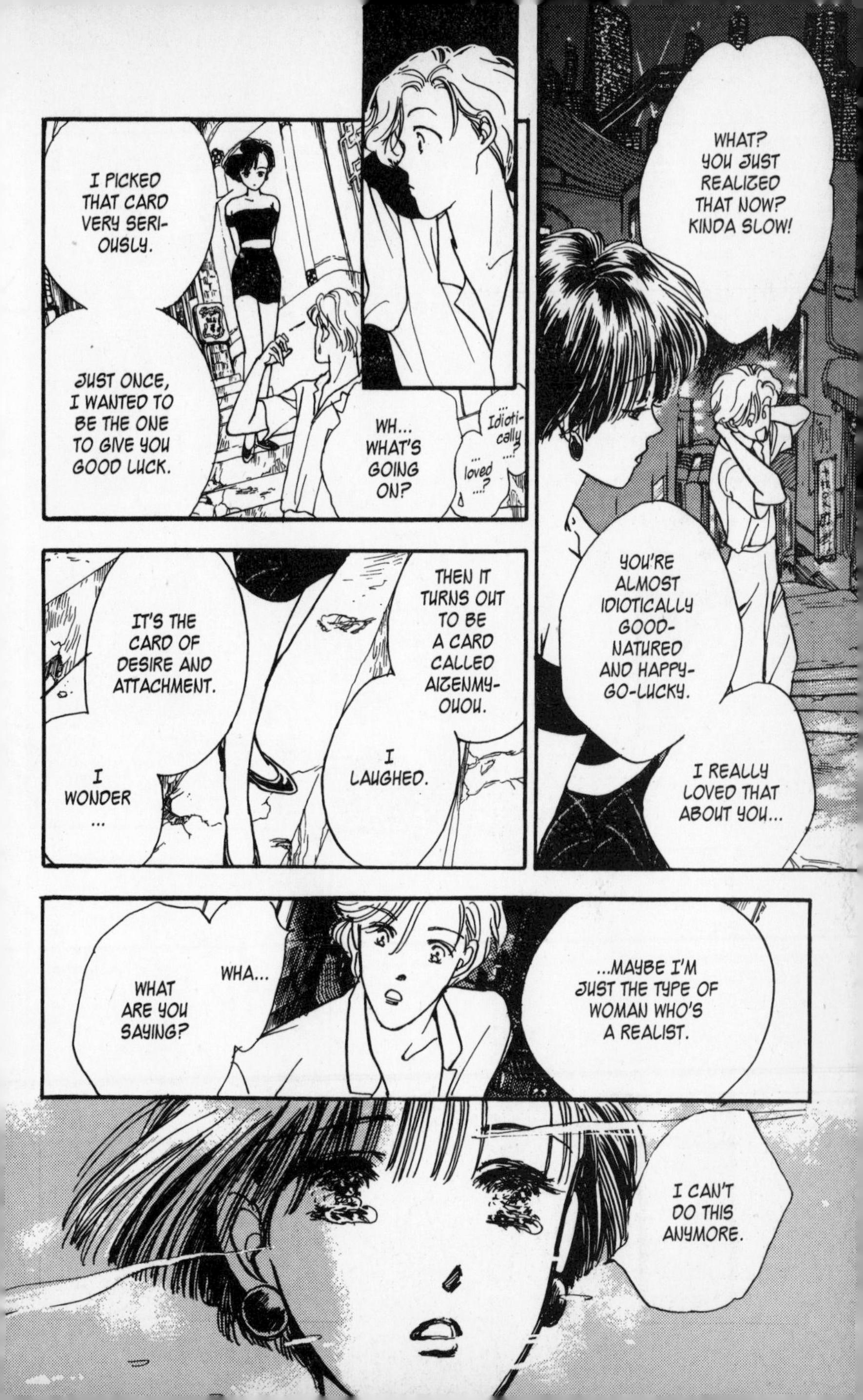
WHAT? YOU JUST REALIZED THAT NOW? KINDA SLOW!
YOU'RE ALMOST IDIOTICALLY GOOD-NATURED AND HAPPY-GO-LUCKY.
I REALLY LOVED THAT ABOUT YOU...
...Idioti-cally...?
...loved...?
WH... WHAT'S GOING ON?
I PICKED THAT CARD VERY SERI-OUSLY.
JUST ONCE, I WANTED TO BE THE ONE TO GIVE YOU GOOD LUCK.
THEN IT TURNS OUT TO BE A CARD CALLED AIZENMYOUOU.
I LAUGHED.
IT'S THE CARD OF DESIRE AND ATTACHMENT.
I WONDER...
...MAYBE I'M JUST THE TYPE OF WOMAN WHO'S A REALIST.
WHA...
WHAT ARE YOU SAYING?
I CAN'T DO THIS ANYMORE.

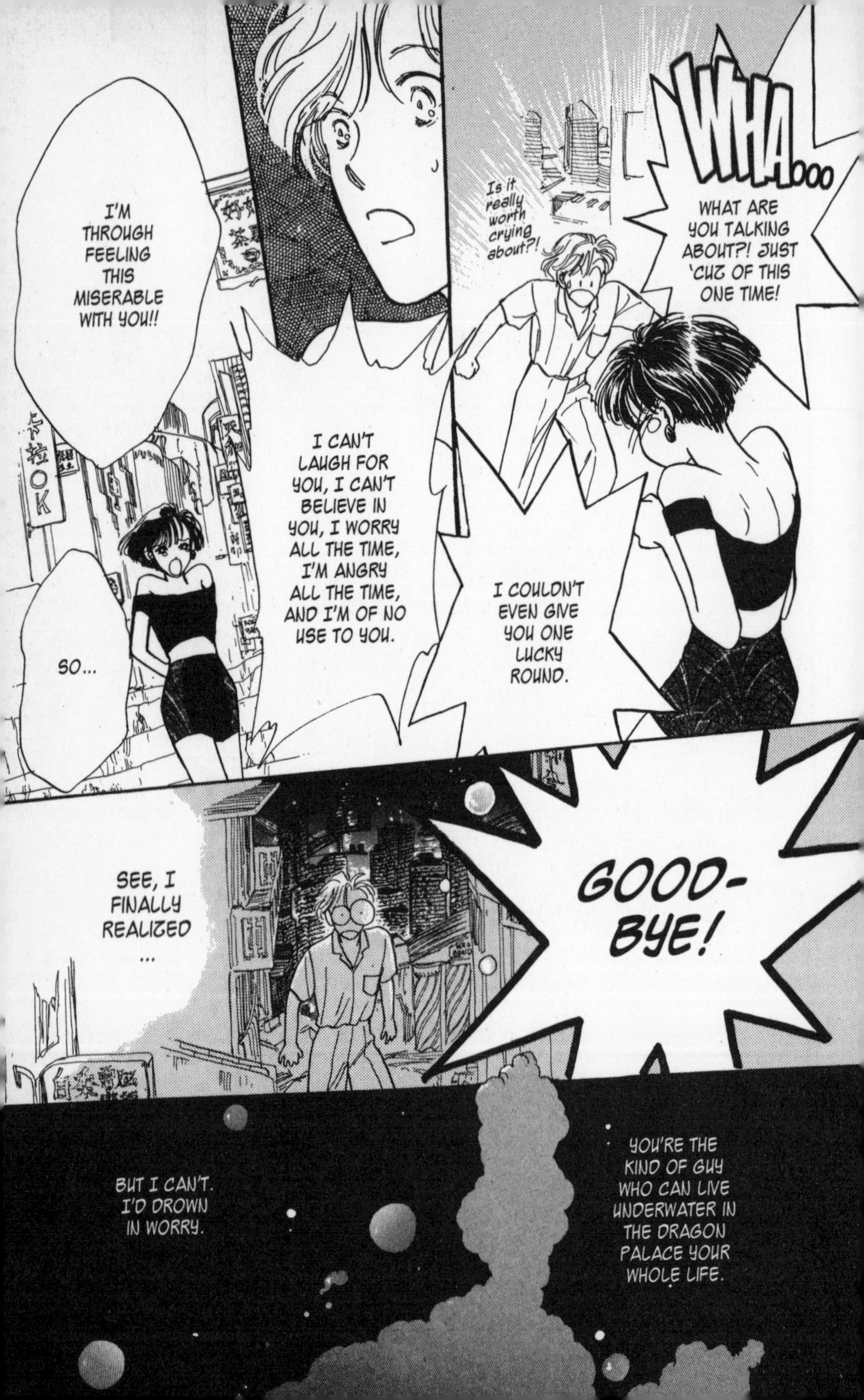
WHA...ooo
Is it really worth crying about?!
WHAT ARE YOU TALKING ABOUT?! JUST 'CUZ OF THIS ONE TIME!
I COULDN'T EVEN GIVE YOU ONE LUCKY ROUND.
I CAN'T LAUGH FOR YOU, I CAN'T BELIEVE IN YOU, I WORRY ALL THE TIME, I'M ANGRY ALL THE TIME, AND I'M OF NO USE TO YOU.
I'M THROUGH FEELING THIS MISERABLE WITH YOU!!
SO...
GOOD-BYE!
SEE, I FINALLY REALIZED ...
YOU'RE THE KIND OF GUY WHO CAN LIVE UNDERWATER IN THE DRAGON PALACE YOUR WHOLE LIFE.
BUT I CAN'T. I'D DROWN IN WORRY.

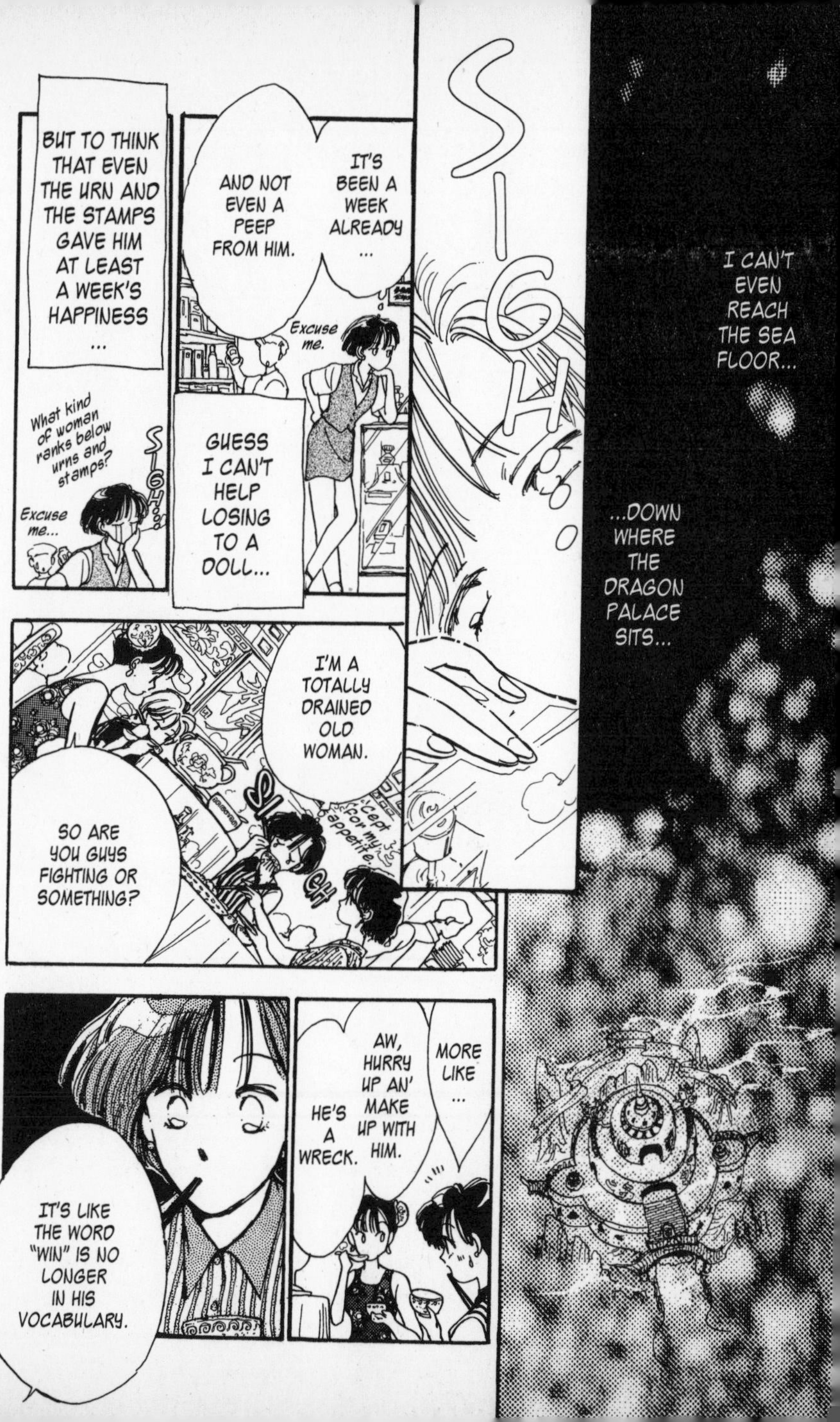
I CAN'T EVEN REACH THE SEA FLOOR...
...DOWN WHERE THE DRAGON PALACE SITS...
SIGH
IT'S BEEN A WEEK ALREADY...
AND NOT EVEN A PEEP FROM HIM.
Excuse me.
GUESS I CAN'T HELP LOSING TO A DOLL...
BUT TO THINK THAT EVEN THE URN AND THE STAMPS GAVE HIM AT LEAST A WEEK'S HAPPINESS...
What kind of woman ranks below urns and stamps?
SIGH...
Excuse me...
I'M A TOTALLY DRAINED OLD WOMAN.
SIGH
'Cept for my appetite.
SO ARE YOU GUYS FIGHTING OR SOMETHING?
MORE LIKE...
AW, HURRY UP AN' MAKE UP WITH HIM.
HE'S A WRECK.
IT'S LIKE THE WORD "WIN" IS NO LONGER IN HIS VOCABULARY.

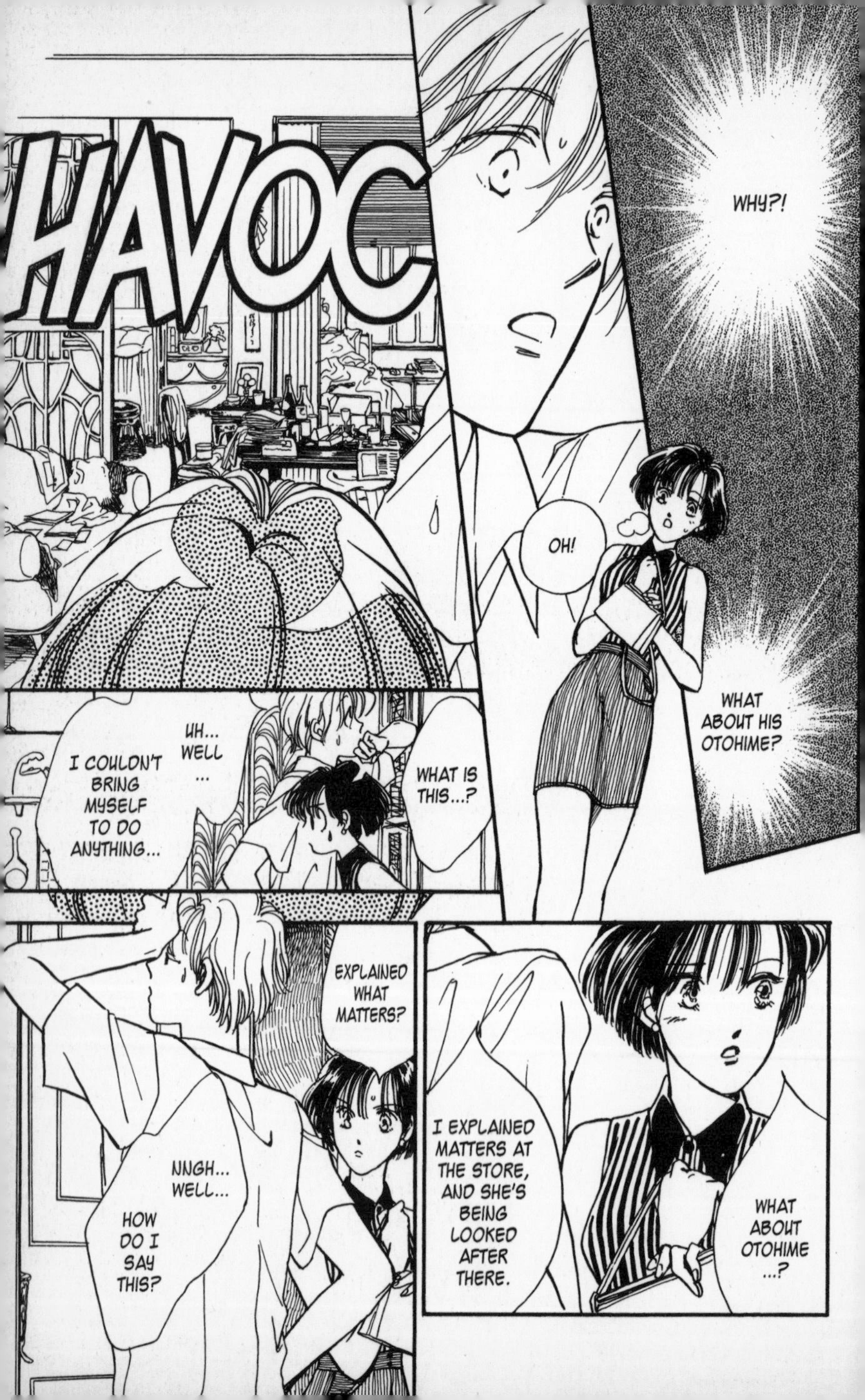
WHY?!
OH!
WHAT ABOUT HIS OTOHIME?
HAVOC
WHAT IS THIS...?
UH... WELL ...
I COULDN'T BRING MYSELF TO DO ANYTHING...
WHAT ABOUT OTOHIME ...?
I EXPLAINED MATTERS AT THE STORE, AND SHE'S BEING LOOKED AFTER THERE.
EXPLAINED WHAT MATTERS?
NNGH... WELL...
HOW DO I SAY THIS?

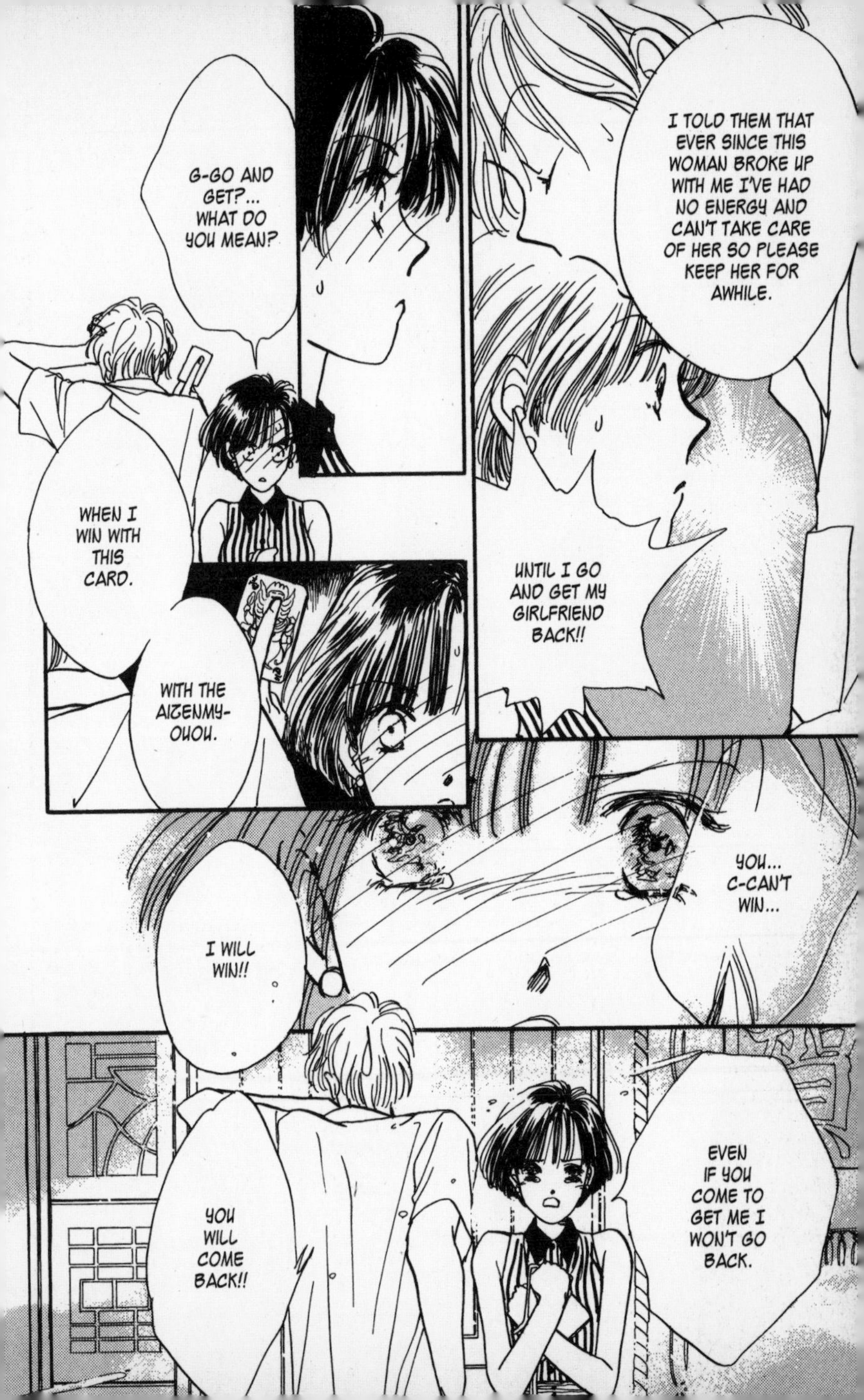
I TOLD THEM THAT EVER SINCE THIS WOMAN BROKE UP WITH ME I'VE HAD NO ENERGY AND CAN'T TAKE CARE OF HER SO PLEASE KEEP HER FOR AWHILE.
UNTIL I GO AND GET MY GIRLFRIEND BACK!!
G-GO AND GET?... WHAT DO YOU MEAN?
WHEN I WIN WITH THIS CARD.
WITH THE AIZENMYOUOU.
YOU... C-CAN'T WIN...
I WILL WIN!!
EVEN IF YOU COME TO GET ME I WON'T GO BACK.
YOU WILL COME BACK!!

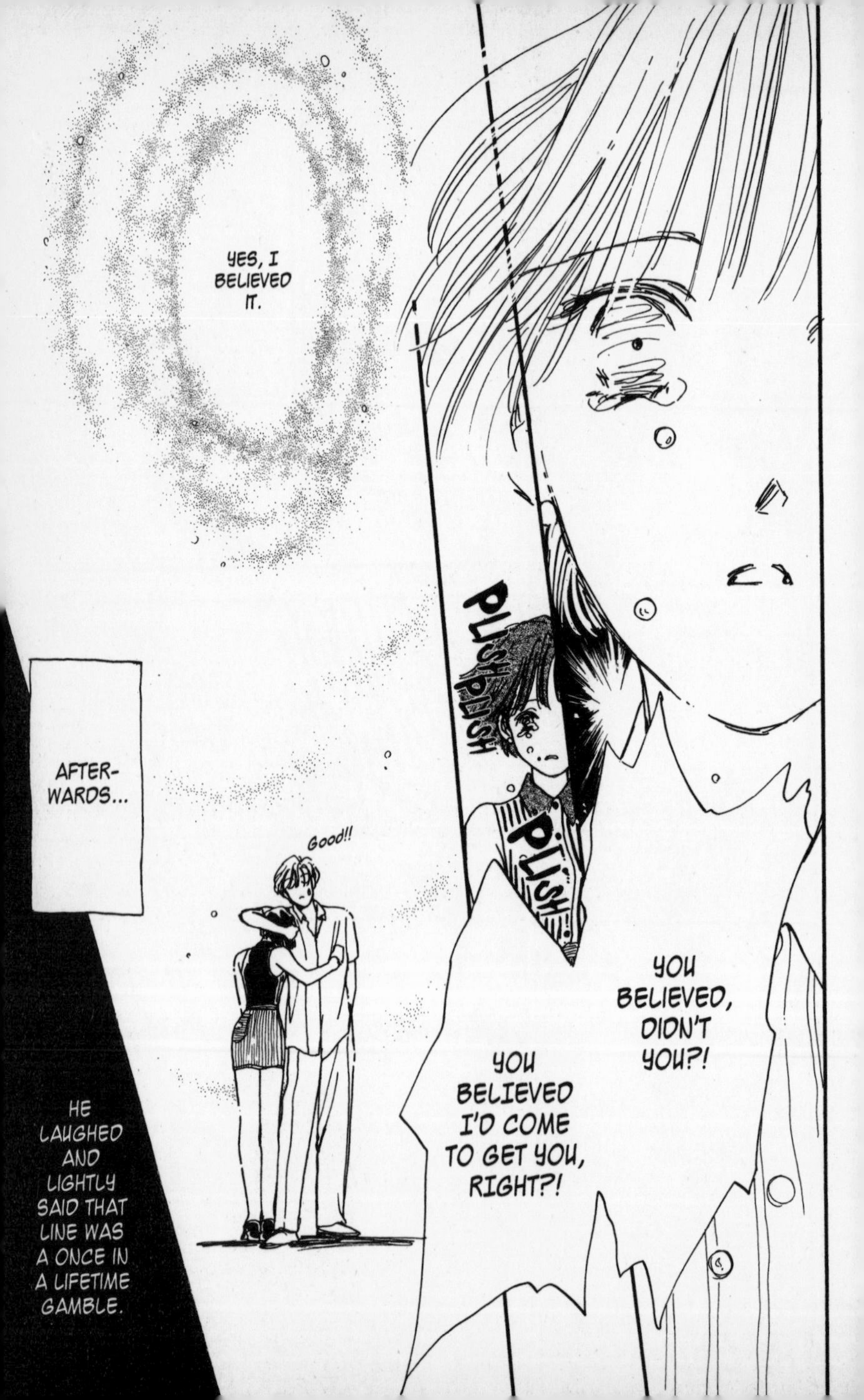
YOU BELIEVED, DIDN'T YOU?!
YOU BELIEVED I'D COME TO GET YOU, RIGHT?!
PLISH PLISH PLISH
PLISH
YES, I BELIEVED IT.
AFTER-WARDS...
Good!!
HE LAUGHED AND LIGHTLY SAID THAT LINE WAS A ONCE IN A LIFETIME GAMBLE.

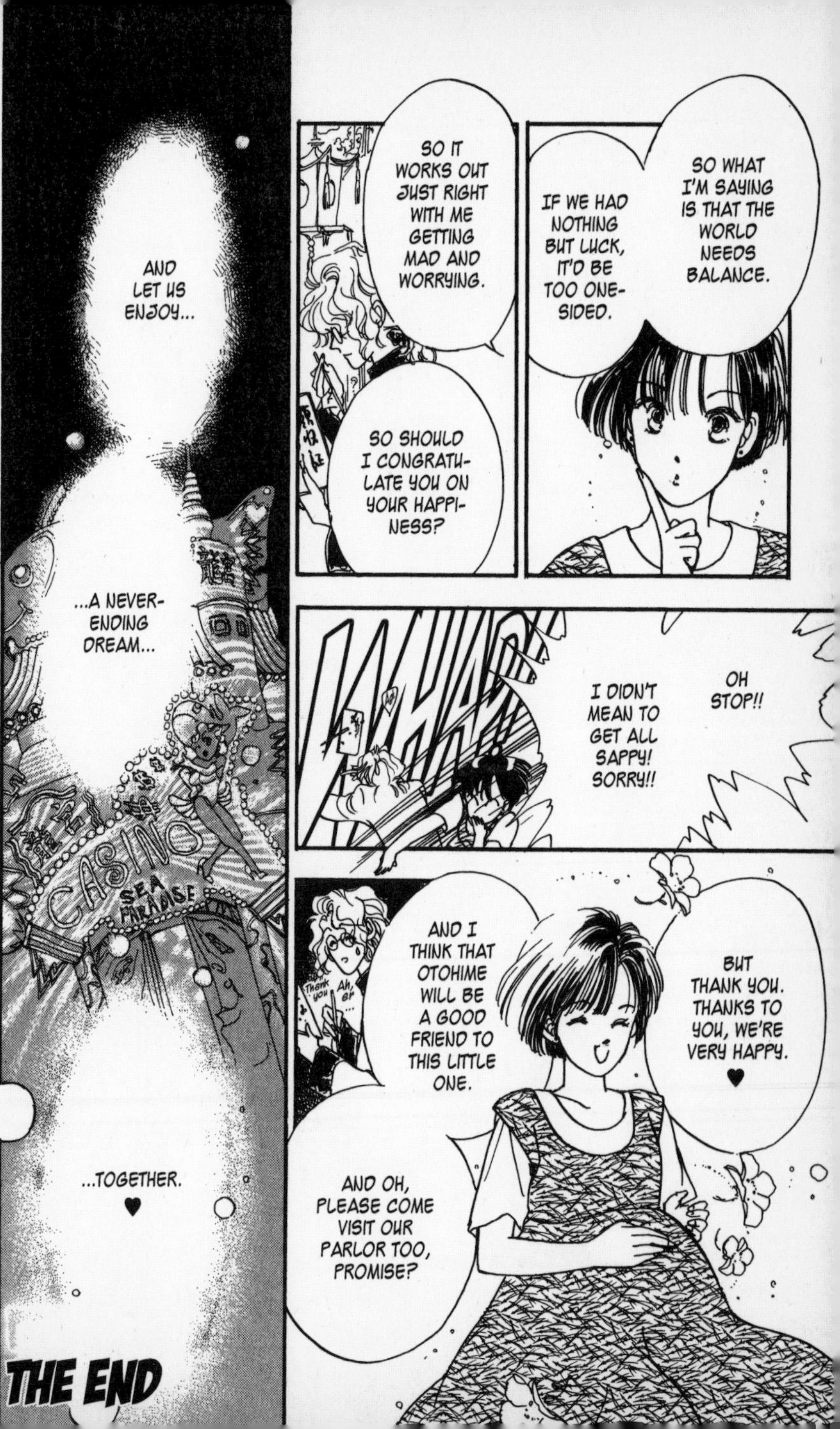
SO WHAT I'M SAYING IS THAT THE WORLD NEEDS BALANCE.
IF WE HAD NOTHING BUT LUCK, IT'D BE TOO ONE-SIDED.
SO IT WORKS OUT JUST RIGHT WITH ME GETTING MAD AND WORRYING.
SO SHOULD I CONGRATULATE YOU ON YOUR HAPPINESS?
OH STOP!!
I DIDN'T MEAN TO GET ALL SAPPY! SORRY!!
BUT THANK YOU. THANKS TO YOU, WE'RE VERY HAPPY. ♥
AND I THINK THAT OTOHIME WILL BE A GOOD FRIEND TO THIS LITTLE ONE.
Thank you
Ah, er ...
AND OH, PLEASE COME VISIT OUR PARLOR TOO, PROMISE?
AND LET US ENJOY...
...A NEVER-ENDING DREAM...
CASINO
SEA PARADISE
...TOGETHER. ♥
THE END

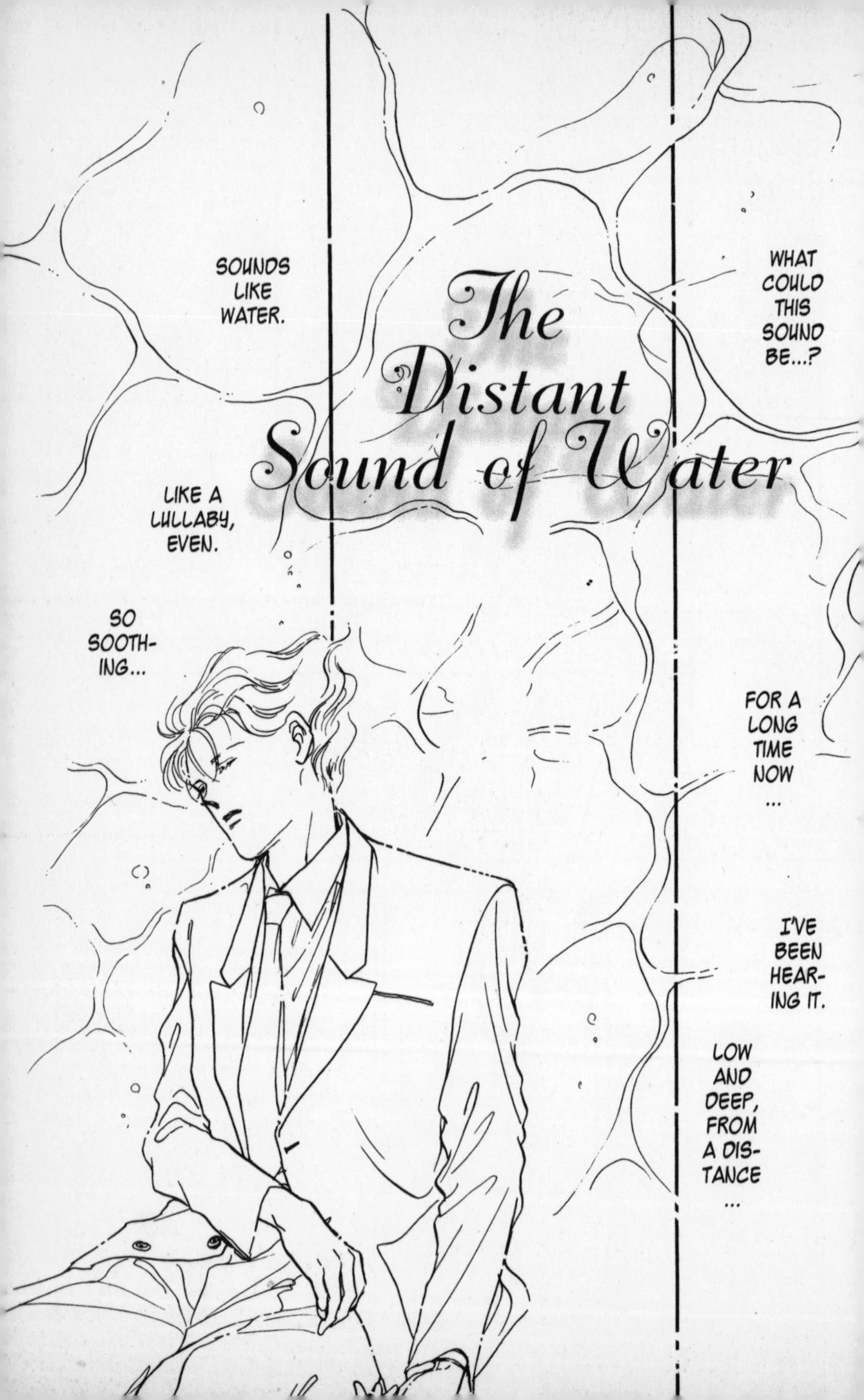
WHAT COULD THIS SOUND BE...?
FOR A LONG TIME NOW...
I'VE BEEN HEARING IT.
LOW AND DEEP, FROM A DISTANCE...
The Distant Sound of Water
SOUNDS LIKE WATER.
LIKE A LULLABY, EVEN.
SO SOOTHING...

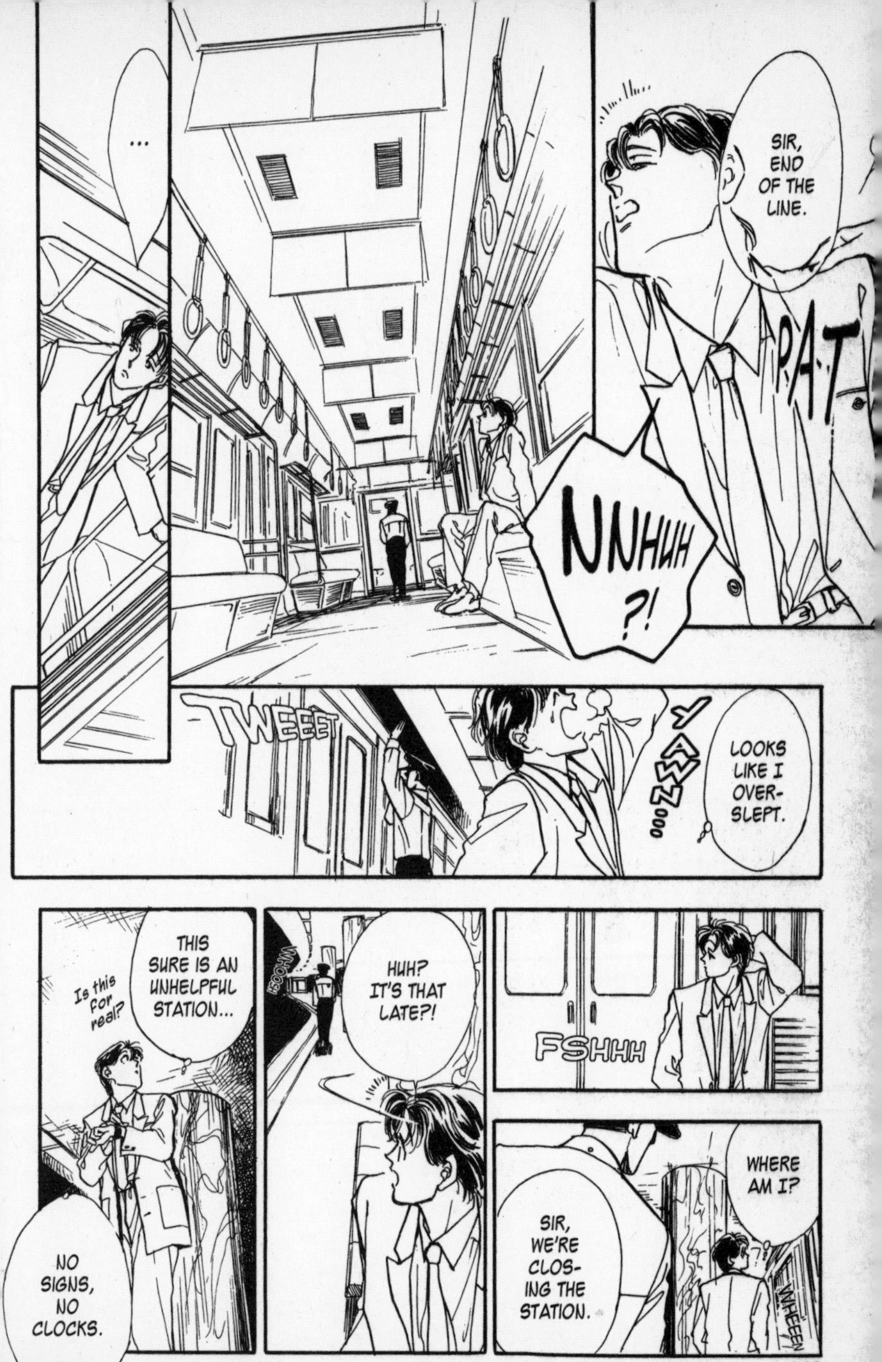
SIR, END OF THE LINE.
PAT
NNHUH ?!
...
YAWNooo
LOOKS LIKE I OVER-SLEPT.
TWEEET
FSHHH
WHERE AM I?
SIR, WE'RE CLOS-ING THE STATION.
WHEEEN
HUH? IT'S THAT LATE?!
WHOOSH
THIS SURE IS AN UNHELPFUL STATION...
Is this for real?
NO SIGNS, NO CLOCKS.

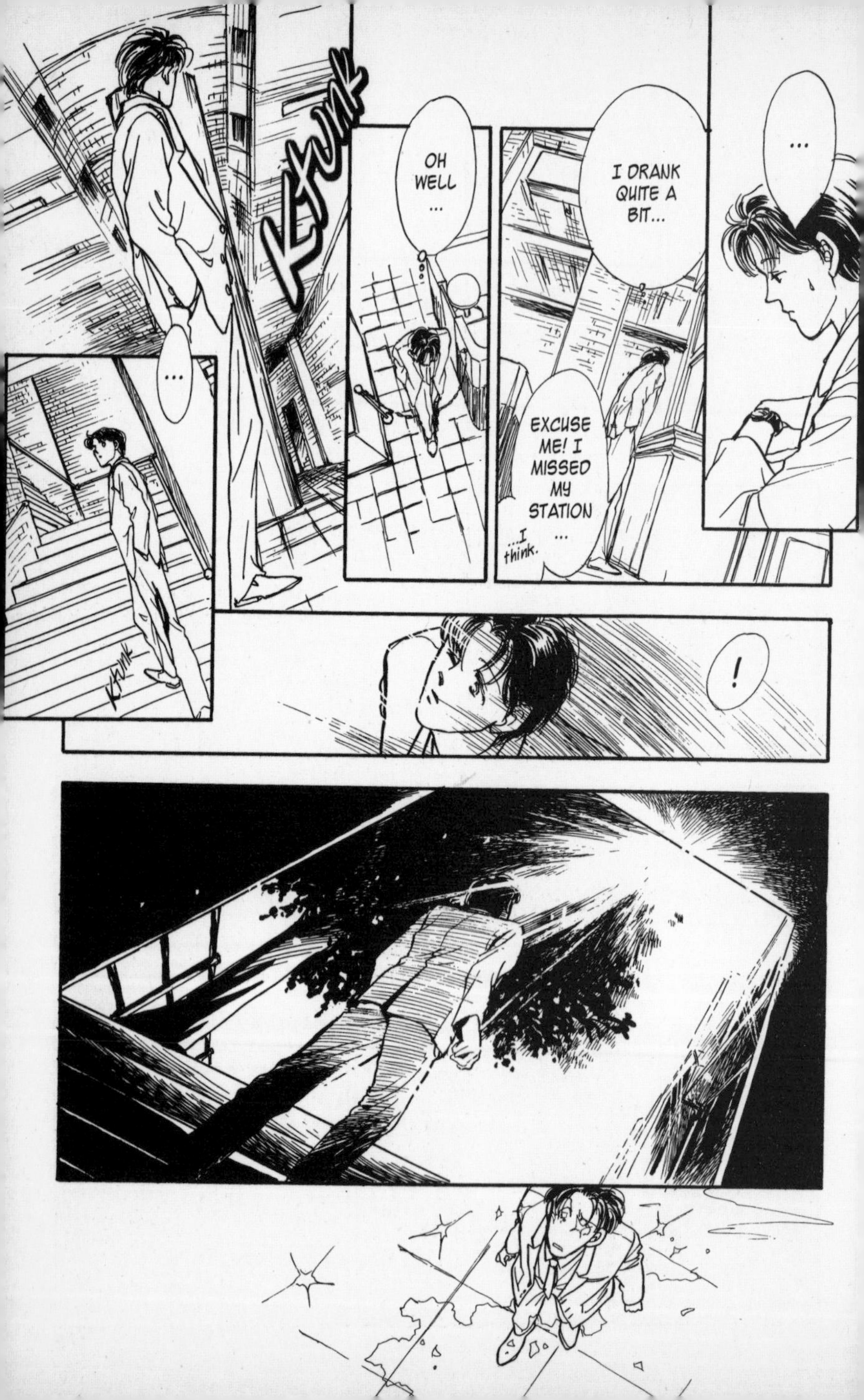
...
I DRANK QUITE A BIT...
EXCUSE ME! I MISSED MY STATION ...
...I think.
OH WELL ...
K-tunk
...
K-tunk
!

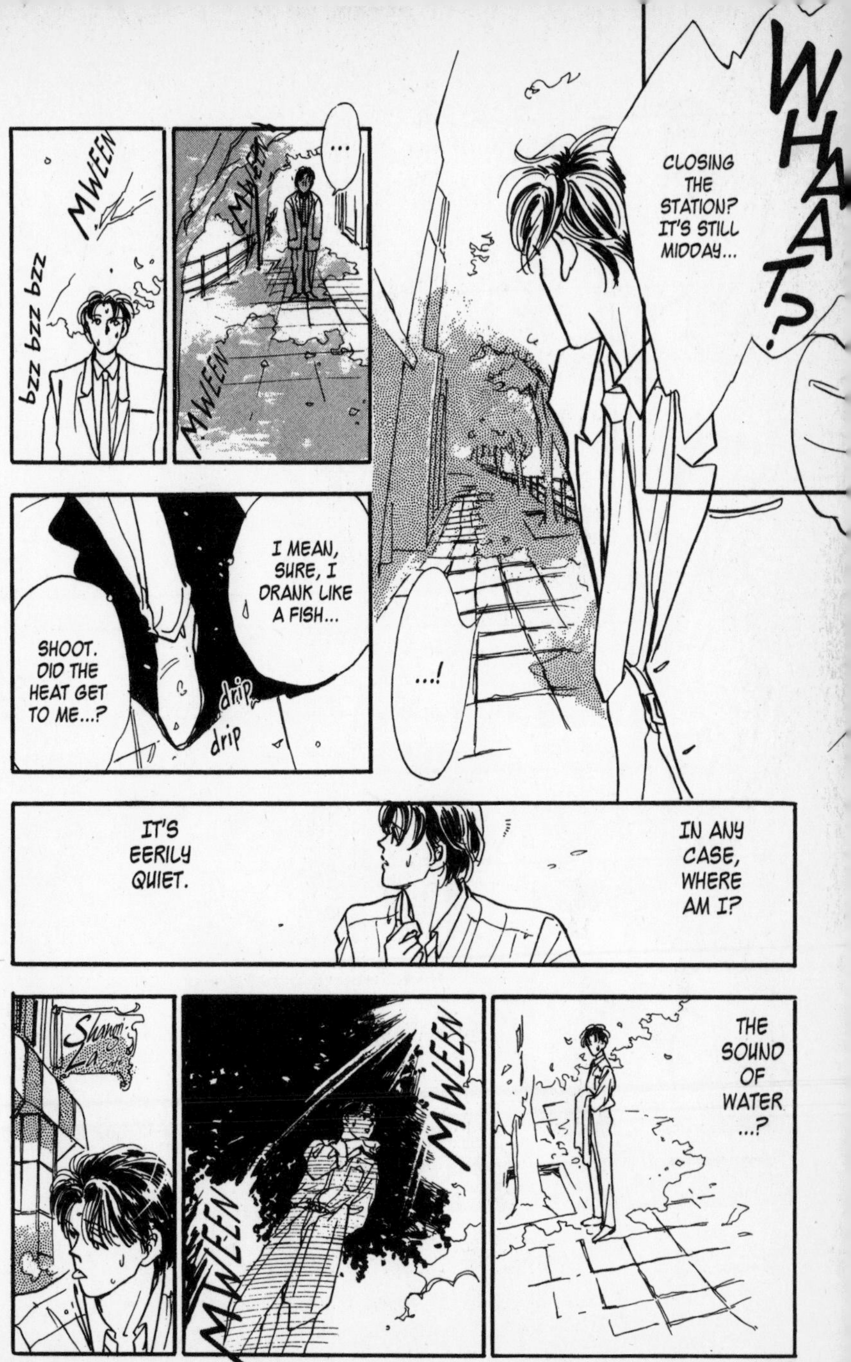
WHAT?
CLOSING THE STATION? IT'S STILL MIDDAY...
...!
...
MWEEN
MWEEN
MWEEN
bzz bzz bzz
I MEAN, SURE, I DRANK LIKE A FISH...
SHOOT. DID THE HEAT GET TO ME...?
drip
drip
IN ANY CASE, WHERE AM I?
IT'S EERILY QUIET.
THE SOUND OF WATER ...?
MWEEN
MWEEN
Shangri-La cafe

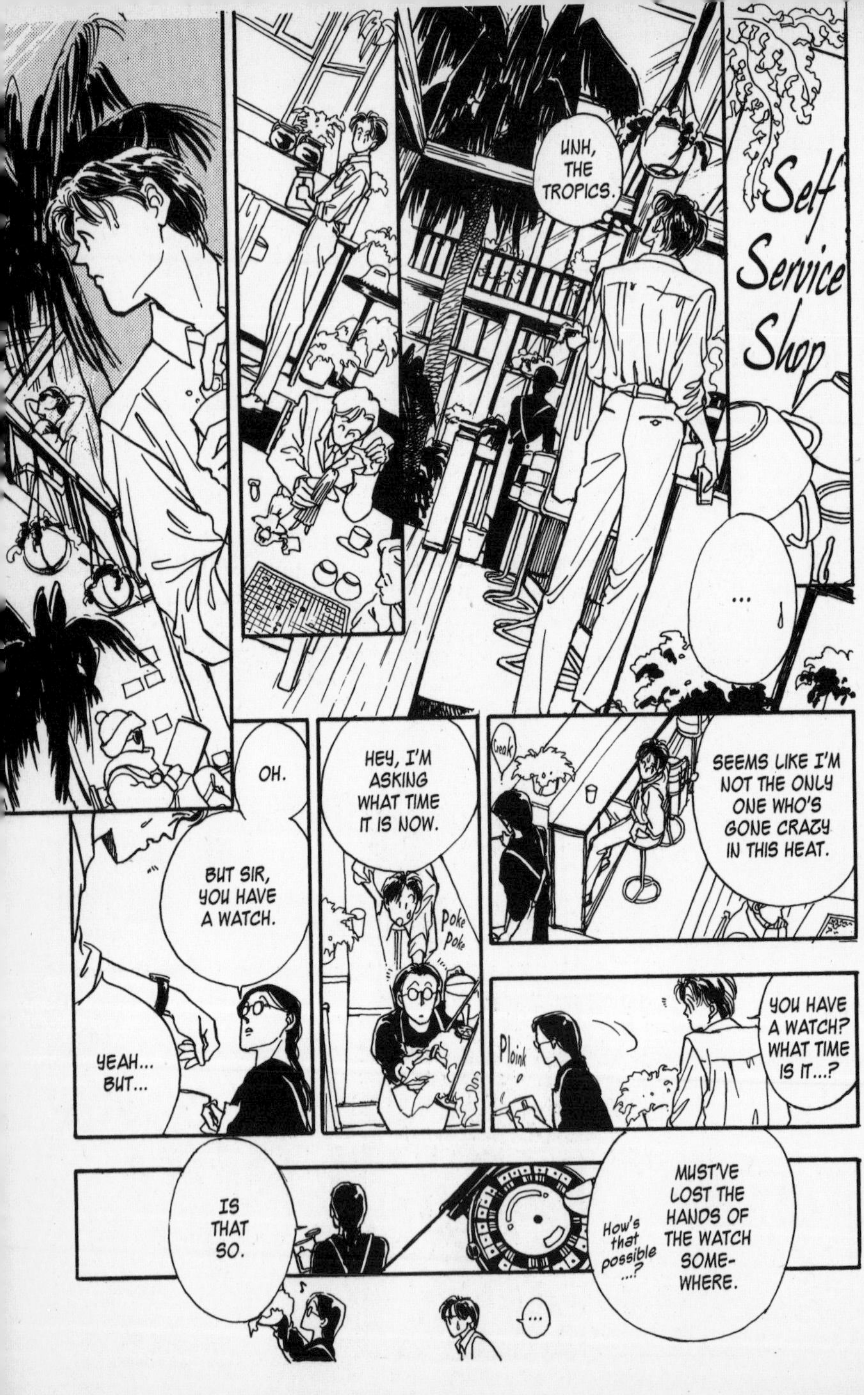
Self Service Shop
UNH, THE TROPICS.
...
Creak
SEEMS LIKE I'M NOT THE ONLY ONE WHO'S GONE CRAZY IN THIS HEAT.
YOU HAVE A WATCH? WHAT TIME IS IT...?
Ploink
HEY, I'M ASKING WHAT TIME IT IS NOW.
Poke Poke
OH.
BUT SIR, YOU HAVE A WATCH.
YEAH... BUT...
MUST'VE LOST THE HANDS OF THE WATCH SOMEWHERE.
How's that possible ...?
IS THAT SO.
...

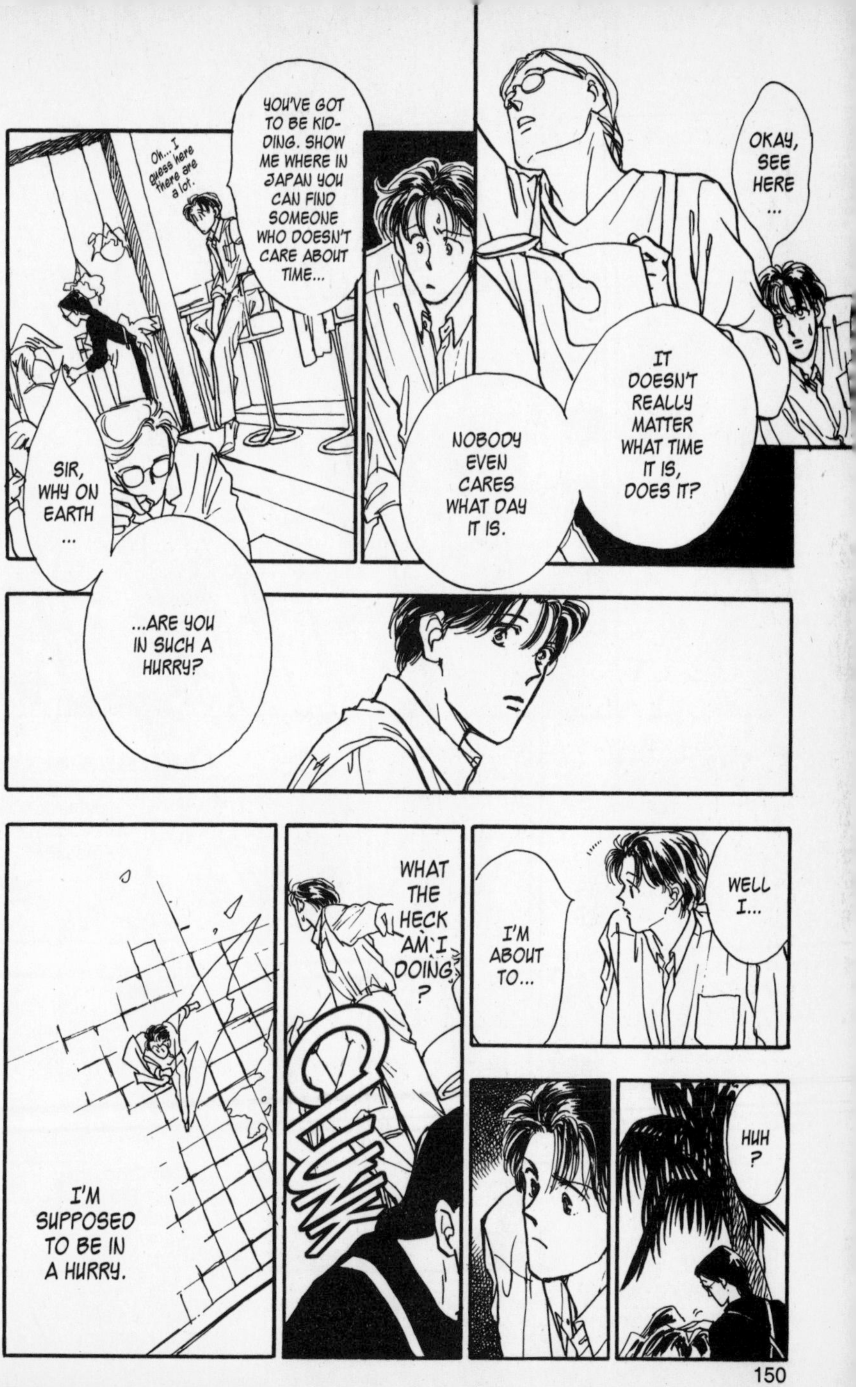
OKAY, SEE HERE ...
IT DOESN'T REALLY MATTER WHAT TIME IT IS, DOES IT?
NOBODY EVEN CARES WHAT DAY IT IS.
YOU'VE GOT TO BE KID-DING. SHOW ME WHERE IN JAPAN YOU CAN FIND SOMEONE WHO DOESN'T CARE ABOUT TIME...
Oh... I guess here there are a lot.
SIR, WHY ON EARTH ...
...ARE YOU IN SUCH A HURRY?
WELL I...
I'M ABOUT TO...
HUH ?
WHAT THE HECK AM I DOING ?
CLUNK
I'M SUPPOSED TO BE IN A HURRY.

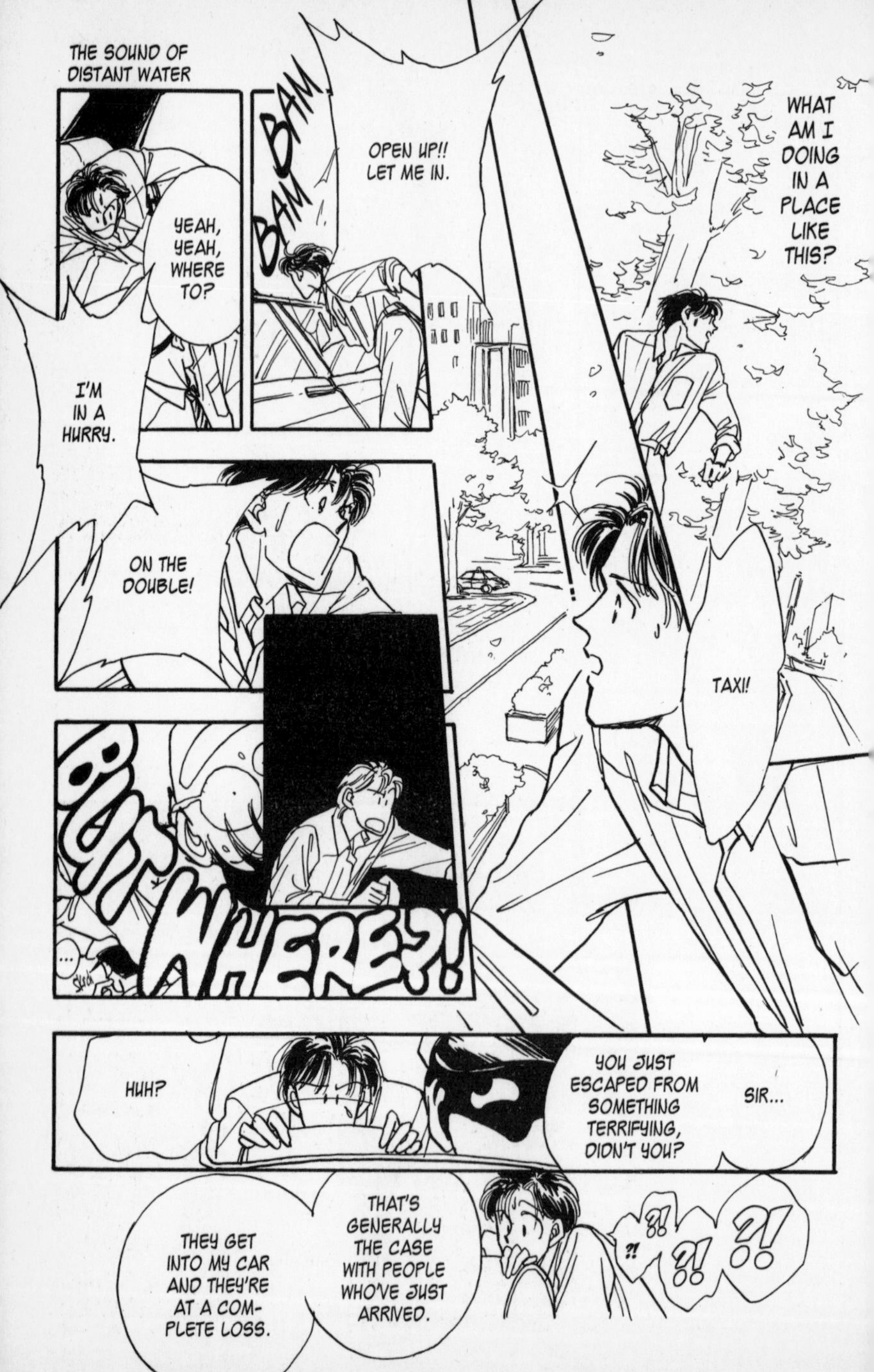
WHAT AM I DOING IN A PLACE LIKE THIS?
TAXI!
THE SOUND OF DISTANT WATER
BAM BAM BAM
OPEN UP!! LET ME IN.
YEAH, YEAH, WHERE TO?
I'M IN A HURRY.
ON THE DOUBLE!
BUT WHERE?!
...
SIR...
YOU JUST ESCAPED FROM SOMETHING TERRIFYING, DIDN'T YOU?
HUH?
?! ?! ?! ?!
THAT'S GENERALLY THE CASE WITH PEOPLE WHO'VE JUST ARRIVED.
THEY GET INTO MY CAR AND THEY'RE AT A COMPLETE LOSS.

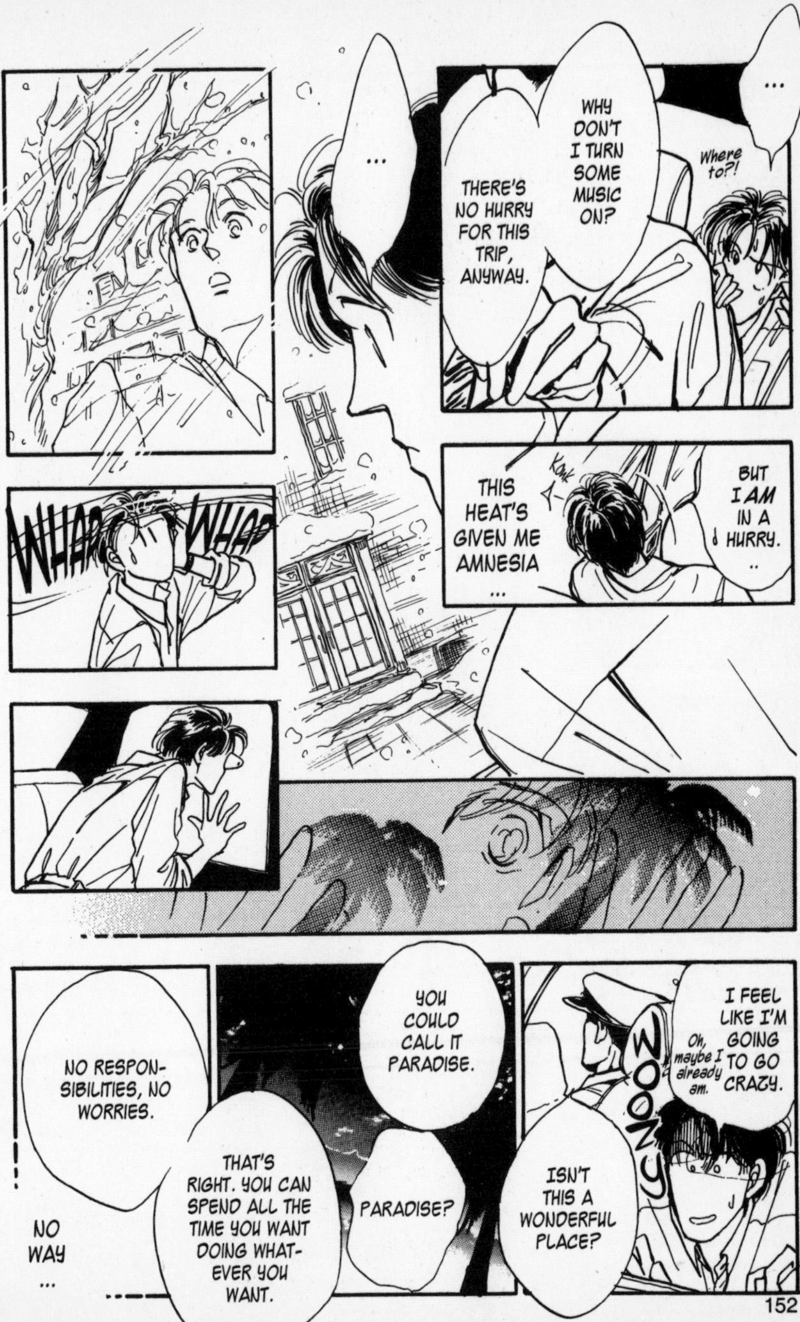
...
Where to?!
WHY DON'T I TURN SOME MUSIC ON?
THERE'S NO HURRY FOR THIS TRIP, ANYWAY.
...
BUT I AM IN A HURRY. ..
Konk
THIS HEAT'S GIVEN ME AMNESIA ...
WHAP WHAP
I FEEL LIKE I'M GOING TO GO CRAZY.
Oh, maybe I already am.
WOONG
ISN'T THIS A WONDERFUL PLACE?
YOU COULD CALL IT PARADISE.
PARADISE?
THAT'S RIGHT. YOU CAN SPEND ALL THE TIME YOU WANT DOING WHAT-EVER YOU WANT.
NO RESPON-SIBILITIES, NO WORRIES.
NO WAY ...

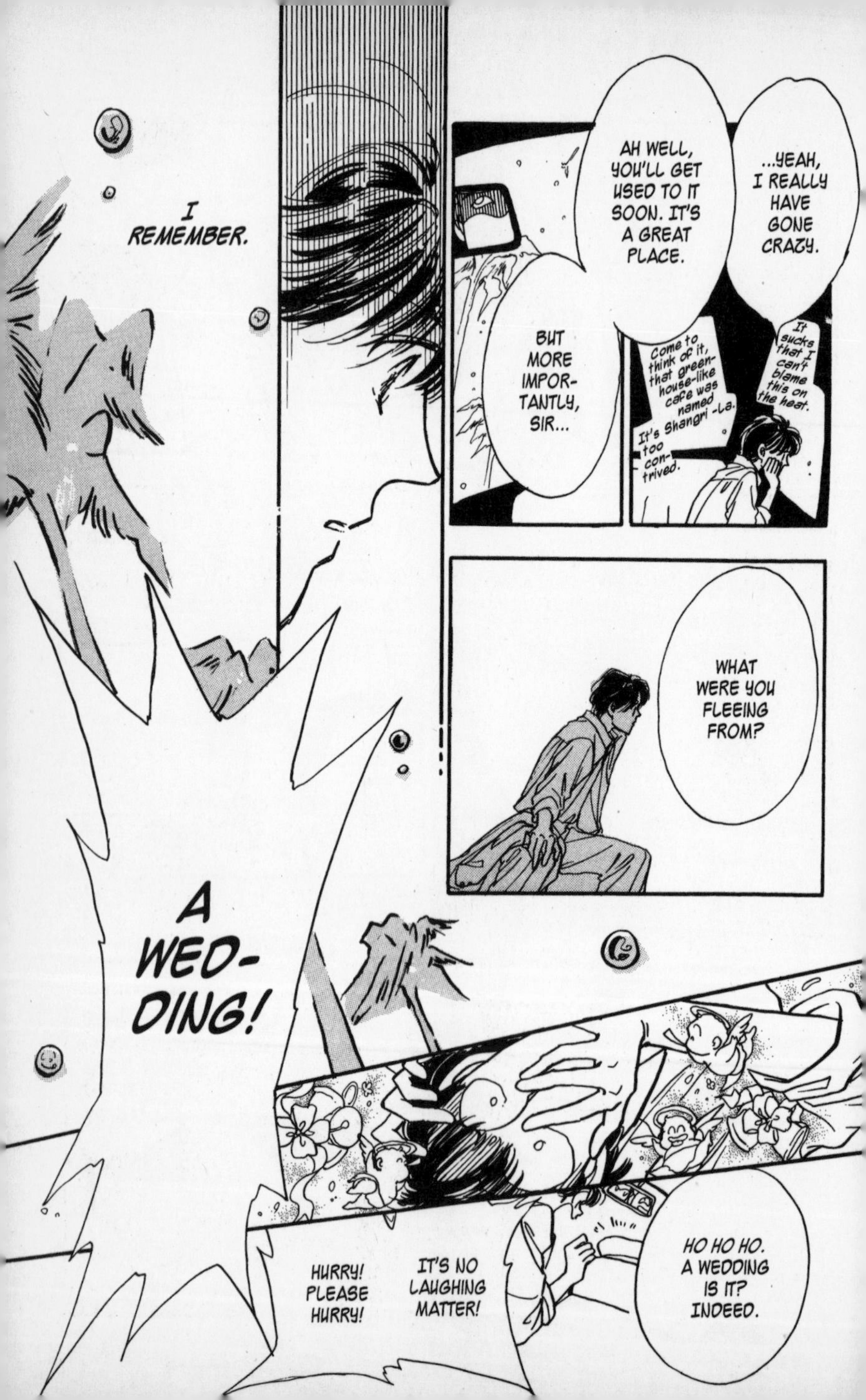
...YEAH, I REALLY HAVE GONE CRAZY.
It sucks that I can't blame this on the heat.
Come to think of it, that green-house-like cafe was named Shangri-La.
It's too con-trived.
AH WELL, YOU'LL GET USED TO IT SOON. IT'S A GREAT PLACE.
BUT MORE IMPOR-TANTLY, SIR...
WHAT WERE YOU FLEEING FROM?
I REMEMBER.
A WED-DING!
HO HO HO. A WEDDING IS IT? INDEED.
IT'S NO LAUGHING MATTER!
HURRY! PLEASE HURRY!

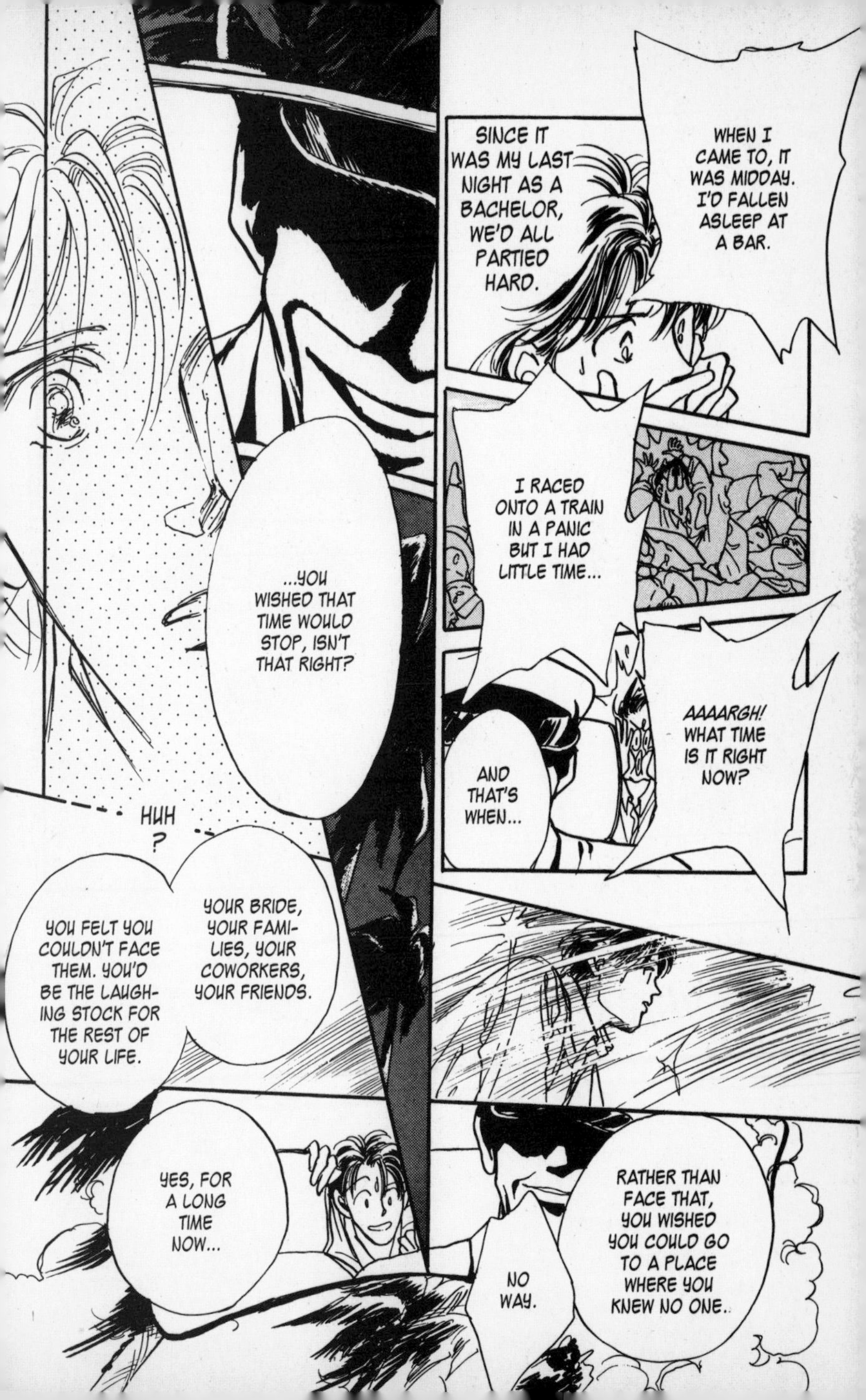
SINCE IT WAS MY LAST NIGHT AS A BACHELOR, WE'D ALL PARTIED HARD.
WHEN I CAME TO, IT WAS MIDDAY. I'D FALLEN ASLEEP AT A BAR.
I RACED ONTO A TRAIN IN A PANIC BUT I HAD LITTLE TIME...
AAAARGH! WHAT TIME IS IT RIGHT NOW?
AND THAT'S WHEN...
...YOU WISHED THAT TIME WOULD STOP, ISN'T THAT RIGHT?
HUH?
YOUR BRIDE, YOUR FAMILIES, YOUR COWORKERS, YOUR FRIENDS.
YOU FELT YOU COULDN'T FACE THEM. YOU'D BE THE LAUGHING STOCK FOR THE REST OF YOUR LIFE.
RATHER THAN FACE THAT, YOU WISHED YOU COULD GO TO A PLACE WHERE YOU KNEW NO ONE..
NO WAY.
YES, FOR A LONG TIME NOW...

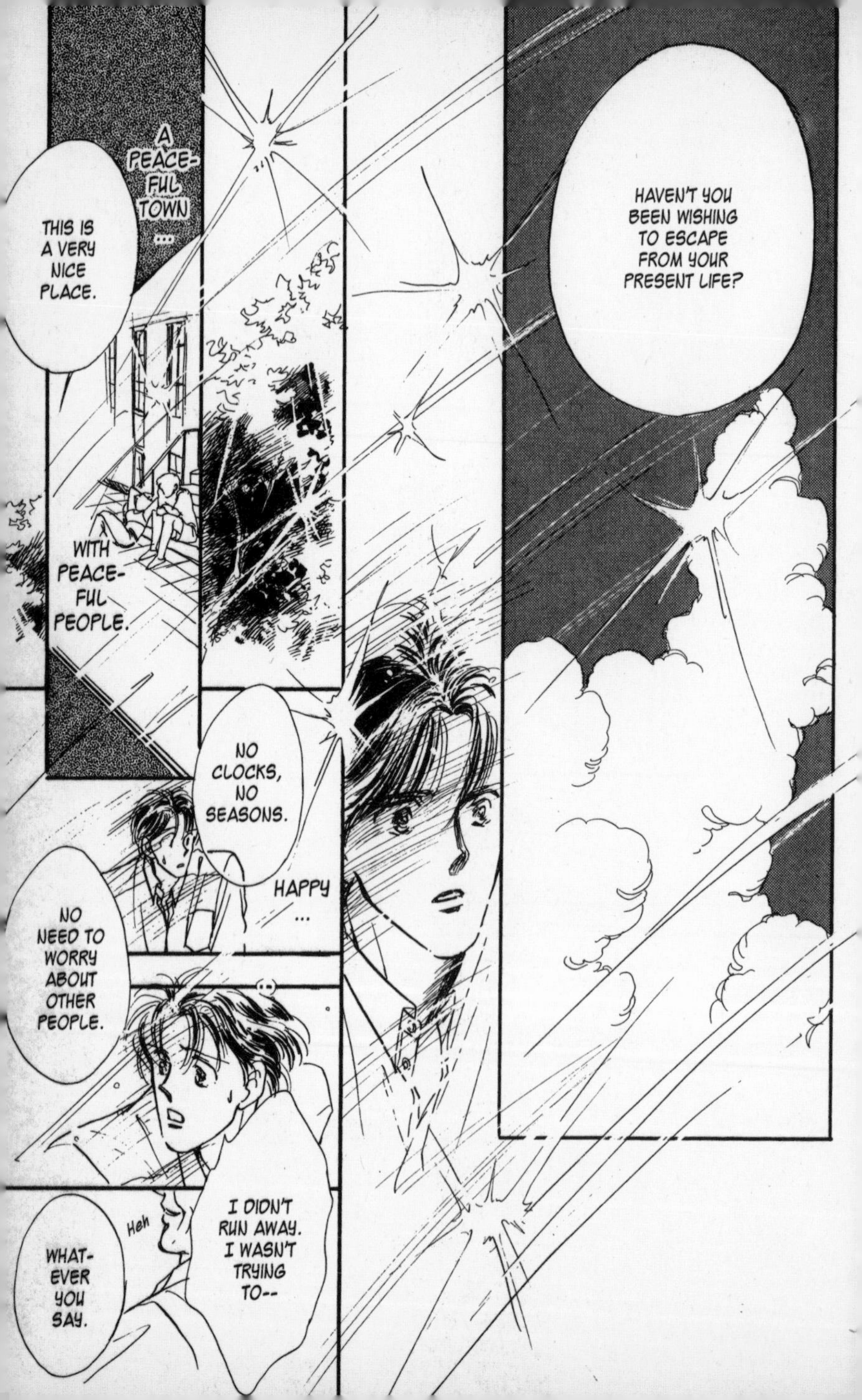
HAVEN'T YOU BEEN WISHING TO ESCAPE FROM YOUR PRESENT LIFE?
A PEACE-FUL TOWN ...
THIS IS A VERY NICE PLACE.
WITH PEACE-FUL PEOPLE.
NO CLOCKS, NO SEASONS.
HAPPY ...
NO NEED TO WORRY ABOUT OTHER PEOPLE.
I DIDN'T RUN AWAY. I WASN'T TRYING TO--
Heh
WHAT-EVER YOU SAY.

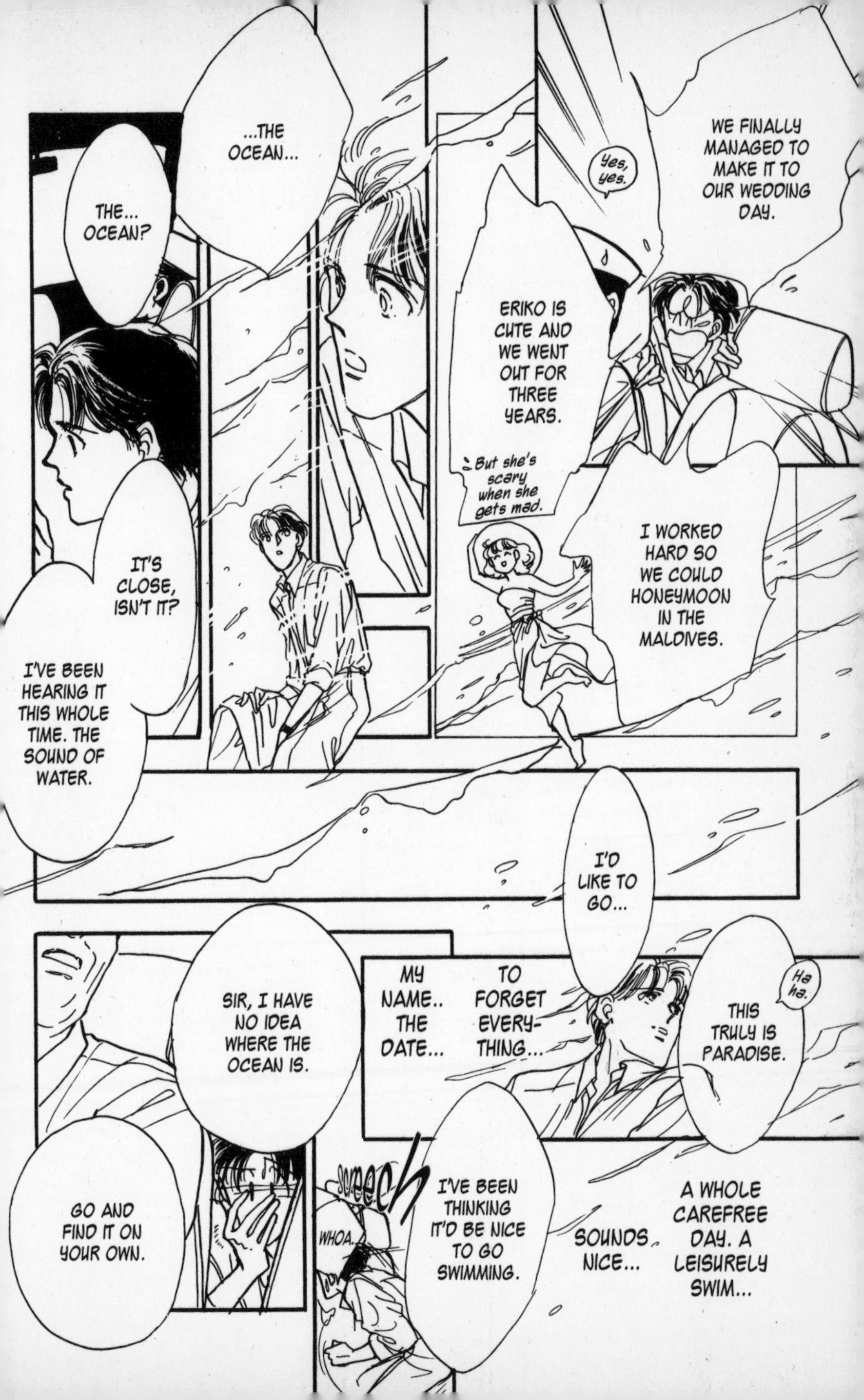
WE FINALLY MANAGED TO MAKE IT TO OUR WEDDING DAY.
Yes, yes.
ERIKO IS CUTE AND WE WENT OUT FOR THREE YEARS.
But she's scary when she gets mad.
I WORKED HARD SO WE COULD HONEYMOON IN THE MALDIVES.
...THE OCEAN...
THE... OCEAN?
IT'S CLOSE, ISN'T IT?
I'VE BEEN HEARING IT THIS WHOLE TIME. THE SOUND OF WATER.
I'D LIKE TO GO...
Ha ha.
THIS TRULY IS PARADISE.
TO FORGET EVERYTHING...
MY NAME.. THE DATE...
A WHOLE CAREFREE DAY. A LEISURELY SWIM...
SOUNDS NICE...
I'VE BEEN THINKING IT'D BE NICE TO GO SWIMMING.
SCREECH
WHOA...
SIR, I HAVE NO IDEA WHERE THE OCEAN IS.
GO AND FIND IT ON YOUR OWN.

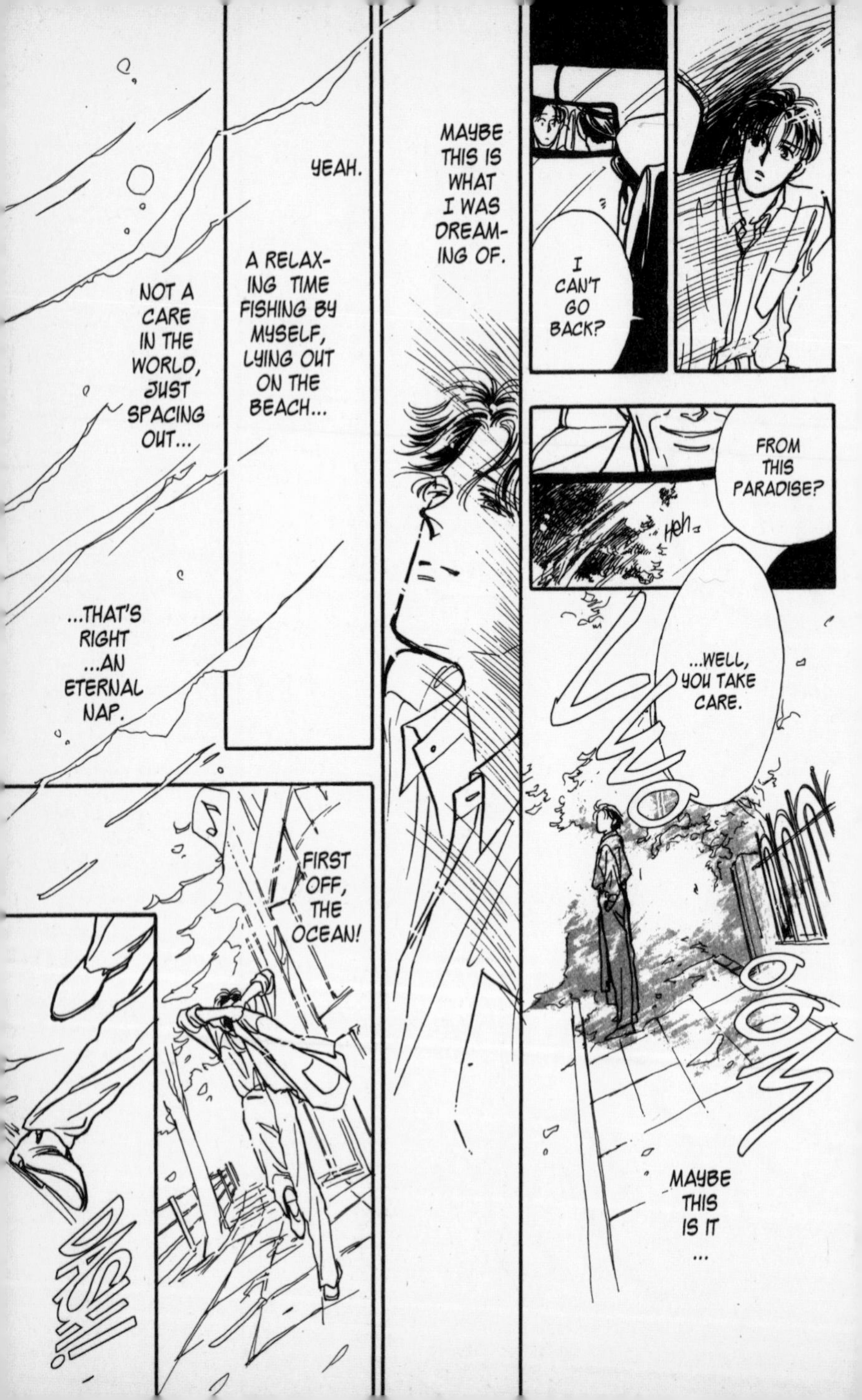
I CAN'T GO BACK?
FROM THIS PARADISE?
heh
...WELL, YOU TAKE CARE.
VWOOOM
MAYBE THIS IS IT ...
MAYBE THIS IS WHAT I WAS DREAMING OF.
YEAH.
A RELAXING TIME FISHING BY MYSELF, LYING OUT ON THE BEACH...
NOT A CARE IN THE WORLD, JUST SPACING OUT...
...THAT'S RIGHT ...AN ETERNAL NAP.
FIRST OFF, THE OCEAN!
DASH!!

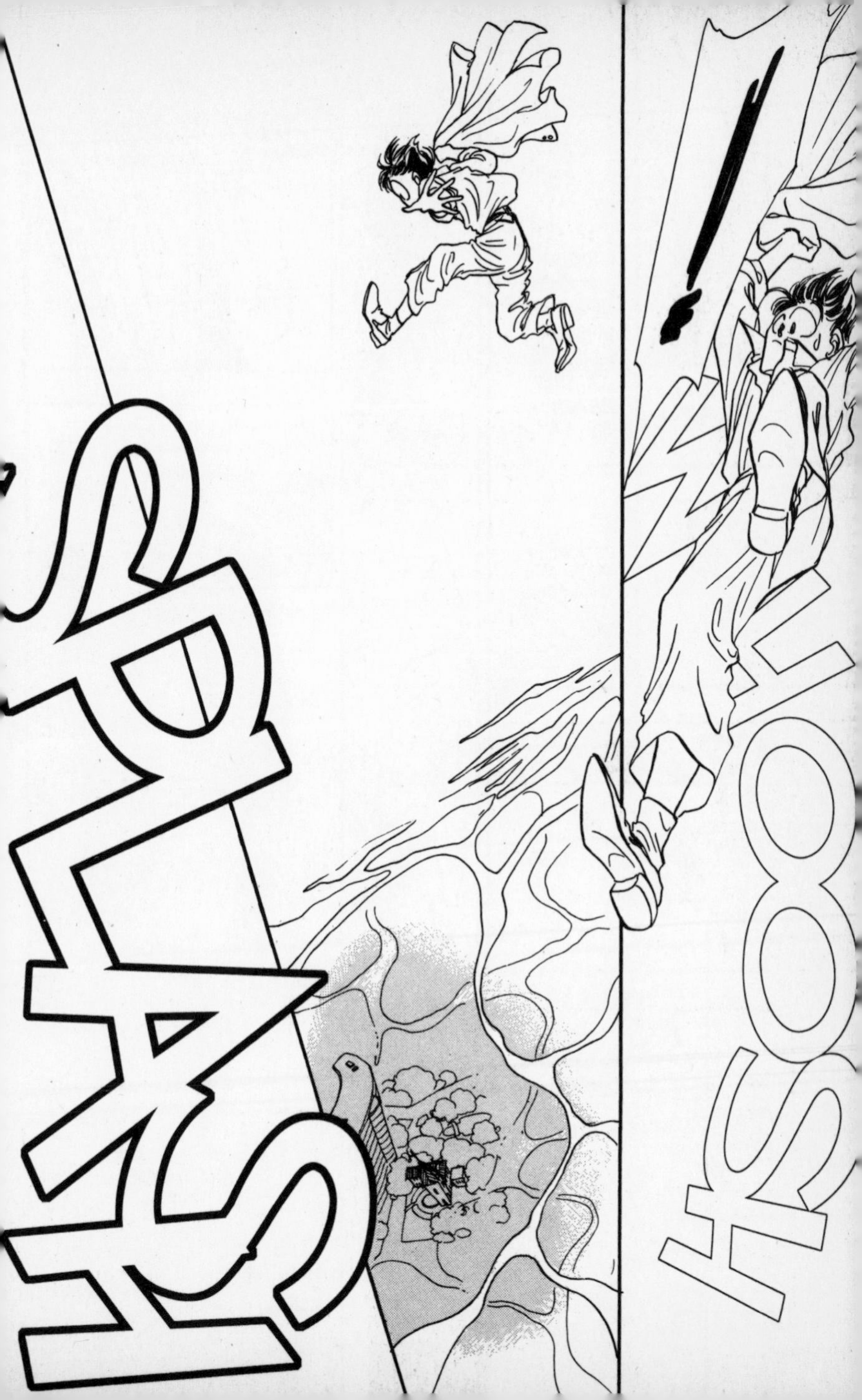
WHOOSH
SPLASH

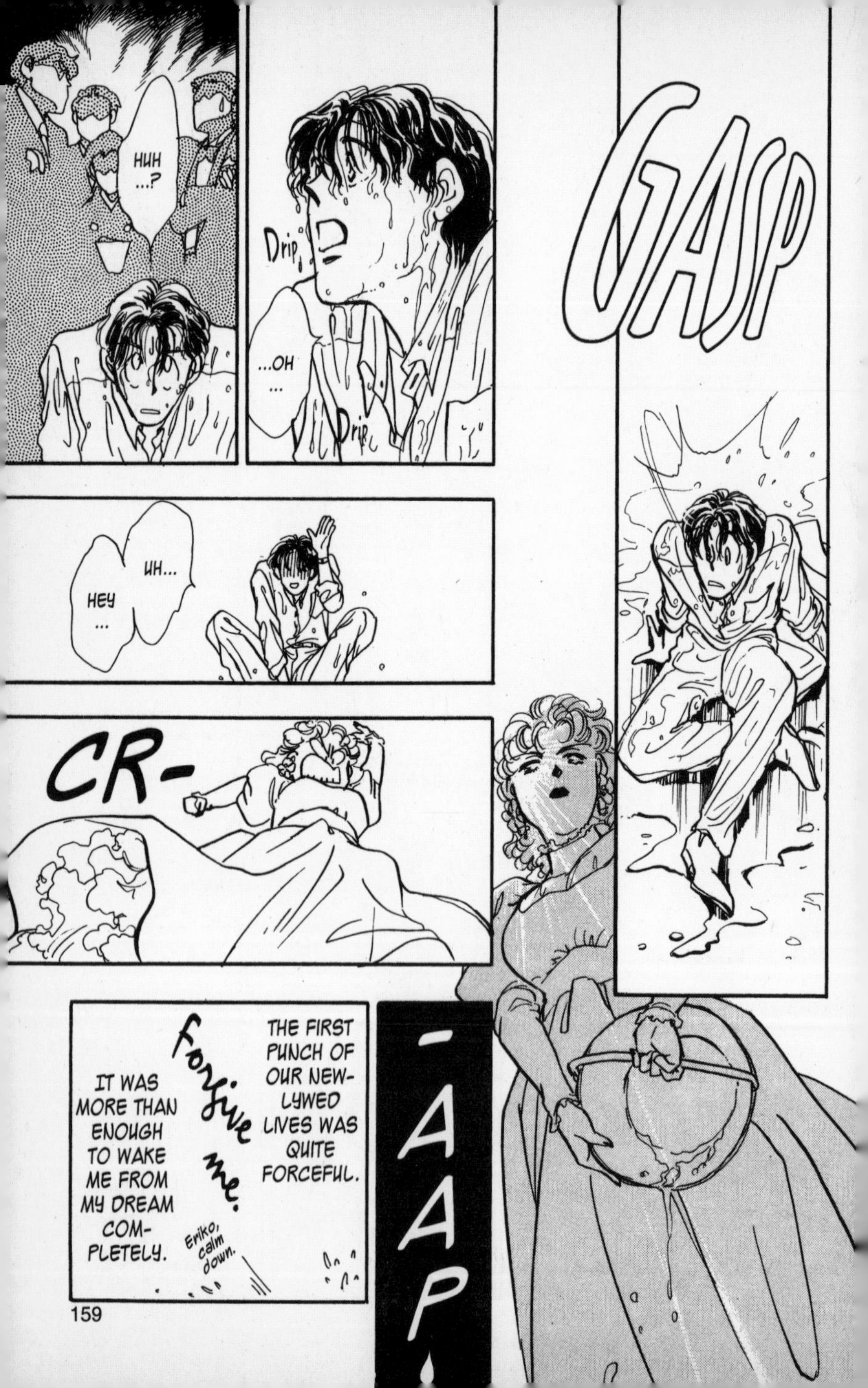

GASP
Drip
...OH ...
Drip
HUH ...?
UH... HEY ...
CR-
-AAP
THE FIRST PUNCH OF OUR NEW-LYWED LIVES WAS QUITE FORCEFUL.
forgive me.
IT WAS MORE THAN ENOUGH TO WAKE ME FROM MY DREAM COM-PLETELY.
Eriko, calm down.

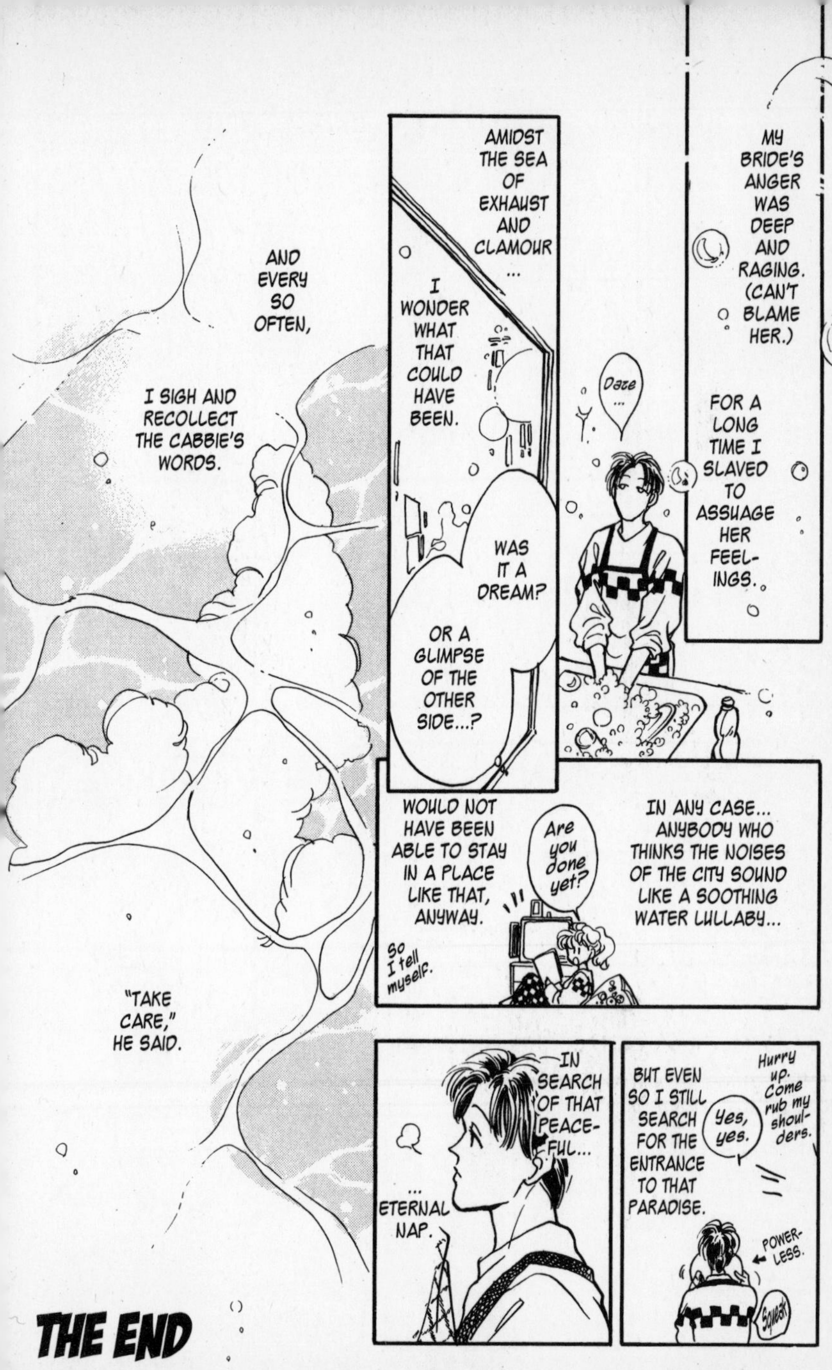
MY BRIDE'S ANGER WAS DEEP AND RAGING. (CAN'T BLAME HER.)
FOR A LONG TIME I SLAVED TO ASSUAGE HER FEELINGS.
Daze...
AMIDST THE SEA OF EXHAUST AND CLAMOUR...
I WONDER WHAT THAT COULD HAVE BEEN.
WAS IT A DREAM?
OR A GLIMPSE OF THE OTHER SIDE...?
IN ANY CASE... ANYBODY WHO THINKS THE NOISES OF THE CITY SOUND LIKE A SOOTHING WATER LULLABY...
Are you done yet?
WOULD NOT HAVE BEEN ABLE TO STAY IN A PLACE LIKE THAT, ANYWAY.
So I tell myself.
Hurry up. Come rub my shoulders.
BUT EVEN SO I STILL SEARCH FOR THE ENTRANCE TO THAT PARADISE.
Yes, yes.
POWER-LESS.
Squeak
IN SEARCH OF THAT PEACE-FUL...
... ETERNAL NAP.
AND EVERY SO OFTEN,
I SIGH AND RECOLLECT THE CABBIE'S WORDS.
"TAKE CARE," HE SAID.
THE END

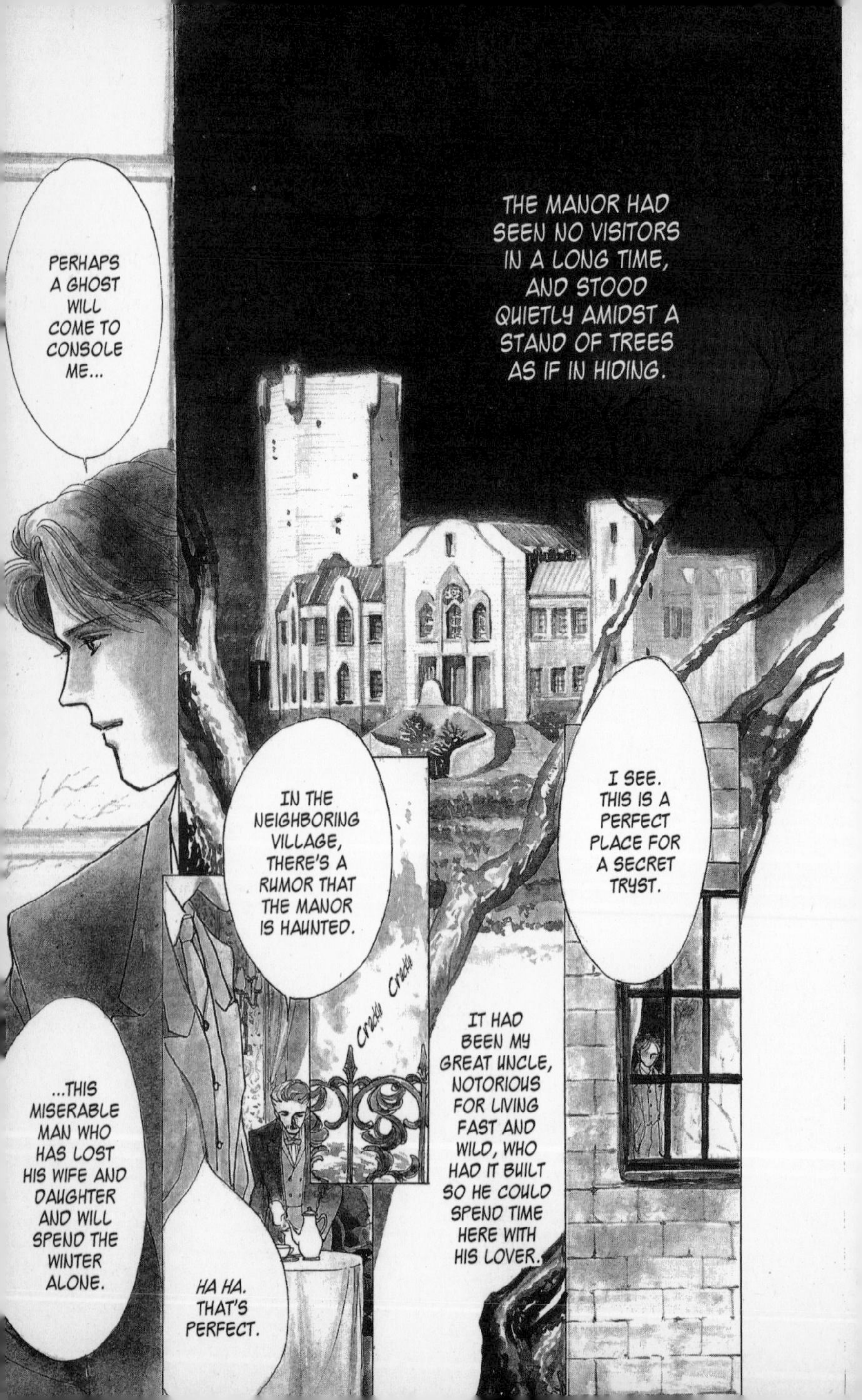
THE MANOR HAD SEEN NO VISITORS IN A LONG TIME, AND STOOD QUIETLY AMIDST A STAND OF TREES AS IF IN HIDING.
I SEE. THIS IS A PERFECT PLACE FOR A SECRET TRYST.
IT HAD BEEN MY GREAT UNCLE, NOTORIOUS FOR LIVING FAST AND WILD, WHO HAD IT BUILT SO HE COULD SPEND TIME HERE WITH HIS LOVER.
IN THE NEIGHBORING VILLAGE, THERE'S A RUMOR THAT THE MANOR IS HAUNTED.
Crackle Crackle
HA HA. THAT'S PERFECT.
PERHAPS A GHOST WILL COME TO CONSOLE ME...
...THIS MISERABLE MAN WHO HAS LOST HIS WIFE AND DAUGHTER AND WILL SPEND THE WINTER ALONE.

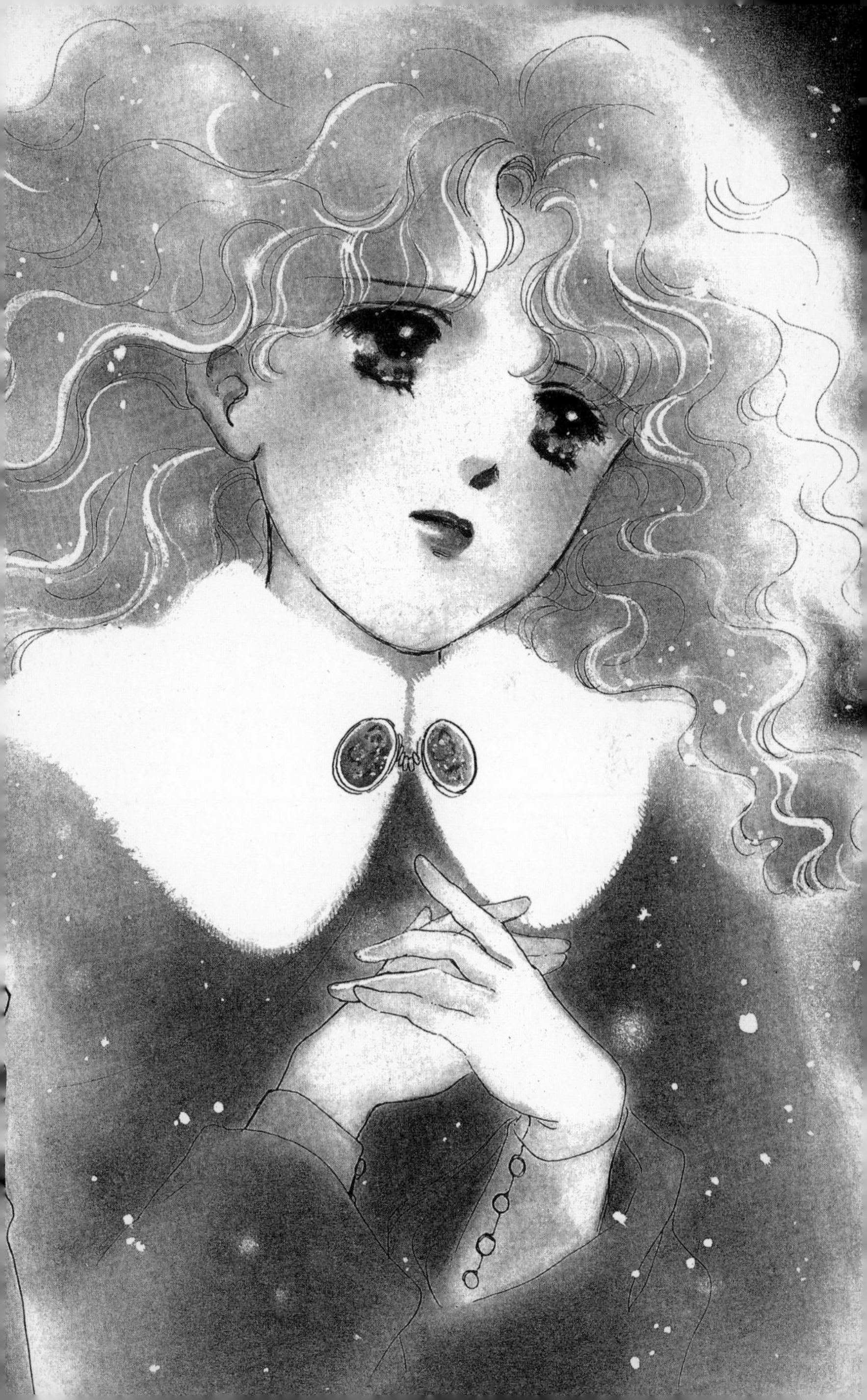

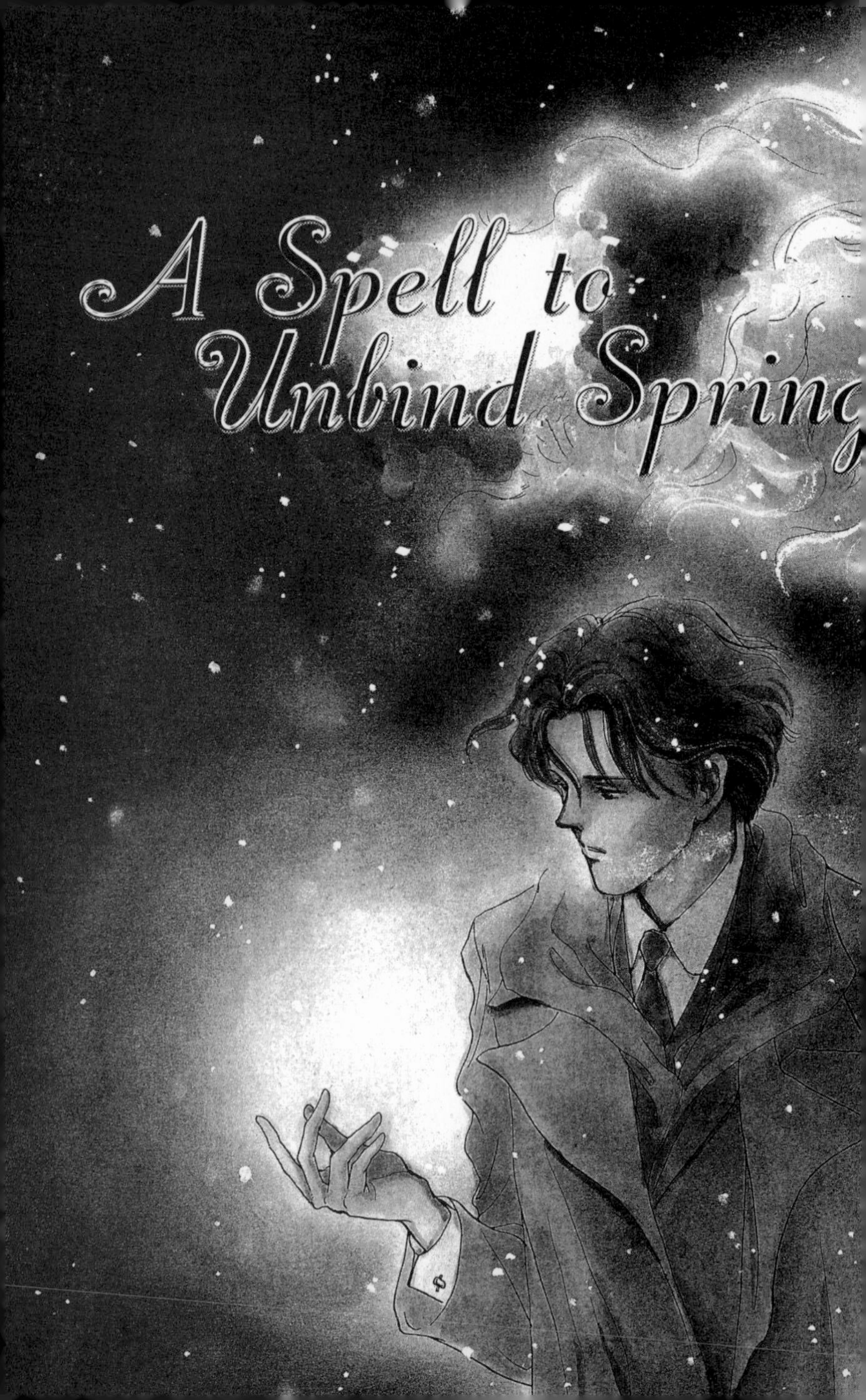
A Spell to
Unbind Spring

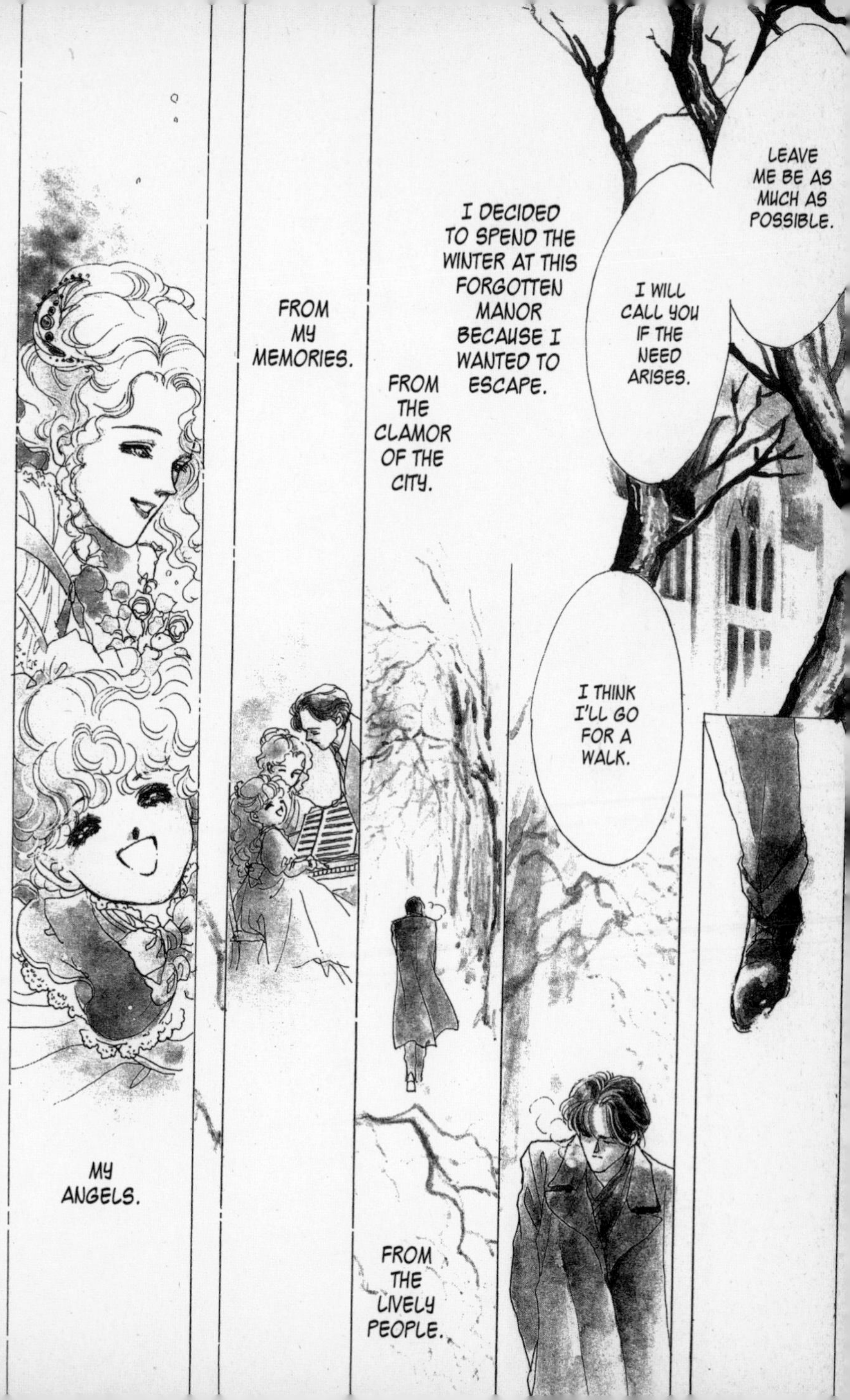
LEAVE ME BE AS MUCH AS POSSIBLE.
I WILL CALL YOU IF THE NEED ARISES.
I THINK I'LL GO FOR A WALK.
I DECIDED TO SPEND THE WINTER AT THIS FORGOTTEN MANOR BECAUSE I WANTED TO ESCAPE.
FROM THE CLAMOR OF THE CITY.
FROM THE LIVELY PEOPLE.
FROM MY MEMORIES.
MY ANGELS.

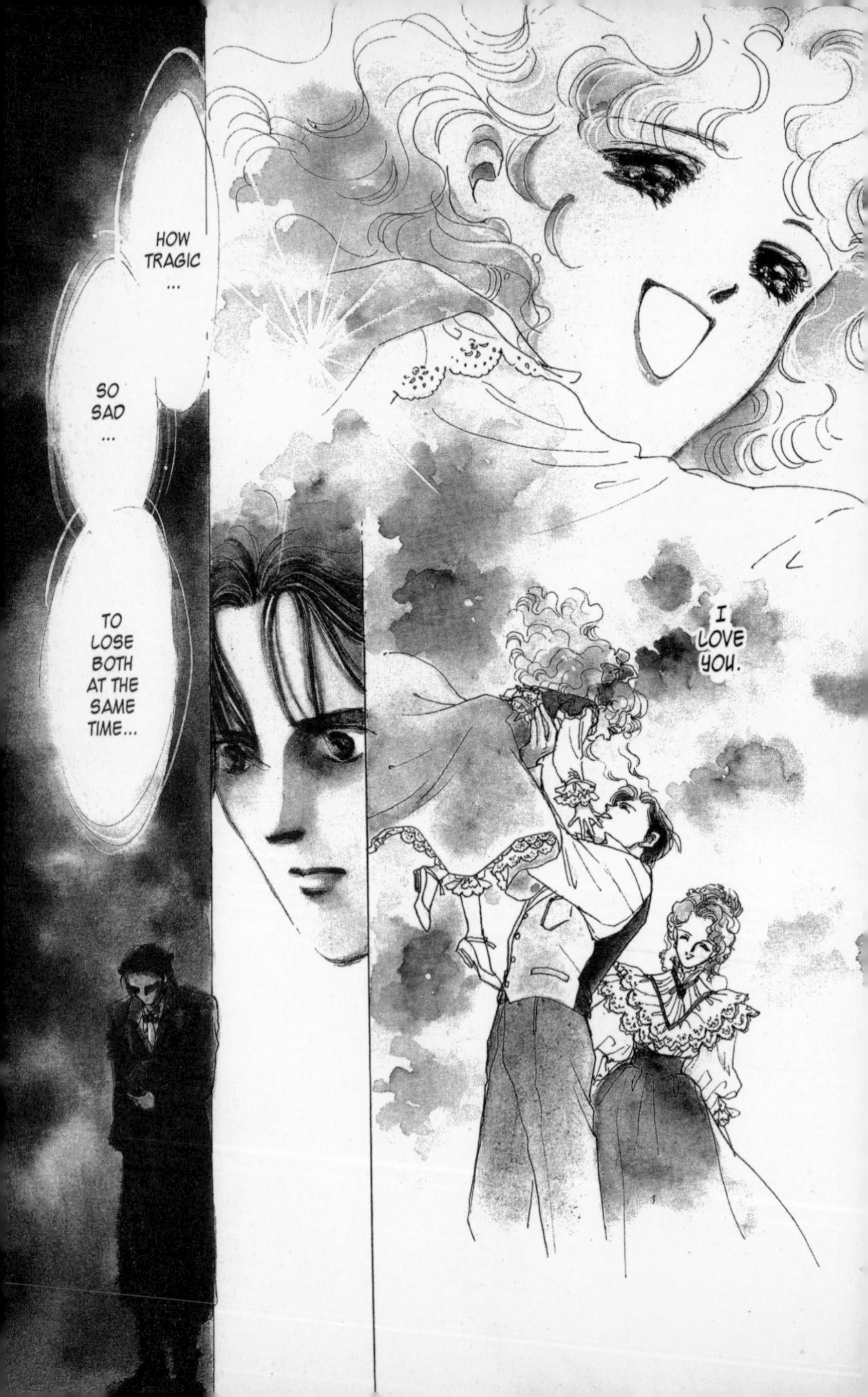
I LOVE YOU.
HOW TRAGIC ...
SO SAD ...
TO LOSE BOTH AT THE SAME TIME...

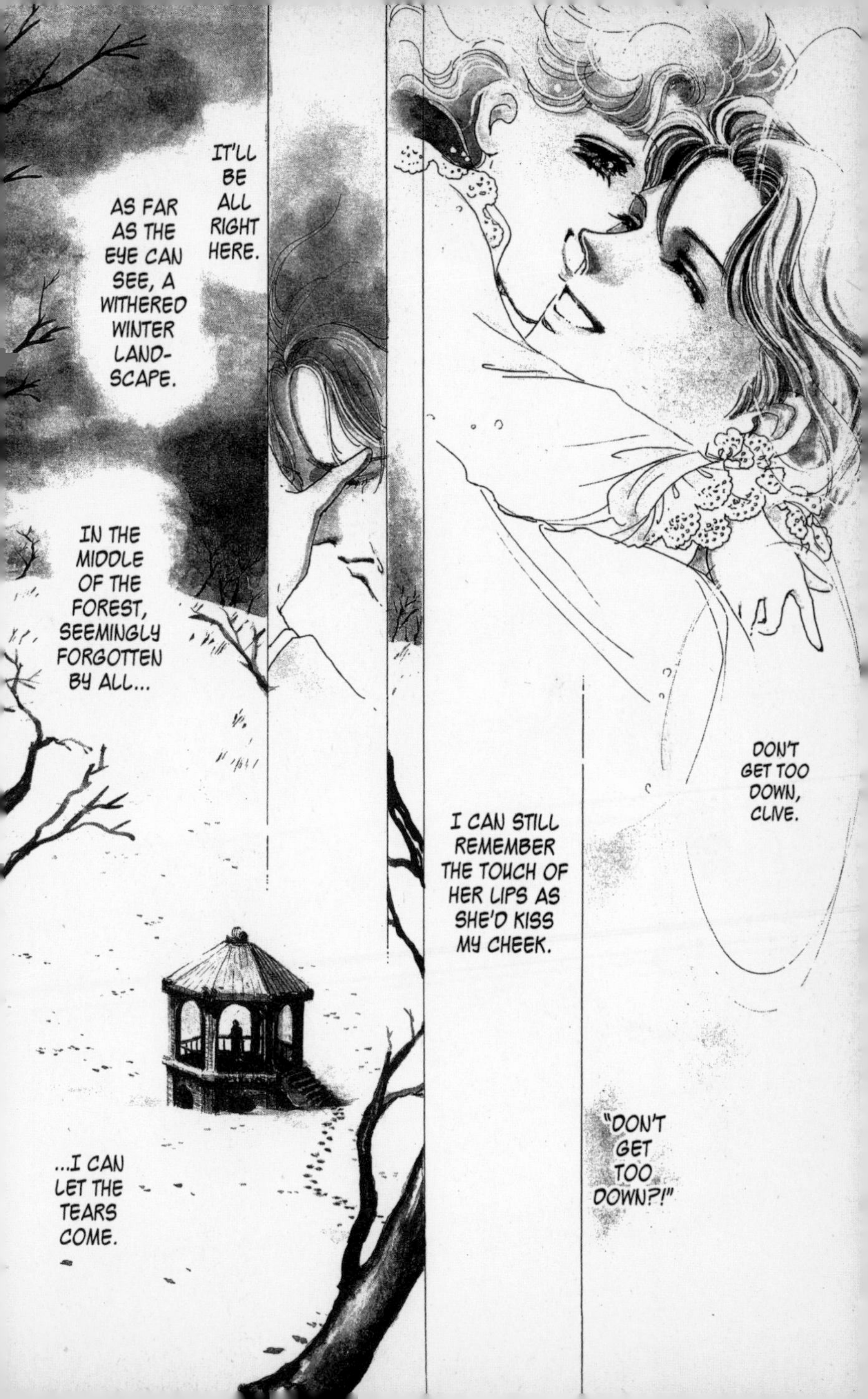
DON'T GET TOO DOWN, CLIVE.
"DON'T GET TOO DOWN?!"
I CAN STILL REMEMBER THE TOUCH OF HER LIPS AS SHE'D KISS MY CHEEK.
IT'LL BE ALL RIGHT HERE.
AS FAR AS THE EYE CAN SEE, A WITHERED WINTER LAND-SCAPE.
IN THE MIDDLE OF THE FOREST, SEEMINGLY FORGOTTEN BY ALL...
...I CAN LET THE TEARS COME.

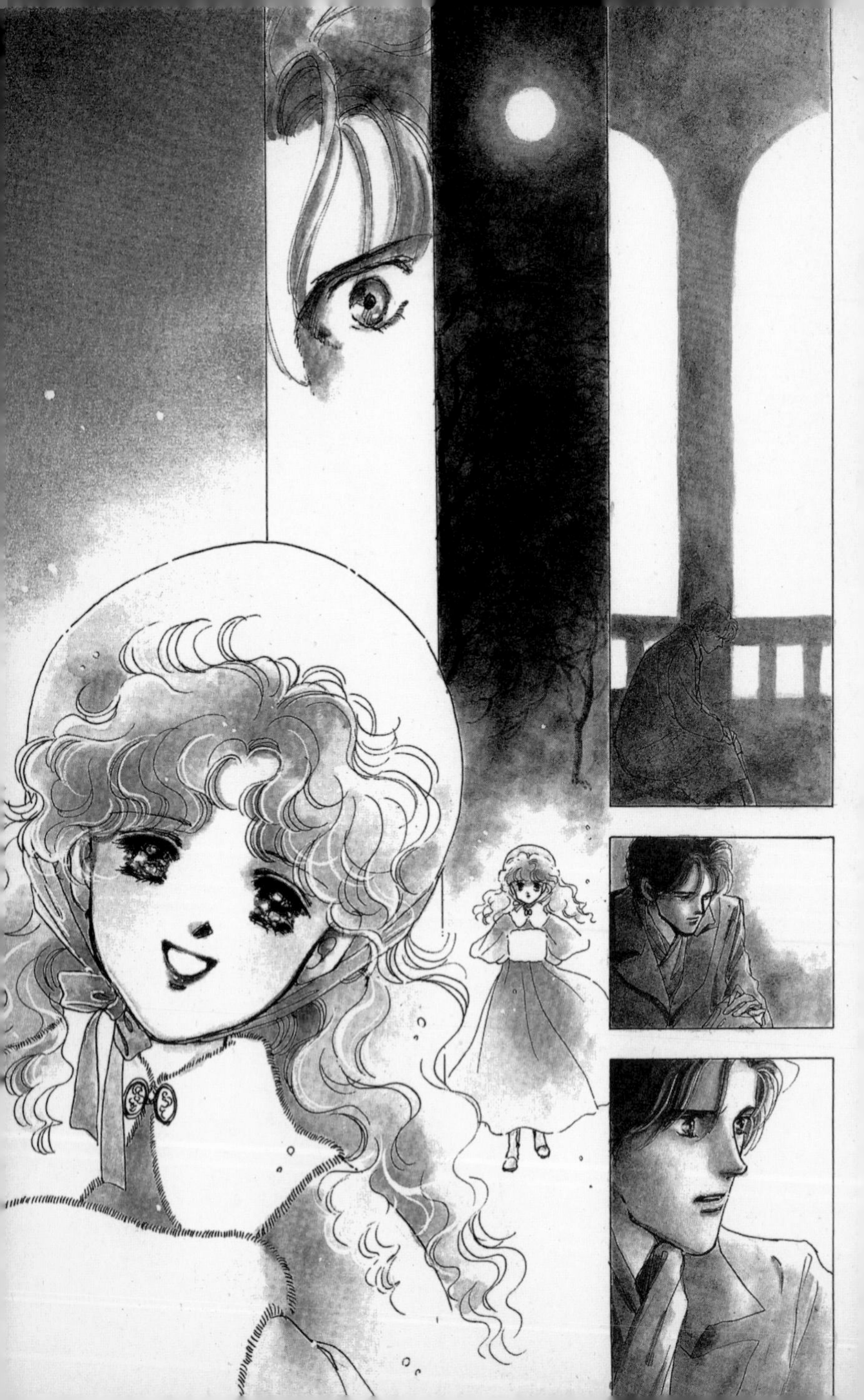

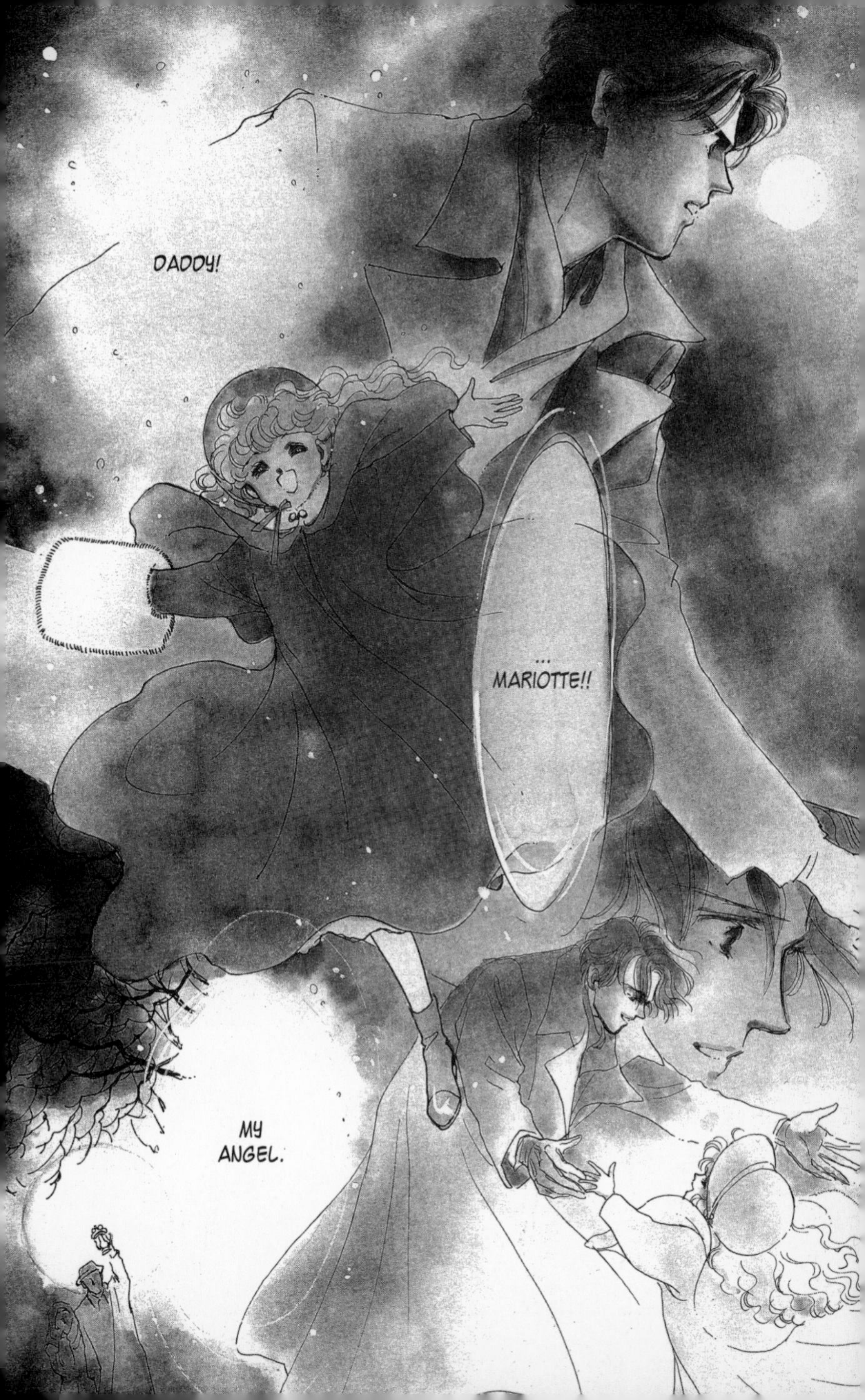
DADDY!
... MARIOTTE!!
MY ANGEL.

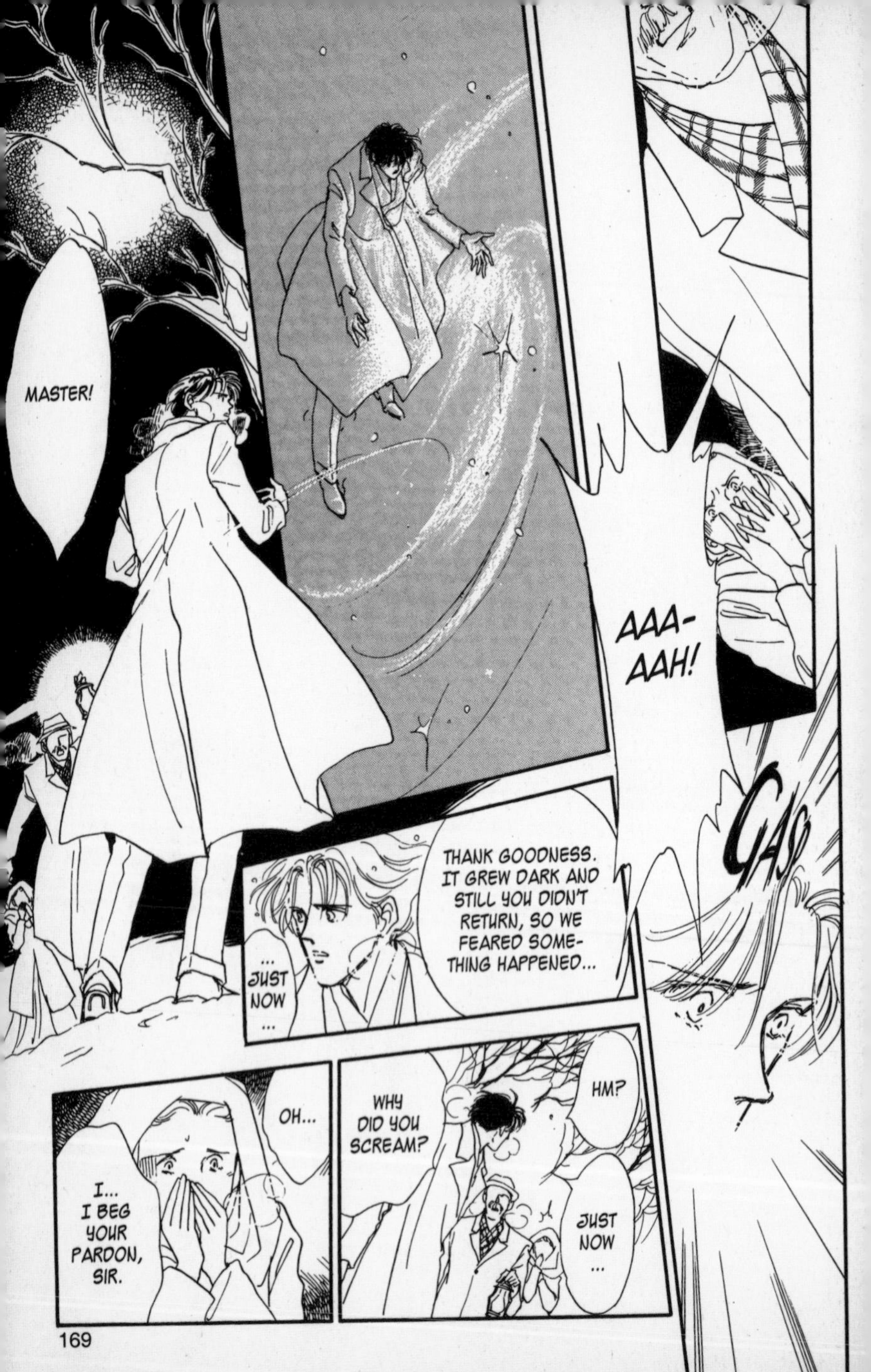
AAA-
AAH!
MASTER!
GAS
THANK GOODNESS. IT GREW DARK AND STILL YOU DIDN'T RETURN, SO WE FEARED SOME-THING HAPPENED...
... JUST NOW ...
HM?
WHY DID YOU SCREAM?
JUST NOW ...
OH...
I... I BEG YOUR PARDON, SIR.

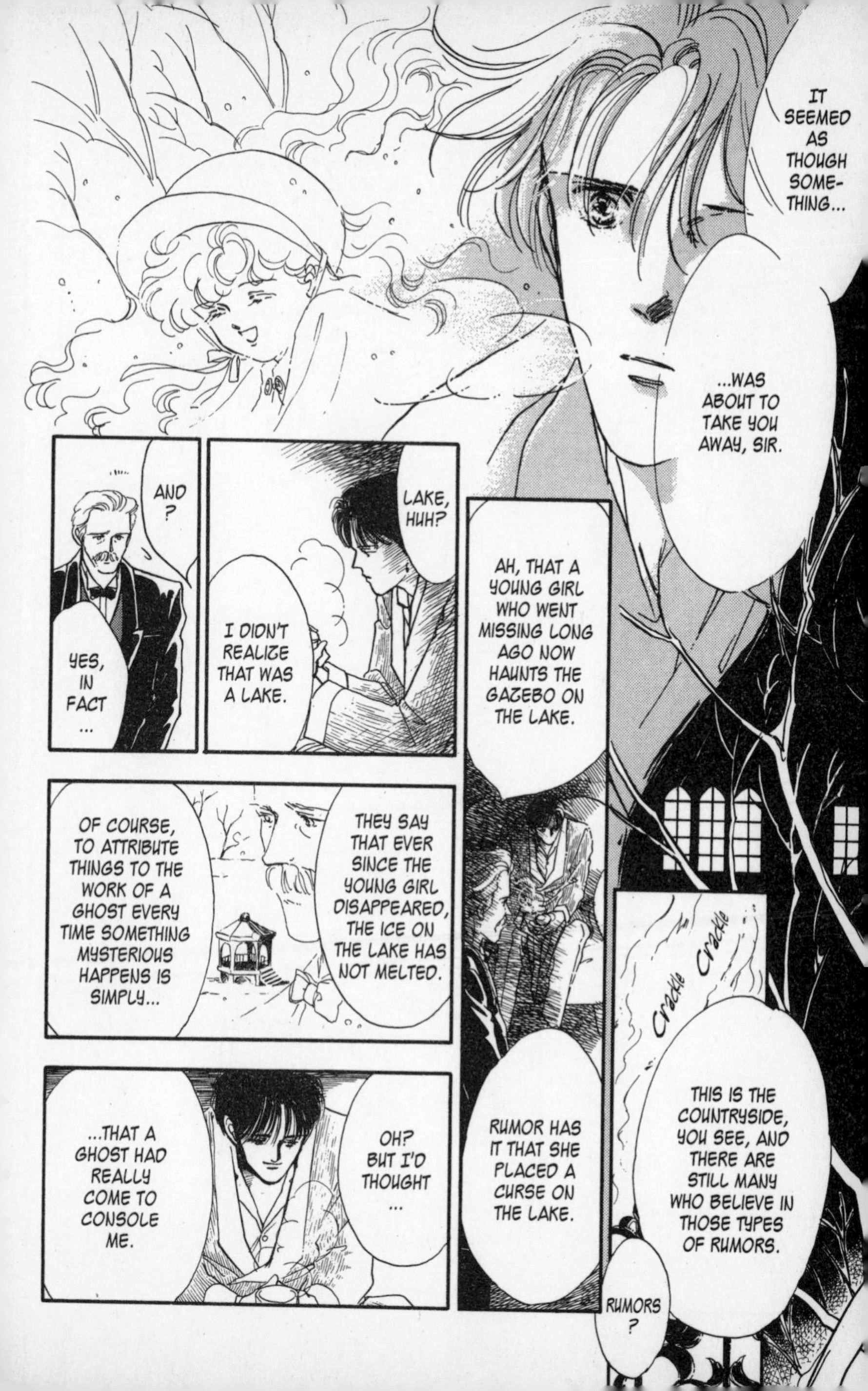
IT SEEMED AS THOUGH SOMETHING...
...WAS ABOUT TO TAKE YOU AWAY, SIR.
LAKE, HUH?
I DIDN'T REALIZE THAT WAS A LAKE.
AND ?
YES, IN FACT ...
AH, THAT A YOUNG GIRL WHO WENT MISSING LONG AGO NOW HAUNTS THE GAZEBO ON THE LAKE.
RUMOR HAS IT THAT SHE PLACED A CURSE ON THE LAKE.
Crackle Crackle
RUMORS ?
THIS IS THE COUNTRYSIDE, YOU SEE, AND THERE ARE STILL MANY WHO BELIEVE IN THOSE TYPES OF RUMORS.
THEY SAY THAT EVER SINCE THE YOUNG GIRL DISAPPEARED, THE ICE ON THE LAKE HAS NOT MELTED.
OF COURSE, TO ATTRIBUTE THINGS TO THE WORK OF A GHOST EVERY TIME SOMETHING MYSTERIOUS HAPPENS IS SIMPLY...
OH? BUT I'D THOUGHT ...
...THAT A GHOST HAD REALLY COME TO CONSOLE ME.

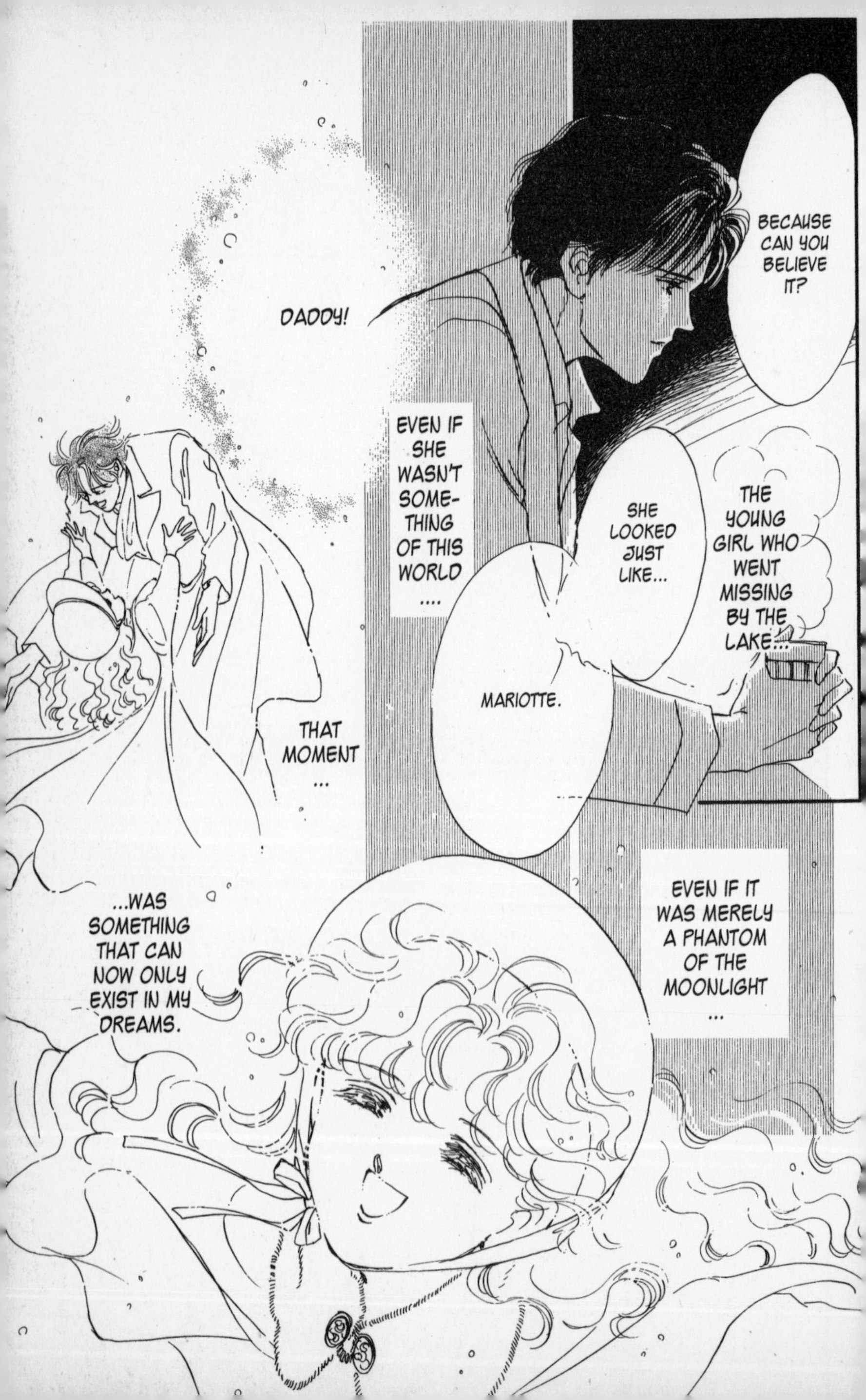
BECAUSE CAN YOU BELIEVE IT?
THE YOUNG GIRL WHO WENT MISSING BY THE LAKE...
SHE LOOKED JUST LIKE...
MARIOTTE.
EVEN IF SHE WASN'T SOMETHING OF THIS WORLD ....
DADDY!
EVEN IF IT WAS MERELY A PHANTOM OF THE MOONLIGHT ...
THAT MOMENT ...
...WAS SOMETHING THAT CAN NOW ONLY EXIST IN MY DREAMS.

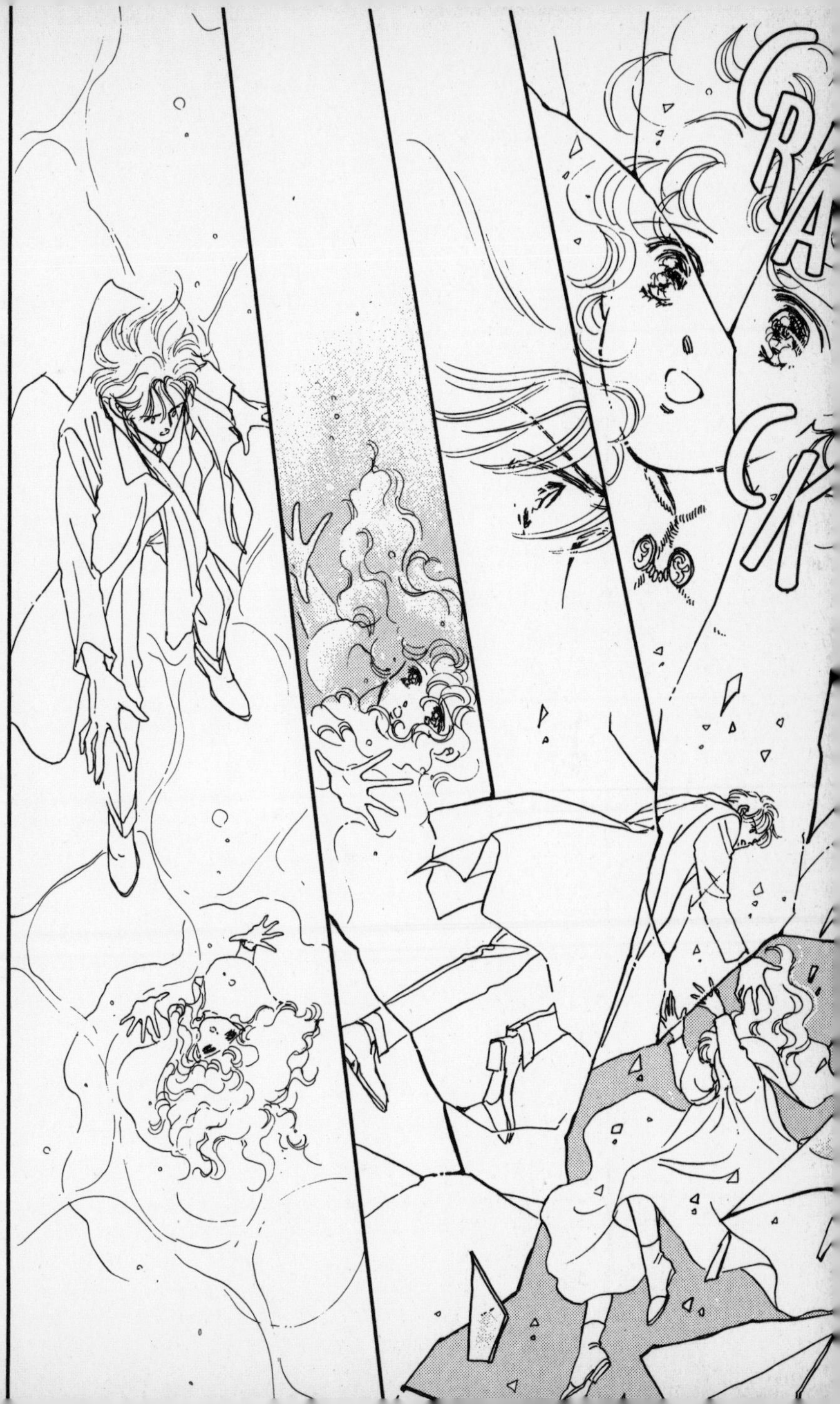
CRACK

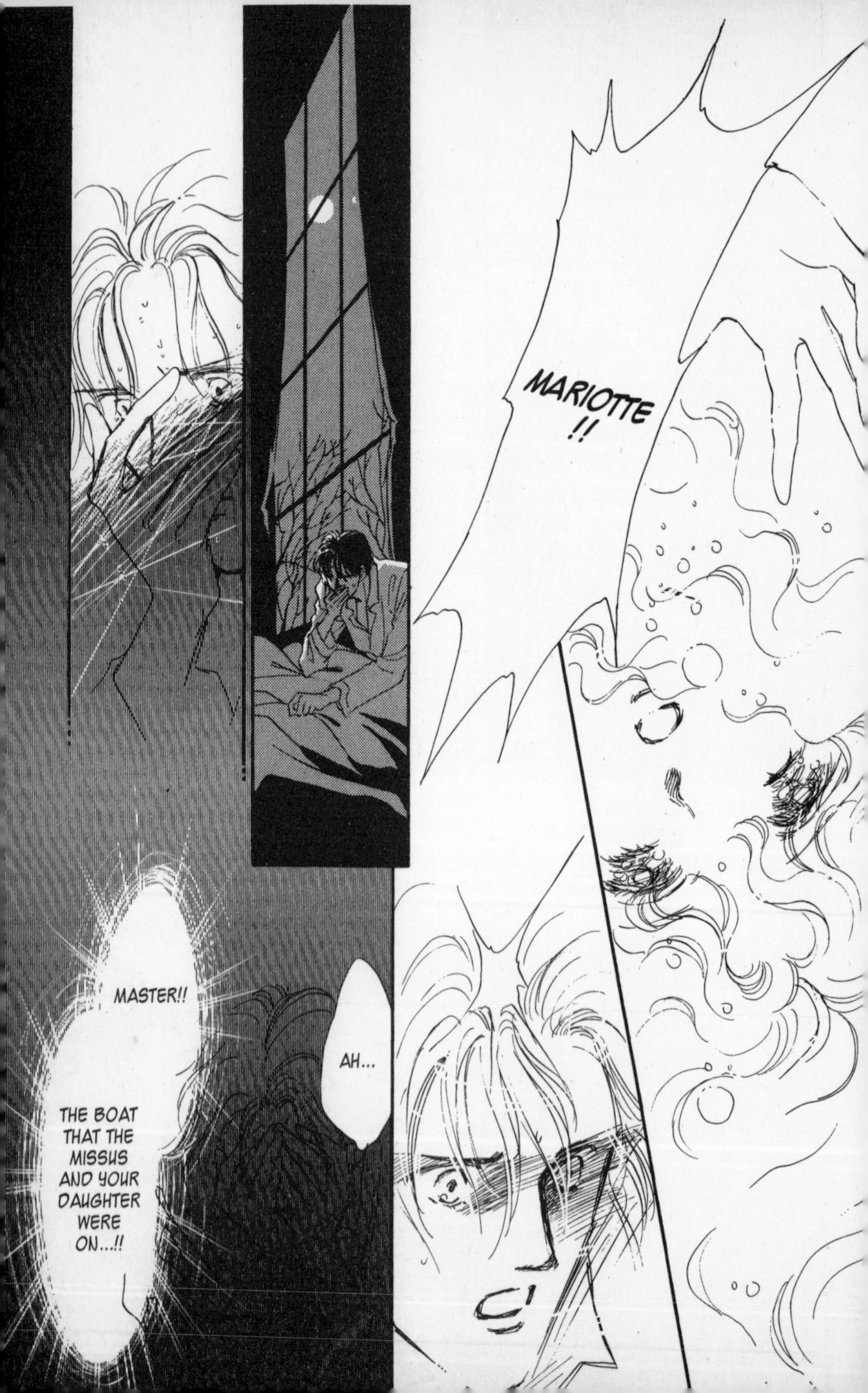
MARIOTTE !!
MASTER!!
THE BOAT THAT THE MISSUS AND YOUR DAUGHTER WERE ON...!!
AH...

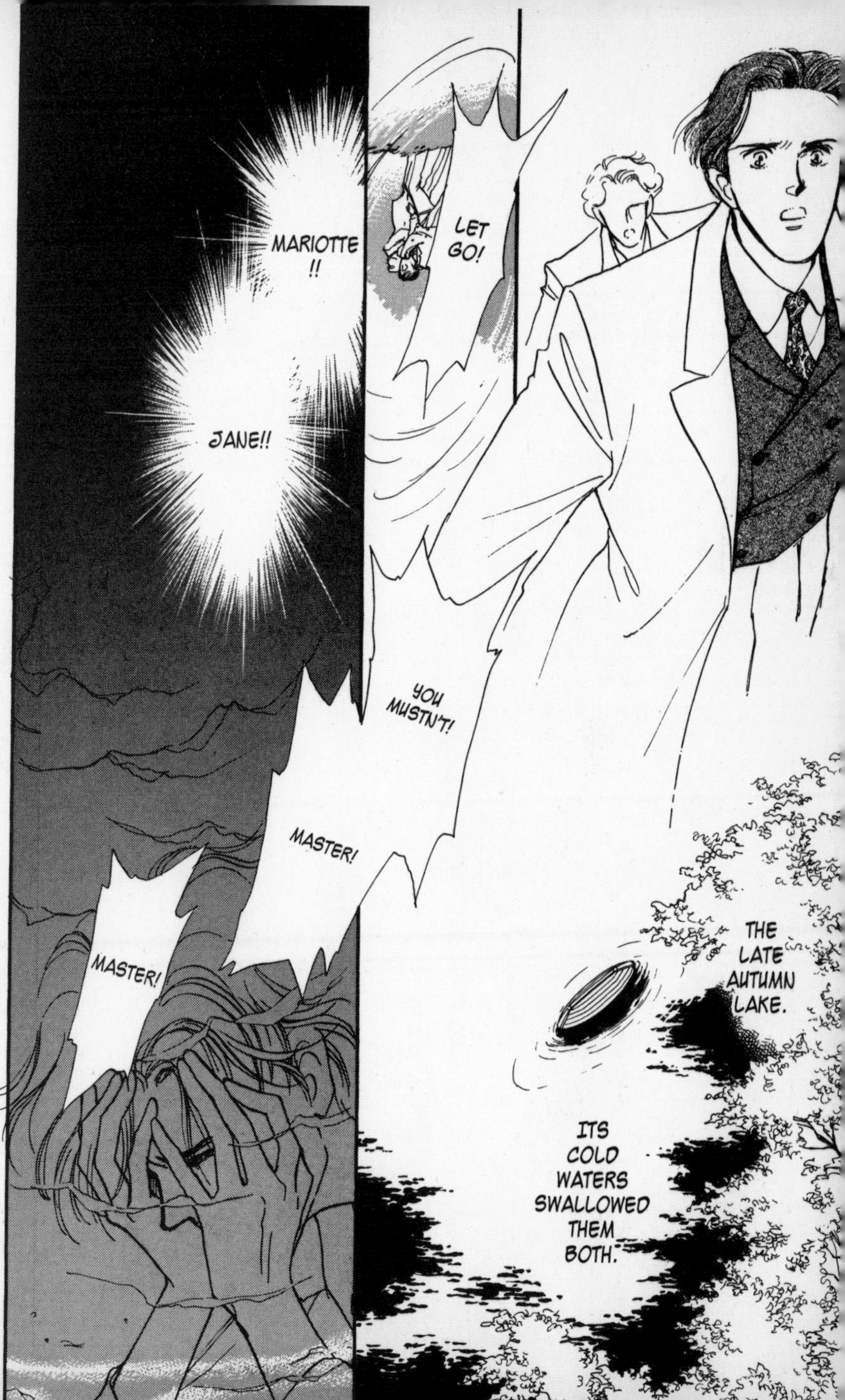
LET GO!
YOU MUSTN'T!
THE LATE AUTUMN LAKE.
ITS COLD WATERS SWALLOWED THEM BOTH.
MARIOTTE !!
JANE!!
MASTER!
MASTER!

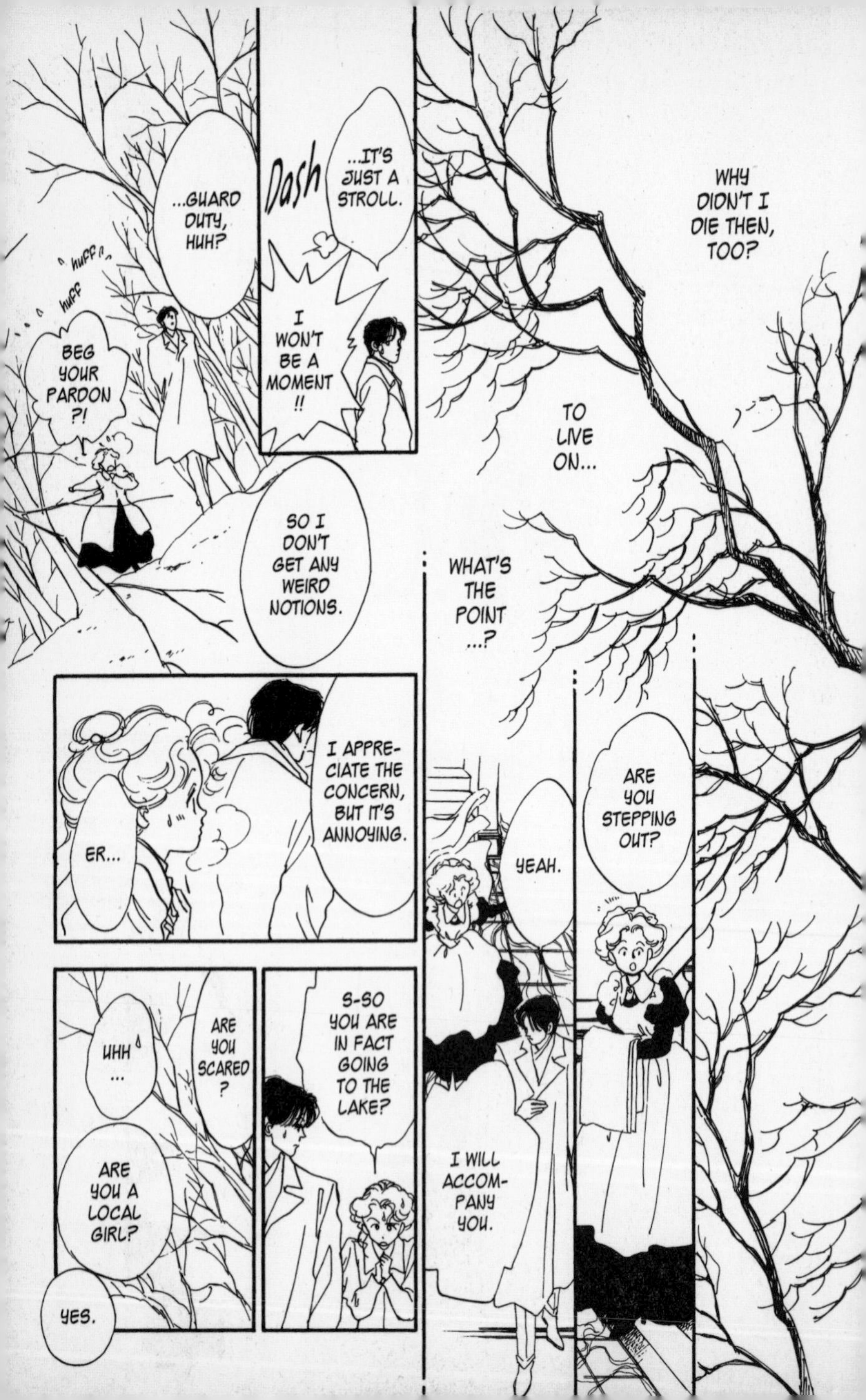

WHY DIDN'T I DIE THEN, TOO?
TO LIVE ON...
WHAT'S THE POINT ...?
ARE YOU STEPPING OUT?
YEAH.
I WILL ACCOMPANY YOU.
...IT'S JUST A STROLL.
Dash
I WON'T BE A MOMENT !!
...GUARD DUTY, HUH?
huff huff
BEG YOUR PARDON ?!
SO I DON'T GET ANY WEIRD NOTIONS.
I APPRECIATE THE CONCERN, BUT IT'S ANNOYING.
ER...
S-SO YOU ARE IN FACT GOING TO THE LAKE?
ARE YOU SCARED ?
UHH ...
ARE YOU A LOCAL GIRL?
YES.

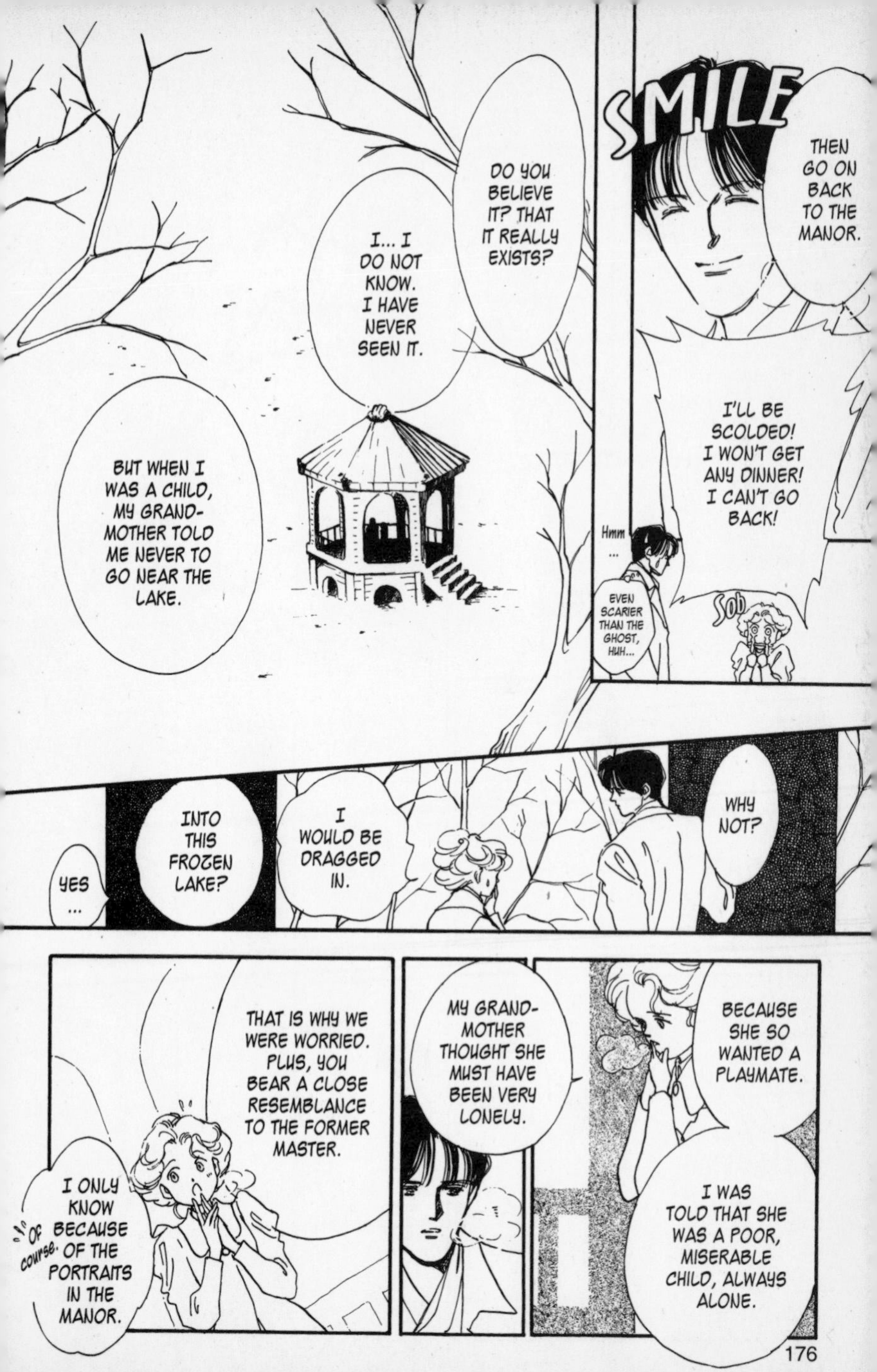
SMILE
THEN GO ON BACK TO THE MANOR.
I'LL BE SCOLDED! I WON'T GET ANY DINNER! I CAN'T GO BACK!
Hmm ...
EVEN SCARIER THAN THE GHOST, HUH...
Sob
DO YOU BELIEVE IT? THAT IT REALLY EXISTS?
I... I DO NOT KNOW. I HAVE NEVER SEEN IT.
BUT WHEN I WAS A CHILD, MY GRAND-MOTHER TOLD ME NEVER TO GO NEAR THE LAKE.
WHY NOT?
I WOULD BE DRAGGED IN.
INTO THIS FROZEN LAKE?
YES ...
BECAUSE SHE SO WANTED A PLAYMATE.
I WAS TOLD THAT SHE WAS A POOR, MISERABLE CHILD, ALWAYS ALONE.
MY GRAND-MOTHER THOUGHT SHE MUST HAVE BEEN VERY LONELY.
THAT IS WHY WE WERE WORRIED. PLUS, YOU BEAR A CLOSE RESEMBLANCE TO THE FORMER MASTER.
OF course.
I ONLY KNOW BECAUSE OF THE PORTRAITS IN THE MANOR.

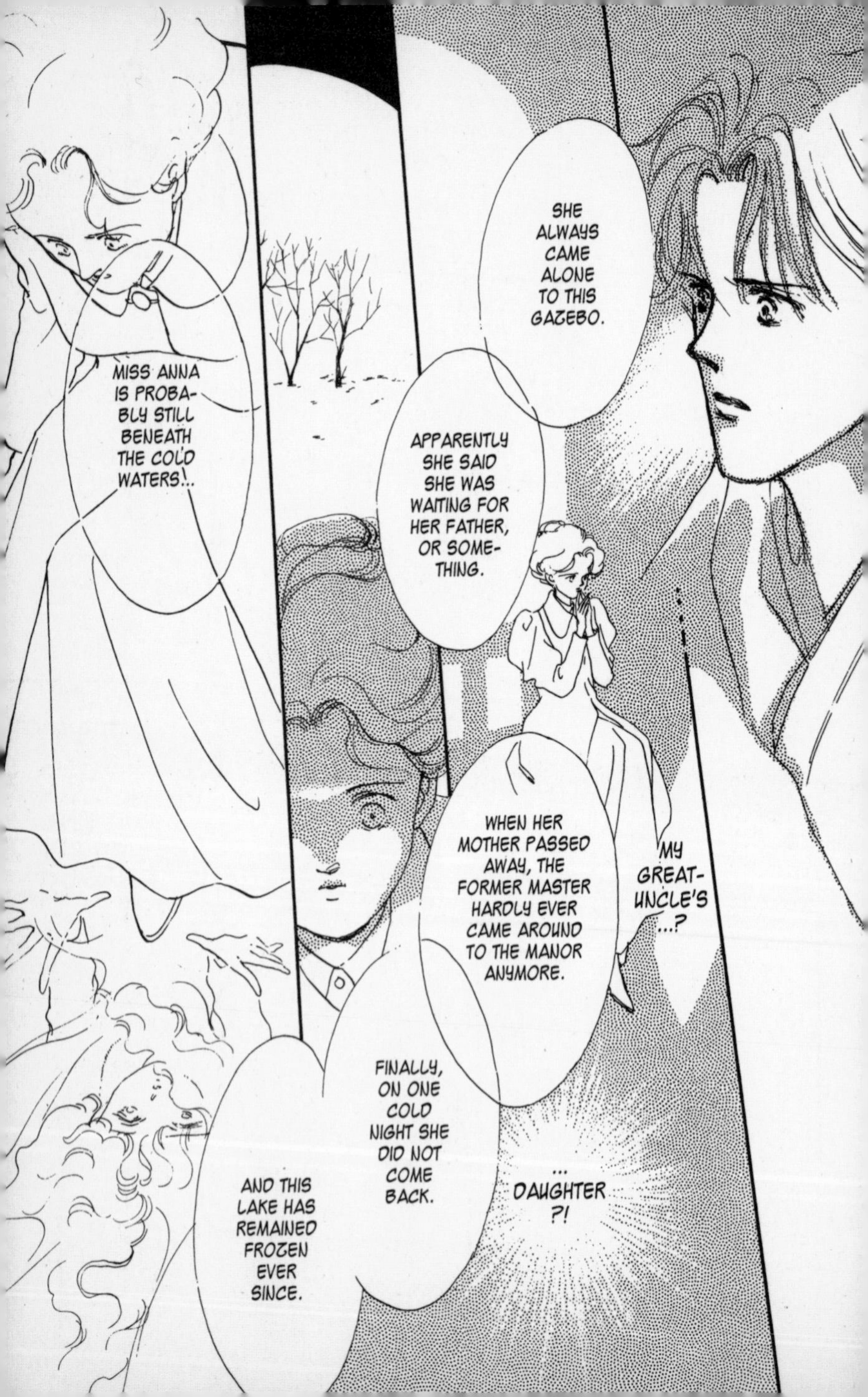
SHE ALWAYS CAME ALONE TO THIS GAZEBO.
APPARENTLY SHE SAID SHE WAS WAITING FOR HER FATHER, OR SOME-THING.
WHEN HER MOTHER PASSED AWAY, THE FORMER MASTER HARDLY EVER CAME AROUND TO THE MANOR ANYMORE.
MY GREAT-UNCLE'S ...?
... DAUGHTER ?!
FINALLY, ON ONE COLD NIGHT SHE DID NOT COME BACK.
AND THIS LAKE HAS REMAINED FROZEN EVER SINCE.
MISS ANNA IS PROBA-BLY STILL BENEATH THE COLD WATERS...

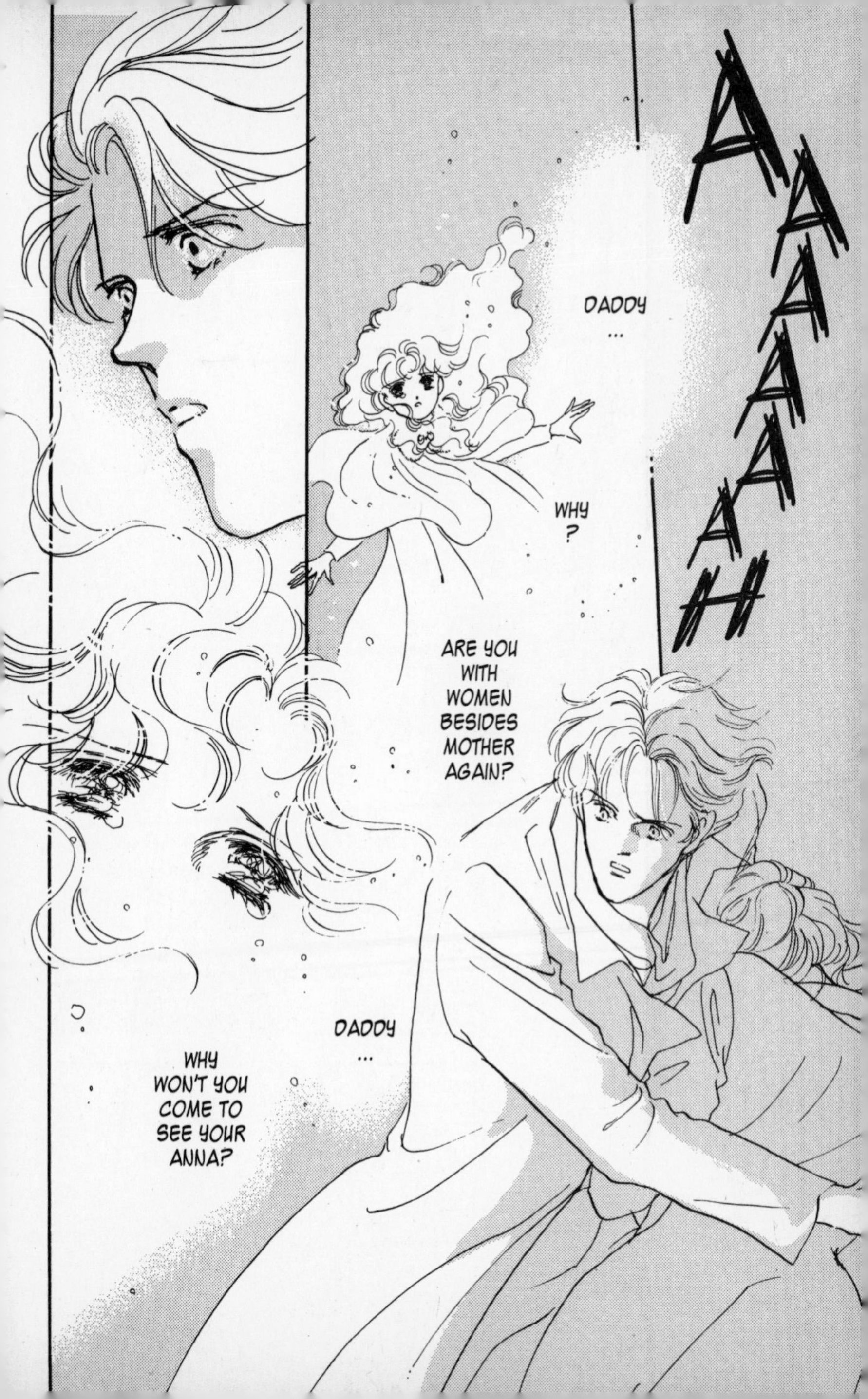
AAAAAAAH
DADDY ...
WHY ?
ARE YOU WITH WOMEN BESIDES MOTHER AGAIN?
DADDY ...
WHY WON'T YOU COME TO SEE YOUR ANNA?

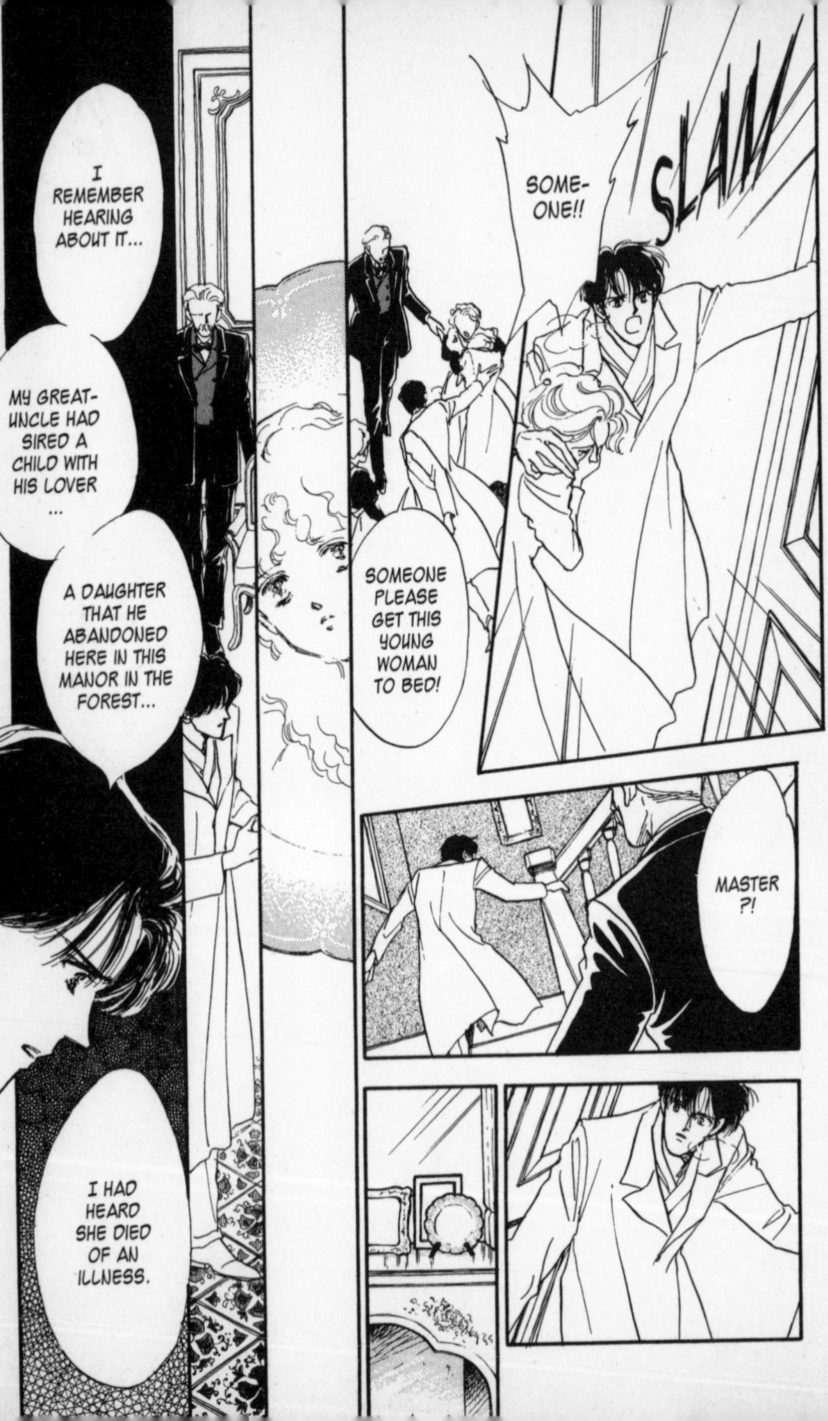
SLAM
SOME-ONE!!
SOMEONE PLEASE GET THIS YOUNG WOMAN TO BED!
MASTER ?!
I REMEMBER HEARING ABOUT IT...
MY GREAT-UNCLE HAD SIRED A CHILD WITH HIS LOVER ...
A DAUGHTER THAT HE ABANDONED HERE IN THIS MANOR IN THE FOREST...
I HAD HEARD SHE DIED OF AN ILLNESS.

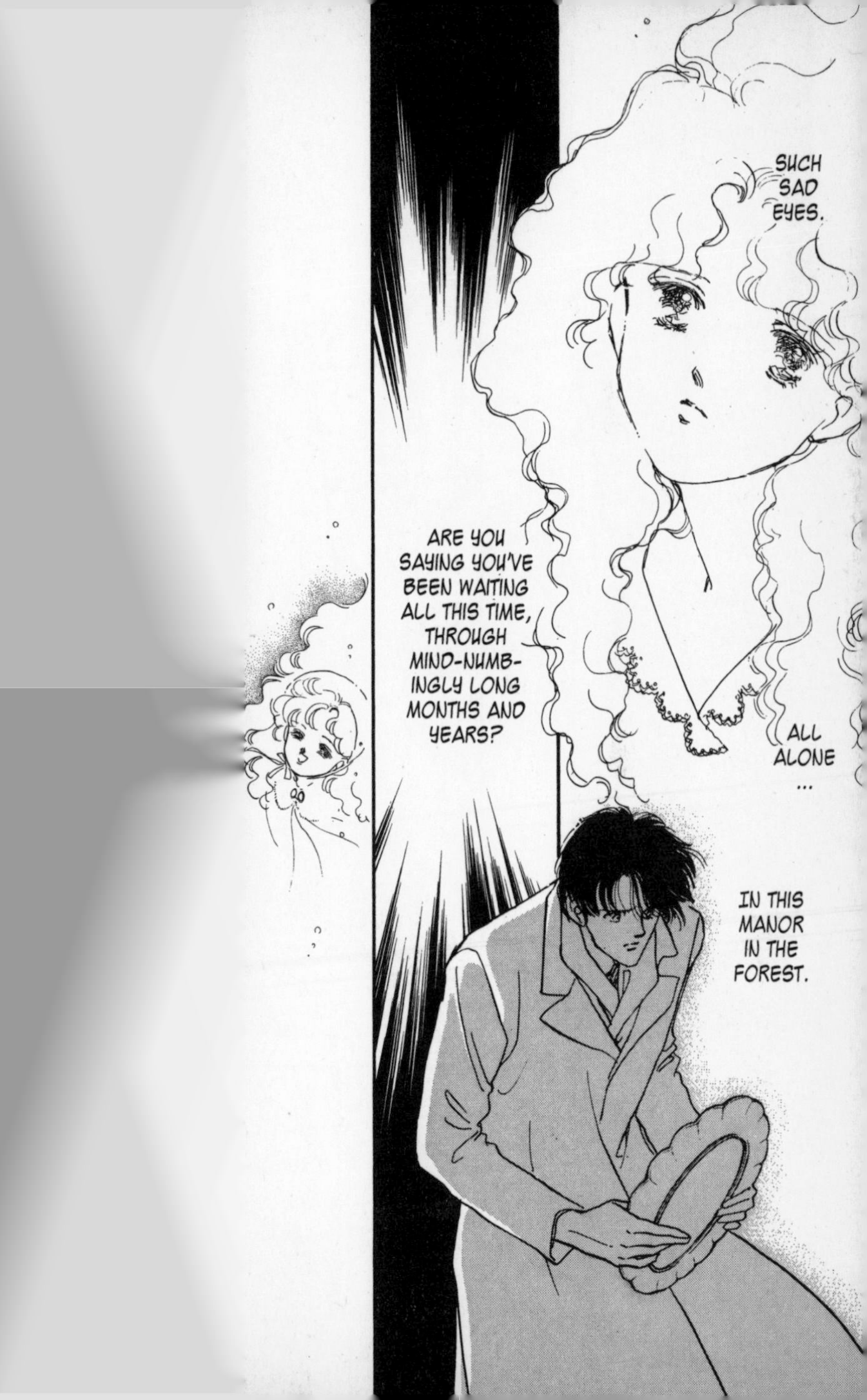
SUCH SAD EYES.
ALL ALONE ...
IN THIS MANOR IN THE FOREST.
ARE YOU SAYING YOU'VE BEEN WAITING ALL THIS TIME, THROUGH MIND-NUMB-INGLY LONG MONTHS AND YEARS?

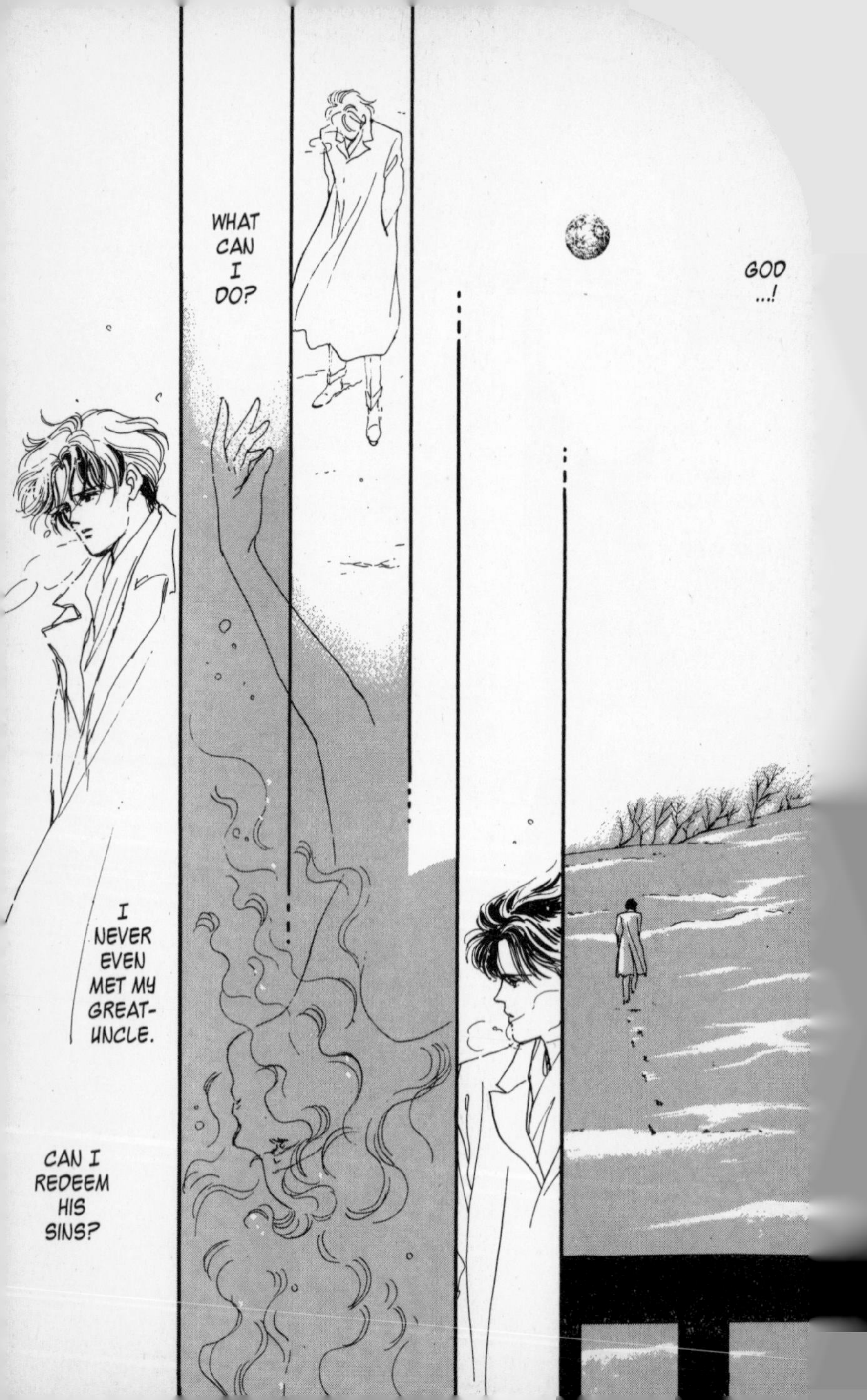
GOD ...!
WHAT CAN I DO?
I NEVER EVEN MET MY GREAT-UNCLE.
CAN I REDEEM HIS SINS?

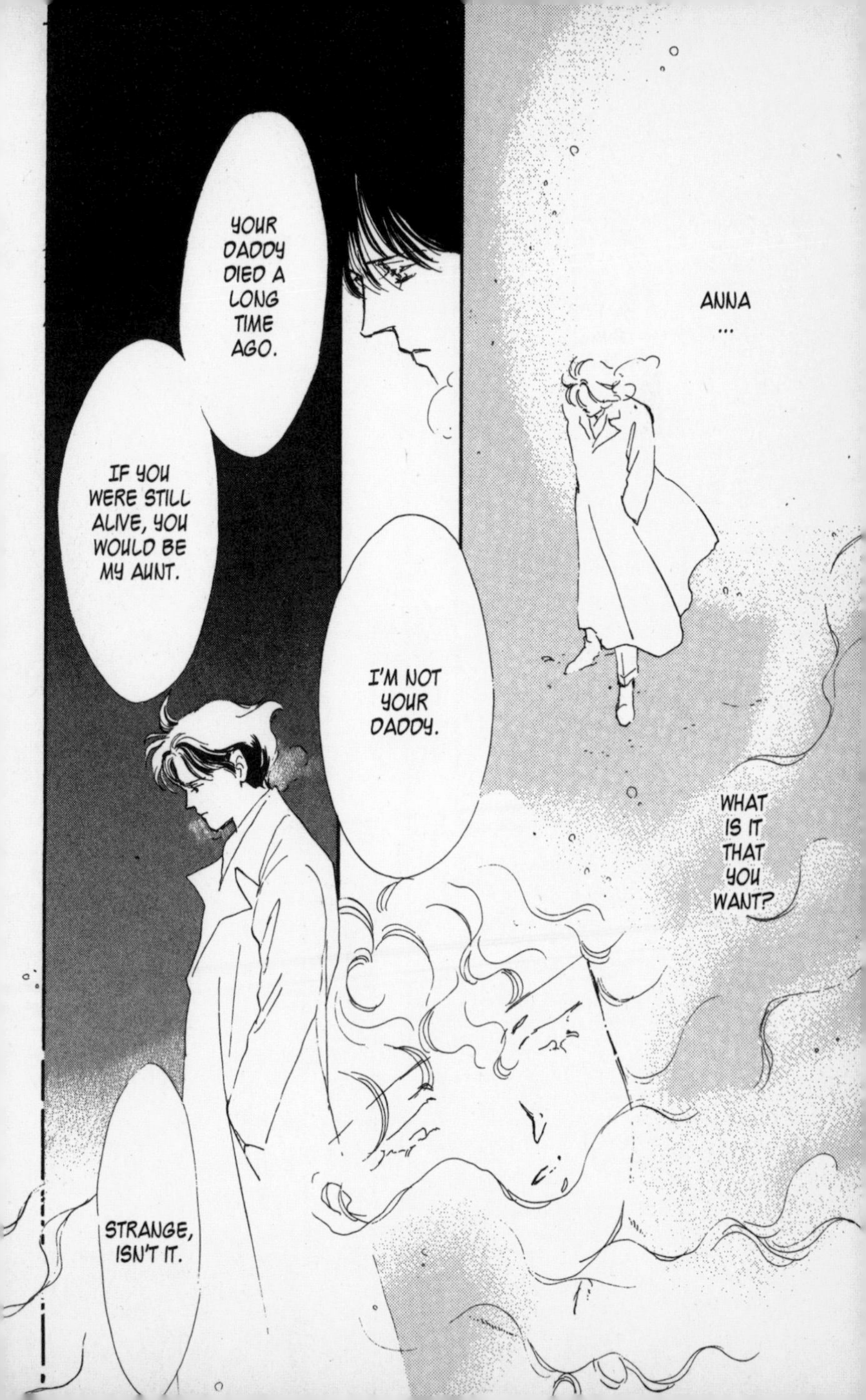
ANNA ...
WHAT IS IT THAT YOU WANT?
YOUR DADDY DIED A LONG TIME AGO.
IF YOU WERE STILL ALIVE, YOU WOULD BE MY AUNT.
I'M NOT YOUR DADDY.
STRANGE, ISN'T IT.

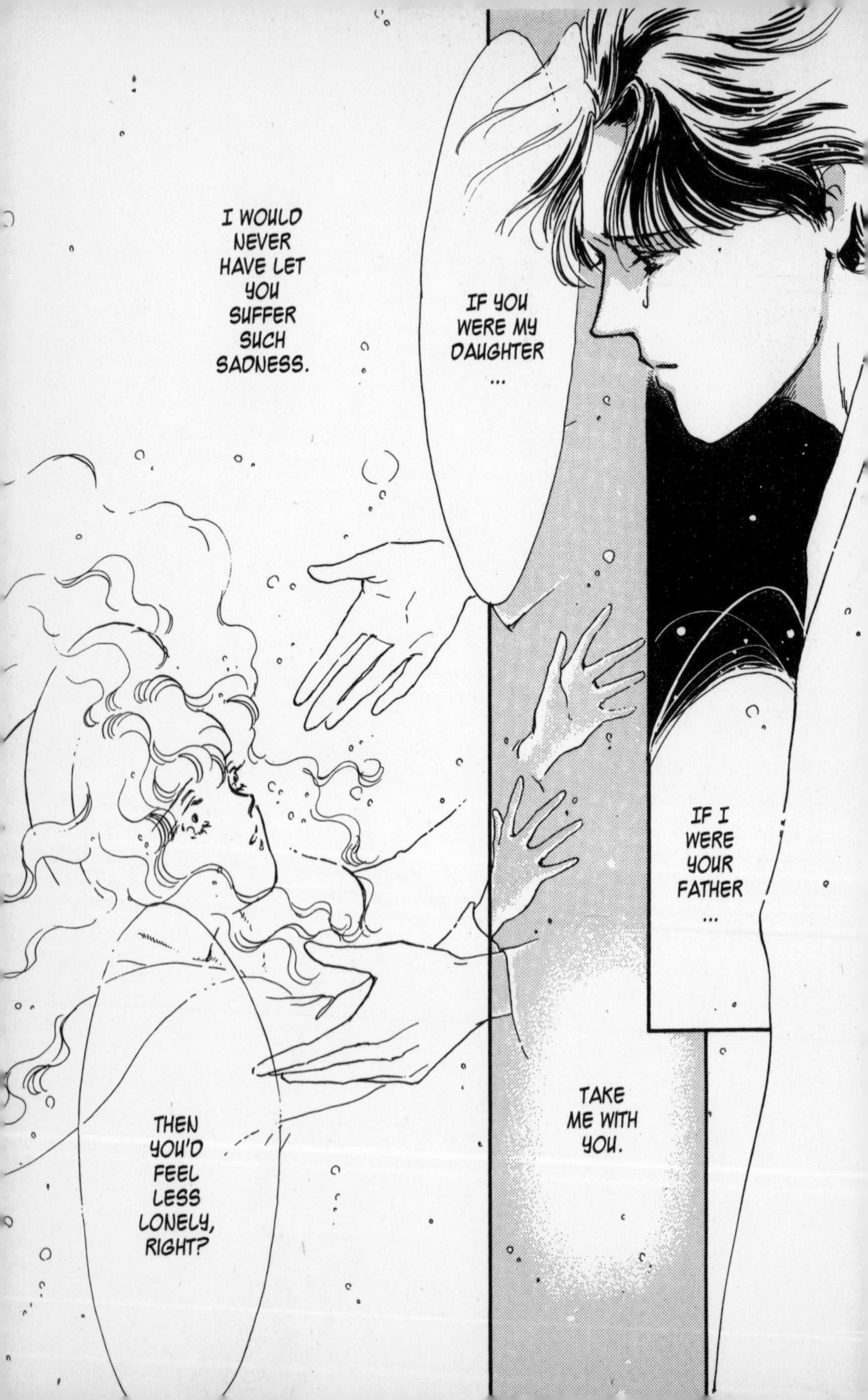
IF YOU WERE MY DAUGHTER ...
I WOULD NEVER HAVE LET YOU SUFFER SUCH SADNESS.
IF I WERE YOUR FATHER ...
TAKE ME WITH YOU.
THEN YOU'D FEEL LESS LONELY, RIGHT?

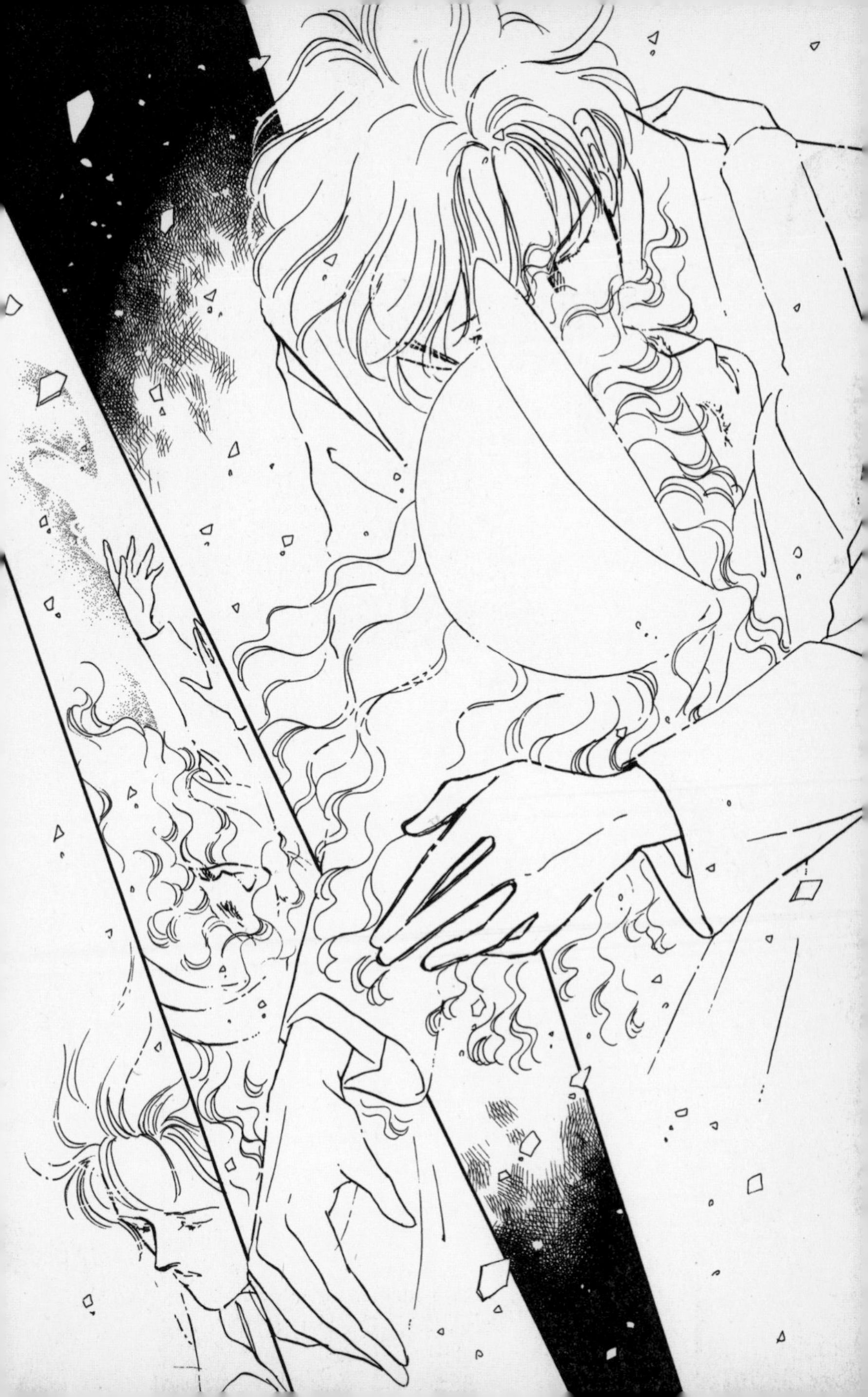

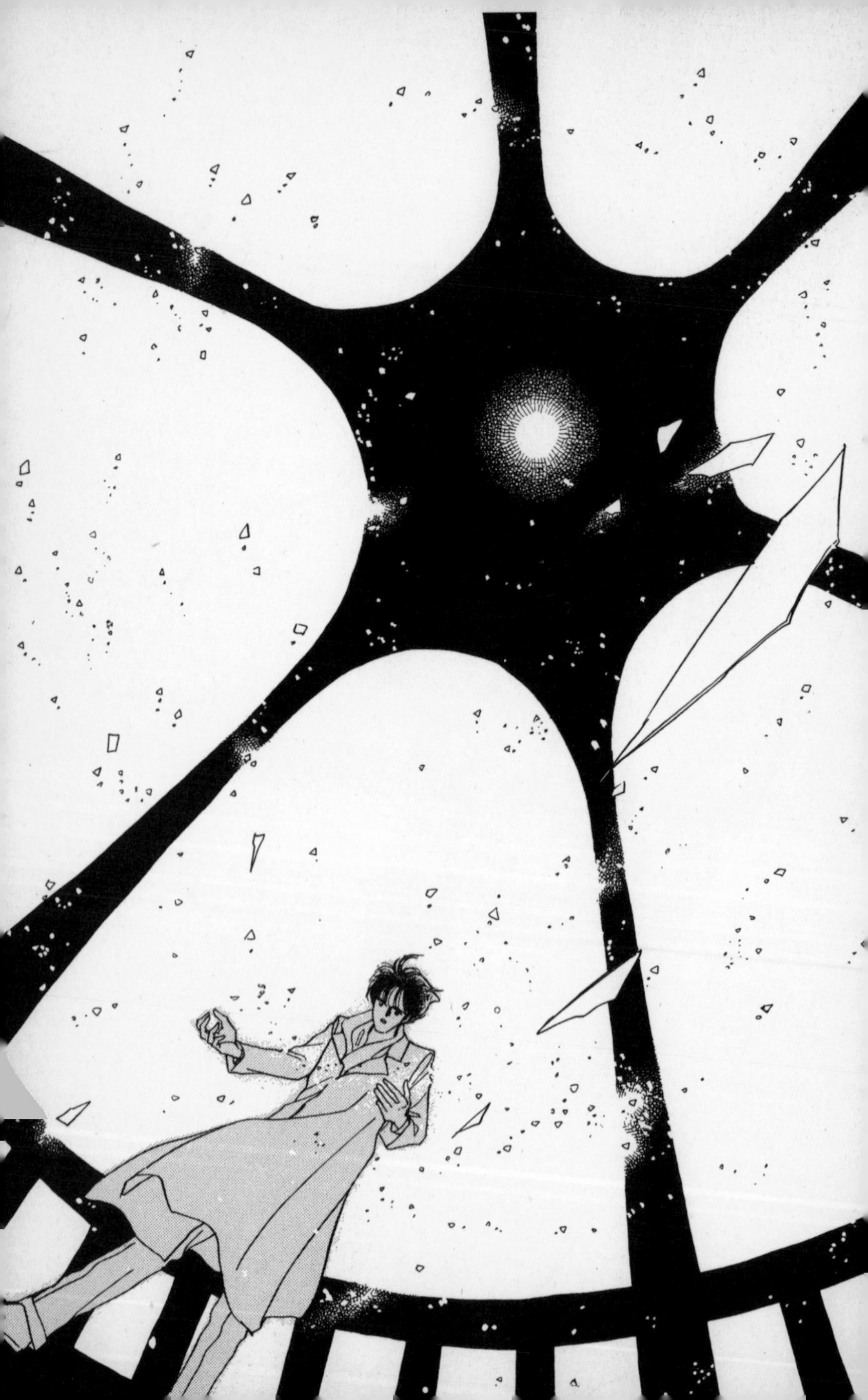

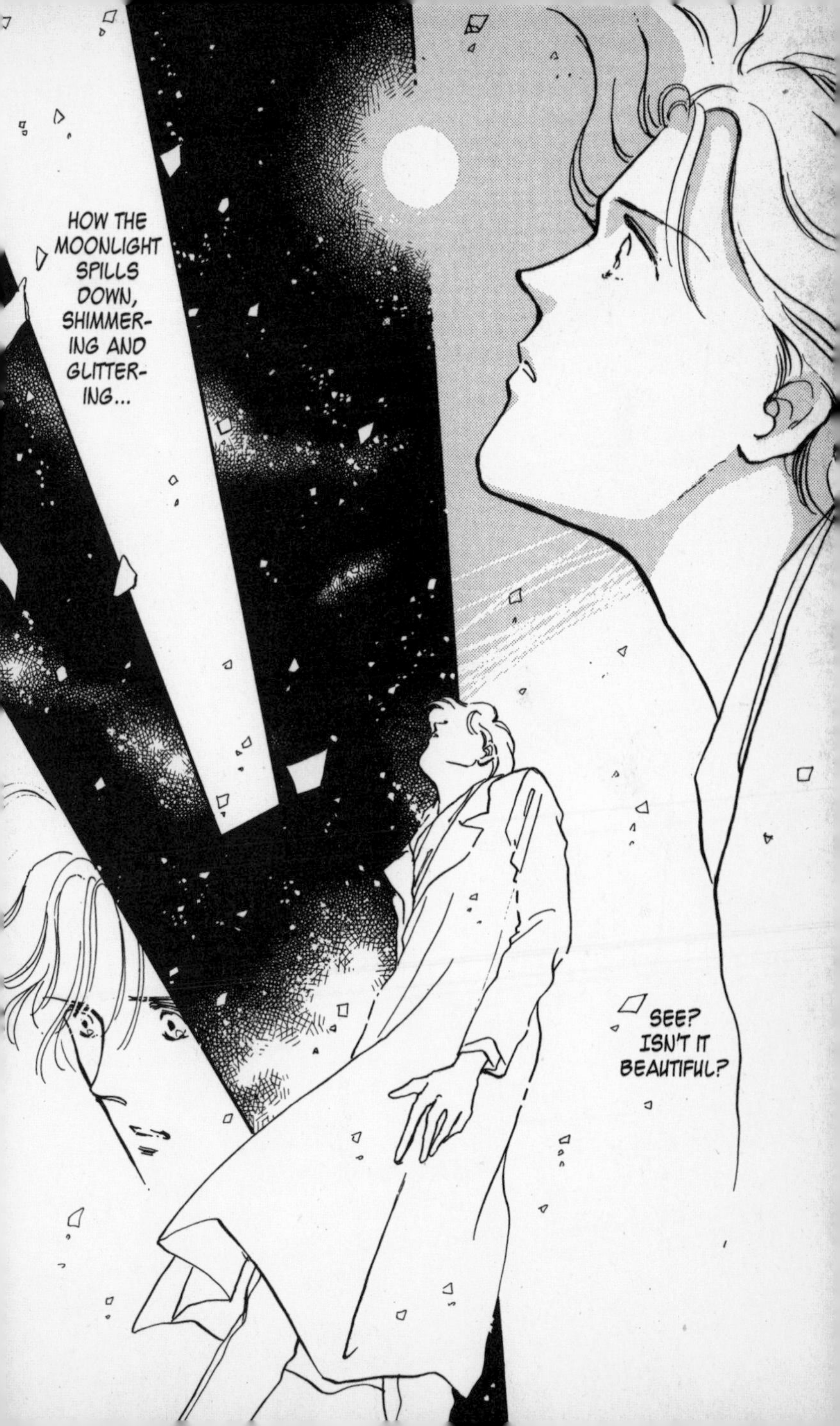
SEE? ISN'T IT BEAUTIFUL?
HOW THE MOONLIGHT SPILLS DOWN, SHIMMERING AND GLITTERING...

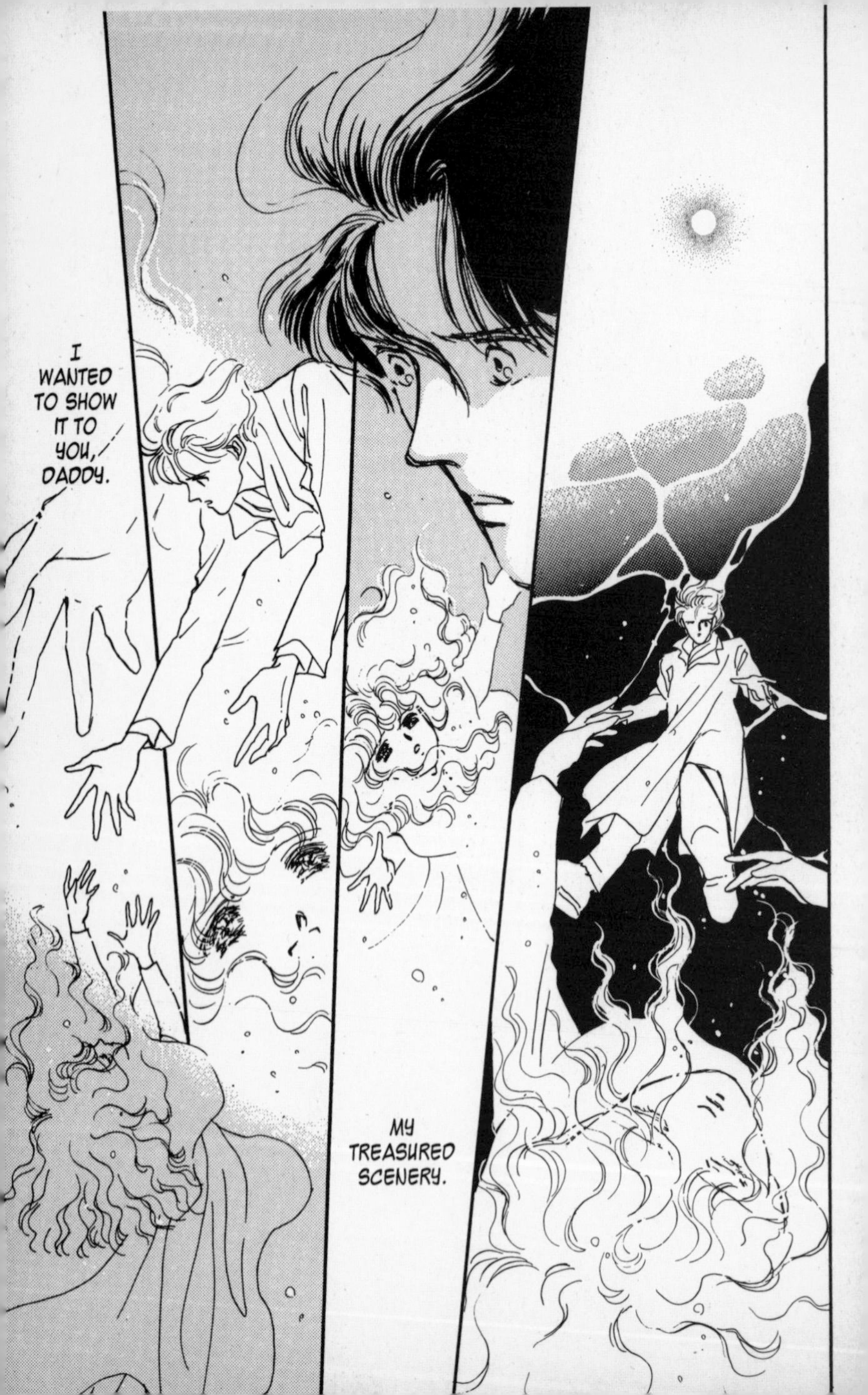
MY TREASURED SCENERY.
I WANTED TO SHOW IT TO YOU, DADDY.

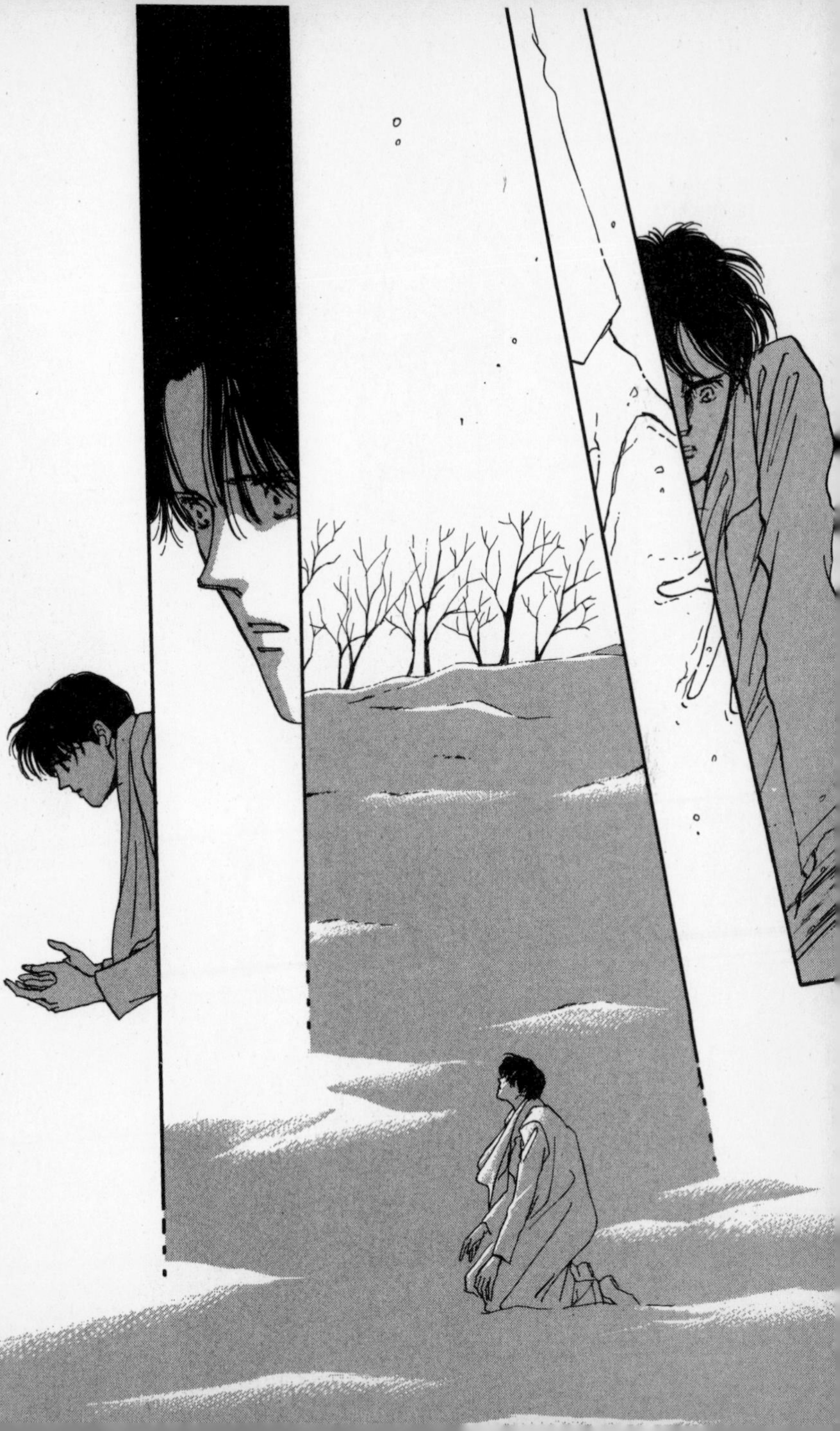

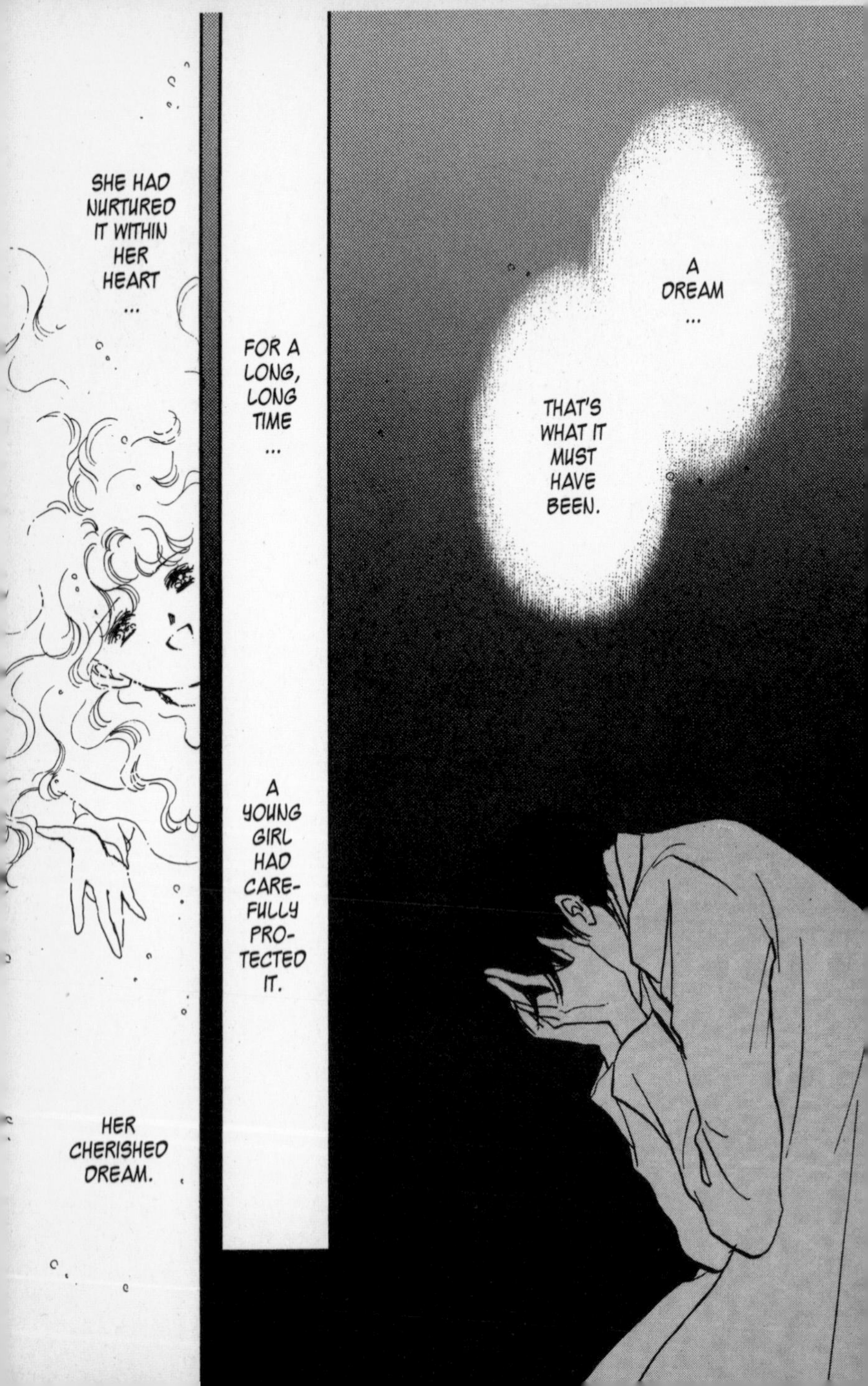
A DREAM ...
THAT'S WHAT IT MUST HAVE BEEN.
FOR A LONG, LONG TIME ...
A YOUNG GIRL HAD CAREFULLY PROTECTED IT.
SHE HAD NURTURED IT WITHIN HER HEART ...
HER CHERISHED DREAM.

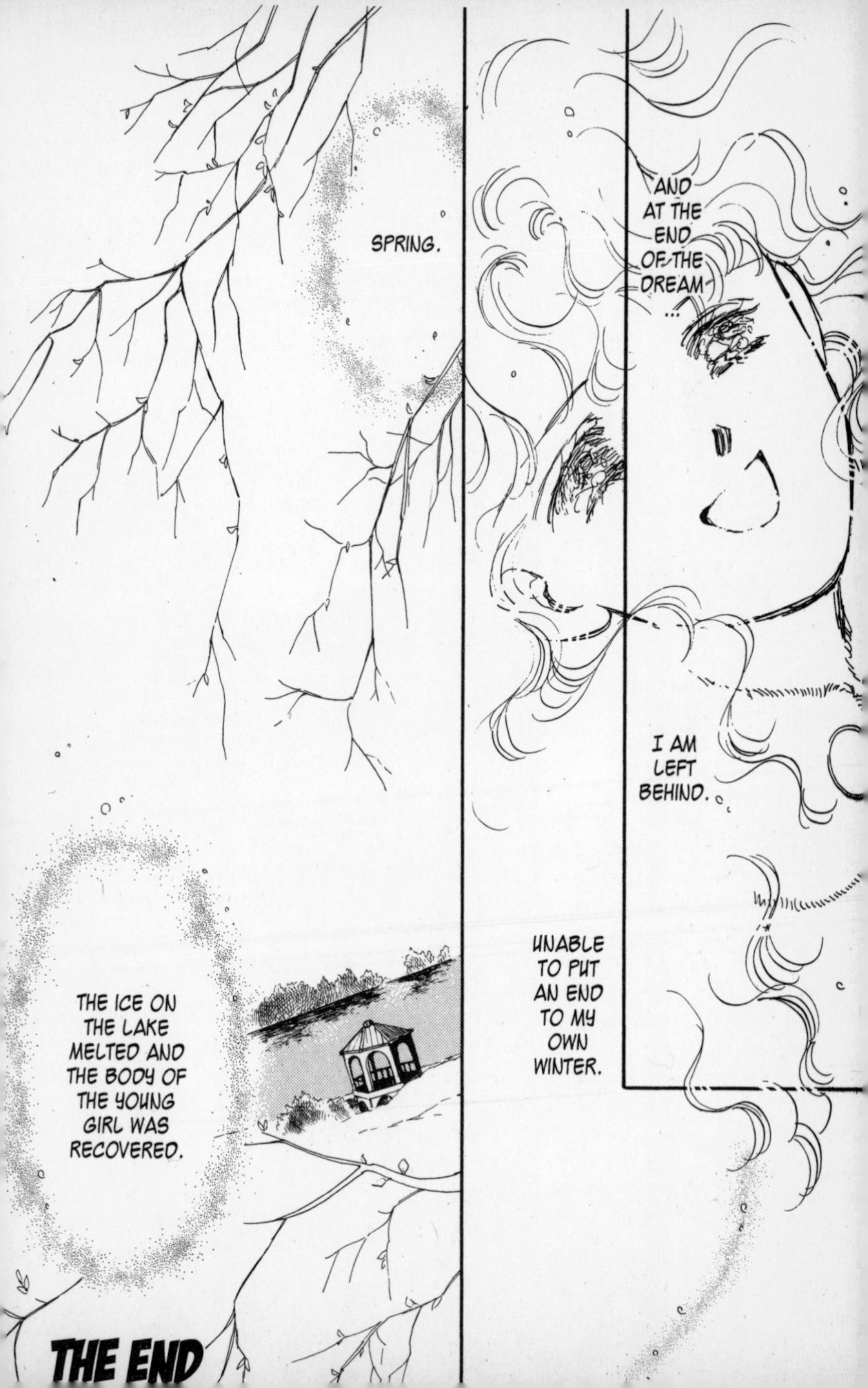
AND AT THE END OF THE DREAM ...
I AM LEFT BEHIND.
UNABLE TO PUT AN END TO MY OWN WINTER.
SPRING.
THE ICE ON THE LAKE MELTED AND THE BODY OF THE YOUNG GIRL WAS RECOVERED.
THE END

Afterword

I boast that I bring fair weather with me. When going on trips or out to see a play, the chance that I'll encounter rain is very low. Some of my friends even leave their umbrellas at home on days where it looks like rain, saying, "I'm with you, so...." When at my best, I've gone to Hong Kong for a week during the rainy season without once seeing rain, but since I'd expected rain I'd taken an umbrella and a raincoat and ended up kicking myself for it. (I'd never before taken an umbrella on a trip.) In such a case, do I consider myself lucky or unlucky? And one winter I went to Hokkaido for snow-viewing and there wasn't any snow at all. So I brag about being a fair weather woman, but it does come with hidden pitfalls. Come to think of it, on days that I have deadlines the weather is often splendid. It's really maddening.

But still, I'm a pretty happy woman, I think to myself. It's to be expected that things don't always go as planned, but since I can take those times and find a way to enjoy it, I think I have it good. People say I have good luck. "I guess I do," I agree. For example, take "Nemurenu Yoru no Kimyou na Hanashi." (Note: These stories were originally published in *Nemurenu Yoru no Kimyou na Hanashi (Mysterious Stories for Sleepless Nights.)* I was just thinking how cool it would be if I could do work in a book like that when they approached me. "Waah! What should I do? What will I draw? I don't have any material or confidence, and I won't be able to make the deadline." They let me do it despite this terrible case of don'ts and won'ts, and now here is a collection of stories gathered into their own graphic novel. Really. I know, it's like life's too easy. I'm sorry.

I'm happy about this graphic novel. There are a lot of things I want to explain and I did think of many things, but it was kind of bothersome so I'm not going to. But mostly I wanted to use this opportunity to thank my editor Mr. Matsuzawa for patiently bearing with me through my don'ts and won'ts, all those who helped with the creation of this work, my friends who cheered me up when I complained, and my readers. I am truly grateful. I hope we will meet again. These days I sigh and think there's no word so ill-suited to me as *gambaru* (persist) but I hope somehow I can *gambaru*. Till we meet again.

Yumiko Kawahara, A lucky day in December, 1994

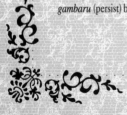

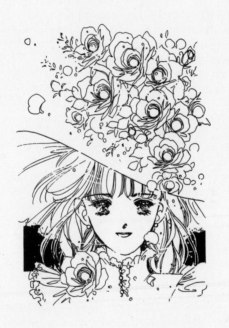

Dolls

Volume 1

Shôjo Edition

English Adaptation/Naoko Amemiya
Translation/Kaori Inoue
Touch-Up & Lettering/Gia Cam Luc
Cover & Graphic Design/Izumi Evers
Editor/Eric Searleman

Managing Editor/Annette Roman
Production Manager/Noboru Watanabe
Editorial Director/Alvin Lu
Sr. Director of Licensing & Acquisitions/Rika Inouye
Vice President of Sales & Marketing/Liza Coppola
Executive Vice President/Hyoe Narita
Publisher/Seiji Horibuchi

Published by VIZ, LLC
P.O. 77010
San Francisco, CA 94107

Shôjo Edition
10 9 8 7 6 5 4 3 2 1
First Printing, October 2004

For advertising rates or media kit,
e-mail advertising@viz.com

 store.viz.com   www.viz.com

EDITOR'S RECOMMENDATIONS

More manga!
More manga!

If you enjoyed this volume of

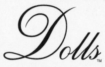

here are three more books we think you'll enjoy:

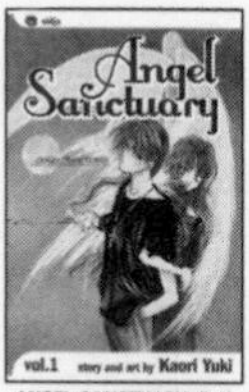

ANGEL SANCTUARY © Kaori
Yuki 1994/HAKUSENSHA, Inc.

Angel Sanctuary
In a war between Heaven and Hell, there's only one thing forbidden: the love between a brother and sister!

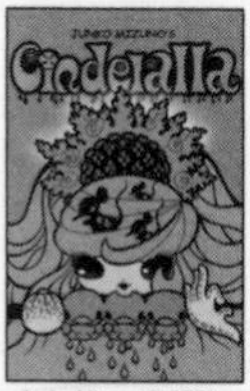

Junko Mizuno © 2002

Junko Mizuno's Cinderalla
Psychedelic, grotesque (and cute!), **Cinderalla** is a mindwarping visual blast. Give it a try… if you dare! Recommended for adults only.

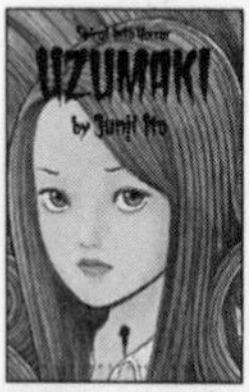

© 1998 Junji
Ito/Shogakukan, Inc.

Uzumaki
A small fishing village falls prey to the hypnotic power of uzumaki. A three-volume classic from Junji Ito. Highly recommended!

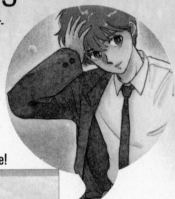

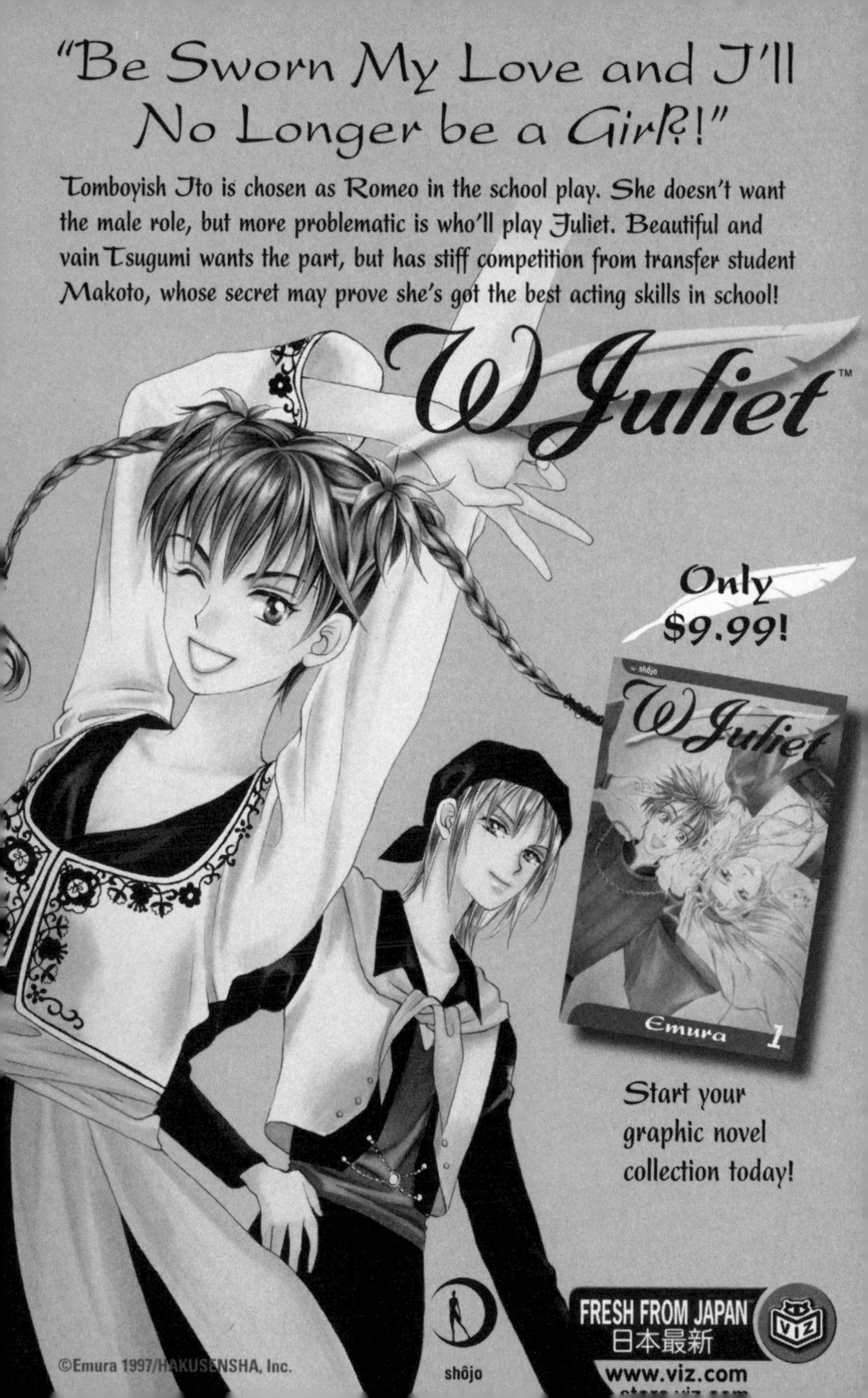
"Be Sworn My Love and I'll No Longer be a Girl?!"
Tomboyish Ito is chosen as Romeo in the school play. She doesn't want the male role, but more problematic is who'll play Juliet. Beautiful and vain Tsugumi wants the part, but has stiff competition from transfer student Makoto, whose secret may prove she's got the best acting skills in school!
W Juliet™
Only $9.99!
shôjo
W Juliet
Emura 1
Start your graphic novel collection today!
©Emura 1997/HAKUSENSHA, Inc.
shôjo
FRESH FROM JAPAN™
日本最新
VIZ
www.viz.com

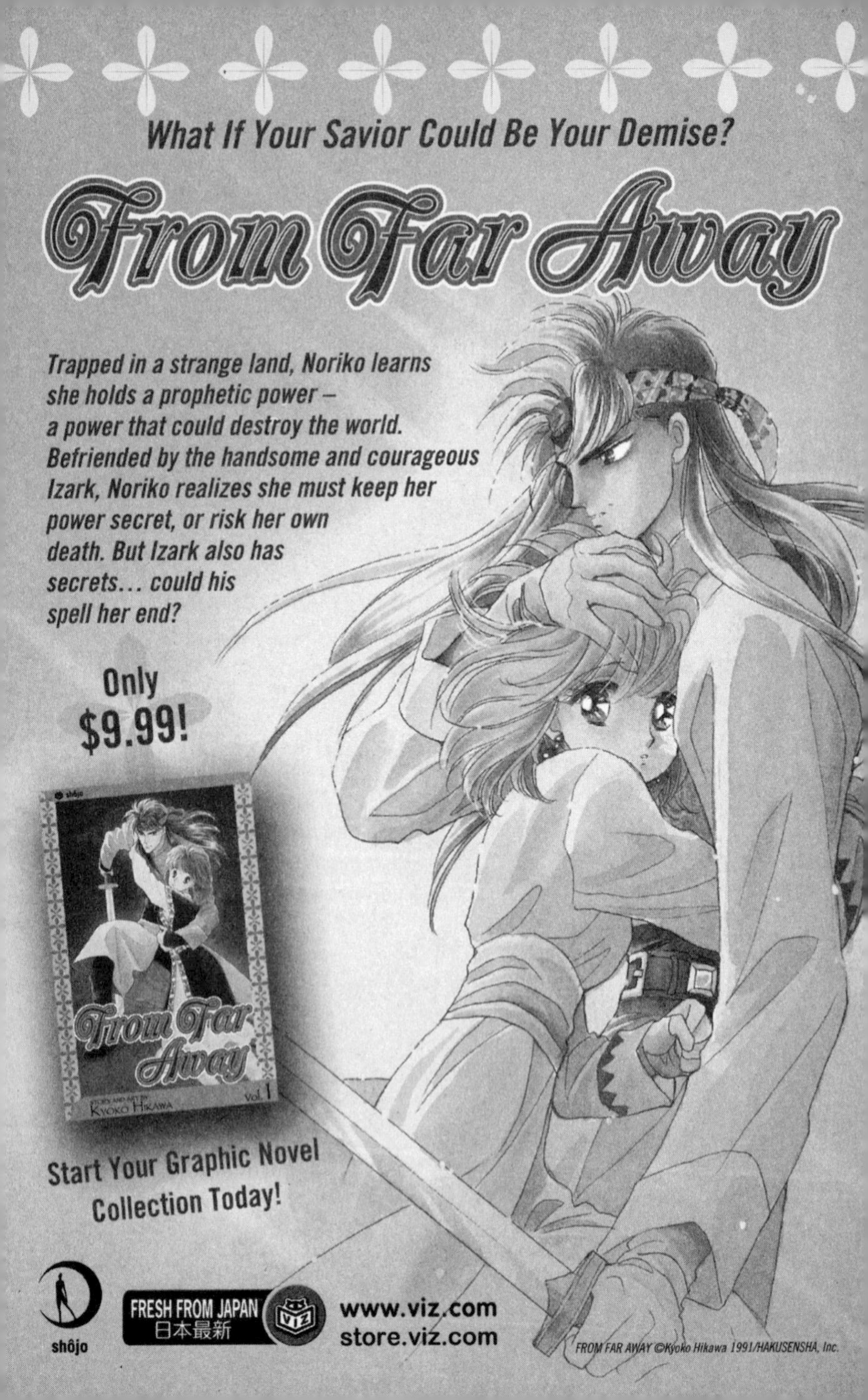
What If Your Savior Could Be Your Demise?
From Far Away
Trapped in a strange land, Noriko learns she holds a prophetic power – a power that could destroy the world. Befriended by the handsome and courageous Izark, Noriko realizes she must keep her power secret, or risk her own death. But Izark also has secrets… could his spell her end?
Only $9.99!
shôjo
From Far Away
STORY AND ART BY KYOKO HIKAWA
Vol. 1
Start Your Graphic Novel Collection Today!
shôjo
FRESH FROM JAPAN 日本最新
VIZ
www.viz.com
store.viz.com
FROM FAR AWAY ©Kyoko Hikawa 1991/HAKUSENSHA, Inc.

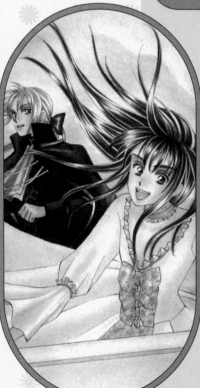
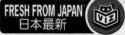

COMPLETE OUR SURVEY AND LET US KNOW WHAT YOU THINK!

☐ Please do NOT send me information about VIZ products, news and events, special offers, or other information.

☐ Please do NOT send me information from VIZ's trusted business partners.

Name: _____

Address: _____

City: _____ State: _____ Zip: _____

E-mail: _____

☐ Male ☐ Female   Date of Birth (mm/dd/yyyy): ___/___/_____   (Under 13? Parental consent required)

What race/ethnicity do you consider yourself? (please check one)

☐ Asian/Pacific Islander ☐ Black/African American ☐ Hispanic/Latino

☐ Native American/Alaskan Native ☐ White/Caucasian ☐ Other: _____

What VIZ product did you purchase? (check all that apply and indicate title purchased)

☐ DVD/VHS _____

☐ Graphic Novel _____

☐ Magazines _____

☐ Merchandise _____

Reason for purchase: (check all that apply)

☐ Special offer ☐ Favorite title ☐ Gift

☐ Recommendation ☐ Other _____

Where did you make your purchase? (please check one)

☐ Comic store ☐ Bookstore ☐ Mass/Grocery Store

☐ Newsstand ☐ Video/Video Game Store ☐ Other: _____

☐ Online (site: _____)

What other VIZ properties have you purchased/own? _____
_____

How many anime and/or manga titles have
VIZ titles? **(please check one from each column)**

ANIME	MANGA	
☐ None	☐ None	
☐ 1-4	☐ 1-4	
☐ 5-10	☐ 5-10	
☐ 11+	☐ 11+	☐ 11+

I find the pricing of VIZ products to be: **(please check one)**

☐ Cheap ☐ Reasonable ☐ Expensive

What genre of manga and anime would you like to see from VIZ? **(please check two)**

☐ Adventure ☐ Comic Strip ☐ Science Fiction ☐ Fighting
☐ Horror ☐ Romance ☐ Fantasy ☐ Sports

What do you think of VIZ's new look?

☐ Love It ☐ It's OK ☐ Hate It ☐ Didn't Notice ☐ No Opinion

Which do you prefer? **(please check one)**

☐ Reading right-to-left
☐ Reading left-to-right

Which do you prefer? **(please check one)**

☐ Sound effects in English
☐ Sound effects in Japanese with English captions
☐ Sound effects in Japanese only with a glossary at the back

THANK YOU! Please send the completed form to:

NJW Research
42 Catharine St.
Poughkeepsie, NY 12601

All information provided will be used for internal purposes only. We promise not to sell or otherwise divulge your information.